Building and planning for industrial storage and distribution

BUILDING AND PLANNING FOR INDUSTRIAL STORAGE AND DISTRIBUTION

Peter Falconer
Jolyon Drury

The Architectural Press, London
Halsted Press Division
John Wiley & Sons, New York

The text of this book as it originally appeared in *The Architects'*
Journal was edited by Susan Dawson, BA, BArch, RIBA

First published in book form in 1975
in Great Britain by
The Architectural Press Ltd
© Peter Falconer and Jolyon Drury, 1975

British edition
ISBN 0 85139 274 1

Published in the USA by
Halsted Press a Division of
John Wiley & Sons Inc.,
New York

Library of Congress Cataloging in Publication Data

Falconer, Peter.
    Building and planning for industrial storage and distribution.

    Bibliography: pp 16, 92, 125, 240.
    Includes index.
    1. Warehouses—Design and construction.
I. Drury, Jolyon, joint author. II. Title.
TS189.6.F34   1976   725'.35   75-28387
ISBN 0 470-25355-X

Printed in Great Britain by
Diemer & Reynolds Ltd, Bedford

Preface

The universal acceptance of the container in materials handling means that this book, written by two architects in the United Kingdom, is directly applicable for industrial facility managers and architects in the United States, the Netherlands, the Middle East, the British Isles, and virtually all industrialised and developing countries.

The authors point out, 'The coming of the container has had the effect of unifying materials handling methods worldwide, and inevitably leads to compatibility requirements on pallet sizes, racking, vehicle design, etc, so that storage and handling methods have to be considered on a worldwide basis if the full economy of the container is to benefit mankind'.

This book also presents further evidence that there is increasing in-depth expertise in an ever widening area of specialised planning and design within the architectural profession. This says that the architect is more than exterior decorator. Increasingly, building owners and facility managers can turn to the architect/manager* for the most objective and professional guidance through all phases of their construction programmes. In turn, the architect/manager* can more and more call on members of the profession for in-depth expertise in specialised areas.

This is not to say that every architect is a specialist, a manager, or even completely competent. Most experienced owners know better. An architect practising in a medium sized city once told a friend, who had inquired if membership in the local architectural society chapter meant that a certain member was a 'good' architect: 'Our society includes all of the good architects and most of the bad ones'. As in any profession, no honest or accurate generalisation can be made regarding capabilities or competence. But, increasingly, there are to be found those high levels of competence in special areas of planning and consultation, design, and construction programme management within the architectural profession or within organisations that are outgrowths of architectural firms.

Underlying this thoroughly detailed work of Messrs Falconer and Drury is a basic concern for cost in the broadest sense. The work's primary concern with the operational philosophies behind storage facility needs, as well as the details of what these facilities must accommodate, points out the concern for the total true costs—or better: profit or loss impact of such facilities. This concern, then, fits well into the managerial expertise related to total cost (including time as a cost function) that must be further nurtured within the architectural profession.

George T. Heery, AIA
Atlanta, Georgia, USA

* Construction Programme Manager

Foreword

The nature of market forces in the field of distribution and the range of technological processes that have been developed to meet them, make the planning of efficient buildings for storage and distribution vital in the industrial sector. Getting it right, however, is an exacting business—particularly when the designer is under pressure to keep costs down by making the correct initial choice, while at the same time having to remain aware that the building must have sufficient built-in flexibility to allow for the economic or technical changes that will inevitably come along during its lifetime. Thus, while storage buildings are normally designed to outlast a pay-back period of 25 years, reaching maximum efficiency at the halfway stage, it can now be predicted that a storage and handling system may change three or more times. It was argued at one time that the answer was a 'throw away' philosophy, with minimum cost buildings designed to be demolished when the storage system became obsolete. But like some developments in storage itself, this concept has been overtaken by external events. Increasing building costs and greater competition on smaller profit margins mean that manufacturing and distributive industry can no longer afford to shut down or reduce its trading for the lengthy periods that may be involved in alteration and rebuilding.

Changes in the hardware and software of distribution affect storage buildings in a number of ways—the lack of weight-bearing capacity on floor or frame, lack of height and width, shortage of room for further expansion, and, above all, insufficient yard space. Planning ahead for considerations of this kind has to be reconciled with often unhelpful and outmoded constraints in the way of legislation and restrictions. There is a world-wide lack of integration—which remains to be overcome—in the way of building codes, fire regulations, the requirements of insurance companies and the rationale of storage design. All these are factors which add to building costs. A similar problem facing the designer is the absence of compatible systems in the way goods are handled. Unit load technology has advanced, but not as much as was first predicted. It is easy for designers to become excited by the concept of modular units fitting smoothly together; in fact it will be some time before pallets, freight containers and demountable body units become universally compatible. Certainly as far as the European rail network is concerned, vagaries of tunnels and handling equipment render nearly similar container designs incompatible when it comes to actual practice. Indeed, there is a good argument for resisting a doctrinaire desire for modular conformity because of the variations in the characteristics of goods and the distributive system. The distributive trade is therefore unlikely to adopt the standard pallet sizes that are to be found in deep-sea shipping.

Although there are, therefore, some unresolved areas in the field of storage and distribution, one can distinguish certain broad trends which the designer will have to take into account in planning his buildings and discussing them with his client, for whom this book is also intended. Thus, in spite of the slowness of progress towards standardisation and the warnings that have to be entered against too inflexible an approach in this respect, there is no doubt that there *will* be increasing standardisation of the size and weight of unit loads, leading to higher stacking, faster handling methods and calling in turn for greater headroom, better floors and higher quality buildings. In line with present trends this means further growth in the development of containers and, in this context, specifically of swop bodies which are really small containers for urban deliveries. Pointers in this direction emerge clearly from planning and environmental pressures which are discouraging heavy transport incursions into towns in favour of container-based 'distribution villages' at the periphery of urban centres and neighbourhoods. The problem here—and it is symptomatic of the range of issues the designer and his client have to face—is that when this is combined with bans against daytime goods traffic movement in towns, there is obviously going to be a good deal of night noise which has to be taken into account when considering location. Recently several operators, subjected to hostile public opinion over this issue, have had to make costly alterations to their loading facilities.

Another important factor is, of course, energy conservation; not only in terms of fuel costs but the growing awareness that this raises a question mark over the concept of throw-away packaging. There is a conflict here between the fact that at present it is actually more economic to throw away packs than to use returnable bottles or drums and thus conserve materials. However, if the balance changes, as is happening with metal containers, the distribution industry will have to accept part of the cost of recovery, with all the accompanying problems of transport, storage and baling, and the associated costs of contamination. This really implies a separate distribution system the costs of which are likely to be reflected in prices to the consumer.

Equally, energy conservation will have a major influence on building design. Already the cost of energy in the form of heating, cooling and refrigeration forms a high proportion of the overall costs of the storage operation. However, good insulation, and a large volume can achieve near steady-state internal conditions in a temperate climate: high buildings can allow for natural cooling without having to resort to large scale plant—increasingly costly to run. At the same time, although for most goods cool environmental conditions are required, this may be at odds with working conditions demanded by the labour force. A similar problem occurs over the actual handling of goods. If the systems are manual, the personnel are going to demand certain standards of heat and light—particularly in the case of night work. These have to be weighed against the cost of automated systems which do not require the same environmental standards, but which involve sums of another sort. Ultimately the decision rests on the throughput and the characteristics of the orders handled: for example, in the foreseeable future, the cheapest and quickest way to pick a large number of small orders and discrete items will be by hand. The task facing the designer of buildings for storage and distribution is therefore to balance the need to produce value in terms of immediate cost-cutting efficiency with a longer term strategy which will provide the flexibility for rapid change in the overall socio-economic situation: also to weigh up simple, low energy solutions against the performance offered by the immensely wide choice of high technology equipment now available in this field. Making the right choice depends, as one might expect, on both client and designer having access to as much information as is practicable. Thus, we have attempted in this guide to storage building design not only to provide sufficient data about mechanical handling and storage systems as they affect the detailed design of buildings but also to offer a considerable degree of background information concerning the reasons for the choice of certain systems and an insight into what effect these decisions can have. We hope that in this way we will help designers to balance criteria of pure operational efficiency for an initial price, with others—increasingly important—of the labour market, social conditions and long-term value. These are all factors in the design of industrial storage buildings for such buildings can never be seen in isolation, but as part of a system of distribution in which economic, social and technological elements interact with the development of our community as a whole.

Introduction :
Scope and form of book

Industrial storage can be a very complex operation; its demands are seldom correctly identified, both because management has failed to anticipate developments in the distribution industry, and because of lack of common education and language between user, building designer, equipment manufacturers and specialist consultants. Few parties understand the relationship between a warehouse and transport and distribution system, or the effects that particular solutions will have on other parts of a project.

Other reasons for costly and unnecessary failures can be traced back to an inaccurate brief from the user and questionable assumptions from consultants. Moreover, few architects understand the problems involved, most lack knowledge to check proposals and relate each part to the whole at all stages of the project.

The choice is clear; either the architectural profession must educate itself up to industry's level, or industrial storage work will be given to package dealers, to the detriment of long term value to the user and to the environment as a whole.

This book provides a skeleton on which architects can build up competence; the intention is not to dictate, with such a fast changing and dynamic industry this would be unrealistic. The information is intended as a guide, to point out where potential failures of interaction can occur, to illustrate the effect of choice of certain types of machinery and equipment on both a particular operation and on the building itself, and to indicate the most suitable consultants to employ for further information.

An architect, as overall co-ordinator, must have sufficient background knowledge to appreciate the actions and problems of specialists.

Therefore, each section of the book which deals with warehouse types—mechanised, bulk, manual, etc—discusses the theory behind the operation of the storage process. Architects should not necessarily become physical distribution management or mechanical handling consultants, but they must have sufficient data to check a user's brief, to understand consultant's reports and what lies behind their decisions, and, if necessary, to question both brief and consultant's decisions, as well as how current and future conditions affect the distribution system as a whole.

Layout of the book

The first three sections—Introduction, Loading bays, and External storage—are applicable to all warehouses, and these retain the usual AJ style.

Later sections deal with specific types of storage buildings, eg Cold storage, Bulk storage, Mechanised storage. Each section contains two technical studies: Storage process and Building function (see Contents list).

Each Technical study Storage process starts with an introduction to explain the role of that particular form of storage in the total distribution context. Next, the user specification is set out, what happens in a particular type of warehouse and why, how it is affected by external factors and the system as a whole, what machinery and control methods are involved, and what should be considered in choosing the storage method and the machinery to implement it. In this way, when Technical study Building function, which deals with the design and elements of the building in detail, is read, a designer should have a basic measure of understanding of the factors contributing to the decisions involved. Personnel provision and any special requirements for their welfare are also discussed in this study. In each section, the list of sub-headings in these technical studies remains the same, with the same title and numbering system. For example, 'Order picking' for each storage process

will appear under sub-heading 16, and 'Security' for each type of building will appear under sub-heading 28. Thus, when the book is complete, it can be read either 'vertically', ie conventionally through a section such as 'Mechanised storage', or 'horizontally', so that a designer can gain a broad knowledge of a particular operation across the industry by finding the particular sub-heading of each storage type. By using these cross references, designers will be able to gather information quickly, identify potential failures of interaction, and learn of any special conditions that can affect design decisions.

Information sheets

One of the most obvious problems when discussing warehousing with designers, consultants and users has been the lack of basic design data for equipment and mobile plant. Each section is backed up by information sheets, giving data of typical dimensions and performance of mobile and static equipment.

These information sheets are also intended to help designers understand how the wide variety of equipment is used so that if necessary they may question a consultant or client's proposal for a type of pallet racking and handling plant in relation to suitability for the product and the effect on the store in relation to the area available.

In this way, an attempt is made to provide sufficient information for architects to be able to make use of their valuable multi-disciplinary expertise, and regain their former versatility in offering a really useful, competent service to industrial clients.

Contents of technical studies

<table>
<tr><td>Technical study:
Storage process</td><td>Technical study:
Building function</td></tr>
<tr><td>1 Introduction.</td><td>22 Structure.</td></tr>
<tr><td>2 Receipt of goods.</td><td>23 Floor.</td></tr>
<tr><td>3 Source of goods.</td><td>24 Building services.</td></tr>
<tr><td>4 Form of transport.</td><td>25 Special services.</td></tr>
<tr><td>5 Control of transport.</td><td>26 Building fabric.</td></tr>
<tr><td>6 Form of goods.</td><td>27 Fire control.</td></tr>
<tr><td>7 Unloading.</td><td>28 Security.</td></tr>
<tr><td>8 Sortation.</td><td>29 External works.</td></tr>
<tr><td>9 Characteristics of goods.</td><td>30 Structure-based plant.</td></tr>
<tr><td>10 Volume calculations.</td><td>31 Mobile plant.</td></tr>
<tr><td>11 Turnover calculations.</td><td>32 Integration of building</td></tr>
<tr><td>12 Variety and flow.</td><td>and plant.</td></tr>
<tr><td>13 Type of storage.</td><td>33 Building process.</td></tr>
<tr><td>14 Stock control.</td><td>34 Management.</td></tr>
<tr><td>15 Stock withdrawal.</td><td>35 Personnel accommodation.</td></tr>
<tr><td>16 Order picking.</td><td>36 Amenity.</td></tr>
<tr><td>17 Picking area.</td><td>37 Security and safety.</td></tr>
<tr><td>18 Load build up.</td><td>38 Circulation and parking.</td></tr>
<tr><td>19 Order and documentation
check.</td><td></td></tr>
<tr><td>20 Loading and dispatch.</td><td></td></tr>
<tr><td>21 Additional data.</td><td></td></tr>
</table>

Authors

PETER FALCONER RIBA (left) is an architect in private practice specialising in industrial and storage buildings and a Council Member of the Materials Handling Institute.

JOLYON DRURY RIBA (right) is an architect in private practice specialising in industrial and storage buildings and a member of the Materials Handling Institute.

List of contents

Sections	Technical studies	Information sheets

Definitions

A

Articulated vehicle A vehicle comprising a motor unit (tractor) and a load carrying unit (trailer): for greater manoeuvrability the front of the trailer is superimposed onto a bearing plate (fifth wheel) mounted at the rear of the tractor chassis. Thus the vehicle can bend in the middle, ie articulate, requiring a much smaller turning circle than a rigid vehicle of a comparable length

B, C

Block stacking Unit loads stacked on top of each other
Bogies More than one axle in tandem
Bridging plates Detachable metal plates designed to bridge gap between dock surface and vehicles of different heights
Buffer An area for goods to accumulate between parts of a system running at different speeds.

Curtain sided vehicle Vehicle fitted with curtain sides to the body for easy sideloading

D

Dock leveller A hinged bridge between the dock surface and different load bed heights of vehicles. Levellers automatically adjust to different vehicle heights and the rise of vehicle springs as it is unloaded

F

Finger dock A raised loading dock set at an acute angle of 80° plus, so that trucks can be either side-loaded or end-loaded in the conventional manner
Flat trailer A semi or drawbar trailer designed as a flat bed, ie no sides; some are dual purpose, being fitted with twist locks for container carrying as well. Flat trailers are still favoured in Britain as hauliers consider them more flexible for bulky loads, achieving maximum tonnage without being restricted by cubic capacity of vans. A skeletal trailer is a flat trailer for containers only, with no floor, only twist locks
Free path A machine not tied to a fixed track

G

Gantry crane A form of crane in which the hoist system is suspended between flat beams
Gross combination weight Weight of vehicle, fully fuelled, plus load, driver and trailer
Groupage The grouping of small loads (often for export) collected by feeder vans and sorted out into bulk shipment

H, I

Hopper A container for granular materials
Hover-pallet A unit load platform, suspended on a cushion of air

Interface Where two elements or conditions meet
ISO container A container designed to the size, capacity and weight agreed by the International Standards Organisation; suitable for road, rail and sea forwarding

L, M, N

Lpg Liquid petroleum gas

Mezzanine An intermediate floor
Mobile shelving Shelving on mobile base running on track

Node The point where elements meet

O, P

On-line Direct control from a computer
Order picking The selection of a variety of goods to make up mixed orders for delivery

Pallet A modular-sized load platform that may be of timber, metal, plastics, paper, and which might be disposable
Palletisation Generic term for unit load using pallets
Platten A unit load base designed only for use in a store
Post pallets Stackable metal framed cages to pallet sizes

R

Raised dock An area of the floor raised to the truck bed level for easy and fast loading and unloading of goods.
Reefer A refrigerated container

S

Skip Unit load for handling waste
Stillage A frame with fixed legs on which a load can be placed and moved
Straddle carrier A container-carrying vehicle that passes over a stack and which can place containers three high
Swarf Metal shavings
Swept turning circle Diameter of outer extremity of vehicle at full lock
Swop body A demountable truck body which can stand on its own legs; the truck chassis can then be used again. In many cases similar to an ISO container, but for closed system use, ie not international

T

TIR *Transportes Internationals Routiers*, a term given by Customs and Excise to a vehicle and load sealed at the loading point to permit travel across frontiers without inspection. The vehicle has been constructed to customs-approved standards, and so carries the TIR plate
'Tilt' trailer A semi-trailer or drawbar trailer with a removable 'tilt', ie a canvas or plastic sheet covered top, so that customs can examine the goods inside quickly without having to unload them. Also used as a generic term for trailers used in international haulage
Tote box A container for small items in a closed system
Tractor A towing unit of articulated lorry
Transtainer A gantry crane for container sorting/stacking
Turning circle Diameter to outer wheel at full lock
Turret truck Free path lifting device for operating at high levels in narrow aisles

U

Unit loads Goods packed onto a modular carriage unit, eg pallet, crate, bin, etc, for efficient mechanical handling

Bibliography

Factory Act 1961, HMSO
Offices, Shops and Railway
Premises Act 1963. HMSO
Rules for Automatic
Sprinkler Installations, 29th
edition, Fire Officer's
Committee, Aldermary
House, Queens Street,
London EC4
BS 2629: 1960. Pallets for
Materials Handling, HMSO.
Department of Employment
Bulletins: 22 Health and
Safety at Work. Dust
explosions in factories;
25 Noise and the Worker;
34 Flame Arrestors and
Explosion Relief; 43 Safety
in Mechanical Handling;
47 Safety in Stacking
Materials, HMSO
HULETT, M. Unit Load
Handling. Gower Press Ltd,
PO Box 5, Epping, £10·00
MECHANICAL
HANDLING, Directory of
Suppliers, 33 Bowling
Green Lane, London EC1
BAILEY, P., D. FARMER,
Managing Materials in
Industry, Gower Press Ltd,
PO Box 5, Epping, £5·75
SAWDY, L., The
Economics of Distribution,
Gower Press Ltd, PO Box 5,
Epping, £4·25
The Costing of Handling
and Storage in Warehouses,
Vol I and II, Department
of Trade and Industry
£4·00
WILLIAMS, C.,
Conventional Warehouses,
HMSO £2·00
WILLIAMS, C., High Bay
Warehouses, HMSO £2·00
BAKER, D. W., Not So
Much a Warehouse,
HMSO £4·00
WILLIAMS, C., Problems
of Fire in High Bay
Warehouses, National
Materials Handling Centre

Acknowledgements

The authors would like to
thank the following for their
help and co-operation:
Bruce Whitehall and staff of
'Mechanical Handling'
B. Carter, National
Maritime Museum
Stockvis Ltd
HTS Transport Ltd
Jane's Freight Containers
'Commercial Motor'
'Materials Handling News'
Crane Fruehauf Ltd
S. G. Jones, Ford Motor Co
W. Jamieson, Chantrill Ltd
J. Sainsbury Ltd
M. Knight, Demag Ltd
A. S. Goldberg, Powder
Advisory Centre
S. Henricksson,
Frigoscandia Ltd
C. C. Wilson, BOAC

Useful addresses

Factory Inspector,
address of Local Inspector
obtainable from Factory
Inspectorate Division,
Baynards House,
1 Chepstow Place,
Westbourne Grove,
London W2 4TF
**Freight Transport
Association,** Sunley House,
Bedford Park, Croydon,
CR9 1XU.
Fire Research Station,
Station Road, Boreham
Wood, Herts.
**National Materials
Handling Centre,**
Cranfield Institute,
Cranfield, Beds.
Petroleum Officer—see
local authority.
**Institute of Materials
Handling,** St Ives House,
St Ives Road, Maidenhead,
Berks.

Credits

Ts Intro 1
1 Heery & Heery
2 Honeysett
3, 4 Meigh
Ts Intro 2
1 Kennington, Little
4, 5 Mechanical Handling
Ts Intro 3
3, 4 National Trust
5 Sam Lambert
6 Maritime Museum
7-13 Architectural Review
Ts Loading 1
7, 8, 11a/b Toomey
12 Stockvis
13 Crane Fruehauf
14 Matral
15 Dexion
16 Joloda
17, 18b Toomey

18a Lancer Boss
19 British Monorail
21 Pengco Ltd
Inf Loading 2
2 TRRL
Inf Loading 3
1, 2 Shephard Meiller
4 Toomey
7a, b Shephard Meiller
8 Powell Duffryn
9 Reynolds Boughton
17 Toomey
Inf Loading 5
2 Hunter
3, 4, 5 Gascoigne, Gush and Dent
6a Stockvis
6b Keyzar Farnworth
7, 8 GGD
9 Power lifts
10 GGD
11a Stockvis, b Loading Systems
12 Newland Conveyors

13 Stanmill
Inf Loading 6
6, 7 Shell
8 Lansing Bagnall
Ts External 1
1 Drury
2a/b Abel Systems Ltd
3 R. Winterton
4, 5 Toomey
6 York Trailer Co
9, 10 R. Winterton
11 Lansing Bagnall
Inf External 1
1a Crane Fruehauf
1b, 2 Drury
Rubery Owen (p.70 bottom)
Inf External 2
1 Crane Fruehauf
2, 3a R. Winterton
3b Rubery Owen
4a/b, 5, 6a/b, 7 Lancer Boss
13, 14, 15, 16 Mafi (UK) Ltd
17, 18 Powell Duffryn
19 Braby
21, 22 Welford Ltd
23a/b Canadian National Railway
24 SNCF Novotrans
Ts Manual 1
1 Toomey
3, 6b WCB Clare's Ltd
9, 10, 11 Toomey
Ts Manual 2
1 Drury
5 Fiat
Inf Manual 1
1 Welconstruct
2 Linvar
Inf Manual 2
1, 2, 3, 4 Dexion
5 Toomey
Inf Manual 4
Climax (p. 104)
Ts Mechanised 1
2 Toomey
3 Chrysler
4 Toomey
6a Mary Kay Cosmetics
6b Heery & Heery
7 Orenstein & Koppel
8, 9 Chantrill
10 Dexion
11 Demag
12 John Laing
13, 14, 15, 44 Lansing Bagnall
6, 18 Dexion
19 British Monorail
20, 21 Toomey
26 Mechanical Handling
27 Cleco
28, 29 George King
30 Bagshaw
32 Post Office
33 Pantin
37-42 Toomey
43 Stewart Bale
Ts Mechanised 2
2a/c, 5 Atcost
9 Toomey
11 BRE
13 Crown Controls Ltd
14 Lansing Bagnall
15 Coventry Climax
16 Pantin
18 Lansing Bagnall
19 Orenstein + Koppell
20 Melford Engineering
21 Falconer
Inf Mechanised 1
1 Dexion
3 Mechanical Handling
5 Hi-lo
Table 1 Boltless Systems Ltd
6 Boltless
7 Mechanical Handling
8, 9, 10, 11 Boltless
12 Dexion
16, 17 Mechanical Handling
19 Mills K.
20 Boltless
21a/b Bruynzeel
22 Spacemaster
24 Dexion
26, 27 John S. Bolles
Inf Mechanised 2
3 Hudswell
5 Rubery Owen
Inf Mechanised 3
1, 2, 3 Mechanical Handling
4, 5, 6, 7 Cascade
8 Hudswell
9, 11 Atlet
12, 13 Climax
14 Ameise
15 Fleet-Line Manutention
Inf Mechanised 4
1 Lawson
3a Möllers
Inf Mechanised 7
5 Goss Handling
6 Power Lifts

Inf Mechanised 8
1, 5 British Monorail
3, 4, 8 Demag
Inf Mechanised 9
1, 2, 4, 5 MGK Engineering
7 A'Court
6 Atcost
8, 9 Lansing Bagnall
Inf Mechanised 10
1, 6 Rapistan
8, 12a Flexiveyor
11 Dexion
13a Möller
16a Teleflex
18-23 Mechanical Handling
29 Dexion
30 Geo. W. King
Ts Auto 1
frontispiece Dexion
2, 3 Ohler/Whylen
5 Williams
6 Mechanical Handling
13 HMSO
15, 16, 19 Eastern Electricity
18 Ohler
21 EB
22, 32 Mills K.
27 Integrated Handling Ltd
28 Eastern Electricity
29 SSI
31 Demag
32, 34, 35 Transrobot Ltd
33 Mechanical Handling
Ts Auto 2
1 Mills K.
2, 3 Eastern Electricity
4 British Steel
5 Lansing Bagnall
6 SSI
8 Mills K.
9 Transrobot Ltd
Inf Auto 1
2 Demag
3 Owen Thorn
4 Dexion
Inf Auto 2
2 EMI
Ts Bulk 1
1a National Water Authority
1b Lykes Lines
2 Charles Roberts
3, 4 Crane Fruehauf
7, 8 Moller
9 Mechanical Handling
11b York Trailer Co
16, 17, 18 Mechanical Handling
20 Bell Lines
Ts Bulk 2
1 Molex
3 Ceretti & Tanfani
4, 5 Dust Control Engineering
6b Ceretti & Tanfani
7a/b Alcoa
9 Redler Conveyors
10 John Laing/Whitbread
11 Redler
12 ABM Carnoustie
13 Scottish & Newcastle Breweries
14 Geo. W. King
Inf Bulk 3
1-6 Möllers
Inf Bulk 4
1 Alcoa
Ts Cold 1
1 Birds Eye
2, 4 Crane Fruehauf
5, 11, 13 Toomey
6 Western Engineering
7 Birds Eye
8 Frigoscandia
9a/b WCB Clare's
10 Birds Eye
12 Lansing Bagnall
14 Foamglass
15 Lansing Bagnall
Ts Cold 2
1 Frigoscandia
4, 5, 7 Toomey
6 Frigoscandia
10 Birds Eye
11 Lansing Bagnall
12 Eaton Yale
13 Danepak, Thetford
Ts Special 1
1 Bruynzeel
2 Crane Fruehauf
6 British Monorail
7, 8 Cleco
Ts Special 2
2 British Monorail
3, 4 Lye Trading
5 Cleco Electrical Industries
6 Matbro
7 Lansing Bagnall
8 W. T. Avery

Appendix Interprocess
1, 2, 3 Geo. W. King

Technical study Introduction 1

Introduction

An introduction to the problems of designing storage buildings, and the role of the project team.

1 The warehouse as part of the distribution system

1.01 Industrial stores are not usually designed to earn profits. Costs incurred are reflected in the production or distribution accounts, and are ultimately passed on to the consumer. Thus as the design of a warehouse affects handling and storage costs, which help to fix commodity prices, the architect bears considerable responsibility to the public. For this reason, a warehouse should be considered as part of the total distribution system from the outset. In many warehouses the operator has asked a consultant to develop a brief orientated towards mechanical handling at the expense of the efficiency of the distribution system; several of these are virtually redundant after only a few years' service **1**.

1.02 It is therefore in the client's interest that the multi-disciplinary expertise of the architect should be used in a total system approach; consultants can then be used for their primary function, to examine the economics and flow patterns of the distribution system in relation to the user's manufacturing and marketing potential, working in parallel with and contributing to the architect's investigation into the best storage arrangement and building type for the required through-puts in relation to the product's packaging, the potential for mechanical handling and the effects of future change.

Warehouse design

1.03 There are no hard and fast rules for warehouse design; policy decisions depend on type of product, the speed that it will pass through the warehouse, the type of outlet and consumer market being served and the distance of travel involved. For example, there are conflicting opinions about whether storage facilities should be centralised. Two very large household names in the retail trade, one in pharmaceuticals, the other in groceries, have similar outlet patterns but

1 '*In many warehouses the operator has asked a consultant to develop a brief oriented towards mechanical handling at the expense of distribution system.*'

employ different distribution systems. One has a central factory and uses several redistribution centres around the country, operated by contractors. The other employs three main bulk storage warehouses, a certain amount of manufacture and processing, and computer ordering for sorting for delivery to individual retail outlets.

1.04 Although this decision is usually based on market research and is the client's responsibility, the pattern can be seriously affected by other factors. The form and unit size in which the product reaches the store is a prime consideration. This will often have been determined by production and marketing considerations, without sufficient regard for the storage medium. By understanding the product and its handling properties, design teams can feed back useful data to the client, resulting in a more efficient package, a reduced cost of packaging materials and higher efficiency of storage and handling systems.

1.05 A good example of this approach is a company which adds a 3 per cent on-cost to parts suppliers' contracts and sends them a detailed packaging specification, including size, shape and materials: this has enabled them to cut warehousing and handling costs considerably. It would be possible to take a supplier to court for breach of contract for unacceptable packaging.

1.06 Equally, transport should be considered as a flexible system, integrated with the warehouse by employing dimensionally co-ordinated unit loads. Even some newly built installations which are considered well-planned have cramped loading bays which choke in peak conditions (the company forgot that suppliers' vehicles were larger than their own, and only provided very constricted manoeuvring space). In the handbook, data have been included on vehicle types and sizes to aid designers planning for transport.

1.07 The architect's job in this field should therefore be the co-ordination of these systems, keeping an overall view of the project and its part in the total manufacturing and distribution system.

2 'The project team should include drivers selected from the floor.'

2 The project team

2.01 The design of such a complex building as a warehouse, combining building fabric and sophisticated plant, can only be carried out by a team. Many plant manufacturers offer package deals, especially for complicated installations such as automated high-bay warehouses. Though very knowledgeable in equipment, they are not concerned with other factors outside this sphere. Professional involvement is therefore vital to protect the client. Each specialist member of the team must keep the others constantly aware of the effect which various decisions will have on the project.

Members of the team

2.02 There is no single form for a project team, but the skeleton team outlined here is a useful guide. Size and complexity of a project will obviously govern the content. The part that each member of the team plays in the development of different zones will be discussed more fully in specialist sections of the handbook. The project team should include:

Basic members
Multi-disciplinary leader (architect)
Representative from client's management[1]
Structural engineer
Quantity surveyor
Mechanical services engineer
Electrical engineer
Public health engineer
Mechanical handling consultant
Transport consultant
Accountant/business consultant[1]
Mechanical handling engineer
Representative of the insurance company involved.

Team members passing through at various stages:
Distribution manager[1]
Existing warehouse manager(s)
Future warehouse manager[1]
Transport manager[1]
Union shop stewards[1]
Warehouseman/operatives/drivers selected from the floor[1] [2]
Local authority representatives, ie building inspector, factory inspector, fire officer, etc.

2.03 No project team, however well organised, can operate efficiently without the client's full support. In most cases of industrial storage building schemes, this is the board of the company concerned. The managing director should be kept active and interested throughout all stages of the project. Management lethargy is easily transmitted down into the client's representatives within the project team, and will adversely affect the efficiency of the whole operation **3**.

The brief
2.04 The development of an accurate and far-sighted brief is essential to the success of a storage project **4**. To ensure that accurate data are to be collected and analysed, *users* must be represented on the team. Often, the management of the company concerned is not the real user. One company put the future warehouse manager in charge of the initial project, assuming that if he was to use the installation, he would exert every effort to see that the planning was satisfactory. This worked well, but was a special case as the projected warehouse was of a scale and importance to merit a supervisor of management rank. It is well worthwhile contacting users at all levels, such as plant operation, transport, handling, and general maintenance. These members of the team will pass through at different stages so that there is little danger of the team reaching an unmanageable number.

2.05 Labour relations are increasingly entering the sphere of the project team. In the final analysis, all industrial projects involve operatives. The project team should continually inform the labour force of what is happening and how decisions will affect them. Usually, this results in useful information and active co-operation in the commissioning period. Unions should be kept informed; one installation incorporated some expensive scissor lifts that have never been used, blacked by a

---

[1] Continuing in team after completion and commissioning of project

union as unsafe. This waste could have been avoided with a little co-operation from each side. However, a shop steward may not be the most expert representative technically, and a balance of union and technically expert personnel should be maintained if possible.

Team action during construction

2.06 The multi-disciplinary team should continue to operate at a high level during construction. The architect should define contractual relationships and responsibilities to all the client's members of the team. Members of the team concerned with specific sections of the project, eg future section store managers, are often tempted to ask subcontractors to install on-site modifications to the system, without referring this to the general contractor or the architect. Long and expensive claims have resulted. The same applies to informing the client about the effect of changes at the construction stage. Minor variations can be assimilated into a contractor's programme, but major system changes can cause havoc.

2.06 Industrial clients often want to install the warehouse plant as soon as it is possible to gain access, so that initial commissioning can take place while other building operations continue. Unless the timing for this operation is agreed at the design stage, the costing agreed in the initial tender and the client kept aware of his contractual responsibility, the project can run into serious trouble—especially where integral storage plant and building structures are involved. The client must understand what is possible at each stage of construction and be aware of the requirements for special access situations, especially before any new internal route system is complete on an existing site. For example, one client had planned his distribution cycle so critically close to the project completion date, that when abnormal winter conditions put back the programme and commissioning by over a month, there was trouble in finding alternative accommodation. It was the architect's responsibility to inform the client that bad weather might hold up building, plant installation and thus commissioning.

Phased developments

2.07 Large projects are often phased developments. The project team in this case has the added responsibility in the design and construction stages of ensuring smooth movements between phases, with as little disruption as possible to the

4 '*The development of an accurate and far-sighted brief is essential to the success of a storage project.*'

storage process already in operation. Phased development for architects is basically a problem of initial planning. For warehousemen, it is one of continuing storage and sorting activities while works continue. The feedback from the initial stages usually results in some modifications to the later phases. Again, contact with the warehouse operatives is essential, both for information and the smooth running of the system as it accelerates to full operating capacity.

Maintenance and costs-in-use

2.08 Even if maintenance and costs-in-use have been considered fully at the design stage as an integral part of the project design, the team should ensure that the correct preventative maintenance procedures are followed. After commissioning, the architect will progressively hand over the responsibility to the management. With complex storage buildings, management should realise the importance of the company core of the team remaining responsible for the continued operation of the project, anyway at first, and that this team is fully aware of the scheme as finally built, with a knowledge of the reasons behind the major decisions.

3 '*Management lethargy is easily transmitted to the project team.*'

Technical study Introduction 2

Storage and distribution as a total system

Building designers must understand the components that form the total storage and distribution function. The relationship between packaging, method of storage, storage plant and building, and transport and distribution systems are so closely enmeshed that they cannot be considered independently in design.

1 The warehouse as a means of control

1.01 The consumer society has generated a complex manufacturing and distribution network and the warehouse acts as a valve within the system for controlling consumer markets. This is achieved by:

a Balancing machine-oriented mass production with irregular or unpredictable demand, for instance the economic manufacturing quantities for packeted goods

b Balancing irregular and seasonal production with round-the-year demand. For example, frozen vegetables or raw, perishable ingredients for continuous production

c Building up stocks for seasonal peak demands

d Acting as a redistribution point between the manufacturer and the retail outlet, ensuring that specific items are constantly available.

Economically, it is desirable to manufacture goods in batches. This conflicts with seasonal demand and the consumer's demand to buy any product throughout the year.

1.02 This is especially important in the present inflationary situation. Distribution costs form roughly a fifth of the retail price of most consumer goods, and are still rising. The warehouse has become an important economic valve, combining cost benefits of batch production with controlled distribution. To keep prices down, distribution costs must be minimised by efficient storage and transport.

2 The European connection

2.01 The effects of Britain joining the EEC are not just of increased areas for sales and distribution, but also of substantially increased competition. Unless storage and distribution systems are considered together, profits will be even harder to come by. Some Dutch and West German companies already run very slick and sophisticated integrated storage and distribution systems, and continental distribution organisations have recently been buying into British companies in increasing numbers. There is a trend towards centralised manufacturing units linked to the storage function on the same site, to reduce costs, especially where a large variety of goods are made. One Swedish cold store construction company, itself running contract refrigerated warehouses, is planning cold store 'villages', attached to linked manufacturing units.

2.02 In the European context, efficient storage must play a larger part in stabilising EEC commodity production and distribution. At present, this shows all the signs of bureaucracy, rather than physical distribution management, especially in the area of dairy products.

3 Storage considered as production cost

3.01 As the demands placed on warehousing and distribution operations increase, management should consider warehousing costs in the same terms as production costs, investing in materials handling and storage equipment to increase efficiency,

1

profit margins, and reduce distribution and warehouse costs. The accent should fall on value and running cost rather than initial cost. The present trend towards rationalising and grouping manufacturing processes **1** is an attempt by central organisations to reduce costs and excessive overheads.

3.02 With the high price of industrial land and the increasing quantities of stock being held to cope with the fluctuations in consumer demand, the whole system, especially the cubic capacity of the warehouse and transport, must be used to the full to reduce operational costs-in-use, and to keep commodity prices down. High costs result from a lack of co-ordination between transport and storage systems, and between a storage system and its enclosure. This applies not only to manufacturers, but also to specialist companies which provide a contract warehousing and distribution service.

4 Packaging, the basis of the storage system

4.01 The method of packaging goods is a major element in the total system. Packaging is becoming more sophisticated; now it not only protects but can also advertise and act as the basic storage unit. The size and type of package determine the character of a unit load, in turn generating the type of transport to be used, in conjunction with the quantities and distances involved. The form of the packaging and unit load contribute to choice of storage function and its continual operating characteristics and potential efficiency. One example of this is expanded plastic used for packaging; this results in a uniform shape of package which is much easier to handle in bulk, and which suits a mechanised storage system. Another example is polythene film, used to 'shrink wrap' pallet loads of goods which used to be packed into boxes; this allows better use of the space provided, more stable stacking and easier checking. However, the fire protection problem is increased (this is discussed more fully in Technical study: Building function).

Specification
4.02 Managements hold very different attitudes towards packaging and handling of goods. Some place full responsibility on the carrier and rely on the common sense of the operatives within the store; others spend a great deal of money on packaging the finished product, but accept valuable components packed in old cardboard boxes; the third, and unfortunately rare, category dictates the standards for both incoming and outgoing packaging with a detailed specification for each type of product.

1 *72 000 m² warehouse and service centre for a department store in Georgia.*

4.03 The specification should include:
1 The best size of the package for storage and distribution of the commodity
2 The number of product units per package, depending on weight, display function, retail requirements
3 The materials in which the product should be packed
4 Graphics and codes for transport and storage identification
5 The number of packages per unit load, and the best stacking patterns for stability and volume
6 The type of unit load best suited to transport and storage eg Europallets, air pallets etc.
7 Method of securing packages to unit load, ie shrink wrapping.
For incoming supplies, this specification should be sent out with the tender documents to the subcontractor. For dispatch, it will save the company a lot of money in the long term. It should be the handling manager's responsibility to dictate these terms to subcontractors and to their own manufacturing departments. One manufacturer finds that a 3 per cent on-cost added to each contract, to ensure correct packaging, is money well spent. The building designer should check that this process is happening, as it is an important aid to the design of the storage system.

5 Transport: an integral part of the storage and distribution system

5.01 The boundaries between transport, storage and mechanical handling are becoming more difficult to distinguish. Containerisation has combined storage and transport, ISO containers, swop bodies and semi-trailers being used for short-term storage **2**. The building designer must understand the full implications of modern transport and its potential as a major and integral part of the storage and handling system.

Road transport and mechanical handling
5.02 Delays in vehicle turnround have been an important and growing cost problem for a long time. Loading bay and marshalling area design will be discussed in section 2. The loading bay is the critical link between the storage system and the transport and distribution systems. Choked space can wreck the successful operation of a warehouse, as slow vehicle turnround causes accumulation in the dock area. By using more mechan-

2

3

4

*2 Containers used as both
storage and transport.
3 Well considered design of
basic package—eg a range of
related interlocking
dimensions.
4, 5 New ideas in handling
aids on vehicles: 4 hydraulic
clamp covering whole length
of semi-trailer's platform, for
handling bricks.*

ised handling facilities on vehicles, the distribution industry
can increase productivity of men and machinery, reduce
operating costs, damages, and ultimately the cost to the
consumer 4.

5.03 To date, however, most British transport operators have
been very conservative about mounting mechanical handling
aids to their vehicles, compared with European practice. The
prevalent attitude is that every extra piece of equipment on a
vehicle increases the taxation weight, so decreasing the payload. Superficially, this is true, but many operators have
found that their turnround times have been so reduced when
handling aids have been employed that productivity has been
more than doubled, allowing the numbers of vehicles to be
reduced.

5.04 Pressure to modernise with handling aids increases as
more shops and factories specify periods when they will not
accept deliveries: this, combined with the new drivers' hours
regulations and city centre restrictions, is forcing deliveries
into shorter periods; this affects not only the peak arrival of
vehicles at a warehouse, but also storage, order picking and
load assembly functions.

5.05 Typical examples of useful on-vehicle handling aids are the
tailboard lift and demountable body units. Tail lifts link
transport with the retail outlet: roll pallets can be unloaded
fast by the driver, pushing the pallet on to the lift, travelling
to pavement level at the press of a button, and pushing the
pallet into the shop. Multiple delivery times and traffic
obstruction have been greatly reduced by this method.

5.06 Demountable truck bodies have made the haulage
vehicle much more flexible. One truck chassis can pick up a
body preloaded at a warehouse, leave it on mounted legs at a
supermarket loading bay, pick up the empty unit, return to the
warehouse and immediately leave with another laden body 7.

5 *portable yard lift.*
6 *This lorry is leaving its swop body on mounted legs at loading bay, and is now ready to receive another.*
7 *Container is lifted to load directly into aircraft hold.*

Further, the bodies can be 'trunk hauled', like containers. A European standard is being prepared for swop bodies for use within the EEC road and rail systems. (See technical study External storage 1.)

6 Total system thinking: an example

6.01 A good example of this can be seen in air cargo and airport catering. Within a very short turnround time, the inventory, stock control, load build-up, transport, delivery and loading into the aircraft is completed. Demountable bodies are mounted on scissor lifts, integral with the lorry, which raise the whole body to aircraft door height. Jumbo jets have galleys that break down into unit loads, allowing fast handling and reduced handling staffing 7.

7 The influence of shop design on the distribution system

7.01 As so many factors are mutually dependent for efficiency, a large scale breakdown or major policy change will disrupt the whole storage and distribution system. An example of this is of a major retail organisation acquiring another large chain of shops. These had been modified to fulfil a function that the existing stores did not meet, but were to be supplied from the former central store. Virtually overnight, the capacity of the system was expected to double, which required an expanded computerised stock control function, a larger and reworked transport fleet, a range of new suppliers adding to the already heavy traffic and increased turnover, putting added pressure on loading bays, sorting areas and load assembly zones.

8 The future

8.01 Warehouse and distribution buildings are likely to be needed beyond the end of this century, although it is already possible to see a trend towards a total transportation system, so well controlled that it can act as the storage system itself. This is not pure science fiction: the control systems, although at present very expensive, are already available. In fact, a system has been planned for a new city in an Eastern bloc country, where the consumer would key an order code into a terminal at his home, and the nearest product of that type would be directed to him immediately from within the transport system, the cost being deducted from a centralised account automatically. This is based on the pneumatic tube principle.
8.02 In the future, pressure to conserve the environment may influence storage system design. But these environmental benefits may be gained only at the expense of price increases; for instance, an alternative transport structure, though environmentally preferable, may be far more expensive to run.

PACIFIC WESTERN

Technical study Introduction 3

Storage buildings: a short history

A short illustrated survey of storage buildings and techniques through the ages.

Storage buildings started when man began to cultivate enough food in the summer to last him through the winter. The Pharaohs had a tightly organised chain of grain warehouses, for which Joseph organised a rigorous method of stock control (see Genesis 41). The Romans had extremely sophisticated trading and distribution methods. Their warehouses often had concrete walls, with wide spanning timber roof trusses. Porticus Aemilia, a granary built in 193 BC, was a concrete vaulted structure built on three levels down a slope, 1. Huge warehouses have also been found at Ostia, the main distribution point for the whole Roman Empire. One example, Horrea Epagathiana, still survives, 2.

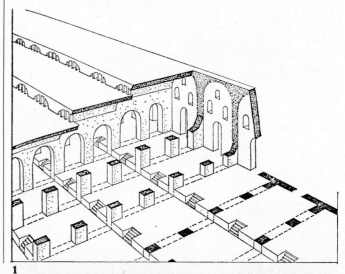

1

2

4

As the Roman Empire
fragmented, international
trade contracted, and the
constant wars meant that
large scale storage was
confined to cellars, in keeps,
or under the great halls of
manors. The most important
medieval storage building
was the tithe barn, built to
hold tithes, a form of tax to
the church, given mainly in
the form of produce. One of
the few surviving tithe barns,
at Great Coxwell, near
Faringdon, 3, 4, is built on a
stone foundation and
measures 46 m × 13 m ×
14 m.

5

6

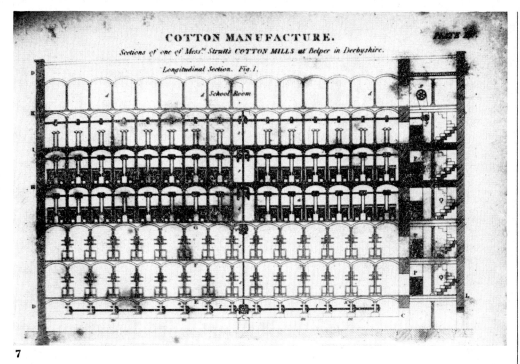

7

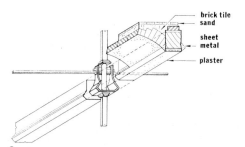

brick tile
sand
sheet metal
plaster

8

The greatest developments in storage buildings came with the Industrial Revolution. Most early warehouses were built from local stone and brick, with timber floors and gable-end hoists, such as these at Lancaster quayside, dating from 1750, 5. Inside the warehouse (a typical interior a tobacco warehouse, is shown in 6), the combination of timber structure, inflammable goods and lighted candles constituted a terrible fire risk.

By the 1790s, an increasing number of fires in cotton mills forced engineers to find an alternative construction. William Strutts's six-storey cotton mill in Derby (1792-3) was the first multi-storey fireproof building. The floors consisted of brick arches springing from heavy timber beams supported by heavy cast-iron pillars, 8. His North Mill at Belper, 7, incorporates all the structural advances made in earlier mills. From this, it was a short step to a predominantly cast iron framework, 9, from which developed the steel frame of the Chicago school in the 1890s.

9

10

11

12

13

14

Mass production techniques of the Industrial Revolution produced a more complex storage demand. Ships had irregular sailings and required buffer collection and groupage points for cargoes to be assembled, and the growing consumer society generated seasonal peaks, in exports and consumer demand.
To cater for this, huge, many-storeyed warehouses were built at the ports. In the 1840s and '50s the Albert and Stanley Docks, at Liverpool, by Jesse Hartley, 10, 11; and warehouses at Bristol, 12, by W. B. Gingell

were built.
Another form of construction, a cast iron framed building, is illustrated by this boathouse, built at Sheerness in 1858-60, 13.
At the same time, the first big grain elevators that so impressed Le Corbusier were going up, showing new standards in monolithic size, and introducing new shapes and bulk-handling technology into industrial storage, 14, 15. In this century, the greatest developments have been in fields of mechanical handling, 16, and transport, 17.
Previously, commodities were stored in sacks, boxes or crates on the floors of multi-storey warehouses; they needed much manual handling, making it difficult to meet manufacturers' and retail traders' demands for faster turnover. Consumer demand fluctuated and commodity ranges increased. The obvious development was to handle the goods as unit loads.
Unit loads had been used for many years; for instance, from the beginning of this

15

16

century, the London and North-Eastern Railway ran lift-off containers interchangeable between road and rail wagons, 18.
Forklift trucks carrying pallets were first used to a significant extent by the US army during World War II.
More recently, palletisation and racking methods have virtually eliminated the multi-storey warehouse. To carry unit loads long distances, the ISO container has been developed, reducing distribution costs and making handling more flexible. Later developments, caused by increased competition and the need to reduce labour and handling costs, are computerised stock control, plant such as fixed-path order pickers, stacker cranes, and high-bay warehouses which allow a very high concentration of goods on the minimum of land.
Commercial economic practice in the West has developed by supplying goods in sufficient quantities to keep prices stable and to generate demand.
Warehouses play an essential part in this, acting as valves which help to stabilise the economy of a community.

Bibliography

SMITH, S. Art and architecture of ancient Egypt. London, 1973, Pelican [9(Ad62)] £4·20
LAWRENCE, A. Greek architecture. London, 1973, Pelican [9(Ad495)] £6·50
KIDSON, P., P. MURRAY and P. THOMPSON, History of English architecture. Harmondsworth, 1965, Pelican [(Ac)] 90p
PEVSNER, N. Pioneers of modern design. Harmondsworth, 1970, Pelican [(Ac)] 80p
LAVEDON, P. French architecture. Harmondsworth, 1956, Pelican [9(Ad44)] 25p
GIEDION, S. The eternal present. London, Vol 1 1962, Vol 2 1964, Oxford University Press [9(Ac)] £3·15
GIEDION, S. Space, time and architecture. London, 1967, Oxford University [9(Ac)] £6
RICHARDS, J. M. The functional tradition in early industrial buildings. London, 1958, The Architectural Press [2(Ac)] £3·00
FLETCHER, BANISTER. A history of architecture on the comparative method. London, 1967, Athlone Press, 17th edition [9(Ac)] £4·50
SKEMPTON, A. W., and H. R. JOHNSON The first iron frames. *The Architectural Review*, 1962, March, pp175-186 [(28) Xh1]

17

18

Technical study Loading 1

Loading bay design

The loading bay is the beginning and end of any production storage process and must be able to handle peak traffic flows, be adaptable to future conditions and operate in all weathers. To achieve this, the architect must co-ordinate the specialist team of management, system designers, mechanical handling and transport and equipment consultants. If he does not, incorrect decisions may be made which are magnified throughout the distribution system. Dimensions of bays, vehicles and equipment are given in Information sheets Loading 1—6.

1 Loading bay position in relation to warehouse perimeter

1.01 Loading bays are frequently placed at the corner of an industrial building where trucks have room to manoeuvre, catering for both incoming and dispatched goods: logically, with a production line and storage process, the loading bay should be positioned as close as possible to the beginning and end of the operation. This, however, duplicates plant; some argue that with contemporary sophisticated communications and handling plant, loading bays might be placed at node points around the building. Advantages and disadvantages of this, compared to a single, long bay are shown in **1**.

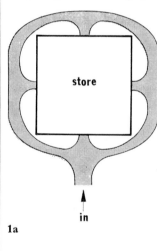

1a

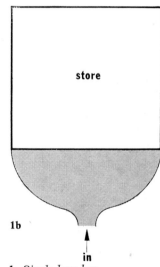

1b

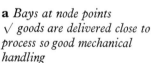

a *Bays at node points*
√ *goods are delivered close to process so good mechanical handling*
× *not flexible—industrial processes may change*
× *perimeter road needed, with turning space for each bay.*
× *other vehicles constricted by trucks manoeuvring to each bay.*

b *Single long bay.*
√ *allows flexible handling and storage.*
√ *fast turnround.*

Large numbers of vehicles operate faster if loading and despatch bays are separated. This is mandatory for customs.

√ = *good point.*
× = *bad point.*

1 *Comparison of loading bay positions.*

1.02 The designer must plan possible layouts, considering:
1 Best flow for vehicles also considering peak conditions, future expansion, and types of vehicle involved
2 The production or storage flow pattern, and possible product packaging and system changes
3 The type of goods involved, considering special features like product incompatibility or fire and corrosion hazards.
1.03 User requirements and site constraints usually restrict

choices, while planning in co-ordination with the systems designer and plant engineer would eliminate inefficient solutions. Computer models can simulate how the design will affect peak build-ups, stoppages, and handling times. These exercises often demonstrate how seemingly insignificant decisions can waste much time and money.

2 Approach roads, marshalling and buffer areas

2.01 Loading bays cannot be designed in isolation, they also require:

1 *An approach road* within the site area, which is separated from the public road by a supervised gate
2 *A marshalling area* where trucks accumulate before getting into the loading bay position. This area is vital, as the particular bay may not be ready in time
3 *A truck buffer area*—a secondary manoeuvring area for large storage buildings where many trucks collect and are sorted for specific loading bays. These areas should be supervised by a traffic office.

Approach roads and marshalling areas
2.02 Where turn round is fast (eg a high turnover wholesale

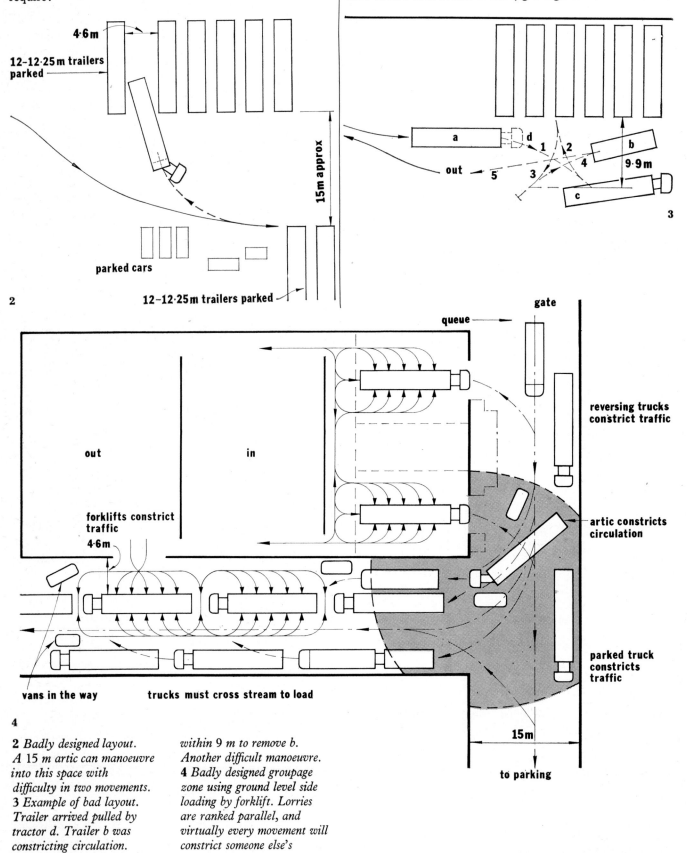

2

3

4

2 *Badly designed layout. A 15 m artic can manoeuvre into this space with difficulty in two movements.*
3 *Example of bad layout. Trailer arrived pulled by tractor d. Trailer b was constricting circulation. Tractor d shunted round*

within 9 m to remove b. Another difficult manoeuvre.
4 *Badly designed groupage zone using ground level side loading by forklift. Lorries are ranked parallel, and virtually every movement will constrict someone else's action.*

warehouse, handling palletised unit loads) the number of loading bays can be reduced by careful marshalling area design. Space savings depend on site and vehicle flow conditions. Cross manoeuvring should be avoided wherever possible, as shunting vehicles, especially in a counter-clockwise flow requiring blind left-hand reversing, have been seen to baulk other incoming or outgoing trucks, slowing the whole cycle and considerably reducing the possible work load **2, 3, 4**. **2.03** To design marshalling areas:

1 Establish probable number of types and calculate peaks of different vehicles. (In break bulk or mixed long distance haulage and local delivery situations, arrival peaks vary.)
2 Examine existing patterns in the area (as vehicle peaks depend on local traffic conditions), the distance that the vehicles have travelled, and the operatives' working day. Future city delivery restrictions will also affect peak distribution. Often a peak of light vans hold up the heavy vehicles, causing jams, so it is best to segregate the flow. With the British rule of the road, a clockwise traffic flow allows articulated vehicles to reverse quickly.
2.04 Dimensions of gate entries, marshalling areas and buffer areas are given in Information sheet Loading 2.

Buffer or accumulation zones
2.05 Buffer zones should always be provided, even for short waits. It is uneconomic to build the maximum number of

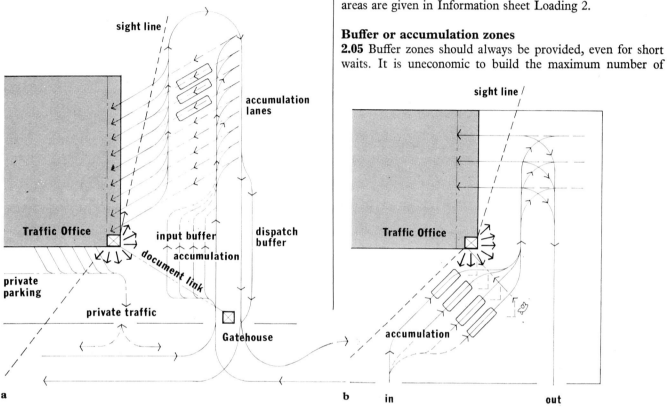

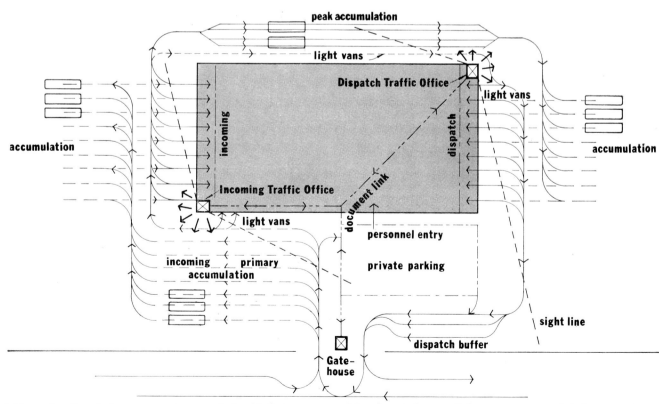

5 *Examples of typical approach road, marshalling and buffer area layout.* **a** *Dual purpose dock with fast turn-round.* **b** *Typical layout for small installation. Truck drivers' route (arrowed) from accumulation bay to traffic office.* **c** *Fast turn-round segregated dock, eg groupage or large scale distribution warehouse layout.*

loading bays required at peak times, and there is always a chance of a breakdown. A buffer area is also useful for document processing. Buffer park size is determined by the estimated turn-round time of different vehicle types, against the projected peak flow. Queueing lanes should be clearly marked with either visual displays or amplified orders for bay allocation. This area should be out of the way of manoeuvring trucks (see Technical studies Mechanised and Automated Storage para 7).

3 Detailed problems of bay design

How many bays?

3.01 This is linked to design of marshalling and buffer space. Number depends on:

1 Product being handled and speed of handling
2 Type of vehicle being loaded
3 Predicted traffic flow
4 Future growth of goods and traffic
5 Financial policy of client.

3.02 Large numbers of bays increase building volume, and thus costs-in-use, and the risks of theft but the marshalling area is smaller and the loading bay buffer is improved. Handling from vehicle into store will be quicker, as the turn-round will be fast, and the handling equipment will be working on a wide front.

3.03 Where expansion is anticipated, the marshalling area should be increased and handling speed in the loading bay should be improved. By increasing the marshalling space, there is a saving in building volume and the overall construction cost will be less; turn-round speed will be higher for lower plant investment. In this situation the handling system, ie forklift trucks, would always operate under pressure, which increases the chance of a breakdown. The designer must co-ordinate with the other consultants in making this decision, as a mistake here can mean the difference between profit and loss for a company.

Straight or angled bays?

3.04 Choice is between 90°, angled or straight through layout, depending on trade handled and characteristics of the unit load. For instance, if curtain-sided vehicles are loaded from block stacks, ground level loading with straight through access is efficient **6**. A large soft drinks company finds that this method still allows the quickest turn-round. (See also Information sheet Loading 2 for dock dimensions.)

3.05 But straight through designs are not suitable for many vehicles and containers, and they hinder future development. They rely on parallel parking, with either ground level or

6 Hand-stacked load of bulk cartons, loaded over the side from forklift truck. Little used now.

raised dock loading. It is often slower to position a truck accurately parallel to a dock than to reverse into an end-loading bay.

3.06 There are several arguments in favour of 90° or angled bays. A 90° bay enables a fast turn round, as the driver can easily see to where he is reversing in his mirrors. A 15 m articulated vehicle needs 21 m in front for manoeuvring at 90°. If there is not enough length between a 90° dock face and the edge of the site, the saw tooth arrangement permits manoeuvring. The angle cut out reduces the loading space, but reversing is slightly less difficult with a clockwise circulation. A balance of speed and flow to space available should be decided by the designer when making the decision on the number of bays and size of the marshalling area.

7 Tight loading bay and parking area with many trailers fitted into a small area.

Do not design with too close tolerances

3.07 In many existing bays the tolerances are so tight that turn-round times have been hampered, and in some cases it is thought that more money is lost from reduced throughput than the initial savings in reducing area of the building **7**. For example in some bays, the driver cannot leave his cab due to the narrow high sides of a sunken dock, or other bays are so close fitting for easy side access with forklift trucks, that the reversing manoeuvre has been seriously slowed down. The solution would have been to have specified hinge-down bridging plates and a wider dock.

Should the loading bay be enclosed?

3.08 Totally enclosed loading bays are uncommon, due to high building costs and costs-in-use. Their advantages are total independence from the outside environment, and a greater control over theft **8**. Other than cost, the major problems are of fume extraction and lighting. Most totally enclosed bays operate straight-through with a door at each end, or are for railway wagon loading.

3.09 The canopied loading bay is normal. All loading bays should give some weather protection, even if truck dock weather seals are fitted. It is usual to provide 4·5 to 6 m of cover, and a translucent roof covering is advisable to achieve adequate illumination on the dock floor. The underside of the structure should not be less than 4·6 m to clear a 2·5 m high container on a skeletal trailer, but higher clearances may be required with special box vans. The canopy should fall towards the building, in order to avoid water flowing onto the vehicles beneath **9**.

Raised or ground level docks?

3.10 Loading bays can be equipped with a raised dock, a sunken road, or trucks and containers can be loaded from ground level by forklift trucks or conveyor belts.

3.11 Sunken roads can lead to problems of reversing and

8 *Totally enclosed loading bay. (Note structural clearances, the van at the dock is about 3·6 m high.) Note good light level without glare, clearly marked bay lines, well painted columns to assist in reversing, extraction* *grill under stairs, and retracted dock leveller. As usual there is a quantity of rubbish and broken pallets, as there is seldom provision in the loading area for its disposal.*

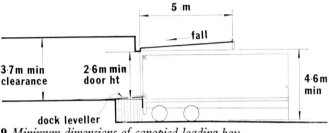

9 *Minimum dimensions of canopied loading bay.*

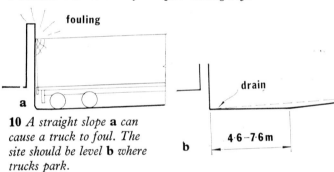

10 *A straight slope **a** can cause a truck to foul. The site should be level **b** where trucks park.*

suspension damage, although allowing a constant level factory or warehouse floor and loading bay. The natural falls of the land on most sites can be used to form a loading bay level change. In sunken road docks, gradients should not exceed 10 per cent and should be level for 4·6 m to 7·6 m before the face of the dock, depending on the size of the vehicles expected. If a slope runs up to a dock face, a container or van can easily foul the structure with its roof before the base has reached the dock, and forklift trucks and pallet trucks can 'ground' on the hump produced by the sloping truck bed **10**.

3.12 Where ice and snow are likely, articulated vehicles can skid and jack-knife on slopes, even at low speeds, and can cause extensive and costly damage to the loading area. Wires sunk into the slope keep the surface above freezing point, or an epoxy resin and granite chip non-slip surface (as being used at traffic junctions in London), can be laid. Drains should be provided in sunken roads as mud, slush and water can accumulate under a dock leveller. Extraction should also be provided, as the extra tractive effort of climbing the slope will produce proportionately more fumes. Loads may also topple down the slope; often to make way for the next vehicle, flat trucks leave the dock with an unsecured load, to rope and sheet up in the buffer zone. Any badly packed pallet has a good chance of falling off on the slope, causing an expensive hold-up.

11a

11b

11a *When a truck stops to load it constricts the road. Manoeuvring forklift trucks then block it completely. Externally stacked goods* *impede loading on both sides.* ***b*** *With two forklifts in operation, the throughway is frequently impassable to heavy vehicles.*

4 Raised dock design

4.01 Raised docks are very efficient for some loading operations and should be used in conjunction with a dock levelling device, as truck bed heights vary from type to type and between unloaded and laden conditions. Some people argue that if nearly all the trucks are of one type, only a few bays need be fitted with leveller plates. Unless the operation is very simple or the future development very clear, this decision is short sighted (for dimensions see Information sheet Loading 1 and 5).

4.02 Containers on skeletal trailers can have floor heights as high as 1·5 m: the normal truck has an average floor height of 1·4 m and urban delivery trucks vary from 1 to 1·2 m. Forklift or pallet trucks, often run on solid tyres, which may be damaged by continuous level change impacts; a dock levelling device is essential to bridge the gap between the dock and all the above heights, without exceeding the maximum gradient of 10 per cent (for details of vehicle heights see Information sheet Loading 1).

4.03 Dock levellers are either hydraulic or counter balance operated, and should be a minimum of 2·2 m wide, with a non-skid surface, and long enough to ensure that a forklift is nearly horizontal when entering a van or container. Permanent adjustable dock levellers are the most practical and safest way of overcoming the problem. Designers should be aware that oversteep gradients can drain electric forklift batteries faster and can cause pallet trucks to run away; these should be specified with a brake for loading bay use **12**.

5 ISO containers and demountable body units

5.01 Most common large vehicles today are enclosed trailers **13**, ISO containers and demountable body units. ISO containers and TIR services have had a marked effect on loading bay and marshalling area design. The vehicles that carry ISO containers are large; their loading also requires different handling and packaging, based on special forklift trucks and unit loads. Due to documentation problems and uncertain delivery for containers on the short sea route into Europe, the present trend is to return to driver-accompanied 'tilt' trailers for this type of service.

14 *Special small forklift truck filling container.*

12 *Powered pallet truck moving up dock leveller.*

13 *Typical enclosed trailers.*

15 *The small forklift exchanges loads with a turret truck at the buffer zone.*

Forklift trucks and loading bays
5.02 There are conflicting opinions on the best loading bay organisation for 'stuffing' and unpacking containers and demountable bodies. By using a raised dock, special forklift trucks can run in and out of the container and transfer the goods directly to and from the storage medium in one operation **14**. Small forklifts designed for container stuffing have only a limited use in stacking goods, and a larger truck has to be used as well. This means a buffer space is needed to transfer loads between forklift and reach truck **15**. If side loading on a raised dock can be justified, the reach truck or turret truck could be used for loading flat trailers and enclosed units direct; the counter argument is that as most traffic in the future will be containerised, there will have to be a load transfer point

between the forklift and reach truck in the store anyway.

5.03 ISO containers and trailers have conflicting loading requirements. The floors of most British trailers are not strong enough to accept forklift trucks; so they require either ground level loading (over the side) or a finger dock—the best compromise for operators required to handle both trailers and containers. A steep, angled, single-sided finger dock (75°-80°), allows either

1 conventional end loading with a dock leveller

2 sideloading without the forklift having to run on the floor, and

3 ground level side loading for bulky objects. The steep angle of the dock reduces both on-dock and truck manoeuvring area, and permits fast turn-round cycle (see Information sheet Loading 2).

5.04 Although the detailed stowage of goods in containers is not within the scope of this handbook, the designer should realise the permutations of pallets and the handling plant required, so that the correct space is allocated for the operation. If forklift trucks are used, notice must be taken of the power plants; petrol and diesel are not suitable for container filling, due to rapid fume build-up. Even liquid petroleum gas produces enough toxic fumes to be dangerous in the constricted space of a container, and may contaminate perishables. Electric traction is best for this work, but then battery charging provision must be made, with the associated acid problems on the floor (see Information sheet Mechanised storage 5. Data on forklift truck sizes is in Information sheet Mechanised storage 3). When designing for container use, wheel loadings of laden forklift trucks or pallet trucks should not exceed 22·7 kN, otherwise the container floor may be damaged. Due to this, designers can choose their loading bay floor surface, knowing that these weights will not be exceeded. A good rule of thumb is that a forklift truck with 2 tonnes lifting capacity is satisfactory, but always check with the mechanical handling consultant.

Pallets and unit loads

5.05 Pallets are the most usual method for loading containers (see Information sheet Mechanised storage 3 Pallets); note that pallet sizes were standardised before containers. Many companies have standardised pallets suitable for road or rail use, which may not suit optimum packing patterns in containers. If rail waggons are to be loaded as well, a store should be provided to hold both 1200 × 1000 mm road transport pallets, 800 × 1200 mm European rail pallets, and any damaged units. It is good practice to provide an easily accessible store for pallets, as some companies wish to collect theirs, and there are always damaged units that soon clutter a loading area if not disposed of. As an alternative to timber pallets, cardboard or plastics sheet may be used, especially for manual loading, which is economic for 'deep sea' routes, owing to the need for full volume packing and for stability. Waste collection areas should be provided for this type of packing from incoming containers. Linked with container 'stuffing' is the need to secure the load, as ships can roll 40° and pitch 20°, so if the cargo does not completely fill the container, some form of packing must be inserted to avoid damage. Designers should also provide easily accessible storage for packing, that can be in the form of timber chocks, straps, or pneumatic bags. If pneumatic securing bags are used, a flexible air line should be provided. This is also useful for supplying hover-pallets, a useful new development that makes use of the flat floors of containers and dock levellers to distribute the load on an air cushion.

Load assembly and 'stuffing'

5.06 In order to ensure full and efficient container 'stuffing', one container length space (12 m) should be provided close to each bay so that loads can be pre-assembled. Where space is tight, half the length (ie 6 m) is considered a minimum.

5.07 Many products cannot be packed together or must be loaded in a special order to avoid uneven weight distribution, poor cargo compatibility or inefficient storage. The pre-assembly area ensures that a cargo is checked and arranged for the best loading and fastest container turn round—this is a further argument for splitting incoming and outgoing loading bays in a large scale operation.

5.08 With forklift truck loading, manoeuvrability is often more important in the approach to a container than inside it. A straight approach is the best design, and reduces the risk of load shedding when cornering, although most patterns approach the loading bay by a gangway running at 90° to the container; this arrangement demands realistic cornering space, taking into consideration load tolerances, without sacrificing too much floor area. The double handling at the load pre-assembly position can be justified, considering that container 'stuffing' is best carried out in one continuous operation. The load assembly area should be well lit, and clearly marked on the floor, with varying container lengths annotated preferably in a separate colour unique for each. In situations of frequent tightly packed, homogenous loads, a roll-in system eg Joloda or Berthelat is very attractive. Forklift trucks or pallet trucks bring the elements of the load to the assembly position, where it is built up on the tracks provided. When the assembly is complete, the whole load is pushed into the container as a unit, liberating the forklift trucks to assemble the next load **16**. This is best used with a raised dock, but it can also be used in

16 *Roll-in system allows container to be loaded in one movement.*

a different form for loading containers from ground level with forklift trucks, the pallets or goods having normally to be manually handled from the container door to the final position. A Joloda track reduces the manual effort considerably, the trucks being removed as the container is filled; however, these demand containers or truck bodies with special grooves in the floor, or the cargo has to be packed on a pallet with sufficient clearance for the retracted track sections to be withdrawn.

5.09 A further ground-based system using forklift trucks is a lifting table, which hoists the forklift so that it can enter the container; these are expensive and can be dangerous if not carefully sited and operated. Vehicle raising lifts are useful in very constricted situations, although they are an expensive answer to a simple problem (see Information sheet Loading 5).

5.10 Ramps allow forklifts to stuff containers direct from ground level **17**. Available with flat tops so that pallets are horizontal when they enter the container, these ramps need a long run-up zone to the rear; with a maximum gradient of 10 per cent, and container floor heights over 1·5 m, plus

17 *Loading ramp for forklift trucks.*

enough turning area for the stuffing truck before it mounts the ramp, 18 m can quickly be lost. These ramps are not very wide, although sufficient for forklifts, they cannot be used for unloading mobile cargo like cars.

Side access

5.11 The increasing use of drop side, tilt top trailers and side door containers have strengthened arguments against using raised dock loading bays. Fork lift trucks can load directly into these from both sides and the rear **18**. Side door

18a

18b

18 *Tilt trailer being* **a** *side-loaded* **b** *end loaded.*

operation in raised docks may be wasteful of building volume, as the full turning width is required throughout the trailer length, unless turret trucks can be used direct. But if high turnover is critical as in groupage areas, side loading with shuttling fork trucks can be very fast. The truck throughput and easier storage cycles offsets volume loss and can reduce number of bays required. This has also resulted in a re-assessment of the straight through access loading bay for ground level operation.

5.12 As well as forklift trucks, special telescopic conveyors are available for loading containers with loose cargo. These can be used with raised docks (roller or belt) or can be mobile and ground based. Containers for use over deep sea routes are often hand 'stuffed' for maximum cube and load stability; if this kind of operation is predicted, designers should provide an area nearby where drop-in conveyor sections can be stored, so as not to inhibit other loading operations. Tilt top containers and open half-height units for coils, reels, and steel work allow overhead loading by gantry cranes **19, 20**. Gantry cranes in loading bay situations are only economic if the company specialises in a product requiring special container types or uses a lift-off type of demountable body system for delivery work. For example, the Ford Motor Company parts store at Daventry uses gantry cranes throughout the loading bays, as many parts are crated, and most of the vehicles used are flat beds. Loading bays should adapt quickly to different container types. It is for the designer to check which form is the most likely for the particular product and predicted receipt/despatch pattern.

5.13 Some trucks may arrive with two 6m containers on one trailer. In this situation, simply operated hydraulic lifting legs are available, powered by a small motor unit. One or both containers have to be transferred to a stillage or a slave trailer for unloading. Space should be provided near the loading bay for this type of equipment. If there will be frequent container handling, large scale plant should be provided.

5.14 For a high throughput of TIR 'tilt' trailers, a slave shunt tractor is useful, allowing the trunk units to drop the incoming trailer in the assembly zone and leave immediately with the outgoing one; all attempts should be made to reduce the number of vehicles 'milling' about.

Lighting

5.15 Unless containers have open tops, there will not be enough light inside to ensure accurate loading, especially in 12 m end loading containers. Mobile or permanent extendible lighting should be provided, with a well lit door zone; ensure that there is no glare to dazzle forklift drivers and cause accidents: special dock lights are available in tough steel housings on resilient mountings. (See Information sheet Loading 5).

Weighbridges

5.16 With the present concern about the overloading of lorries and in increase in spot checks by DOE, designers may be asked to incorporate some form of weighing equipment in the loading bay area. There are several methods of weighing trucks and containers; a full weighbridge in the assembly area, can assess gross weight and axle distribution. Another system is a hand portable set of scales which weighs the truck wheel by wheel; it is disputed whether the total load can be accurately weighed by this method. One development with potential is an automatic axle weighing and computation device in the truck itself, which can also guide the distribution of loading in the container and could eliminate dock weighing. Alternatively, goods can be weighed out of the containers by a device attached to the dock leveller, that weighs the forklift truck and the load as it passes over the top.

19 *Daventry parts store, loading with overhead cranes.*

20 *Gantry with fork attachment (far side of truck) unloading pallets.*

6 Bays for refrigerated vehicles

6.01 As a rule, the floor of any refrigerated vehicle is 50 to 102 mm higher than its normal counterpart, due to the insulation. Refrigerated containers or 'reefers', are equipped with gas cooling or integral or clip-on refrigeration machinery. Large scale reefer operations are discussed in Section 8 Cold storage. Refrigeration units are powered either by a small internal combustion engine that is left running in the dock or by electric compressors which require plug points (sometimes low voltage). There can be a fume build-up problem under the loading bay canopy and extraction plant should be up-graded.

7 Demountable body systems

7.01 As more companies realise the great potential efficiency of demountable body units for local and long distance distribution, designers will be asked to integrate these units with loading bays and yards. Demountable truck bodies can be treated as containers fitted with wind-down or hinge-down legs. This is not as simple as articulated vehicle operation, but can be more flexible, especially where access is restricted.

7.02 Demountable bodies can increase the utility of a truck chassis many time because vehicle turn round is as quick as the time taken to change one body for another **21**. Some bodies are equipped with ISO type top corner locks and are built to an ISO standard size for system interchangeability. There are many swop body systems in operation, including demountable skeletal units, so that a container can be left supported on legs for unloading. Numbers of modular sized bodies are often trunk hauled by articulated vehicles and transferred to small local delivery chassis at strategic points, which either deliver direct to the retail outlet or leave the body there as a unit, taking the empty body back to a marshalling area to be picked up by the returning vehicle.

7.03 A further variation which is proving popular because of its increased flexibility, is to employ a lorry and drawbar trailer with modular 'swop' bodies. This doubles the use of the former as the trailer is dropped in a convenient position in a town, and the lorry is driven on to a further destination, where it in turn leaves its bodies for local delivery vehicles, picks up the empties, and then returns to the trailer. The truck then changes its empty bodies for the full ones on the trailer, and starts the delivery process again. Finally, the truck returns to pick up the trailer and returns to base. This has all been achieved by one man.

7.04 The effect on loading bay design is much the same as for

ISO containers in groupage and break-bulk situations. The vehicle entry requirement is similar, as both trunker trucks and local small chassis are liable to use the installation. The buffer area is important, as trunk to local vehicle transfer takes up space. Some demountable bodies are equipped with clip-on or integral tailboard lifts. Often, roll pallets and castored cages are used for retail delivery work, and because they are easily handled, they have been used to load at ground level, by pushing the castored cages onto tailboard lifts of the waiting bodies, powered from a plug. Alternatively, the tailboard lifts can act as a mobile dock leveller by pushing the cages or pallet truck onto the tail lift at dock level, raising the lift to floor height, and rolling them into position. It is not good practice to dispense with dock levellers as few vehicles are equipped in this way and operators tend to forget that suppliers' vehicles are larger than their own. Demountable bodies are often used for short term storage: the implications of this are covered in Technical study External storage 1.

8 Future vehicle sizes

8.01 As yet, the EEC transport authority is undecided at what figure to fix the European gross weights for trucks. Articulated vehicles may be limited to 40 tonnes, enabling 12 m containers to be carried, and truck and drawbar trailer outfits at 44 to 46 tonnes. Overall sizes will not increase over the present limits, and axle loadings will not exceed 11 tonnes, although 13 tonnes is used in France. The drawbar combination is already popular in Britain, especially for light commodities.

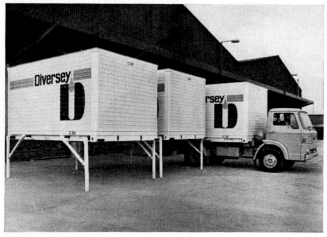

21 *Local delivery vehicle picking up swop body at loading dock.*

Information sheet Loading 1

Vehicle sizes weights and turning circles

This sheet gives information on common types of commercial vehicles. For vehicle dimensions and axle loadings for for the US and Australia, see Appendix 1, page 281.

1 Vehicle dimensions

1.01 Table I illustrates the most common types of commercial vehicles, and gives basic data necessary for design of loading bays. Diagrams of typical vehicles are given to enable designers to spot the specific type used in the storage system they are designing for. The type of vehicle used will depend on type of unit load (see Technical study Storage process para 4 to 6). The precise limits of dimensions in table I are shown in key diagrams **1a** and **b**.

Axle weights

1.02 Table I shows weights of each axle, and gross combination weight, of typical loaded vehicles.

1.03 Single axle weights are measured through the centre of the wheel. The combined weight of twin axles (or bogies) are measured through the centre point between axles.

1.04 Separate axle weights are provided, as they may sometimes be necessary in design, in calculating loading for existing structures, or in situations where tractor and trailer are separated.

Gross combination weight

1.05 The *combined* weights of tractor, trailer, maximum load and driver equal the gross combination weight.

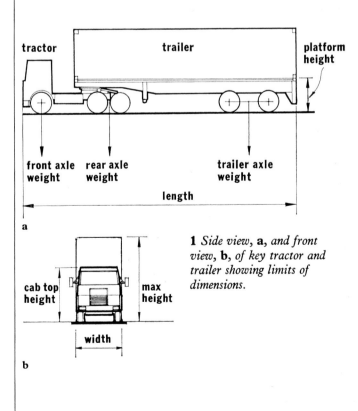

1 *Side view,* **a,** *and front view,* **b,** *of key tractor and trailer showing limits of dimensions.*

Table I Sizes, weights and turning circles of road transport vehicles

	Length (m)	Width[1] (m)	Cab top height (m)	Maximum height[2] (m)	Platform height (m)	Front axle weight (tonnes)	Rear tractor axle or bogie weight (tonnes)	Trailer axle or bogie weight (tonnes)	Gross combination weight (tonnes)	Turning circle diameter (m)	Swept turning circle diameter[3] (m)
Five-axle articulated with refrigerated body	15	2·5	2·74	3·93	1·32*	5·5	10·1	16·9	32·5	24-30	(15·54)
Four-axle articulated with wide spread trailer axles	15	2·5	2·74	4·22	1·32*	5·5	10·1	16·9	32·5	24-30	(15·54)
Tractor with twin steer front bogie	15	2·5	2·48	4·04	1·37*	8·2 (bogie)	9·7	14·6	32·5	24-30	(16·5)
Three-axle tractor. Second steering axle as part of rear bogie. With widespread trailer axles, this is suitable for unevenly laden containers.	15	2·5	2·74	4·22	1·32*	3·7/3·9	10·1	14·8	32·5	24-30	(14·0)
Three-axle tractor. Typical TIR outfit (Figures in brackets show European weights)	15	2·5	2·92	4·12	1·40	3·7 (6·5)	12·6 (15·5)	16·2 (16)	32·5 (38)	24-30	(15·54)

1 Not including mirrors, which can increase width to 3·1 m max.
2 Includes 2·44 m container or fixed body. Varies with springs, wheel and frame depth.
3 Swept turning circle diameter column, figures in brackets refer to the swept turning circle of tractor unit only (without trailer).
* These trailers can carry containers; add 150 mm for height of container floor.

Table I Sizes, weights and turning circles of road transport vehicles—*continued*

	Length (m)	Width[1] (m)	Cab top height (m)	Maximum height[2] (m)	Platform height (m)	Front axle weight (tonnes)	Rear tractor axle or bogie weight (tonnes)	Trailer axle or bogie weight (tonnes)	Gross combination weight (tonnes)	Turning circle diameter (m)	Swept turning circle diameter[3] (m)
Articulated pantechnicon van *High volume for light goods.*	14	2·5	2·54	4·27	0·46	4·5	9·9	9·9	24·3	24-30	(14·0)
Articulated tanker *Holds 28 640 litres.*	15	2·5	2·74	3·81	1·37	5·4	10·1	17	32·5	24-30	(15·9)
High capacity tipper *For coal, ash etc. Sand tippers are shallower. Maximum raised height 9·2 m.*	14	2·5	2·74	3·96	—	5·7	10·1	16·7	32·5	24-30	(13·1)
Powder tanker *Bottom discharge is type shown. Pneumatic discharge and tippers also available.*	15	2·5	2·74	3·96	1·37	5·7	10·1	16·7	32·5	24-30	(15·9)
Three-axle truck, two-axle trailer (drawbar trailer) *Most types in UK have only two axles each. This is typical European vehicle. (Figures in brackets show European weights.)*	18	2·5	2·92	4·12	1·40*	6·1 (6)	16·3 (18)	4/6·1 (8/8)	32·5 (38)	20·7	21·1

[1] Not including mirrors, which can increase width to 3·1 m max.
[2] Includes 2·44 m container or fixed body. Varies with springs, wheel and frame depth.
[3] Swept turning circle diameter column, figures in brackets refer to the swept turning circle of tractor unit only (without trailer).
* These trailers can carry containers; add 150 mm for height of container floor.

Table I Sizes, weights and turning circles of road transport vehicles—*continued*

	Length (m)	Width¹ (m)	Cab top height (m)	Maximum height² (m)	Platform height (m)	Front axle weight (tonnes)	Rear tractor axle or bogie weight (tonnes)	Trailer axle or bogie weight (tonnes)	Gross combination weight (tonnes)	Turning circle diameter (m)	Swept turning circle diameter³ (m)
Two-axle truck, three-axle trailer (drawbar trailer) *Typical European vehicle.*	18	2·5	2·92	4·12	1·40	6·1 (6)	10·1 (10)	8·1/8·1 (6·75/15·25)	32·5 (38)	16·5	17·7
Four-axle rigid *These types can now gross 32 tonnes; usually tankers or tippers.*	9·75	2·5	2·64	3·51	1·37	11·9 (bogie)	18·5	—	30·4	25·6	26·5
Three-axle articulated tanker *Holds 18 180 litres. Useful in restricted forecourts.*	12	2·5	2·43	3·20	1·32	4·8	9·4	10·1	24·3	24-30	(13·4)
Three-axle rigid *Includes tippers, tankers, mixers.*	8	2·5	2·64	3·05	1·63	6·1	18·2	—	24·3	23·2	24·4
Three-axle rigid tipper or skip lorry *If under 5·64 m outer axle spread, 20·2 tonnes on road (see IS Loading 3).*	7	2·5	—	3·35	—	6	18	—	24	17·4	18·9

¹ Not including mirrors, which can increase width to 3·1 m max.
² Includes 2·44 m container or fixed body. Varies with springs, wheel and frame depth.
³ Swept turning circle diameter column, figures in brackets refer to the swept turning circle of tractor unit only (without trailer).
* These trailers can carry containers; add 150 mm for height of container floor.

Table I Sizes, weights and turning circles of road transport vehicles—*continued*

	Length (m)	Width¹ (m)	Cab top height (m)	Maximum height² (m)	Platform height (m)	Front axle weight (tonnes)	Rear tractor axle or bogie weight (tonnes)	Trailer axle or bogie combination weight (tonnes)	Gross combination weight (tonnes)	Turning circle diameter (m)	Swept turning circle diameter³ (m)
Pantechnicon *For large light goods.*	10·5-11	2·5	—	4·23	0·46	6·1	10·1	—	16·2	20·1	21·3
16 tonne rigid *Popular type.*	8·5	2·5	2·43	3·58	1·16	6·1	10·1	—	16·2	21	22
Tipper *Same size for two-axle skip lorries, truck mixers. (Maximum raised height 4·8 m).*	6·3	2·5	—	2·64	1·22	6·1	10·1	—	16·2	18·3	18·9
Van (1 tonne) *Rear engine. Smaller vans as for cars (see AJ Metric Handbook 1973, p55).*	4·4	1·78	1·93	—	0·43	1	1·5	—	2·5	12·2	12·8
Van (2 tonne) *Long wheelbase shown, as for bread delivery, laundry etc.*	6	2·24	2·82	—	0·76	1·6	3·2	—	4·8	13·1	14
Brewer's dray *Three-axle, 400 mm wheels for low height loading. Swop body.*	6·5	2·29	2·29	—	0·92	3·5	8·6	—	12·1	14·3	15·2

¹ Not including mirrors, which can increase width to 3·1 m max.
² Includes 2·44 m container or fixed body. Varies with springs, wheel and frame depth.
³ Swept turning circle diameter column, figures in brackets refer to the swept turning circle of tractor unit only (without trailer).
* These trailers can carry containers; add 150 mm for height of container floor

	Length	Width[1]	Cab top height	Maximum height[2]	Platform height	Front axle weight	Rear tractor axle or bogie weight	Trailer axle or bogie weight	Gross combination weight	Turning circle diameter	Swept turning circle diameter[3]
	(m)	(m)	(m)	(m)	(m)	(tonnes)	(tonnes)	(tonnes)	(tonnes)	(m)	(m)
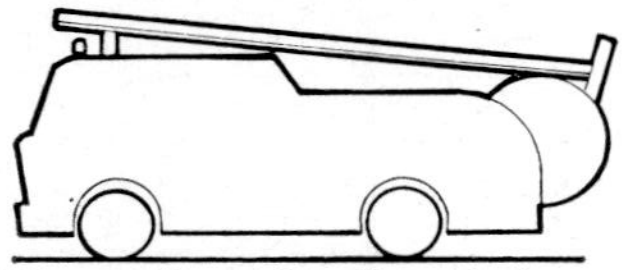 **Fire appliance (medium size)** *For larger types, use 16 tonne rigid dimensions.*	8	2·29	3·4	3·4	—	3·5	4·8	—	8·3	15·2	16·2
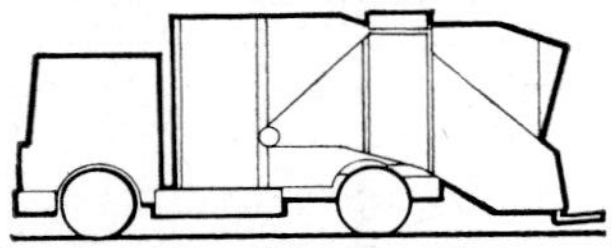 **Dustcart (medium capacity)**	7·4	2·29	3·20	4·0	0·46	4	6·8	—	10·8	14	15·2
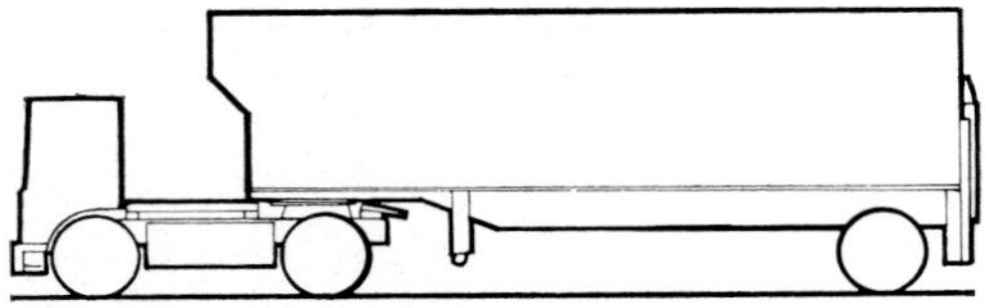 **Articulated van** *Typical van serving supermarkets. Fitted with cooler and tail lift, this unit would carry roll pallets.*	12·5	2·5	2·74	4·0	1·32	4·8	9·4	10·1	24·3	24·30	(13·4)

Table I Sizes, weights and turning circles of road transport vehicles—*continued*

[1] Not including mirrors, which can increase width to 3·1 m max.
[2] Includes 2·44 m container or fixed body. Varies with springs, wheel and frame depth.
[3] Swept turning circle diameter column, figures in brackets refer to the swept turning circle of tractor unit only (without trailer).
* These trailers can carry containers; add 150 mm for height of container floor.

2 Turning circles

2.01 Table I shows dimensions for turning circle diameter, and swept turning circle diameter.

2.02 Turning circle diameter is the *minimum* path of outer front tyre used in calculating kerb clearances.

2.03 Swept turning circle diameter is the *minimum* path of outer front overhang used in calculating building-to-building clearance.

2.04 Articulated vehicle turning circles are inexact because, when turning with tractor at 90 degrees to trailer, the actual radius depends on relative distance between centre line of king pin and centre line of trailer bogie, both of which can be varied on some trailers. Therefore swept turning circles for tractors only (ie, without trailers) are included.

Drawbar combinations

2.05 Turning circles given are of the rigid truck, but drawbar trailers follow within that circle.

2.06 All dimensions of turning and swept turning circle diameters are absolute minimum. Both articulated trailers and drawbar trailers pivot on their bogies, causing considerable tyre wear and road surface damage (if frequent). These minimum dimensions should **not** be used as a planning standard but are for information only. For planning standards, see Information sheet Loading 2.

Vehicle cut-in

2.06 Swept turning circles give the outer radius. Vehicle cut-in **2**, **3**, shows clearances within the circle which must be left for body or trailer cut-in. See also gate entry diagrams, Information sheet Loading 2, which combine clearances for swept turning circles and cut-in.

2.07 Diagrams **2** and **3** illustrate typical cut-in and turning dimensions for a 30·4 tonne four axle rigid truck, and a 15 m long 32·5 tonne articulated combination. Although turning circles are given for vehicle types illustrated in table 1, there are occasions where the detailed cut-in dimensions are required for forecourt and loading bay planning for vehicles unsimilar to diagrams **2** and **3**.

The following diagrams and formulae enable accurate turning diagrams to be built up for any commercial vehicle types: this can be particularly useful when faced with constricted space for manoeuvring and where a calculation based on a predominance of a particular vehicle type is acceptable.

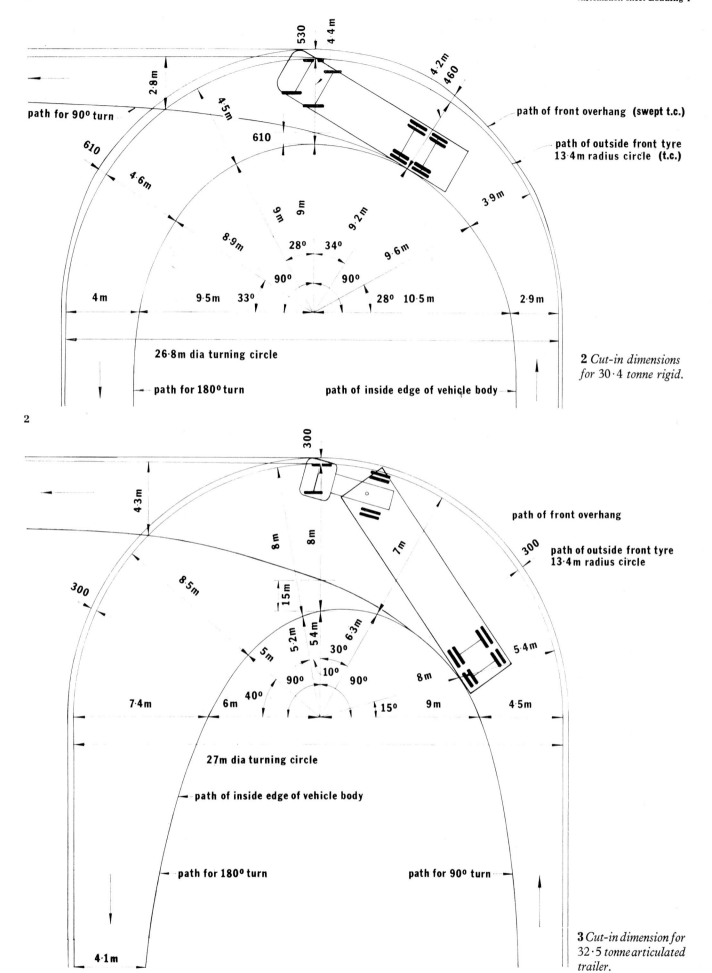

2 Cut-in dimensions for 30·4 tonne rigid.

path for 90° turn

path of front overhang (swept t.c.)

path of outside front tyre 13·4 m radius circle (t.c.)

26·8 m dia turning circle

path for 180° turn

path of inside edge of vehicle body

3 Cut-in dimension for 32·5 tonne articulated trailer.

path for 90° turn

path of front overhang

path of outside front tyre 13·4 m radius circle

27 m dia turning circle

path of inside edge of vehicle body

path for 180° turn

path for 90° turn

2

3

3 Dimensions of US and Australian vehicles

3.01 The typical vehicle dimensions and weights illustrated by vehicle types in table I refer mostly to European standards and regulations. The permitted sizes and axle weights are more complicated in the USA and Australia, however, as in both these federations vehicle legislation is state controlled. In order that designers can have the flexibility to design forecourts and loading bay areas throughout the USA and Australia, the tables in Appendix I on page 281 show individual state requirements for maximum vehicle weights, gross combination weights, maximum axle loadings and size limitations. It will be noticed that in some US states two or three trailers are allowed to be towed on interstate or specially designated highways: called 'double bottoms' or 'triple bottoms', these vehicles are an articulated truck towing one or two additional trailers. These vehicles are becoming increasingly popular in the USA, and in some parts of Australia, ('road trains'). Designers will increasingly work on projects including interchange stations, where 'road trains' are broken down for conventional haulage. Diagrams **4** and **5** illustrate how a 'short double bottom' cuts in less on a bend than a 15 m articulated truck.

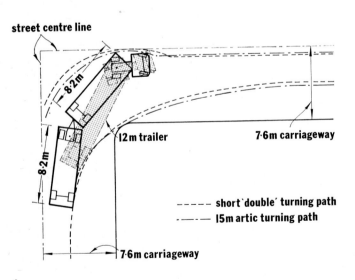

street centre line

8·2 m

12 m trailer

8·2 m

7·6 m carriageway

------ **short 'double' turning path**

-·-·- **15 m artic turning path**

7·6 m carriageway

4

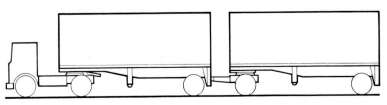

5

4 Calculations to determine road widths for different types of vehicle

For practical purposes the maximum amount of cut in and maximum turning width may be calculated using the following.

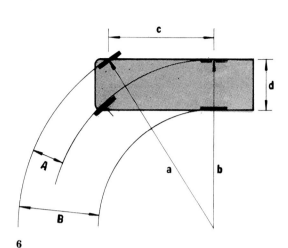

6

6 *A rigid vehicle.*

4.01 A rigid vehicle

$A = a - b$ and $B = a - b + d$
where $b = \sqrt{a^2 - c^2}$

Symbols used to define the maximum cut in and turning width for a rigid vehicle:

a = Outside turning radius of 1st axle

b = Outside turning radius of rear axle

c = Wheel base

d = Vehicle width

A = Cut in

B = Turning width

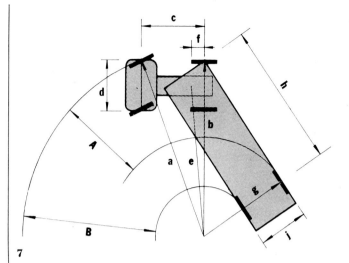

7

7 *An articulated vehicle.*

4.02 An articulated vehicle

$A = a - g$ and $B = a - g + j$
where $g = \sqrt{e^2 - h^2 + \frac{1}{2}j}$

Symbols used to define the maximum cut in and turning width for an articulated vehicle:

a = Outside turning radius of 1st axle

b = Outside turning radius of rear tractor axle $= \sqrt{a^2 - c^2}$

(if a tandem axle bogie, through the centre line between the axles)

c = Wheelbase of tractor

d = Vehicle tractor width

e = Turning radius of king pin $= \sqrt{(b - \frac{1}{2}d)^2 + f^2}$

f = Distance of king pin in front of tractor rear axle

g = Outside turning radius of trailer rear axle

(if a tandem axle bogie, this is through the centre line between the axles, or if a tri-axle bogie, this is through the centre line of the centre axle)

h = Wheelbase of trailer

j   = Width of trailer

A = Cut in

B = Turning width

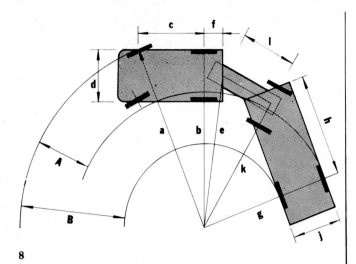

8

8 *A draw-bar trailer combination.*

4.03 A draw-bar trailer combination

$A = a - g$ and $B = a - g + j$
where $g = \sqrt{K^2 - h^2} + \frac{1}{2}j$

Symbols used to define the maximum cut in and turning width for a draw-bar trailer combination:

a = Outside turning radius of 1st axle

b = Outside turning radius of rear tractor axle = $\sqrt{a^2 - c^2}$
(see note in diagram 4.02)

c = Wheelbase of tractor

d = Tractor width

e = Turning radius of coupling = $\sqrt{(b - \frac{1}{2}d)^2 + f^2}$

f = Distance from rear tractor axle to coupling

g = Outside turning radius of trailer rear axle
(see note in diagram 4.02)

h = Trailer wheelbase

j = Trailer width

k = Turning radius of trailer steering axle = $\sqrt{e^2 - l^2}$

l = Draw bar length

A = Cut in

B = Turning width

Information sheet Loading 2

Loading bay layout and gate entries

This sheet gives dimensions of loading bay layouts and gate entries.

1 Loading bay layouts

1.01 **3** to **10** illustrate normal operating conditions in loading bays. Each diagram has a broken line representing absolute minimum clearances (where shunting is likely) and an unbroken line representing preferred dimensions which allow easy manoeuvring and prevent jams. A dotted line shows space for fast turn-round. Scales are shown in metres.

1.02 For general requirements of the immediate loading bay zone and marshalling areas, refer to Technical study Loading 1. For internal store spatial requirements and their influence on bay spacings (eg width required for the preassembly of roll pallets in food distribution warehouses) refer to Technical studies Storage Process, paras 4, 5. For detailed dimensions see **1, 2a, b.**

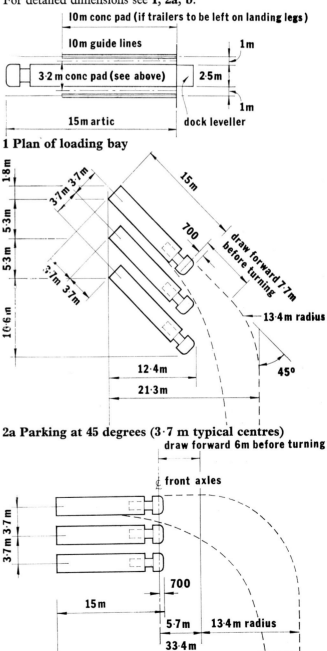

1 Plan of loading bay

2a Parking at 45 degrees (3·7 m typical centres)

2b Parking at 90 degrees (3·7 m typical centres)

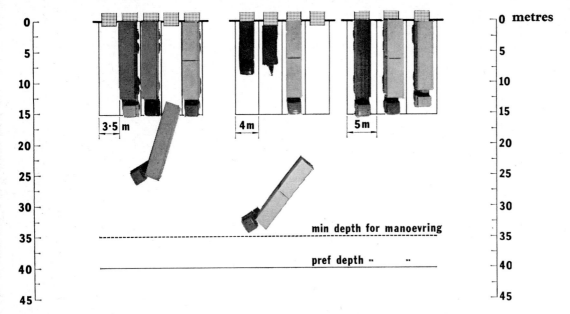

min depth for manoevring

pref depth ··   ··

3 (left) 90° dock 3·5 m bay spacing
For end-loading vehicles, where lateral space is at a
premium, loads are carried away from the dock to another
zone, as all dock space is required for forklift manoeuvring.
(The Freight Transport Association suggests a 3·3 m
minimum bay width, which is considered tight with the
swing-out demanded by 15 m artics.) On principle, narrower
bays mean that the truck driver needs more depth in front
of the bay to move out before he can swing round. Eg
in the 3·5 m bay (left) an articulated container truck is
turning out as sharply as it can for the clearances. If the
bays were 3·3 m, only 1 m would be saved longitudinally
over five bays, but the draw forward area must be nearly
5 m greater to provide swing-out clearance; this can hinder
the next vehicle manoeuvring to use the bay.

3 (centre) 90° dock spacing
For bays with busy cross-dock forklift circulation eg cold
stores. Where fast turnround is also required, 4·5 m bays
are preferable. A reefer container truck is reversing into
the 4 m bay.

3 (right) 90° dock, 5 m bay spacing
For preloading accumulation of roll pallets in distribution
warehouses. Actual dimension will depend on needs of the
accumulation area behind the dock. 35 m from dock face is
the absolute minimum. (33·4 m is possible, as some
operators will state, but allows no clearance for error and is
not recommended.) Continuous line at 40 m shows that a
small increase in depth of marshalling area can accelerate
manoeuvring, by allowing artics to pass. (42 m plus is
preferable for manoeuvring drawbar trailers.)

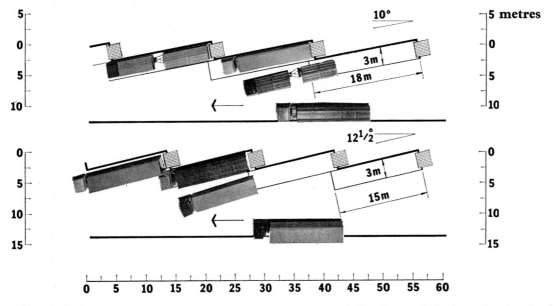

4 Finger docks
A useful way of solving the conflicting requirements of
end-loaded containers which allow forklifts to run on their
floors, and 'tilt' trailers most of which do not have
floors strong enough to accept forklifts and so need side
loading. Groupage and haulage operators find this a real
problem. The finger dock allows conventional end-loading,
dock level over-the-side handling, and ground level
over-the-side handling for awkward and bulky loads.
The upper diagram illustrates 80 degree 18 m × 3 m bays.
The width can be narrow, as side-loading vehicles will
reverse as close as possible to the dock face. The steep
angle of the dock means reversing is easy.

A drawbar outfit is shown leaving the far right bay, with an
artic waiting to take its place, close up to the perimeter to
swing the trailer bogie into position for reversing.
The lower diagram is a 77½° finger dock, with 15 m bays,
for a standard artic fleet needing both end- and side-loading
(use 18 m bays for general purpose work). The 77½° angle
means a slight increase in depth, but space for an extra bay in
the same length. The 15 m raised dock is only long enough for
the usable trailer length (12 m artic, 15·5 drawbar) so that
cab access is possible. British and Continental vehicles will
conflict—if most vehicles are Continental, it would save
manoeuvring time to reverse the flow.
A 5 m canopy would cover all loading operations.

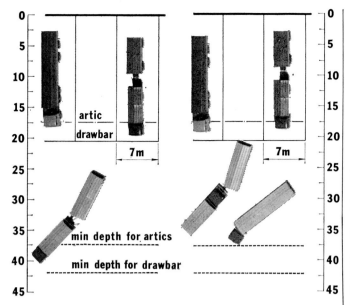

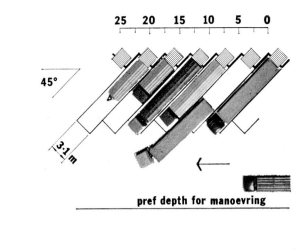

5 Bays for internal loading from each side from floor level

7 m clearance is minimum for two forklifts to load a vehicle from each side. This is typical of a groupage centre, where most traffic is tilt topped trailers for TIR work. The bays show rear forklift clearance, and space required for 15 and 18 m long vehicles. In the loading bay, the dotted line is minimum length for artics, the continuous line is minimum length for trucks with drawbar trailers.

On the left, a truck with trailer is positioning to drop the trailer, so that the truck can turn round and 'nose' the trailer into the bay (as the centre vehicle is doing). If bays are segregated by pillars and door piers, the trucks need to draw further forward before turning to clear the structure.

7 45° dock, 3·1 m bay spacing

Compare with **6**; for the same number of bays, the length is increased, but the depth of the manoeuvring area is substantially decreased to 25 m. This is useful in constricted sites. Note clockwise direction of flow for British trucks; the driver can quickly reverse on his 'view' side. (Inevitably, Continental vehicles have to reverse on their blind side.) **7** shows the sort of mixture of articulated units, drawbar combinations and container trucks that is liable to be found at a general purpose warehouse. The 3·1 m bay width is an absolute minimum; it is less than with 90° bays, as the swing-out clearance is not so critical. Wider bays are preferable, especially where drawbar units are expected, which are more difficult to reverse. **7** shows an articulated vehicle turning out as steeply as the trailer clearance allows.

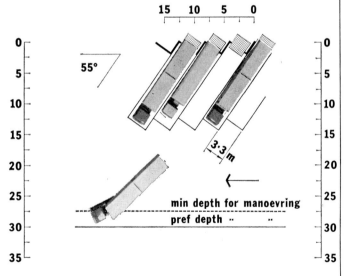

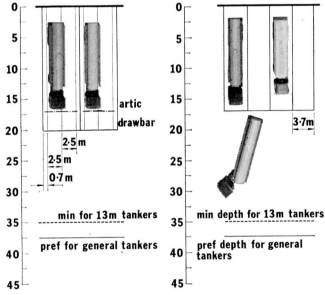

6 55° dock 3·3 m wide

This dock was recommended by the Freight Transport Association, after operational research. 10° difference between **6** and **7** means smaller width but larger marshalling area. The FTA suggests that 11 m from the front of the bays is the minimum for manoeuvring; this is tight. 13 m is preferable, but is still tight, a 15 m artic really needs 16 m for fast, continuous manoeuvring.

Angled docks will change the pattern of movement on the dock. They allow a narrower forklift manoeuvring cross route, but forklifts serving long rows of vehicles can cause heavy on-dock traffic with a linear distribution, rather than forklifts shuttling within the confines of a vehicle's width as with 90° bays.

8 (right) 3·7 m end-loading tanker bays

A conventional 90° bay, with additional clearance to allow personnel to remove hoses laid along tank side. Rear clearance allows connection to valve points without the operator fouling tanker or valve assembly. See Technical study Bulk Storage, paras 4, 5.

8 (left) Side-loading tanker bays

0·7 m clearance on nearside of tankers for valve connection, and 2·5 m on offside for pipe sections stored on the side of the tank. Some tankers allow connection from either side. 13 m tankers are shown. Bay lengths are 15 m for artics, and 18 m for drawbar tankers, popular in Europe (2 m allowed at back of bay for valve clearance). Often straight through bays are used for tankers; allow preferred clearance on each side of bay.

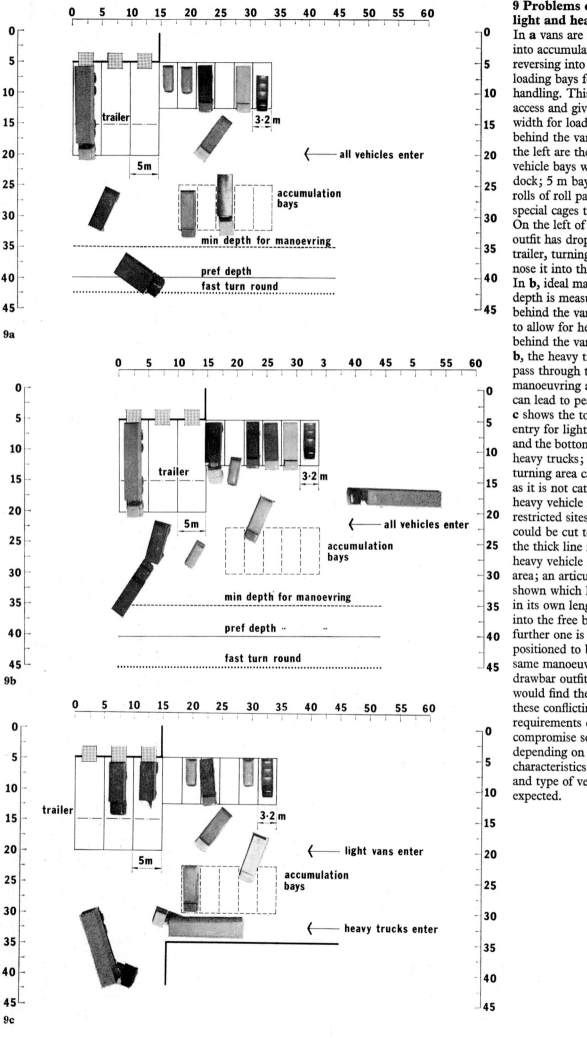

9a

9b

9c

9 Problems of mixed light and heavy traffic

In **a** vans are manoeuvring into accumulation bays, and reversing into 3·2 m wide loading bays for manual handling. This allows driver access and gives sufficient width for load accumulation behind the van doors. To the left are the trunk vehicle bays with a raised dock; 5 m bays allow rolls of roll pallets or special cages to accumulate. On the left of **a**, a drawbar outfit has dropped its trailer, turning round to nose it into the bay. In **b**, ideal manoeuvring depth is measured from 5 m behind the van loading bays to allow for heaps of goods behind the vans. In **a** and **b**, the heavy trucks have to pass through the light van manoeuvring area, which can lead to peak congestion. **c** shows the top arrowed entry for light vehicles only, and the bottom for segregated heavy trucks; the van turning area can be smaller, as it is not catering for heavy vehicle movement. In restricted sites, the access could be cut to the depth of the thick line in **c** up to the heavy vehicle manoeuvring area; an articulated unit is shown which has just turned in its own length to reverse into the free bay, and a further one is waiting positioned to begin the same manoeuvre. The drawbar outfit in the bay would find the area tight; these conflicting requirements dictate a compromise solution, depending on site characteristics and the sizes and type of vehicles expected.

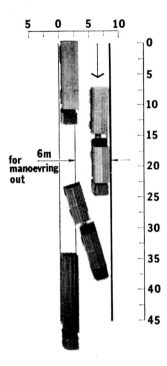

10 Straight through dock for single-sided side loading
Often used for steel stock and other lengthy goods. Loading is on the offside for accurate vehicle positioning, and to allow the driver to descend away from the traffic. 7 m clearance is for forklift manoeuvring. 6 m road width is adequate for passing and drawing out.

2 Gate entries

2.01 The width of the gate and its depth from the back of the pavement line depends on the type of road, its width and frequency of use. The further back the gate from the roadway, the narrower it can be.

2.02 12 to **15** show conventional road widths of 9·1 m, 6·1 m and 3·5 m. The narrowest is not suitable even for private one-way approach roads if a 90° turn is to be made, unless a substantial manoeuvring area is provided in front of the gate entry.

2.03 Shaded areas in **12** to **15** represent typical 15 m artic vehicle path. Information to calculate other vehicle paths is given in Information sheet Loading 1. In all cases, the the most realistic solution has been taken, with the truck swinging out on to the oncoming lane to achieve the required turning circle. If this is unacceptable due to the speed and weight of traffic coming the other way, the effect will be as for the narrowest road shown, greatly increasing the width of the cross-over and the depth of the gate back from the road.

12 shows a one-way street. This is a typical town warehouse entry. For use can be made of the width of the carriageway for swing out to gain the required turning clearance.

13 shows a two-way street, with vehicles entering and leaving from both directions. To allow the gate to be as near to the pavement line as possible, the trucks have to swing across the oncoming traffic when turning left. This is common practice. If unacceptable, the gate has to be further back and the cross-over wider; ie the truck will use the narrower road widths.

If two-way traffic is of sufficient frequency to merit a wide entry gate **14**, this allows simultaneous movement. A typical situation is shown where complete clearance at all cut-in points between the two vehicles would be wasteful. This is a typical situation of a warehouse at the end of a service road.

15 is suitable for busy two-way traffic approaching from both directions. In some cases, such as entries to container ports and groupage centres, the traffic volume is sufficient to merit

clearance for simultaneous movement for entry and exit in both directions. A typical situation has been illustrated, where the clearances are sufficient for movement but not enough for vehicles to pass when actually making the 90° turn. This would increase the width of the entry by over 50 per cent and would also demand that the gate position intrudes further into the site.

The diagrams are considered acceptable for slow speed work, where there is good visibility. For this reason, boundaries should be in the form of wiremesh fencing, rather than walls, to allow for long distance sight lines; incoming vehicle drivers can see outgoing vehicles before they enter the gate zone: this prevents vehicles being caught when swinging across oncoming traffic. If high speed cornering and full passing on the bend are required, this should be considered as highway engineering, and is not a gate entry situation. Contact the DOE for highway standards.

Artic roll-over

2.04 Tests[1] have shown that a heavily and highly laden articulated vehicle will roll over at low speeds without warning to the driver once a certain speed is reached on a curve of a particular radius **11**. Considerable care should be taken by designers to plan approaches to warehouses, factories and container areas to prevent this occurring. The Transport and Road Research Laboratory have evolved a formula to calculate acceptable curve radii in relation to maximum speed.

Minimum turning radius in metres
$$= \frac{\text{(speed in metres per second)}^2}{0 \cdot 15 \times 9 \cdot 81}$$

where 0·15 g is the maximum lateral acceleration to be used in planning, and 9·81 is metres per second.

Example: if speed is 20 km per hour (5·5 m per sec), then minimum turning radius in metres is
$$\frac{5 \cdot 5^2}{0 \cdot 15 \times 9 \cdot 81} = 20 \cdot 55 \text{ m radius}$$

Obviously the value of planning these radii are lost if vehicle speeds are not limited. One method of controlling speed, which also improves security, is to make vehicles stop at a gate-house.

11 *Artic rolling over while rounding bend at low speed.*

1 Road width requirements of commercial vehicles when cornering. Transport and Road Research Laboratory Report No. 608, DOE, HMSO 1973

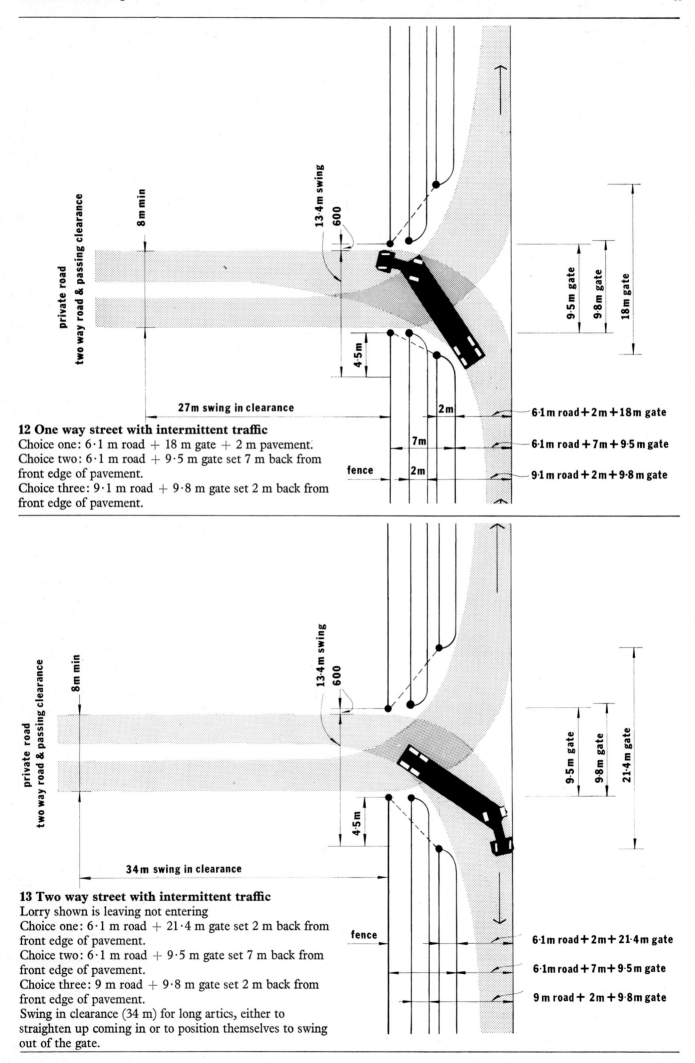

private road
two way road & passing clearance

8 m min

13·4 m swing

600

9·5 m gate

9·8 m gate

18 m gate

4·5 m

27m swing in clearance

2 m

6·1 m road + 2 m + 18 m gate

7 m

6·1 m road + 7 m + 9·5 m gate

fence

2 m

9·1 m road + 2 m + 9·8 m gate

12 One way street with intermittent traffic

Choice one: 6·1 m road + 18 m gate + 2 m pavement.
Choice two: 6·1 m road + 9·5 m gate set 7 m back from
front edge of pavement.
Choice three: 9·1 m road + 9·8 m gate set 2 m back from
front edge of pavement.

private road
two way road & passing clearance

8 m min

13·4 m swing

600

9·5 m gate

9·8 m gate

21·4 m gate

4·5 m

34m swing in clearance

fence

6·1 m road + 2 m + 21·4 m gate

6·1m road + 7 m + 9·5 m gate

9 m road + 2 m + 9·8 m gate

13 Two way street with intermittent traffic

Lorry shown is leaving not entering

Choice one: 6·1 m road + 21·4 m gate set 2 m back from
front edge of pavement.
Choice two: 6·1 m road + 9·5 m gate set 7 m back from
front edge of pavement.
Choice three: 9 m road + 9·8 m gate set 2 m back from
front edge of pavement.
Swing in clearance (34 m) for long artics, either to
straighten up coming in or to position themselves to swing
out of the gate.

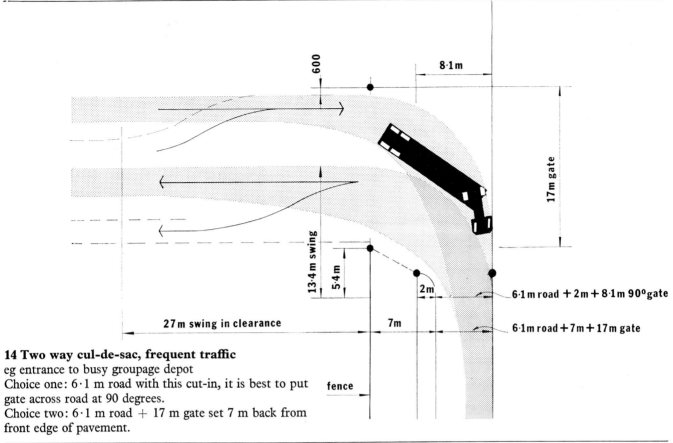

14 Two way cul-de-sac, frequent traffic
eg entrance to busy groupage depot
Choice one: 6·1 m road with this cut-in, it is best to put
gate across road at 90 degrees.
Choice two: 6·1 m road + 17 m gate set 7 m back from
front edge of pavement.

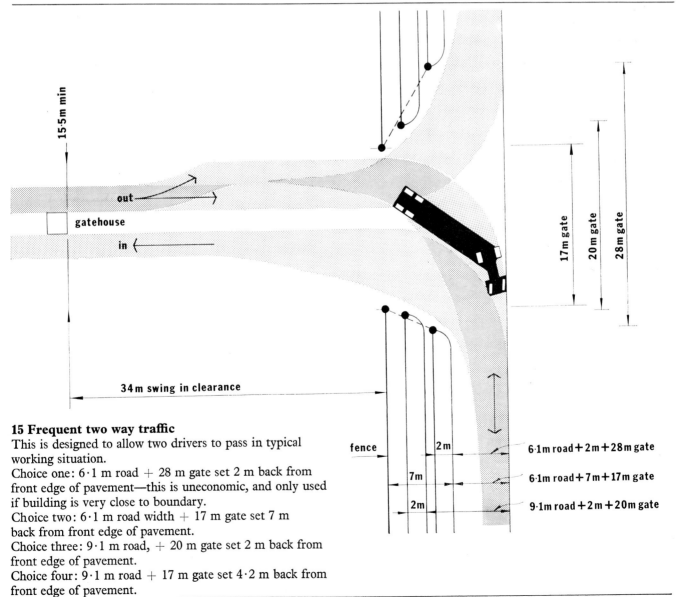

15 Frequent two way traffic
This is designed to allow two drivers to pass in typical
working situation.
Choice one: 6·1 m road + 28 m gate set 2 m back from
front edge of pavement—this is uneconomic, and only used
if building is very close to boundary.
Choice two: 6·1 m road width + 17 m gate set 7 m
back from front edge of pavement.
Choice three: 9·1 m road, + 20 m gate set 2 m back from
front edge of pavement.
Choice four: 9·1 m road + 17 m gate set 4·2 m back from
front edge of pavement.

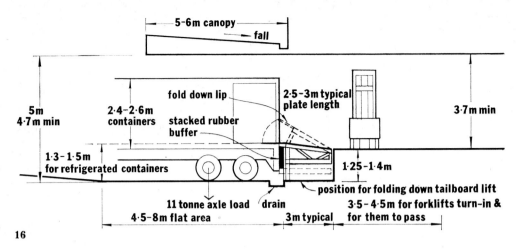

5–6m canopy

fall

fold down lip

2·5–3m typical plate length

stacked rubber buffer

5m
4·7m min

2·4–2·6m containers

3·7m min

1·3–1·5m for refrigerated containers

1·25–1·4m

position for folding down tailboard lift

11 tonne axle load   drain

4·5–8m flat area   3m typical

3·5–4·5m for forklifts turn-in & for them to pass

16

16 *Section through typical loading bay.*

17

17 *Herringbone loading dock: note how lateral dimension of vehicle manoeuvring area is reduced.*

Information sheet Loading 3

Waste handling equipment

This sheet gives information on types and dimensions of waste handling equipment.

1 Introduction

1.01 As the public becomes more aware of the dangers from pollution by industrial waste products, it is likely that new legislation will prohibit dumping of toxic, corrosive and dangerous products into drainage systems, onto waste land or into rivers. Specialist companies are now available with national container hire and collection services for waste products, who take on the responsibility for processing the waste and its eventual disposal. Much research is needed on the recycling of waste products, to reduce the drain on natural resources, and into the possibility of generating power from products that have to be destroyed.

1.02 This information sheet illustrates the type of equipment available for waste handling, and the planning requirements for its inclusion in buildings. It is not only concerned with industrial by-products, but with refuse collected in warehouses and supermarkets, generated by the increasing use of disposable packaging. It could also apply to residential areas, which may soon have centrally placed compaction plant feeding containers, reducing the large amount of open space devoted to turning areas for refuse vehicles, and as a result of the diminishing labour resources for refuse collection.

2 Waste handling equipment

Compaction machinery

2.01 Most waste material from industrial storage areas is dumped into a skip, which is carted away by a skip lorry. Before it is dumped into the skip, waste may be reduced in bulk by a compactor. Compactors are either built-in, or, for smaller installations, are mobile and can be carried like a skip from building to building as required. Skips used with compactors are always enclosed skips, unlike the familiar open skips used in the construction industry.

2.02 Static compactors are available in a large range of capacities. The most common type, as used in hospitals, warehouses and housing areas, is not space consuming, and loads at compaction densities of 550 kg/m³ into 3 to 8 m³ skips **1**. Accessories are marketed to suit special requirements, such as hydraulic tipping mechanisms for large, wheeled bins **2**, and chutes and hoppers for hand loading. Compaction is operated by hydraulic power, activated by an electric pump, on normal three-phase supply.

2.03 Compactors can be placed either in or outside the building **3**. If internally mounted, the machine can be sealed against smells and vermin; a typical unit will fit in a space 17·7 m long (excluding the skip), 5·2 m wide, allowing for space for the operator (see **5**). Planning depends on the waste collection system used, for instance whether mechanical sweepers will be dumping from the base of their collection hoppers into a compactor set in a pit, or whether wheeled bins are tipped hydraulically into the compactor, set at floor level. The collection skip position must be at the same level as the compactor's outlet, and it is often the collection vehicle's access and the provision for the skip that finally decides the planning for the compactor space. If the collection system for the compactor is not sealed, the input position should be clearly marked, well guarded and fitted

1

2

3

1 *Static compactor and skip placed inside the building.*
2 *Device for tipping* 1100 *litre bins into compactor.*
3 *Static compactor and skip placed outside the building and fed by chute from first floor.*
4 *This is a well planned and generous area for a lift-on type of compactor skip, with ample manoeuvring area and headroom. A skip is attached to a static compaction machine; the bin tipping device can be seen on the rear wall.*

4

with easily seen safety cut-out points; space should be left round the compactor, for collecting spillage. Design of waste disposal areas is shown in **4, 5**.

2.04 Approaches at both input and skip positions should be clearly lit. Skips designed for pressure packing are sized according to the application and the capacity of the compactor, and although of similar appearance, vary in detail according to the collection method for the vehicle. Contact the user about preferences, and expansion potential.

Skip collection vehicles

2.05 These employ two basic methods—winch or drag-on, and lift-on. Lift systems are the conventional skips used in the building industry, with hydraulic side arms which swing over the skip and lift it up onto the flat bed of the vehicle **6**. The disadvantage here is in internal positions, where a high ceiling clearance is required (up to 5·5 m) **8**. Refuse areas have been seen which require the skip collection vehicle to drag the skip out to gain lifting clearance, and to push the empty unit into position. This wrecks the floor surface quickly, and can damage the skip, the compactor and the vehicle.

2.06 The drag-on system is more suitable for confined situations. The skip is either dragged on with a hydraulic arm, or winched up guides on the vehicle's chassis. In both cases the truck can remain outside the skip chamber, and can position the empty unit accurately onto the compactor, under full control. The skip is usually fitted with a roller at the rear end for partial support as it is dragged towards the vehicle, the front having been lifted clear; some trucks are also fitted with a roller that is lowered as a stabiliser during the lifting operation. Check that the weight transmitted through this will not crack the floor. Vehicles used are normally in the 16·2 tonne gross class, with two axles. The larger skips, up to 26·7 m³ capacity, are collected by 22·3 to 30·4 tonne three- and four-axle rigids, depending on the weight of compacted material. Typical turning circles are:
16·2 tonne two-axle rigid; 3·8 m wheelbase; 18·28 m
24·3 tonne three-axle rigid; 18·28 m
30·4 tonne four-axle rigid; 21·34 m
For a centralised, large scale compactor, eg for a hospital

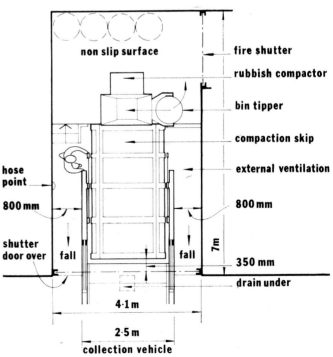

5 *Dimensions of waste handling area with compaction skip. The collection vehicle is a lift-on* type. 7 m typical for small containers and normal handling space (manual).

complex, articulated vehicles are beginning to be used in conjunction with large capacity drag-on skips.

Special purpose skips and tanks

2.07 Because of increasing public concern about dangerous liquids, tank units have been produced for handling by skip carrying vehicles. Both basic skip systems can be used for this; the tanks tend to be specifically designed for the liquid concerned. Contact the factory inspector, fire officer, petroleum officer, the user's insurers and the disposal contractor about special connection points and emergency provision. In case of accidental spillage, tank areas should have wash down facilities and interceptor gulleys. Special purpose skips are used for materials like hot solids and swarf. Swarf handling is now more sophisticated, with oil recovery and compression into bales being increasingly used.

2.08 Some operators prefer to collect refuse in vehicles equipped with their own compaction machinery, from conventional bin skips. Skip areas for uncompacted refuse should have provision for washing down, and a non-slip surface. Hydraulic bin tippers are available, although some operators prefer to build a ramp to tip in the refuse. One system employs bins that are handled by a forklift truck, which lifts the bin and tips it over the skip.

2.09 One form of skip collection by a compactor vehicle, the Dumpmaster, has arms that allow the vehicle to be nosed up to the container, pick it up in full view of the driver, and then reverse to a position with sufficient headroom for the arms to raise the skip over the top of its compactor for discharge **8**. The truck then replaces the skip in position. A new machine, the Lo-skip, can carry ordinary or compaction skips in low headroom, confined areas, and can operate under 2·1 m minimum clearances. This could be useful in applications such as the collection of waste from old premises with low slung pipes **9**.

2.10 When designing for skips with side connection points, design the space with sufficient width to allow the driver to fix the chains, with the skip off centre.

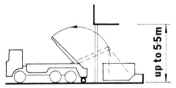

drag-on reduced headroom
6a

lift-on high headroom
6b

6 *Headroom dimensions of*
a *drag-on skip;* **b** *lift-on skip.*
7a *lift-on skip;* **b** *drag-on skip.*
8 *Front-loading skip collection vehicle.*
9 *Skip collection vehicle for areas with low headroom.*

7a

7b

8

9

Information sheet Loading 4

Industrial doors

This sheet gives information on types of doors for internal and external use.

1 Use

1.01 While doors to industrial storage buildings are primarily for access, they also have to provide security, weather protection and thermal insulation. The ways the doors will be used depends on the type of storage; some remain open all day, some, eg in cold stores, continuously open and close while others seldom open, eg for waste collection skip bays. There is a wide range of door types and sizes, with specifications tailored to particular applications. Table I gives typical door types in general use, with their principal applications. **1** to **4** illustrate some typical doors in use.

External doors

1.02 The two types are: doors enclosing a ground level loading area, through which vehicles pass for over-the-side loading, and doors attached to loading banks.

1.03 Ground level doors for wide openings can be sliding, sliding-folding (the most usual), and vertical roller or telescopic shutter types. Sliding and sliding-folding doors can be powered, but require guide rails at the base that are liable to become filled with dirt, and present a drainage problem.

1.04 Horizontally sliding doors are useful where handling plant will pass through frequently. Sliding/folding or horizontally sliding/shutter doors only need open to the width of vehicle passing through, so the minimum area is open to elements. Vertical nesting doors or roller shutters need to open to the full width and height of the vehicle, resulting in greater heat loss, more dust, and rain intrusion. Also, if a panel of a sliding-folding door is damaged, it is usually still openable, whereas if a nesting door is damaged, eg by forklift mast, the whole door jams. Ground level doors should have an external canopy for weather protection extending at least 5 m forward of the opening and 3 m on either side. The canopy will reduce the amount of water brought into the warehouse by delivery vehicles, helping to keep the floor dry (forklift trucks can skid on damp, smooth floor surfaces). A drain channel with a grill pattern to squeeze moisture out of tyres fitted outside the door rail has been used successfully.

1.05 Doors large enough to accept ISO containers on skeletal trailers and big box vans, require power assistance; check that there is manual provision in case of power cuts; in some cases this is difficult.

Doors for raised dock loading bays

1.06 Raised dock loading bays are discussed in Technical study Loading 1 and in Storage process, para 6, 7.

1.07 There are two types of external doors for raised docks: 1; a door incorporated into a dock shelter, or similar construction surrounding each dock leveller. The vehicle reverses into position within the dock shelter, itself forming a weather seal; a roller shutter door is then wound up, and the dock leveller adjusted to the truck's floor level. This door is often used in cold stores, incorporating insulated door panels. With insulation, it is impractical to use roller shutters, so the door usually follows guides parallel with the dock ceiling; this requires low output heaters to prevent the mechanism icing in cold stores.

Table I Typical doors, costs and applications (costs at 1975 prices)

Type	Material and maximum sizes. Width × height (m)			Approximate cost for door 3 m × 4.5 m		Electric hydraulic or pneumatic	Special requirements	Ideal applications	Suitability for fire doors	Resistance to damage	Insulated doors
	St	Tm	Al	Manual	Mechanical						
Sliding shutter	30×6			£500	£690	Yes	Track in floor is vulnerable to damage	Wide openings where vehicles manoeuvre; where security is important	Poor on large doors	Good	No
Up-and-over	9·1×6	6×6	9·1×6	£400	£690	Yes	Not ideal above 9·1 m width between jambs	Garages and loading banks; good security	Average	Good	Good
Roller shutters	9·1×6	7·6×6	9·1×6	£380	£630	Yes	Not ideal above 9·1 m in width between jambs	Garages, loading banks; fair security	Poor	Average	No
Sliding doors		No limit		£310	£500	Yes	Room to slide into when open. Bottom guide required on wider openings	For economy or where clear opening is not required; fair security	Good	Good	Good
Hinged doors	9·1×9	6×6	7·6×7·6	£310	Difficult to apply £500	Not ideal	Strong jambs, level floors and space outside building for when door is open	Where a cheap, small, secure door is required; good security	Good	Good	Good
Sectional	6·4×6·7	6·4×6·4	7·3×6·7	£350	£590	Yes	Clear space above and behind door lintel supports for guides	Garages and loading docks; good security	Fair	Average	Fair
Collapsible gates	15·2×6	Not suitable	9·1×6	£440	£630	Yes	Guide in threshold required	Where security and vision are required	Impossible	Poor	No
Flexible doors	3×4·5 made of rubber or plastic in steel frame			£380	—	—	Firm side fixing. Limited air pressure	For internal use where a draught stopper is required for busy openings; also as secondary closers to external door openings which can then be left open during working hours yet allow fork trucks to push through	Not suitable	Good	No

St = Steel
Tm = Timber
Al = Aluminium

2; (less frequently used). The dock is left open to the elements, and the doors fitted to the warehouse entry positions. This does not provide efficient weather protection when the loading dock is in use, and can constrict circulation, as well as being liable to impact damage.

Internal doors

1.08 These must allow forklift trucks and similar plant to move through; they are often opened by pressure pads or photo-electric cells. Impact doors are also useful; these are manufactured from a flexible material, usually reinforced rubber. These are used where draught stopping and vehicle movement are more important than security. Impact doors can keep out draughts between zones and between a loading dock and the store, and are sometimes fitted behind sliding or shutter doors, left open during normal operation, but shut for security at night. Impact doors do little to prevent heat loss. If used on a two-way flow circulation route, they should be fitted with see-through panels and pads activating a warning siren. Doors to isolate fire zones are normally roller shutter or sliding on an inclined track, activated by fusible links.

Security

1.09 While all doors can be made secure against intruders, the cost of providing security locks, thief-proof hinges and a strengthened door can be very high; check the requirements of the user's insurer. Large doors have been pulled from their mountings by determined thieves who attach chains and haul them out with a lorry. There are sophisticated alarm systems for use with large doors, but some are troublesome, such as light beams which are activated by any bird that is caught inside the warehouse.

1.10 For cold store door requirements, see Section 8, Cold storage.

1.11 There is no substitute for a properly constructed personnel door alongside a vehicle entrance. Machinery and personnel should be segregated where possible, and although there are ingenious solutions of wicket doors in the main door structure, a separate door gives more security and can have full fire escape rating, with easy operation and no risk of fouling.

Manufacturers

1.12 A comprehensive list of industrial door manufacturers can be found in *Specification*, Architectural Press, published annually.

1 *Sectional overhead doors.*

Industrial storage

Information sheet Loading 5

Loading dock equipment

This sheet gives information on types and makes of equipment used in the loading dock.

1 Dock levellers

1.01 Dock levellers are not a luxury. Only by the correct choice and application of equipment can a loading bay reach its full potential **1**. Always consider dock leveller investment in terms of long term costs to the user, of the potential increase in numbers of vehicles handled, of pallet truck and forklift truck battery life and tyre bills. Steep gradients, short leveller plates and tight turns on chequer plate ramps to save space are not an economy.

1.02 There are several types of dock leveller, designed to suit specific requirements.

Conventional dock levellers

1.03 The gradient should never exceed 1 in 10. Length of dock leveller plate is a function of height differential between the vehicle and the dock surface. Container floors can be 1·55 m above the ground, and vehicles can rise 150 mm as they are unloaded.

1.04 There are three types of leveller operation: Counter-balanced, mechanical and hydraulic. Counter-balanced levellers tend to be considered old-fashioned, and can suffer from bounce under load conditions. They require deep pits to accept weights. Mechanical dock levellers **2** are the most popular in Britain. They work on a spring loading principle. Pits can be very shallow (430 mm from one manufacturer). These are well tried units and are virtually maintenance free after initial spring adjustment. Hydraulic levellers **3** are the norm in Europe. They are more expensive than mechanical types, and are particularly suited to heavy duty operation. Because they are quiet in operation, they can be used in urban areas, where the 'clang' of a mechanical leveller hitting the truck deck during night loading would be unacceptable to local residents. Hydraulic levellers usually employ individual pump units: new standards in reliability in hydraulics allow the use of centralised pumps for a range of levellers without fear of total breakdown. Consider cost of hydraulic pipework against individual small pumps: the latter has proved to be cheaper in the past.

1

1 *Typical loading bay. Dock levellers are spaced apart to allow loads to accumulate behind vans, as there is* *limited rear space.*

Builder's work

1.05 Few dock leveller manufacturers include for builder's work in their quotations, either for forming the pit, or for drilling and grouting fixing points. Leveller pits can be costly. Check the leveller's tolerances from the manufacturer; usually pits have to be very accurate. Installation problems seldom occur when manufacturers can supply a sub-frame for building in. Top plates can also be manufactured without excessive side clearances (up to 40 mm).

Free-standing levellers

1.06 If enough space is available, consider free-standing dock levellers **4**. These are standard levellers mounted in a steel sub-frame with integral legs, standing in front of the raised dock. In some cases, this has been cheaper than forming pits, especially in existing buildings. Free-standing levellers cost about £100 more than the basic unit.

1.07 Where existing premises need a higher dock to suit the high container floors, a very long leveller plate is often required to meet the maximum 1 in 10 gradient. This is often uneconomic: a successful solution could be to build a free-standing gradient of chequer plate out from the dock face, equipped with a standard free-standing leveller. This can be angled to suit vehicle reversing lines in constricted premises.

1.08 Most levellers are available in 1·8 m and 2·1 m widths. Dock levellers are mostly equipped with spring-loaded lip plates **5**. These fold back on impact to form a bumper surface, and a flush finish when not in operation. They spring up and out, directly the leveller plate is lifted to meet a vehicle. It is worth specifying these for security, as when the leveller is not in use, and the lip is folded flush with the dock, a roller shutter door can be located into a pocket in the leveller surface, and a strong, intruder-proof barrier is formed.

1.09 Specify dock levellers that can tilt, for trucks also tilt on their springs as they are unloaded. If the leveller cannot tilt, the loading equipment's tyres will be damaged and the loads may topple over.

Flush folding dock levellers

1.10 The folding dock leveller **6** is useful where no pit can be formed or where most vehicles suit the height of the dock and the cost of a full leveller installation would not be justified. This unit is face mounted directly into the concrete, and is equipped with big buffer pads, so that trucks can reverse right up to the dock face. The plate is spring loaded, and is lifted vertically by an operative as the truck backs onto the pads. It then hinges down to form a bridging plate (usually 1·8 m wide). These are basically folding dock-to-vehicle bridge plates and should not be used where any great variation between vehicle floor heights is anticipated. When the vehicle leaves, the leveller folds back vertically flush with dock face.

Mobile dock levellers

1.11 In areas with constricted manoeuvring space, quick turn round is often more important than the simultaneous unloading of several vehicles. A mobile dock leveller **7** is available, which is basically a hydraulic dock leveller running on a carriage mounted on rails, bolted to the dock face. Its advantage is that valuable time need not be wasted by big trucks struggling to manoeuvre accurately in a tight space. Another successful application is in bays used mostly by light vans, where time would be wasted shunting vans to make

2 *Mechanical dock leveller in raised position, showing connections and depth of pit required.*

3 *Hydraulic dock leveller. These are for light vans and so are nearer the ground than usual.*

4 *Dock levellers added to*

existing tobacco warehouses to allow rear loading of containers or side loading of flat trailers.

5 *Typical dock leveller showing lip plate in retracted position and bumper pads.*

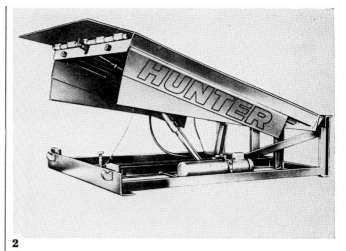

2

3

4

5

way for a large vehicle. The truck can position wherever there is room and the leveller be slid along to its rear door position **8**. When not in use, the plate can be lifted nearly vertical, and the unit pushed to an unobtrusive corner. These are useful for railside operation, allowing flexibility in positioning.

Elevating docks and lift tables

1.12 These are small scissor lifts, and are available as mobile units. They are especially useful when converting existing premises. Typical uses include:
1 Where the warehouse floor is at ground level, and there is no room for a ramp, or no money for a raised dock to be built.
2 Where the existing dock is too low for modern vehicles and there is neither room for a long leveller plate, nor for a free-standing dock extension with a leveller **10**. The elevating dock can be positioned at the best angle to suit the reversing line, and can be fitted with shaped side plates to meet the angle of the existing dock when lowered. Full sized units to lift up forklift trucks are available. Elevating stop bars prevent pallet trucks rolling off during lifting: they can be controlled from the ground or by a man riding up with the table.
3 When building a raised loading dock in a ground level warehouse. The elevating dock bridges the gap between warehouse floor and dock surface, saving space and adding flexibility over a ramp.

1.13 Mobile versions **9** are useful in urban areas, for handling numbers of roll pallets at shop or school premises. They are in direct competition with vehicles equipped with tailboard lifts. Not all suppliers' vehicles have tail lifts, and they are often out of action due to bent guide rails caused by drivers backing into docks too hard. Power is usually from an integral electric motor/hydraulic pump unit, from mains supply or battery. Ten-second operating cycles are possible: maintenance is low. Typical cost of an elevating dock is £1500.

2 Bumper pads

2.01 Vehicles can impose high impact loadings to docks, even at low speeds. To prevent damage, stacked rubber composition bumper pads should be fitted to the dock. This is not a luxury, a 177 kN kg trailer travelling at 2 kph will cause an impact of about 667 kN kg. 25 mm of cushioning will reduce this to 78 kN. Reinforced concrete docks have disintegrated under constant impact. Check with the leveller manufacturer about the correct height and pitch for fixing (see **5**).

7

8

9

6a

6b

10

6a *Folding dock leveller for use in constricted space.*
6b *Dock board takes up small variations in height.*
7 *Mobile dock leveller can slide along rails bolted to dock face. Useful for old*
buildings where trucks have difficulty in positioning accurately.
8 *Mobile dock leveller.*
9 *Mobile dock leveller loading roll pallets.*
10 *Elevating dock used where the old dock (left) is too low, and a dock leveller would reach too steep a gradient in the space available.*

3 Dock shelters

3.01 A typical dock shelter **11** consists of a flexible material, eg reinforced polythene sheet, bonded to a steel frame, standing proud of the building face, with a truckside face of rubber pads or a pneumatic seal. This is placed over a dock leveller position to form a hermetic seal between an enclosed loading dock and a box trailer or container. This is necessary for cold storage areas and in handling perishable foodstuffs and electronic equipment. There is no need for a canopy. Advantages are weather protection, security and dust protection. Management often considers them a luxury for our temperate climate and cost. Check unit cost against that of a canopy. Extending shelters are also available for railside use.

4 Dock lights

4.01 12·1 m containers and 12 m vans are too long for effective light penetration. Accidents and damage have occurred due to lack of light and glare caused by the difference between internal and external light levels. Integral container lights are frequently broken. Spring-loaded dock lights are useful. They are available with one to three joints, and with extended lengths of up to 2·3 m.

5 Loading ramps

5.01 These are useful for loading vehicles by forklift truck or powered pallet truck from ground level. They are usually made of steel in one or two sections, mounted on a mobile frame with securing jacks that screw down to the ground. Because the gradient must not exceed 1 in 10, they are space consuming in operation and when stored. They are too narrow (1·8 m) for unloading cars from containers (see Technical study Loading 1, **17**).

6 Extending conveyors

6.01 These are for 'stuffing' containers and trucks manually to achieve maximum volume **12**. The conveyors can be dock or ground mounted. They can move vertically, turn on their axis, and extend to the end of a container, retracting as the vehicle is loaded. Especially useful in groupage depots, where deep sea services require maximum volume loading. They are used extensively in Europe for loading rail wagons with goods like sacks. (See Technical study Bulk Storage and Information sheet Mechanised Storage 8 and 9.)

11a *Enclosed loading bay with dock shelter: retracted leveller with shutter door locked into leveller plate.* **b** *Flexible sheet type dock shelter.*
12 *Extendible conveyor loading a container to maximum possible volume.*
13 *Detachable remote controlled forks can enter containers to place pallets without the forklift driver leaving his seat.*

11a

11b

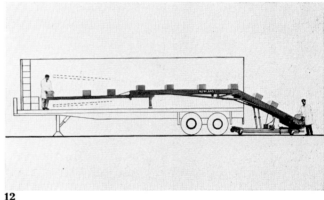

12

13

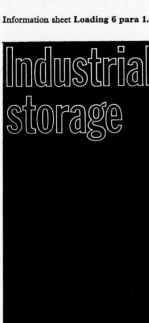

Information sheet Loading 6

Railway layouts

This sheet gives design data on layouts of railway wagon track. It is to be used for general guidance only, as British Rail should be consulted about any detailed plans for linking storage with railway tracks.

1 Dimensions of rail wagons and track

1.01 This information sheet is not intended to act as a basis of design for rail track alignment, curve radii or points design. British Rail should always be contacted concerning any advance plans to link a warehouse to nearby railway tracks. Each 'territory', which replaces the old rail region, has a civil engineering depot, and there is also a civil engineering department for each division. These departments are always pleased to provide guidance for designers planning rail access points and sidings.

1.02 A guide to designing spaces surrounding rail wagons is shown in **1**. Walls, foot and pipe bridges, and platforms (if straight), must be clear of these controlling dimensions. It is safer to plan track foundations for the maximum axle loadings of a typical wagon in use of 25·4 tonnes. **2** shows lengths and overhangs in relation to the wheel base; this data is useful in calculating cut-in and swing-out on curves, so that adequate clearance is allowed for personnel or plant between the trucks and a wall. Some BR lines and sidings have restrictions on loading: check this with BR before proceeding with design. Remember if planning unloading on a curved siding, that the camber of the track is liable to lower the base of door runners on box vans by several millimetres; make sure that this will not foul platform edges on the cut-in.

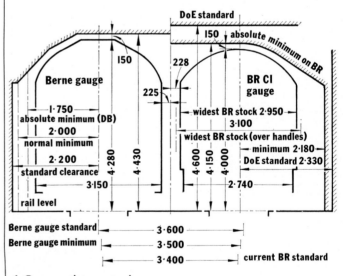

1 *Cross section comparing typical British and European (Berne gauge) standards for rolling stock giving controlling dimensions for use in railway planning: design elements (bridges, platforms, etc) must be clear of these profiles.*

1.03 If using dry goods, the type of wagon most likely to be received are high speed, two axle, side loading vans, designed especially for forklift access with palletised dry goods. These have a maximum load and truck weight of 35·5 tonnes, and long, sliding doors. The container-carrying flat trucks are approximately 19 m long, and are bogey units with 17·7 tonne axle loads. A bridge plate is needed for forklift access to wagon mounted side door containers; the 2·4 m container width is approximately 300 mm less than a normal wagon.

Truck and platform height
1.04 There may be a problem of relating levels of the new 'Lowliner' container flat trucks **3**. These are designed to carry 2·59 m high containers within the loading gauge. Conventional container flat trucks and Freightliner trucks have a rail-to-bed height of a nominal 965·2 mm, but this can vary 50 mm between wagon types whereas the 'Lowliner' is only 836·6 mm. 100 mm average depth of container floor should be added to these dimensions for forklift access. Sideloading allows little tolerance for floor height variation if forklifts are to be used freely. If different types of trucks are delivered, an operator will be faced with unloading one of the truck types manually. The alternatives are:
1 Remove all containers from rail trucks before unloading.
2 Run forklifts at ground level; this requires some manual intervention to push pallets to the container door, which is likely anyway, especially if full volume stuffing is required for deep sea services.
3 Install the dock to 'Lowliner' height, and have a raised section, using a scissor lift for example. British Rail container wagons come in units of three, with a total length of approximately 59·3 m, buffer to buffer, so this would be expensive.
Solution 2 seems the most flexible, but negates the use of the new two-axle trucks designed for pallet handling from a raised dock. Designers should therefore carefully examine the type of traffic to be handled before they make a decision on the platform height.
1.05 Shunting methods are discussed in Technical study Bulk Storage, para 4. Winch systems are also available. A small machine like a motorised wheel barrow is useful for individual truck handling. There is a BR code for wagon handling, so check any shunting ideas for private use with them.
1.06 Certain unit loads may require special fixing methods **4**; check with manufacturer.

Fuel tankers
1.07 Possibly the most frequent type of railway access met by designers today is for fuel tankers. There are large numbers of privately owned tank wagons in operation carrying oil fuel, oil and chemical products, and bulk powders. With the recent trouble experienced with road tanker crashes involving acid and caustic product spillage, more of this traffic will return to the railway, both in bulk tankers, and in tank containers on skeletal wagons.
1.08 For oil fuels the design of reception areas for tank wagons is comparatively simple **4, 5**. The oil companies have consultancy departments to advise customers in planning their reception areas. As long as there is continuity at rail joints, wagons are earthed to the tracks through their wheels, and need no further earthing points for pumping heavy fuel or spirit. Heavy fuel oil tankers are insulated, but not heated; the refinery or distribution tank depot calculate the journey length and unloading period and load the oil sufficiently hot to remain pumpable on arrival. It is also unusual to supply any heating to valves, pipe work or pumps at the reception point, and the pipes are emptied by

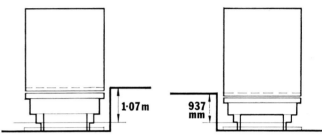

axle load tonnes	min overhang m	min wheelbase m	min dimensions adj wagons m
17·7	1·06	3·65	2·13
25·4	1·52	4·5	3·04

2a

axle load tonnes	min over -hang m	min wheel -base m	min distance between inner wheels m	min wheel -base m	min dimensions adj wagons m
14·2	1·37	1·8	4·87	1·8	2·74
25·4	1·5	2·0	9·1	2·0	3·04

2b

conventional container　　　　　　**2·59m container 'Lowliner'**

1·07m　　　　**937 mm**

dimensions from top of rail to typical container floor
3

2a *Two-axle wagon dimensions and* **b** *bogie wagon dimensions.*
3 *Container wagon floors have different heights, and may also vary up to 100 mm in laden and unladen condition.*

4 *Five-tonne platform loads of bricks secured to container train.*

6

positive displacement pumps; any residue left is cleared by the next load. Pumps operate in the open with meter points, so that the customer can check wagon capacity against loading tickets from the refinery **6**. It is not advisable to provide access to wagon hatches, as is done for road tankers. Rail wagons are self venting, and the fuel tankers do not need cleaning on customer's premises. These checks are performed at the refinery.

1.09 The design of modern joint valves and pipe fittings precludes most spillage; usually, a little sand laid on the ballast is sufficient for spillage collection.

Lighting

1.10 Adequate lighting must be provided for night deliveries. One oil company tried lighting on gantries, which were found to be too high and cast a shadow on connection points. Plug-height lights proved to be a glare source. One solution is to place light towers between the connection plug positions **5**.

Plug positions

1.11 British Rail's minimum for considering a number of wagons as a separate train is five to six units. Tankers are unloaded simultaneously from multiple plug positions **6, 7**; fuel oil tankers have been designed so that the connection points are at constant centres, ie if a large bogey truck is used, it would fit onto the same plugs as two rigid chassis units.

Fire

1.12 There is little fire problem with fuel oil but all electric equipment must be flameproof. If low flash products are to be handled, contact the factory inspector, petroleum officer and the local fire officer. This also applies to areas for handling caustic, corrosive or explosive powder products.

Powder tankers

1.13 Powder tankers either discharge by gravity, or are vacuum assisted. These units tend to be owned by the manufacturers, who will supply any data required for designing the handling equipment most suitable for their product.

7

5 *Section through tanker reception point, showing minimum centres for double sided unloading.*
6 *Double sided discharge area with underground pipes and drain channels.*
7 *Detail of plug point.*
8 *A roll pallet/tractor/forklift system specially developed for rail wagons.*

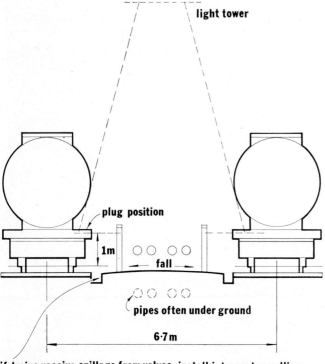

if drains receive spillage from valves, install interceptor gullies
5

8

Technical study External storage 1

Design of container handling areas

External storage, in the context of this handbook, means the short-term storage of ISO containers and demountable truck bodies. The planning of this important and comparatively new type of storage is described in detail, as mistakes can be very costly in wasted plant, effort and area. This section does not cover external storage on the ground of non-containerised loads, such as building materials. Planning of such simple storage areas is described in the Manual and Mechanised storage sections.

1 The potential of containers and demountable bodies

1.01 The ISO container should have revolutionised the transport, storage and packaging industries. The potential of a standard range of box sizes for most commodities is enormous. It should mean that intermodal handling is cut to a minimum, costs are reduced, and turn-round is speeded up because modular units and advanced mechanical handling techniques are used. This potential is not being realised. The responsibility for this rests jointly with the business community, shippers and designers. Misunderstanding of the physical characteristics of container handling has caused waste throughout the industry **1**. Size standards laid down by the International Standards Organisation are being abused. For instance it was widely predicted that 20ft × 8ft × 8ft (6 m × 2·4 m × 2·4 m) containers would become the standard unit, but now the most popular is the 40ft (12 m) unit, with a marked preference for 8ft 6in (2·6 m) height. This extra 6in over the original standard, sponsored by the US trucking industry, allows 8 per cent greater cubic capacity and an average of 2270 kg potential extra payload; the larger size has caused problems on sea (due to the rigid cellular nature of ships) and rail (due to lower European rail loading gauges). With the proposed 4 m height limit for lorries in EEC countries, 8ft 6in (2·6 m) high containers will be difficult to transport. A further complication

1 *Different heights of ISO containers makes stacking difficult.*

in Europe has been the introduction of 2·6 m × 2·6 m section containers, designed specifically for the West German rail system. Outwardly similar to ISO containers, they have caused confusion at groupage depots, as they will not fit onto standard skeletal trailers.

1.02 In spite of these shortcomings, the ISO container is the most adaptable unit of goods transport available. Within the basic frame, tanks, bins, tipping bodies, hoppers, pressure vessels and many special forms can be built (see Information sheet External storage 1). Containers can be stacked three or four high when full, and six high when empty, reducing the ground area previously needed for storage by semitrailers. However, the heavy plant required to handle containers needs manoeuvring space and savings may not be as great as anticipated, due to bad planning.

1.03 The potential of the container as a total system is not being used. There has been much over-investment in land-based plant, skeletal trailers, cranes, straddle carriers and in the numbers of containers themselves. It is unfortunately common to see large areas of European container bases under-utilised and full of expensive, idle plant.

1.04 The problem is increased by the storage potential of standing containers. Mobile, plug-in refrigeration units enable perishable goods to be stored for some time before breaking-bulk or trucking out to the consumer. Industry was quick to realise that their own stores could be greatly reduced if goods could be left in other operators' containers. Where ISO containers are efficient for intercontinental operations, they are bulky for local delivery work and impose a heavy weight penalty.

Demountable bodies

1.05 ISO containers are an open system of heavy construction, for 'deep sea' use and for stacking three or four high when loaded. Demountable bodies are on the same principle, but are a closed system (ie no standard size) and of lighter construction (so cannot be stacked).

1.06 General trends in size are towards 13ft (3·9 m) lengths, so that three can fit on a 40ft (12 m) trailer **2a**, and 10ft (3 m) lengths, so that two can fit on the lorry and two on the trailer of a drawbar outfit.

1.07 Demountable body units enable a truck chassis to be used continuously, with turn-round times as fast as it takes to drop one body and pick up another, not necessarily of the same type. Modular demountable truck bodies offer a very high efficiency trucking system, and it is easy and cheap to store them on integral legs **2b**.

Future conditions

1.08 Designers should plan with future vehicle weights and configurations in mind. As yet, the EEC transport authority is undecided at what figure to fix European gross vehicle weights. It is likely that articulated vehicles will be limited to 40·6 tonnes, allowing a full 40ft (12 m) container to be carried; and truck and drawbar trailer combinations will be rated at 44 to 47 tonnes allowing two full 20ft (6 m) containers to be carried. Designers should note that overall sizes are not likely to increase.

2 Design

Approach roads

2.01 At terminal points in the system—factory, store, or marshalling area—allowance should be made for heavy trucks to arrive in peak conditions. To ensure smooth traffic flow, a computer model to simulate the surrounding roads and daily traffic flow conditions can now be made. Analysis of differing traffic flows would show where peak build-ups and stoppages will occur, and thus where road improvements should be. In several cases, a container-handling area has been re-sited due to the great cost of local road improvements

2a

2b

2a *Three swop bodies on one trailer,* **b** *Swop body is parked on legs, while truck moves out from beneath.*

required to handle future peak traffic conditions. Usually there is a morning and afternoon truck peak, and with future city traffic restrictions, there is a good chance of a night peak as well.

Buffer areas

2.02 Buffer parking and assembly space should be provided for peak build-up and emergency holding for incoming and outgoing traffic. Areas should be provided, especially in groupage depots, for pooled container and skeletal trailer facilities. 'Tilt' trailers and containers on skeletal trailers can choke the loading bank area, unless planned from the outset. For demountable bodies, space should be left for parked chassis and unused body units. Designer or consultant should analyse flow at an early stage and compare cost/efficiency of layouts not only in terms of vehicle turn-round, but in handling plant efficiency in the buffer area. If a buffer zone is not provided and a truck breaks down in peak conditions, major blockages always occur in the assembly position and soon affect major transport links.

2.03 Buffer areas are also important for documentation. Designers sometimes forget that containers have to be checked so that they can be routed to the correct stack area. At present, container codes are checked manually, but scanner readers are being developed that can read numbers on the side and ends of the container, and this, linked with a self-checking computerised bill of loading, would simplify present documentation. The manual system requires a physical check; either the container moves past a fixed point, or a mobile checkpoint moves round the assembly area, often linked with closed-circuit television. The automated system requires containers to pass a scanner beam, and should be carefully positioned so that the traffic flow is not impaired and the buffer space can operate efficiently. Clearly marked lanes, stopping points and a clear visual display instruction system for drivers can help a great deal. Avoid tight turns and route-crossing points hidden by container stacks. Serious accidents have occurred by fast-moving handling plant colliding with a turning vehicle, partially hidden behind a block of containers. Essentially routing should be one way with clearly marked priorities. A clockwise periphery route is the most effective in Britain as drivers are always in a position to see what is happening in the container stacks. If automated handling plant (eg wire-guided straddle carriers) is used, road vehicles need not enter the stack areas, moving only to peripheral assembly zones.

Down draughts
2.04 High stacks of empty containers can become unstable in buffet and eddy conditions, and the funnel effect of stacks can produce high velocity down-draughts **3**. Injury has resulted by personnel being pushed against containers, and the accuracy of the plant in placing can be impaired.

Parking
2.05 Parking surfaces in container areas should be well drained, so that water does not build up in container stacks, caught between falls and container bases. Falls and cambers can impair the speed of alignment of sideloaders and straddle carriers. Containers should not rest on an apex, as there is risk of serious structural damage to the bottom container in the stack. Areas for container stacking should be designed for loadings of not less than 50 kN/m², with aisles for special wheeled plant, weighing about 100 tonnes with a fully laden 40ft (12 m) container. On corners or when braking, where skidding with plant would be disastrous, a non-slip surface should be laid. The type of epoxy-based granite chip surface now being used for junctions in London is not cheap, but is money well spent. Dimensions of parking areas are decided by the type of handling plant, and are illustrated in Information sheet External storage 2.

'Reefer' parking
2.06 Parking areas for 'reefer' (ie refrigerated) containers require special conditions. Several plug-in systems are available. One accepts stacked containers attached to a central spine, others rely on ground connection points. When left on skeletal trailers, electric power or cooling gas points are usually provided at strategic positions for a group of four containers back to back. These areas should be well lit and carefully marked out, leaving a walkway for personnel to connect the plugs safely. Plug positions should be well marked, preferably in luminous paint, and well protected from impact, **4**, **5**. (This subject will be handled in more detail in Section 9 Cold storage).

Personnel
2.07 Some personnel will always be required to work in container areas. Future installations will be more likely to have 'white collar' workers for operating automated systems. Well designed personnel facilities have led to cost benefits, due to a good management/personnel relationships and improved standards of operation. Large-scale container areas are not

3

3 *Container stacks overturned by wind.*
4 *Detail of a refrigerated vehicle plug point. These allow the trucks to act as external storage without running their engines or using up their batteries. Note drain, protective curb and spring-loaded cable reels.*
5 *Well planned truck park for refrigeration lorries, with plug-in positions for integral refrigeration units, clearly identified bays, and raised area to protect the plug points and allow safe personnel movement.*   **4**

conducive to human occupation, and lack of forethought can lead to costly industrial disputes.

Inland container areas

2.08 These are of three types: the inland container port and groupage area, the large industry marshalling zone, and the conventional small-factory or warehouse yard. All three share the basic problems, but with a difference in scale. Inland container groupage areas, such as the London International Freight Terminal at Stratford have similar conditions to a sea port, with the added problem of transferring units to various types of transport, ie truck-to-train, truck-to-truck. These areas also attract agents' and importers' accommodation, requiring break-bulk facilities, so generating more traffic and a security problem. The change in type of transport means peak conditions for both rail and road movement; these do not often coincide, as container trains are scheduled out of passenger peaks, and especially in break-bulk situations, local delivery vehicle peaks occur at the start of the working day and after the lunch break.

2.09 In urban situations, overcrowding can prove very costly (for instance where the best container stack organisation constricts the operation of the break-bulk zone and vice versa). Although this often does not seem important, as the groupage and break-bulk area is probably handling a small percentage of the total traffic by value, a constriction in the approach or buffer to this zone can generate long vehicle hold-ups, the smaller vehicles baulking the large container trucks, so putting a brake on the whole system.

2.10 There are no hard-and-fast rules for organising groupage areas, but the following points are important:

1 Free-flowing traffic is critical

2 Manoeuvring space must be provided for the largest Continental outfits

3 Areas should be provided for: parked TIR 'tilt' trailers and containers on skeletals; Continental drivers to rest in their cabs; unsheeting 'tilt' trailers and containers **6**. If a side access bay is to be used, space should be provided for dropping the sides of the trailer; for Customs to check seals before leaving the site; and for a segregated area to contain light feeder vans.

2.11 The sites that tend to be allocated are often 'left-overs' or old railway yards, by nature a triangle or bent rectangle. These sites do not lend easily to the grid distribution generated by containers and their handling plant.

Environmental problems

2.12 There are environmental side issues in urban areas that often become lost in the design of the handling system. For instance, stacks of empty containers act like drums in heavy rain, their shape amplifying the noise in the immediate neighbourhood and producing discomfort for local residents. Wind can also be an annoyance. Security is a serious problem, not only because of theft but also because of personal safety. Children like to play near big machines, and container stacks and handling plant are very tempting. The expenditure on a carefully designed perimeter barrier is a definite cost benefit, compared with the costs granted against a maimed child. Reduced insurance premiums are offered for well-designed security systems; this must not be treated as an afterthought. Perimeter barriers can also be used for noise attenuation and visual relief in urban situations **7**.

3 Demountable bodies as storage

3.01 Demountable truck bodies are often used as cheap, short-term storage. Most types of swop-body systems are automatically dropped by the truck and have integral hinge or wind-down legs **8**. One type requires a gantry for removal from the prime mover, and another a system of rails. The storage potential of these units is very valuable and saves expensive warehousing, eliminates double handling and takes

6

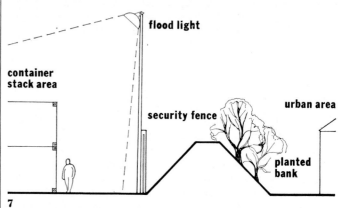

7

6 *Two 20ft (6 m) 'tilt' containers, one with sides lowered.*
7 *Screening of containers*

in urban areas.
8 *Hydraulic landing legs for demountable body.*

8

the goods to the exact position where they will be required. The bodies cannot be stacked like ISO containers, but they can be block-parked very close indeed; there is no need for straddle, carrier or crane access, but only for the truck chassis to reverse under the body. A buffer zone should also be provided, with manoeuvring space for both truck and local delivery vehicles. Several swop bodies can be trunk-hauled by only one vehicle, to an urban marshalling point for transfer to small delivery vehicles carrying one body each. Trunk vehicles are either articulated or (as is becoming more popular, due to their potentially greater cubic capacity) truck and draw-bar trailer outfits. Swop bodies are often block-parked in urban marshalling areas, for short-term storage, and local delivery vans pick them up as required on a first-in, first-out principle, much as pallets can be handled in a warehouse. (See Technical study Mechanised storage 1.)

4 Security

4.01 Great care should be taken over the security of external storage areas, as it is easy for an intruder to be missed amid and underneath the tightly parked body units **9**. Efforts should also be made to prevent children from gaining access and playing in these areas, as serious accidents have occurred due to drivers' vision being restricted. A well-designed fence and a high level of gantry lighting help. The lighting is not wasted, as with the increase of daytime city delivery restrictions, there will probably be many more night movements **10**. For employees' safety, and the fast coupling and deposit of bodies, clear markings should be placed on the ground, ensuring a pre-determined parking pattern. Traffic flow should be one-way and clearly marked out.

5 Personnel accommodation

5.01 In swop body parks, as in container-handling areas, some form of personnel accommodation is likely to be required; this is liable to be in the form of an office, wc and washing facilities. At major interchange points, with numbers of long-distance vehicles passing through, rest and vending facilities should be provided for the drivers. This is no luxury; it gives an incentive for drivers not to waste time in cafés on the road, which in turn reduces the risk of theft. Some form of covered provision should also be made for basic truck and body maintenance, even if it is of a 'driver-does-it-himself' nature. The securing locks and lifting systems on demountable body trucks can break down, and bodies become damaged in tight urban areas. An under-ceiling clearance of 5 m is required, allowing access to a chassis with a lifted body. A roof-mounted chain hoist is useful for removing jammed bodies. Electrical points, water and an airline should be provided, with a store for basic equipment like jacks and portable hydraulic pumps.

9

10

9 *Typical strong security fence with outward sloping top section.*
10 *Large light tower: note also large areas required for container handling. Behind are two container cranes.*
11 *A sideloader carrying 6 m containers. In the background is a loader for 12 m containers.*

11

6 Check list

	Whom to contact
Can the local roads support the future goods traffic?	Local authority, DOE, transport consultant
What type of traffic is expected?	Shippers, management
What quantity of future traffic? Growth?	Business consultant
Will break-bulk facilities be required?	Management
Should vehicle types be split?	System designer
Position of buffer/assembly area	System designer
Road/rail peaks	British Rail—local authority, shippers, transport consultant
Type of container stack and area required	Mechanical handling consultants, shippers
600 40ft (12 m) containers plus processing = 4·45 hectares 3000 40ft (12 m) containers plus processing = 20 to 25 hectares	
Optimum circulation. Clear markings	System designer
Vehicle/plant segregation in rail sidings	Mechanical handling consultants, British Rail
Security, road surface, aisle distribution, personnel, pilferage, entry control	Police, management, system designer
Prevailing wind, local weather	Meteorological Office
Surrounding environment, urban areas: visual, aural environment	Local authority, management
Personnel accommodation	Management
Maintenance facility, plant parking	Plant manager, plant manufacturer, management.

Information sheet External storage 1

Containers

This information sheet describes the range of sizes of ISO containers, types available, and typical uses.

1 Sizes

1.01 As explained in Technical study External storage 1, container sizes are to remain in imperial, due to pressure from the US trucking industry. Sizes are therefore given in imperial, with rounded-up metric equivalents in brackets.

2 Types

2.01 Types of containers, with sizes, materials and uses are shown in table I.

1a

1a 40*ft* (12 *m*) *container being lifted by crane. Twist locks can be seen at corners and* **b**.

1b

3 Method of moving

3.01 Containers are lifted, secured and stacked by 'twist locks' on the corner castings **1**. Containers can be stacked six high when empty, three or four high when laden, depending on weight and lifting equipment. Some are fitted with 350 mm wide × 100 mm deep forklift pockets at the base (positioned at 900 mm centres equidistant from centre line of container) **2**. (See Information Sheet External storage 2).

4 Capacities

4.01 Maximum capacity for 20ft (6 m) container = 20 tonnes
Maximum capacity for 40ft (12 m) container = 30 tonnes
It is unusual for 20ft (6 m) units to gross more than 12 to 15 tonnes, or for 40ft (12 m) units to rise over 20 tonnes. Only full cube packed commodities (eg tinned fruit juice) result in 20 tonnes, 20ft (6 m) containers. Most container handling machinery is not designed for continual handling of maximum loads.

5 Identification

5.01 Coding and identification is marked in standard positions on end doors and sides. They give type of container, its owner, its size and capacity, and its unique serial number.

2 *A tilt-top 20ft (6 m) container with forklift pockets and regulation identification on standard side position.*

Types, sizes and uses of ISO containers

End door and side and end door container

L			W			H		
ft	in	(m)	ft	in	(m)	ft	in	(m)
20		(6·09)	8		(2·43)	8		(2·43)
30		(9·14)				8	6	(2·59)
40		(12·19)						

Materials and construction
Steel, aluminium, plastics-faced ply with steel frame

Use
General dry goods. Side and end door containers are useful where loading area is constricted for large trucks or for railway use

Tilt top container

L			W			H		
ft	in	(m)	ft	in	(m)	ft	in	(m)
20		(6·09)	8		(2·43)	8		(2·43)
30		(9·14)				8	6	(2·59)
40		(12·19)						

Materials and construction
Steel with open top, covered with composite plastics 'tilt' with end doors

Use
For loading long steel or paper reels with an overhead crane, and for outsize loads for deck cargo

Tilt container

L			W			H		
ft in	(m)		ft in	(m)		ft in	(m)	
20	(6·09)		8	(2·43)		8	(2·43)	
30	(9·14)							
40	(12·19)							

Materials and construction
Steel frames with low sides, 'tilt' frames and complete 'tilt' covering in composite plastics. Skeletal end doors and detachable corner posts. Some have fold-down end-panels for standing when empty (four fit within one normal container size)

Use
For bulky goods more suited to side loading, or with special unloading and handling circumstances (eg vehicle tyres, metal coil). Also aids customs examination

Tilt is top container illustrated

Half height container

L			W			H		
ft in	(m)		ft in	(m)		ft in	(m)	
20	(6·09)		8	(2·43)		4	(1·21)	
40	(12·19)							

Materials and construction
Steel or aluminium with 'tilt' top and end doors. Some skeletal, ie above with post and rail sides for carrying steel

Use
For open top or with tilt for steel bars, high weight goods (eg chemical drums)

Bulk container

L			W			H		
ft in	(m)		ft in	(m)		ft in	(m)	
20	(6·09)		8	(2·43)		8	(2·43)	
30	(9·14)							
40	(12·19)							

Materials and construction
Steel or aluminium container with strong end doors. Some have metal sheet roofs with hatches, some with 'tilt' tops. Some end doors have hatches for powder handling. Can be mounted on tippers (as in illustration) or fitted with pneumatic discharge equipment. Also available with plastic liners thrown away after discharge

Use
For increasing trade in bulk materials

Tank container

L			W			H		
ft	in	(m)	ft	in	(m)	ft	in	(m)
20		(6·09)	8		(2·43)	8		(2·43)
30		(9·14)						
40		(12·19)						

Materials and construction
Steel or aluminium tanks mounted on ISO subframes

Use
For bulk liquids and powders. Some tanks are pressurised, heated, or insulated

Insulated container

L			W			H		
ft	in	(m)	ft	in	(m)	ft	in	(m)
20		(6·09)	8		(2·43)	8		(2·43)
30		(9·14)						
40		(12·19)						

Materials and construction
Steel, aluminium or plastic faced ply with insulation. End door ,and side and end door types

Use
For goods needing temperature controlled environment during transit
(*Similar in appearance to standard container*)

Reefer 'refrigerated' container

L			W			H		
ft	in	(m)	ft	in	(m)	ft	in	(m)
20		(6·09)	8		(2·43)	8		(2·43)
30		(9·14)						
40		(12·19)				8	6	(2·59)

Materials and construction
Two types: 1 Autonomous, ie fitted with own refrigeration source on front bulkhead. These are plugged into power sources on ship and vehicle. One type carries cooling cylinder with structure. 2 Non-autonomous, ie container is plugged into central refrigeration source while on ship or in park, and container insulation maintains temperature during delivery. More popular type

Use
For refrigerated goods

Special containers

L			W			H		
ft	in	(m)	ft	in	(m)	ft	in	(m)
40		(12·19)	8		(2·43)	8	6	(2·59)
	8	(2·43)	8		(2·43)	8		(2·43)
35		(10 66)	8		(2·43)	8		(2·43)

Materials and construction
Side door unit with ramp inside. 'Auto-perch', 'Geest' container, 'Sealand' container

Use
Specialist duties eg
car carrier, coil carrier

Industrial storage

Information sheet External storage 2

Container handling plant

This sheet describes plant used to handle containers in both large and small installations.

1 Types of container handling plant

1.01 Container handling systems range from gantry and 'Transtainer' cranes to straddle carriers and forklift trucks. As ISO containers are large, their handling plant must be large as well. The designer should be able to anticipate how areas are used, and so design for the plant from the outset. The choice of a particular handling method is related to type of traffic (eg ship to shore, train to truck or truck to ground), number of containers handled per hour, and the distance of travel which depends on the size and shape of the site, and the potential for expansion.

Gantry cranes
1.02 Gantry cranes are mostly used for unloading containers from ships, and at a smaller scale, for high density rail interchanges. Specially designed for container traffic, they are capable of substantial cantilever lifting, with spreaders mounted on rotating tables, so that the containers can be aligned straight into a stack or onto a vehicle **1**. These are expensive pieces of plant, and generate linear planning. Designers must be careful not to plan cross routes where a stoppage might interfere with crane movement.

1

2

1 *Gantry crane.*   **2** *Mobile gantry.*

Mobile gantry cranes

1.03 This type is basically a gantry crane on rubber tyres, combining the mobility of straddle carriers, although slower, with the wide spans and height of a gantry crane **2**. These too, tend to generate linear planning, although they can steer out of track and 'crab' if required. Mobile gantries also have a spreader on a revolving table, as it is thought that the operator can realign a container quicker than the time taken to shunt a large vehicle to an accurate position. One advantage of mobile gantries over gantry cranes and straddle carriers is their ability to unload railway waggons and transfer the container directly to the stack or to another mode of transport, while being capable of quick movement to another task at a different part of the site (see **8**). If cross movement is anticipated, the designer should plan the container area with some form of grid so that a wheel width is left at all times.

Straddle carriers

1.04 Straddle carriers are efficient in linear stacking situations up to three containers high **3**. Developed from smaller types originally designed for the timber trade, the container-carrying straddle carriers are fast and manoeuvrable, but are expensive to buy and operate. The industry is worried by the high maintenance costs and 'down' time of sophisticated machines, but on the whole they are versatile. They work on the principle of driving over the top of a container, and positioning a spreader beam onto the top casting. This spreader is usually adjustable for 20, 30 and 40ft (6, 9 and 12 m) containers. Although manually operated at present, wire-guided models are being developed which with scanner code readers and photo-electric positioning devices, could become fully automated in the foreseeable future, eliminating the present criticism of high operator positions causing slow alignment.

Forklift trucks

1.05 Forklift trucks can be used for container handling, but not all containers have fork tunnels. Most operators equip their forklifts with high level spreader beams as well **4**. When using these machines, the forks must be 2·4 m long or be fitted with 2·4 m sleeves, ensuring evenly distributed support, otherwise serious damage to a container floor can result. When using 2·4 m forks or sleeves, care should be taken that the rated capacity at the 1·2 m load centres is not exceeded. Normal types of forklift trucks can be used for empty container handling and stacking. For laden units, a special heavy duty truck is required. A useful development for empty container handling is the slewing mast truck, that can place the container at 90° to the direction of travel, load like a normal fork truck, and travel in aisles like a side loader (see Information sheet Mechanised storage 1).

Side loaders

1.06 The side loader is very useful in container areas, and like forklift trucks, there are special models designed for container handling **5**. These machines lift a container from the ground, or from a truck, or stack, traverse the mast, and so place it on to the wide platform for stability **6**. They are capable of fast travel in aisles no wider than themselves **7**. Models are available with small turning circles, enabling them to fit into very tight stacks (see Information sheet Mechanised storage 1).

3a

3b

4a

3a *Two parked straddle carriers. Container crane in the background.* **b** *Straddle carrier stacking containers three high.*

4 *Container carrying forklift trucks* **b** *can also stack containers two high when laden, and higher when empty,* **a**.

4b

2 Which system makes the most of site potential?

2.01 To reach an optimum solution, evaluate each particular situation carefully, eliminating systems that are unsuitable. Some operators claim that straddle carriers are not as efficient as mobile gantries; straddle carriers demand large turning aisles and wheel width spaces, whereas a mobile gantry can span over 10 container stacks in block **10**. The straddle carrier is faster, but wastes space; the mobile gantry has to be fed by tractor train, forklift truck or side loader. Aisles between container stacks are useful for visual number checks, where block stacking can lead to confusion. All container stacks should be organised into high, medium and low speed lines to increase efficiency, with these areas clearly marked out. Some argue that an aisle system built up by a mobile gantry is most efficient, while those using sideloaders claim greater speed and efficiency than straddle carriers (side loaders can stack three high and double stack, requiring an aisle of their own width only every second row). Side loaders can also block stack containers for one destination, for gantry crane removal **11**. For slower work cycles and short distance travel from rail or road waggon to stack, a forklift truck is efficient especially if it can be used for other jobs.

6a

6b

5

5 (*left*) 20-*tonne* (*right*) 30-*tonne sideloader.*
6a, b *Sideloader placing container onto vehicle trailer.*

7 *Sideloader stacking containers in parallel.*

7

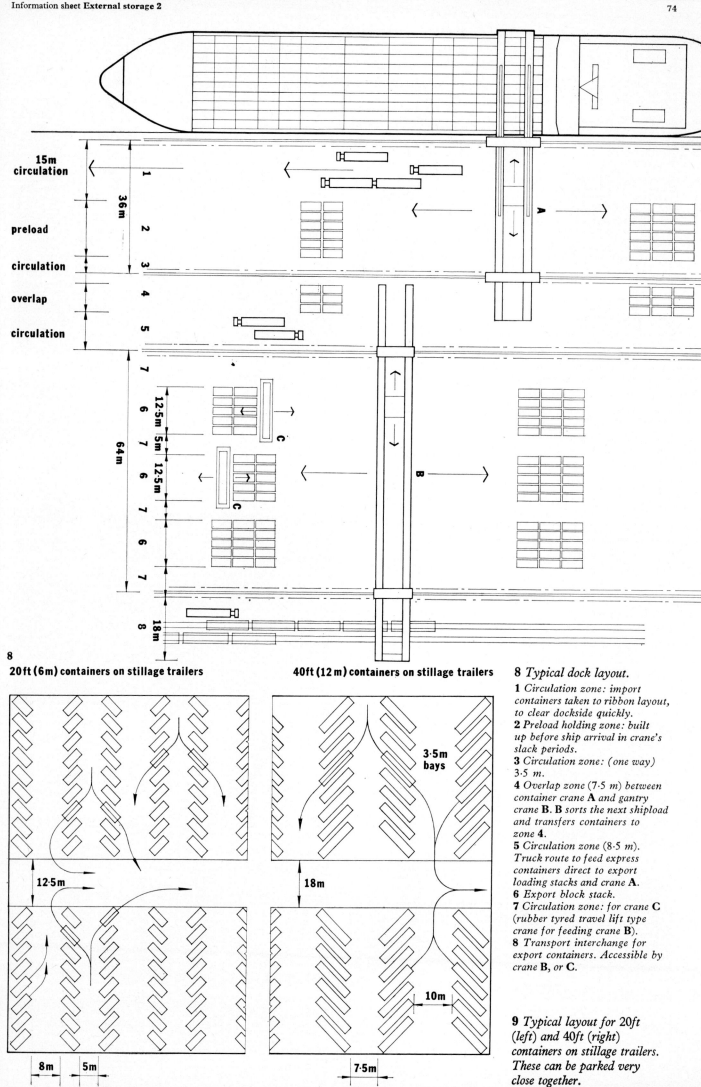

8

20 ft (6m) containers on stillage trailers

40 ft (12 m) containers on stillage trailers

8 *Typical dock layout.*

1 *Circulation zone: import containers taken to ribbon layout, to clear dockside quickly.*
2 *Preload holding zone: built up before ship arrival in crane's slack periods.*
3 *Circulation zone: (one way) 3·5 m.*
4 *Overlap zone (7·5 m) between container crane* **A** *and gantry crane* **B**. **B** *sorts the next shipload and transfers containers to zone* **4**.
5 *Circulation zone (8·5 m). Truck route to feed express containers direct to export loading stacks and crane* **A**.
6 *Export block stack.*
7 *Circulation zone: for crane* **C** *(rubber tyred travel lift type crane for feeding crane* **B**).
8 *Transport interchange for export containers. Accessible by crane* **B**, *or* **C**.

9 *Typical layout for 20ft (left) and 40ft (right) containers on stillage trailers. These can be parked very close together.*

9

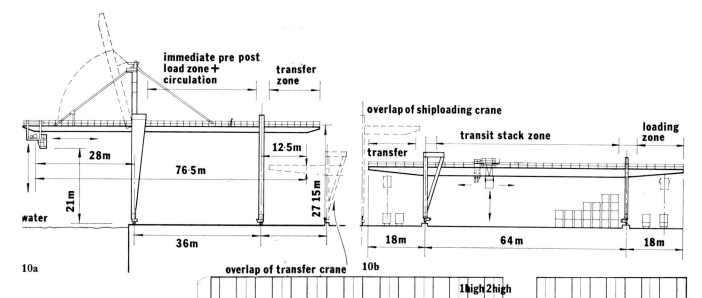

10a

10b

10a *Shiploading container crane (portainer),* **b** *Gantry crane (transtainer) for sorting containers and feeding shiploading crane.*

11 *Typical inland container area for sideloaders. 20ft (6 m) containers are shown. Sideloaders can load truck and rail wagons direct, as well as stack. Top left, ribbon layout is for fast selection ie imports. Top right, block layout where high individual selectivity is not important.*

12 *Typical layout using sideloaders in a port with fast turnover, or clearance depot. Top left, layout for import ribbon stack or where containers have to be selected quickly. They are stacked alternately one and two high, so that only one container need be moved to reach another. Bottom left, lower selectivity ribbon layout. Sideloaders can operate on bad surfaces.*

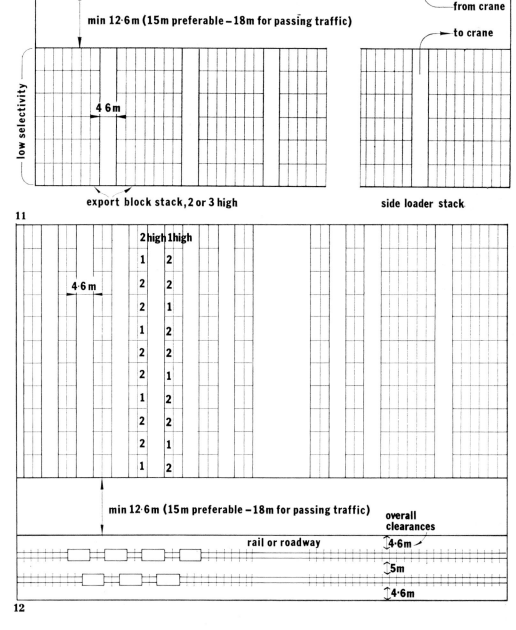

11

12

13

14

15

16

2.02 Other sections of the industry, particularly stevedores, prefer the stillage trailer system **13, 14, 15**—this can be used with break-bulk flat trucks and stillages as well as articulated straddle lifters. These units are popular in inland container terminals, and for feeding 'Transtainer' cranes **16**. Side transfer machinery is useful in a stack to rail/road or road/rail situation. Container lifting side transfer plant is usually based on a semitrailer, which will carry the container from the pick-up position to the stack like a normal lorry. The best systems are a good combination of these machines, each performing a specific function, and working to a calculated cycle for maximum utility. The designer must be aware of each system's potential, yet plan a flexible system so that change can quickly be accommodated.

3 Maintenance

3.01 All this sophisticated plant requires parking and maintenance areas close to the activity. Once the handling system has been decided, the designer should contact the plant manufacturer and ascertain any special maintenance requirements. If straddle carriers are brought into buildings, the door should be at least 10 m high. Maintaining these units often demands hydraulic platforms and gantry cranes within the building.

4 Simple container handling systems

4.01 Many factories or warehouses only handle containers in small numbers and at infrequent intervals. Unless the plant can be used for other purposes, expensive container-carrying forklift trucks or side loaders are uneconomic. There are several cheap and simple systems for the small operator. The best method is not to remove the container from the skeletal trailer at all (see Technical study Loading 1). If two 20ft (6 m) containers arrive on one 12 m trailer, however, one will have to be removed for unloading. If there is a mobile crane on site of sufficient capacity, this can be used with a special lifting frame, or spreader. There are simple mobile gantries on the market, that lift ISO containers from their top or bottom corner castings, and will place the unit on a slave trailer or onto the ground. Most of these do not move when lifting a container, the vehicle backing underneath **17, 18**. Some gantries are designed for 20ft (6 m) containers, and are used in tandem for 40ft (12 m) units, and others are capable of handling all sizes, with adjustable spreader beams. Also popular are portable hydraulic lifting legs, which can be handled by one man and are usually powered by a small portable hydraulic pump/motor unit. These legs are clipped onto the corner castings, and then lift the container off the truck and onto the ground. Castors to clip onto container castings are also available **20**.

4.02 For short-distance horizontal transport in small installations, forklift trucks of 3 to 5 tonnes capacity can be equipped with special roller bottom forks to push the container sideways, or a special low level trolley can be attached to the forks. Alternatively, if break-bulk and loose-load operation is normal, a special low level trailer can be attached to stillage trailer tugs or tractors, which can also carry normal palletised goods (see **2.02**). Hover-pallets have a great potential in the low cost field, but they require a smooth, flat surface. Developments in this field, that seem

13 *Tug towing stillage trailer with ISO container (see **9**).*
14 *Heavy duty forklifts can be adapted to handle stillage trailers (roll-on/roll-off load).*
15 *Close-up of tug with*
elevated fifth wheel coupling.
16 *Stillage trailer with ISO 'flat' for loads unsuitable for containers for roll-on/roll-off use.*

ideal, include small, high-lift pads, attached to each bottom-corner casting, and linked to a central air source which when detached, could be used simply for handling conventional pallets.

5 On-vehicle handling aids

5.01 Certain types of externally stored goods, especially goods for the building industry are more suitable for flat-bed trailers. Vehicles equipped with integral cranes and forklifts allow autonomous handling at both storage and delivery premises **19, 21, 22**.

20

17

21

18

19

22

17 *Hydraulic mobile gantry.*
18 *'Four-poster' mobile manual gantry.*
19 *Artic tractor with integral forklift.*
20 *Detail of container wheel.*
21 *Artic tractor with self-loading crane.*

22 *Typical sliding trailer loading crane. Useful for many general-purpose goods.*

23a

24

6 'Piggy back' and 'Kangaroo' systems

6.01 The 'Piggy back' system, used in the US employs either gantry cranes or a special wheeled lifting machine, the Sideporter or Piggy-backer, which places the semi-trailer directly onto the railwagon. These machines can quickly adapt to handle ISO containers. Also in the US there is a system of transferring box vans, 'Flexivans', from trucks to trains—the rear of the trailer rests on a turntable on the flat car, the trailer's running gear is removed, and a special tractor swings the body through 90°.

6.02 'Kangaroo' is a European rail-based system, similar to 'Piggy back' except that due to the lower loading gauge, the wheels of the trailer are in deeper wells. A special loading tractor drives the trailers up ramps and over the flat trucks until the correct position, when the well is lowered, and the trailer secured. If a 'Kangaroo' terminal is incorporated in the container area, as is possible in inland situations, a large marshalling zone should be provided at the end of the sidings, clearly marked in lanes for the parking of incoming and outgoing trailers **23, 24.**

6.03 Various side loading devices are available for road/rail interchange, where the truck is driven next to the railwaggon, and there is direct transfer. As these systems are usually integral with the carrying vehicle and as they run parallel to the rail tracks, there are few problems for designers, except ensuring that the hardstanding next to the rail track is capable of taking hydraulic stabiliser point loads during transfer.

23 *Canadian 'Piggy back' system* **a** *drives the trailer directly onto railway wagon,* **b** *transcontinental train of 'piggy-backs'.*
24 *Kangaroo 'tilt' trailer being loaded onto rail wagon by special tractor.*

23b

Technical study Manual storage 1

Storage process

Although the bulk of the handbook is directed at a broad range of storage methods, many of them mechanised, so as to provide a reference for designers engaged throughout this field, for many architects, much of the material may seem to reflect a scale and level of complication considerably above the experience of their practice. The manual storage section provides guidance to those designing small scale industrial storage facilities and for those involved in planning for the handling and storage of components and work in progress in small factories, whose needs are also discussed in Appendix 2.

1 Introduction

1.01 There are two types of manually oriented systems: purely manual, and manual with hand guided and operated mechanical handling aids.

Manual systems are still most effective where there are:
infrequent handling demands,
confined and congested areas,
need to consolidate cargo to fit every available space,
diverse load shapes,
awkward and fragile loads,
grouping of non-standard small goods.

1.02 The second type of operation is often found on a small scale as part of more sophisticated types of storage, and within manufacturing processes.

Man as machine

1.03 Successful planning of a manual storage building or zone depends on dimensional control based on human measurements, a good working environment, and understanding of how a man is used as 'handling plant'. Designers tend to consider man only in terms of intellectual and environmental needs, not as a hardworking industrial machine. Compared with lifting and carrying mechanical plant men are inefficient, as they have low power-to-weight ratio and variable performance **1**. This inefficiency is balanced by a

1 *Man lifting next to a forklift truck. A forklift can use a straight lift, but a man* *has to bend his knees to keep his back straight.*

man's ability to do two or more things at once. As with machinery, there are different grades of man; but whereas strength and control can be combined in a sophisticated machine, the strongest men often lack a high level of intellect and control. An average warehouseman can, simultaneously, carry an awkwardly shaped, damaged parcel up a flight of twisting stairs, compensate for the shape of the parcel in relation to clearance in the stair-well, keep a hand over the damaged section to prevent further spillage and think of the paper work and the next process. This versatility is at the same time man's great advantage over a machine. He can handle a wide range of aids, and is limited only by the weight and size of the object to be handled. The human hand has 22 possible separate movements, coupled with a very flexible, cushioned yet strong outer skin, enabling a wide variety of shapes to be easily and carefully handled. A machine needs clamps and other complex attachments. In order picking, for instance, man is still the most effective tool available, in that he can simultaneously carry out a clerical function with manual selection and visual distinction.

1.04 Although computers can produce detailed picking sequences and can check the pickers' accuracy, a man can still pick small goods more efficiently than a machine. This is especially true in the case of small loads, less than pallet size, for which the high cost of automated selection mechanism is often unjustified.

1.05 In consistency of performance, man compares badly with a machine. He can be thoughtless and irresponsible and also cause malicious damage. Inconsistency is usually caused by fatigue; ideally the work should spread a man's output evenly over a shift rather than exhaust him in one huge effort. Unlike machines, man's efficiency decreases after 'recharging' (ie taking a meal) and his overall effectiveness decreases steeply over the period of the shift.

1.06 Because man is limited to carrying comparatively small loads, unit cost per ton of cargo handled is high compared with a machine. Man's first cost involves only a pair of overalls, gloves and the cost of an advertisement, but running costs can prove very expensive; redundant machines can be sold, personnel have to be paid redundancy money. An old or outmoded machine can be scrapped; man often has to be paid a pension.

1.07 Boredom can be a special hazard for anyone engaged on repetitive work. Order picking with stock lists introduces a measure of interest, and some companies introduce a productivity bonus as a further incentive. The designer of manual systems has the responsibility of designing for man not only as a machine, with specific motions to perform, but also as a person. Bad working conditions are often at the root of industrial unrest.

2 Source of goods

2.01 Typical businesses which are satisfactorily served by manually oriented storage processes are:
parcels groupage for carriers,
cash-and-carry stores serving the smaller retailer,
spares depots,
small component stores for specialist production,
furniture repositories,
interprocess storage and handling in small factories.
The goods originate from a large number of private and industrial sources or, in the case of spares depots, from the production side of the company concerned. Only in the latter case can the package size and material be controlled.

3 Form of transport

3.01 All types of road transport vehicles from the smallest van to the largest trunk lorries are used. Large consignments of parcels can be delivered by rail. Large cubic capacity trucks are increasingly used for inter-city distribution. Such vehicles require a large manoeuvring area, posing a problem in restricted yards. If quantity supply is anticipated, maximum-sized vehicles can be expected; this is often forgotten by firms who use predominantly small vans, ie parcels groupage and cash-and-carry operations.

4 Control of transport

4.01 The problems are: 1 how to control numerous light vans arriving all at once, and 2 how to cope with light and heavy traffic arriving at the same time. Trunk vehicles cannot manoeuvre if vans are parked at random while awaiting their turn at loading bays. Designers should allot space for vans to accumulate in an orderly manner in peak periods. Clear directional markings help, eg a one-way flow pattern and clearly painted parking bays. Many light vans have sliding entrance doors for drivers, so accumulation spacing can be close, but space should be available to open swing rear doors before reaching the dock (see Information sheet Loading 2).

Separate areas for trunk vehicles
4.02 If trunk vehicle delivery and collection is regular, and local delivery is by light vans, it is worth installing a segregated dock area for large trucks. Vans have lower floor heights than trunk vehicles (see Technical study Loading 1), and can be quickly unloaded by hand from ground level. Semi-trailers and box vans are too high for this, and need either a ramp, a forklift truck to load 'over the side', or a raised section of the dock fitted with a dock leveller plate. All this is expensive if trunk vehicles are comparatively infrequent.

4.03 In order not to constrict either access for vans or operation of the loading bay the trunk vehicle area should be towards the ends of the bay **2**. It is seldom worth segregating incoming truck operation from collection as the same vehicle is usually involved.

Demountable bodies
4.04 The present European trend for parcels work is towards 'swop' bodies mounted on drawbar trailer combinations. The lorry parks first its trailer and next its own demountable body, both of which can be unloaded (and reloaded) later. The lorry then picks up previously loaded bodies and trailers and leaves at once. Four heavy vehicle bays are required for this, alternate pairs being used (empty bays can be used for other suppliers' vehicles). If many demountable bodies are used the client could employ a type that is lowered right to floor level for conventional pallet truck loading.

Gate entries
4.05 The gate to a public road should be opposite the trunk vehicle bay, to ease manoeuvring, but if the yard is short this can restrict entry of vans **4, 5**. Balance must be achieved between the expected number of vans, peak assembly, entry of heavy vehicles and conditions of the public road (local authorities often will not allow access gates near bus bays, corners, etc). Check with client, transport contractors, police and local authority (see Information sheet Loading 2).

5 Receipt of goods

5.01 Handling operations in a parcels groupage depot are subject to severe peaks and troughs. Greatest peaks in are usually in the evening, when most goods are ready for collection at the senders' premises. The same evening as much

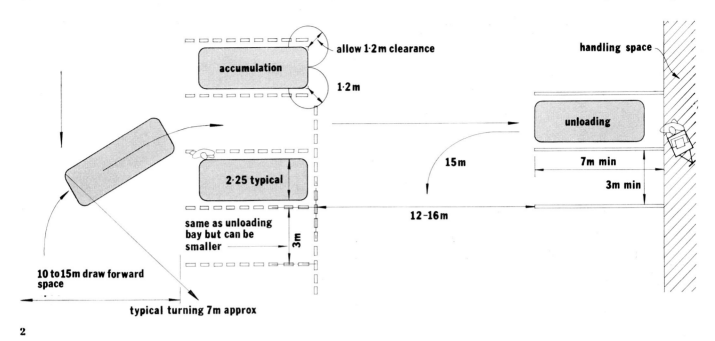

allow 1·2m clearance

accumulation

1·2 m

handling space

unloading

7m min

3m min

2·25 typical

15m

same as unloading bay but can be smaller

3m

12–16m

10 to15m draw forward space

typical turning 7m approx

2

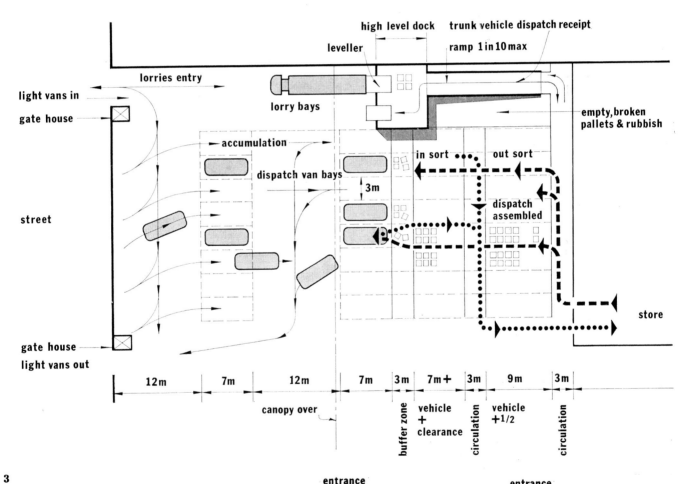

high level dock   trunk vehicle dispatch receipt

leveller   ramp 1in10 max

lorries entry

light vans in

gate house

lorry bays

empty, broken pallets & rubbish

accumulation

in sort   out sort

dispatch van bays

3m

dispatch assembled

street

gate house

light vans out

store

12m	7m	12m	7m	3m	7m+	3m	9m	3m

canopy over

buffer zone

vehicle + clearance

circulation

vehicle +1/2

circulation

3

2 *Minimum dimensions for parking accumulating vans, allowing for rear door swing.*
3 *Typical van and accumulation parking area.*
4 *Choice of circulation patterns for van accumulation and parking. Typical dimensions* **a,** *26 to 30 m.* **b,** *36 to 40 m.*

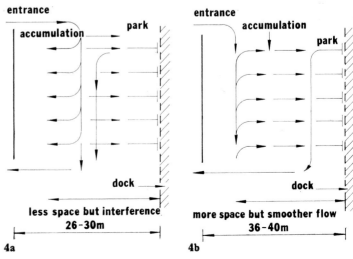

entrance

accumulation

park

entrance

accumulation

park

dock

dock

less space but interference 26–30m

more space but smoother flow 36–40m

4a   **4b**

traffic as possible must be sorted and reloaded on to *outward* trunk vehicles for overnight trunking. Providing for peaks inflates handling costs, as much of the equipment and personnel will be redundant during off-peak hours. The client should arrange with main senders to spread traffic over a greater proportion of the day. Such problems should not arise with bulk goods received for spares, cash-and-carry operations, or components for production.

6 Form of goods

6.01 Small packages in trunk vehicles are usually packed in roll pallets or stacking cages, and are occasionally stacked on standard road pallets. Some mechanical handling aid will be required (eg pedestrian controlled reach truck and pallet trucks). If the vehicle has a tail lift, then the raised section will not be required **5**. A mobile lift is also useful as a link element (see Information sheet Loading 5). Examples of goods also in this section are boxes of spares, newspaper bundles, cages or post pallets of components, and special loads such as radio isotopes. Goods from local delivery vehicles are likely to be irregularly shaped parcels, often badly packed.

7 Unloading

7.01 Small delivery rounds in large towns are so complicated by small consignments that detailed knowledge of the geography and industrial behaviour of the area is necessary to avoid undue delays. In cities vehicles frequently deliver parcels on the outward run and collect on the inward. Local delivery drivers often help to unload their vehicle at the store (this is useful as queries, incomplete orders, damaged packages can be dealt with on the spot) **6**. It is difficult to mechanise unloading parcels from small delivery vehicles, so a sizable buffer area for primary manual sorting is required. This buffer zone should be planned carefully, otherwise outgoing goods can hamper off-loading and sorting.

Primary sortation
7.02 There are several methods of first sorting goods:
1 Some companies unload at random into wheeled cages which are then removed at once to a sorting area, and taken in rotation. This clears the dock quickly.
2 Other methods include light mobile belt units, taking individual parcels directly out of the loading area; or fixed belts for larger handling operation.
3 Conveyors are limited in that traffic has to be manhandled at least four times between arrival and dispatch. Mobile conveyors are quickly removable by one man **8**.
4 Fixed belts inhibit cross-circulation unless flush with the floor and if flush can cause back trouble in operatives by forcing them to swing heavy packages from vans on to the belt.
5 Floor level sliding slat or plate conveyors do not impede cross-movement, and are capable of being looped to any number of sorting stations (see Information sheet Mechanised storage for details of conveyors).
Packets are often damaged by being thrown out of a van on to ground level equipment; shocks of 140 G have been measured. The type of goods and degree of protection provided by the packing will decide the system used between van and sorting area.
7.03 To unload roll pallets or standard road pallets from trunk vehicles, a raised dock section for reach truck and pallet truck is required. This can be avoided if the trunk vehicle is fitted with a tailboard lift for roll pallets, or if the trailer is fitted with curtain or sliding sides so that pallets can be unloaded over the side. The floor remains flat throughout, and in the latter case the trunk vehicle can be parked anywhere.

Goods handling after unloading
7.04 In one method, goods are recorded, checked and stored

5

6a   6b

7

5 *Van with built-in tail lift.*
6a, b *Local deliveries are difficult to mechanise; where small premises do not justify raised docks, tailboard lifts can help.*
7 *Typical small warehouse for parcels distribution.*

8

9

10

8 *Retractable flexible conveyor.*
9 *Manual identification and storage in roll pallets.*

10 *Tote bins for small components. These are being picked on to a conveyor.*

at once, still in unit form. Unless two lift trucks are used turnround is slow, but avoids double handling. The second method is to unload into a buffer area with checking and breakdown prior to storage, freeing the lift truck for full, unloading activity. This also frees loading bays more quickly.
7.05 Portable, extendable container-stuffing belts are useful in trunk vehicle loading areas. One end of the belt is placed in the truck and the other end over a cage or laid direct to personnel in the sorting area. After unloading, belts are retracted and wheeled out of the way of light vans.

8 Characteristics of goods

8.01 Often goods are handled manually because they are fragile or delicate. Packaging should be considered at the design stage to avoid, for instance, delivery of delicate electronics components in old, battered cardboard boxes. The handling manager must decide whether to repack the goods in the warehouse to make maximum use of available space (repacking is space consuming and can hinder sorting personnel) (see Technical study Introduction 2).
8.02 If goods are easily damaged, designers should not install systems that can cause damage, eg gravity conveyors from mezzanine floors.

9 Sorting

9.01 Parcels are usually grouped for onward transit with some sorted for local redelivery. Spares are sorted into sections based on speed of withdrawal and proximity to use. Components are sorted for the process involved and speed of use.
9.02 Manual sorting consists of taking a package, identifying it and either building up a unit load, or placing the object with a unique coding for separate storage. Usually operatives pick packets with coded labels from a conveyor and stack them for storage into bins or cages **9**; a certain amount of throwing is often involved. This is costly in damage, wasteful of personnel, and floors become congested. In small installations goods are sorted direct from vehicles into bins or cages and stored. Much waste paper is generated from splitting packages, repacking, and superfluous material. A skip and press should be provided in easy reach of this area. Allow for operatives moving round with barrows; also for empty pallets and cages, and for trolley parking. Usually trolleys are left in unsuitable places and can cause injury. Small components and spares are packed into tote bins which stack neatly and do not waste much space **10** (see Information sheet Manual storage 1). Include a stacking area for empty bins.

10 Volume calculations

10.01 Volume of parcels groupage is highly seasonal. Volumes spares and components can be calculated from the projected manufacturing cycle or sales forecast.

11 Turnover calculations

11.01 For parcels groupage calculation of turnover is based on speed of collection and reshipment cycles. Some overseas groupage requires long lead times prior to final sorting for collection for forwarding. Carriers can calculate this from their schedules. For spares, turnover calculation requires more detailed knowledge of the product turnover, not always available. Motor car spares are a typical example, spares for obsolete models being slow moving (and so wasteful of space if this factor is not considered from the outset). Maximum turnover in car spares occurs for two years after discontinuation of a model. For successful manual picking, goods with the highest turnover will be placed nearest to personnel and delivery points. The client should ensure that the correct rating is given to groups of products.

12 Variety and flow

12.01 In the smallest installations, when goods are needed, a man is dispatched with a barrow to fetch them. However, there will probably be many varieties of goods and packages. Volume is difficult to calculate, as it is the volume taken by packaging not the weight of the commodity that affects location of the store. In small scale cash-and-carry operations, for instance, block storage is needed as well as racked and shelved goods. (Eg large boxes of breakfast cereals are popular in summer and have high turnover, high volume and low weight: powdered soups for winter consumption are usually packed in sachets in shrink wrapped trays, have low volume, high weight, and have to be stored in subsections of flavour.) Designers should bear the clients' seasonal trade variations in mind when allotting space in racks and shelves and consider adaptable rack/shelf systems.

13 Type of storage

13.01 Manually operated storage usually combines bulk stock and order picking. In operations such as cash-and-carry, a pedestrian controlled reach truck places pallets of goods on three level racking. The top two levels are replenishment stock for the base section, used for direct picking. Another system (often used on the Continent) is a bulk rack area backing up a live storage picking face, where packages are unpacked from the 'outer' and placed in gravity flow lanes, so that customers can pick the commodities required in an environment more like a large supermarket than a warehouse **11**.

13.02 Spares and components are often stored in tote bins, cartons or cages, for direct picking and replenishment from bulk stock, often block stacked in the same area. Drawers and mobile shelf units are also used. (See Information sheet Manual storage). These methods allow many small parts to be stored in a confined space, and yet be equally accessible. Racks should be carefully positioned for personnel to stack and pick stock without overreaching or twisting under load to cause themselves injury. Racks should be spaced far enough apart for those working in the rack area to move freely without colliding with passing barrows. This dimension will be governed by the type of barrow and the operation; ie if drawers are involved, the operative will intrude further into the aisle (for dimensions see Information sheets Manual storage).

13.03 Mezzanines can double volume where usable height is limited by human dimensions. This involves goods lifts and inter-floor belts. (See Technical study Mechanised storage).

14 Stock control

14.01 Stock control is usually manual, unless the parent company is big enough to require a line link to a central computer for distribution planning. Normally the picker walks down the racks with a barrow and a picking list, each aisle having a letter, and each space a number. Manual stock control is by cards allocated to each rack or shelf position, recording type of goods and number of units in a box of small goods. When goods are picked, the picking card will return to the office where stock cards are updated. Where replenishment is the aisle operatives' responsibility, a stock card is put in a pocket on the side of the rack; this is updated after each picking operation (this method can lead to pilfering).

14.02 Coding of racks is affected by initial design decisions. In a long and narrow building, fast moving goods will all be in racks at the loading bay end of the building. If the building is wide with short racks, a whole rack nearest the sortation area will be devoted to fast moving goods **13. a, b**

14.03 Stock control can affect design from the start; for instance if the trade requires many fast-moving lines to be quickly accessible to the sorting area, short racks would be planned with the aisles at 90° to the dock face. The designer should discuss stock control with the client at an early stage in the design process.

11 *Gravity flow picking face.*

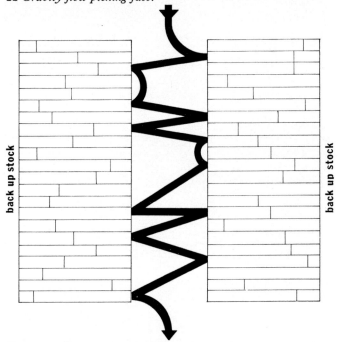

12 a, b *Different types of order picking.*

12a *Used for low to medium variety and high throughput.*

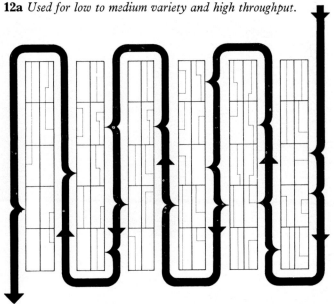

12b *Used for high variety and varied throughput.*

15 Stock withdrawal

15.01 Manual withdrawal of stock is mostly order picking. Some full pallet loads can be expected for dispatch. Aisles must be wide enough to accept pedestrian controlled reach and pallet trucks, without endangering other picking personnel. One- and two-way access to racking is discussed in 16 'Order picking'.

16 Order picking

16.01 Order picking depends on human efficiency. For small quantities, eg in a trade motor spares store, one operator will pick the unit and carry it direct to the service counter. If larger orders are being assembled, as in a cash-and-carry store, a cage or trolley will be dragged round, or sometimes an empty pallet on a pallet truck. Order picking tends to take up more aisle width than stacking, as the operation of identification, withdrawal and swing to place the load on a trolley requires a wider pitch from the rack face (see Technical study Manual storage 2, para 6).

17 Picking area

17.01 The picking area is usually synonymous with the rack or shelf storage zone in these small buildings. If the rack area is used, enough space must be left for pickers and trolleys to pass other personnel in action. If many small goods are picked from bulk cartons, consider alternate aisles with double-sided access **12a**. This is not efficient volumetrically but enables reach trucks and personnel to operate safely unharassed by movement to replenish shelves.

17.02 Picking efficiency and service to customers is more important in these stores than maximum utilisation of volume. This system applies only where there is high constant turnover; normally there are sufficient slack periods for stock replenishment not to interfere with picking.

18 Load build-up

18.01 City delivery drivers should load their own vehicles, as they know the local area and delivery cycle. Group loads well

in advance of the vehicles' arrival and segregate this area for incoming sorting. Clearly marked lanes (related to numbered areas) for each van bay are useful when assembling loads. The most personnel can do is pick the correct goods and assemble trolleys so that they can be either wheeled to the vehicle for direct loading, or taken to a belt end after unloading is completed.

18.02 Provide space for empty trolleys; if large deliveries are anticipated, roll pallets will be used and will collect in this area for transfer. Security is important (see para 28).

19 Order and documents check

19.01 Documents will be checked during load build-up in small scale operations. Provide room for the checker to walk round assembled goods, and to examine random packages without snagging racking or trolleys.

20 Loading and dispatch

20.01 Small goods delivery rounds in cities are complicated by small consignments, and heavy daily and seasonal peaks. These peaks will necessitate fast moving between unloading and loading for the next round. The evening peak is inward only; the morning peak can be in both directions and occurs when the first returning vehicles coincide with the next batch for midday deliveries. Loading bays quickly become choked with vans and heaps of pallets and empty cages. A flow system with clearly defined and marked areas should be designed, to integrate with the load build-up zone (see Technical study Manual storage 2).

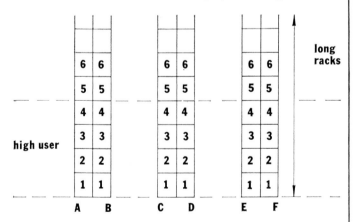

13a

13a Pallet positions coded by user speed across a whole zone. In a narrow building, this presents fast moving stock in the most accessible area. Picking as 12a.

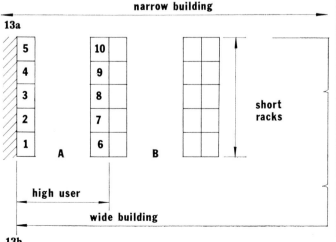

13b

13b In a wide building, whole racks or groups of racks can be organised by turnover speed. This tends to be used when a large number of stock lines are involved. Picking as 12b.

Technical study Manual storage 2

Building function

22 Structure

22.01 Simple systems require a simple building. A manually orientated system may not remain so for ever, so flexibility will allow for change to a mechanised operation later.

22.02 Protection from the weather is important for personnel operating in the loading zone. It can be achieved either by putting the vans inside the building during loading or by building an external canopy. The former is seldom practicable as turnround times may be short **1** and the build-up of fumes requires extraction plant. However, where manual loading takes some time and only one or two vehicles are handled simultaneously, the first method can solve many problems, including security.

22.03 Structurally, a canopy is a simple solution, needing only a column-free span over the rear of the vehicle area, large enough to cover a van and low enough to prevent normal driving rain to reach the loading area (5 m to 6 m long $\times$ 3 m to 3·5 m high) **3**. This conflicts with the height requirements, 4 m to 5 m, for trunk vehicles. If special bays are provided, the canopy in that area can be higher (see Technical study Loading 1). The open canopy does not solve the problem of cold and draughts; drivers loading their own vehicles can suffer severe discomfort, increasing turnround times **2**. Warm-air curtains are expensive and will not stand up to high winds and pressure differences. The problem is not just a matter of continuing the building structure over the loading bay.

22.04 In some installations the picking staff's productivity has been considerably reduced by draughts and cold spots in the rack and load assembly areas. Such lack of planning forethought can lead to industrial unrest, absenteeism and serious accidents caused by loss of concentration in uncomfortable conditions **2**.

1 *Congestion caused by peaks of feeder vans with short turnround times.*

2 One result of a cold loading area. Efficiency is reduced in bad conditions.

23 Floor

23.01 The floors for these buildings pose no problems unless spilt oil or chemical products are involved. A 12·5 mm monolithic granolithic topping is excellent for normal duty.

24 Building services

24.01 In a manually operated installation, environmental control is very important. Human comfort, compliance with the Factory Act and the possibility of accidents, which rises in discomfort conditions of both heat, cold and draughts, must be considered. As personnel will be operating at all hours within the store, their efficiency will be considerably reduced if the heating, lighting and ventilation are not excellent. The cumulative cost of loss of throughput will considerably outweigh any savings on the initial cost of environmental control. In open canopy loading bays a hot air blower will reduce heat loss and penetration of cold air, but it will also create minor dust storms by blowing dirt, and is expensive to run. Radiant panels are effective and cheaper to operate.

Heating and ventilation
24.02 The Factory Act 1961 stipulates 'that reasonable working temperatures be maintained'. Designers should plan for temperatures of 19°C in light duty areas, ie load assembly and order picking, and 15°C in heavy lifting areas or parts of the store intermittently used. Both blown air and radiant heat have proved effective in manual storage installations. Lightweight buildings are susceptible to excessive heat gains caused by insolation, which can normally be controlled only by ventilation.
24.03 Usually one to two air changes per hour are acceptable in warehouses, but in areas of intensive manual work the aim should be for air movement between 0·16 and 0·51 m/sec. It is air movement which gives a feeling of comfort rather than replacement of extracted air. Adequate ventilation and heating will also eliminate condensation from the structure—drips can seriously damage stored goods in cartons. Properly insulated roof and wall cladding will reduce this possibility and allow operatives to work efficiently in comfort. Fumes must be extracted from the loading bay area, especially if it is also used for assembling loads. (See also Technical study, Mechanised storage, para 24.)

Lighting
24.04 Temperature control is closely linked with lighting. Even light levels are essential for accurate picking and eliminating fatigue (caused by glare from light sources reflected by racking and loads). Sloping rooflights exposed to direct sun require $4\frac{1}{2}$ times the ventilation needed by north-facing rooflights with the same roof insulation. The IES *Code* suggests a minimum lighting level of 100 lux for the loading area, and 200 lux for small goods racks and sorting and dispatch functions: 400 lux is suggested for issue counters. Order picking of small parts from tote boxes or drawers also requires 400 lux. In manual sorting where loading bays are likely to be used as a check point and in primary sorting areas, 200 lux should be the design objective.
24.05 Psychologically, where order picking takes place, some communication to the outside world is important, as it has been found that operatives are more contented if they can see what the weather is like outside. (See also Technical study, Mechanised storage 2, which covers Building Services in much more detail: para 24).

25 Special services
25.01 These are required only where electric pallet and reach trucks are operated. (For battery recharging areas see Information sheet, Mechanised storage 5.)

26 Building fabric
26.0 There is little chance of damage through handling in this type of storage. As many of these buildings are in urban areas, the treatment will not only act as an advertising medium but can also attract business. It is no good the company spending a great deal of money on an expensive painting on their delivery vans if the building does not continue the image. This may seem obvious to designers but it has proved not to be so with management.

27 Fire control
27.01 As in any large public building full of people, exits are likely to be difficult and constricted. Routes to escape doors must be kept free from obstruction by plant or racking. Even though many installations will be below 2000 m² in area, most insurance companies will insist on sprinklers everywhere, especially if vans are to be brought into the building.[1]

28 Security
28.01 This is a particular problem with manual systems, especially where consumer commodities are concerned. Shrink-wrapped goods have not helped, as picking staff can see all goods on pallets. In 'cash and carry' stores, with many small vans entering the loading bay in peak periods, people sometimes 'forget' the cash side of the operation. By insisting on load/documentation check prior to loading into the vehicle, such 'forgetfulness' at the dock can be eliminated.
28.02 Inside the store security is more difficult. Amenity areas should not be planned where operatives can reach lockers and the outside without being seen. One company found the position of the lavatories a problem, where they also served the loading bay and opened directly to the exterior; some losses resulted from this. Locker areas should not be positioned where people can slip out of the picking area unseen. Some companies demand the right of search at any time, but usually only as a last resort after some error in design has resulted in theft. There should be no areas within the working area where goods could be hidden; not only small consumer goods such as lipsticks or bottles will disappear but also large objects—as one wholesaler reported, whole sides of bacon. A strong fence round the installation will deter casual intruders, and parking areas should be planned so that vans left near the walls do not act as stepping stones to windows and the boundary fence.

29 External works

29.01 The position of the entry gate in relation to the loading dock is very important, especially in constricted urban areas. The siting of the gate should be based on the manoeuvring dimensions of trunk vehicles, their segregation from light vans and office parking, and the position allocated for heavy vehicles in the loading bay. All truck areas should be well drained; and in the case of ground level unloading for light vans, drainage and provision against driving rain should be carefully considered **3a, b, c, d.**

29.02 If night-time operation is planned (fairly common in parcels groupage operations) the yard should be well lit. Illumination of all dark corners will reduce security problems. There should be no glare, and lamp standards should be placed where they cannot constrict vehicles (large articulated trucks cut in on corners. See Information sheet Loading 1.) If an awkward corner might be a traffic hazard, a well positioned mirror helps, but beware of glare and impact damage by passing vans.

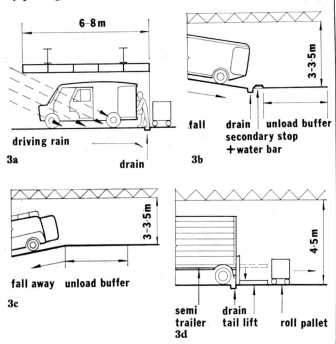

3a Light van handling area with canopy over. **b** Detail at edge of loading area for manually unloading light vans (exaggerated fall towards the handling area). Buffer area 2·5-3·5 m. **c** Light van

handling area and unloading buffer (exaggerated fallaway from handling area). **d** Ground level handling for trunk semi-trailers fitted with tail lift.

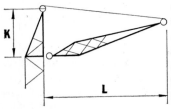

4 No crane manufacturer would use a power lever-arm of load: arm ratio higher than 1 : 3 **a**. Because the human spine is designed for upright rigidity, man has to contend with a ratio of 1:8.

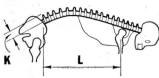

5 Man lifting correctly in light van.

30 Structure-based plant

30.01 This is dealt with in Technical study Mechanised storage 1, para 30.

31 Mobile plant

Man as machine

31.01 The human body is an energy-using machine whose efficiency varies with the amount of strain imposed by the task. Man, like any machine, is subject to physical limitations, but his vary according to fitness, skill and technique. But, unlike machinery that can be put straight to work, man needs to be trained for lifting and picking. This is essential in avoiding injury and assuring a high level of productivity. As both lifting and carrying agent and operator, man can compensate for shifts and load movement, and can work out how to carry very heavy loads by using his own weight and centre of gravity. Removal men do this all the time.

31.02 Man's spine is not as mechanically efficient as a lifting or carrying machine, and the maximum load lifted frequently should be not more than 25 kg when lifted by *any* method. A fatigue factor, which should be introduced through the shift, can further reduce this figure by 25 per cent. A load of 25 kg is not much: every day men can be seen lifting more than 50 kg, for instance unloading cement bags. These operatives run a risk of severe permanent injury. The Factory Act 1961[1] states: 'A person shall not be employed to lift, carry or move any load so heavy as likely to cause injury to him.' This is vague, and it has been proved dangerous to leave the responsibility to management[4].

31.03 Many warehouse operators do not understand the limitations of the human physique, and financial incentive often wins over an operative's common sense. It is the designer's responsibility to provide a system with the handling aids necessary to avoid overstrain. At the same time, man's mechanical characteristics must be the criterion for designing the storage system itself. Lifting and carrying incurs both continuous heavy muscular strain and intermittent high peak strain in the back and on the heart. The recommended method for lifting is with a straight back, using the powerful thigh muscles for the main effort. Clearance must be left for this. Reaching is an especial problem; racks and shelves should never cause overreaching during order picking. The spine is even less suited to tensile loads, and a jerk to dislodge goods can make a disc slip out. If high shelves must be used, provide steps, moving platform or mezzanine floor. Without steps, pickers will tend to use their barrows, which can be dangerous.

Other mobile plant
31.04 This includes trolleys, barrows, roll pallets, manually powered pallet trucks, pedestrian controlled but powered pallet trucks and pedestrian controlled reach trucks. Other aids are crowbars, which enable a man to move very heavy weights on the lever principle (this can ruin concrete floors) and various types of grippers (see Information sheet Manual storage 3 for handling aids).

32 Integration of building and plant

32.01 A building for manual storage is likely to be a simple building that may not require integration of building and plant except for handling plant for feeding backup stock to order pickers **6ab**.

33 Maintenance

33.01 A plant maintenance area is needed for battery charging for pedestrian controlled, powered pallet and reach trucks. In this area a strip of acid-resistant finish should be laid as ordinary granolithic screed can break up under acid corrosion, especially when it is rolled in by solid tyres. The second maintenance area is for mending pallets and roll pallets. Castors are especially badly treated. This area should adjoin the zone reserved for broken units, which never seems big enough. Fabric maintenance should be considered from the outset; for example, guards fitted to corners will save much damage to both building and delivery vans (see Information sheet Loading 5). Rubbish disposal is also important. For large amounts of paper and board a small baler would be useful if worked into the circulation pattern; it could be installed in a corner of the loading bay.

34 Management

34.01 Representatives from the floor and shop stewards should be involved throughout the design process. There have been examples of areas planned according to the pre-conceived notions of designers and management never being used, because the unions barred them as either unsafe or unusable for the intended purpose. (See Technical study Introduction 1.)

35 Personnel accommodation

35.01 A high standard of accommodation for personnel is very important psychologically. Lockers should be provided with heating for drying wet outdoor clothes and be secure for personal effects.

Office accommodation
35.02 This is larger in proportion to store area than in more sophisticated and mechanised systems owing to the large amount of manually processed paper work that the groupage and 'cash and carry' trade generates. Designers should also consider car parking space for office staff, and the internal environment in view of heavy traffic passing the windows.

36 Amenity

36.01 The Offices, Shops and Railway Premises Act 1963[2] forbids operatives to eat meals in a room containing poisonous substances. Although the type of store dealt with here is unlikely to contain such substances, rest periods and meals should in any case be taken outside the storage zone. A room equipped with a tea and coffee dispensing machine and seating has proved beneficial. Amenities for drivers should

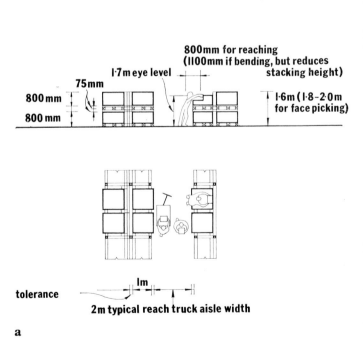

tolerance

800mm
800mm
75mm
1·7m eye level
800mm for reaching (1100mm if bending, but reduces stacking height)
1·6m (1·8-2·0m for face picking)

1m
2m typical reach truck aisle width

a

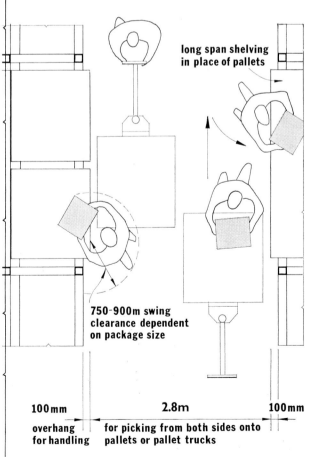

long span shelving in place of pallets

750-900m swing clearance dependent on package size

100mm
overhang for handling
2.8m
for picking from both sides onto pallets or pallet trucks
100mm

b

6 *Order picking from pallets.* **a** *for picking from both sides onto a trolley, a one-way operation. For design clearances for pallets in racking, see page* 141.

b *for picking from both sides onto pallet trucks with a two-way cycle (2·8 m width is for intense personnel activity).*

also be provided and, preferably, separate lavatory and washing accommodation with external access. As described in para 28, if the amenity area is open to both store and the outside and is not overlooked by offices, pilfering will be difficult to control.

37 Security and safety

37.01 If a raised dock is used for trunk vehicles, safety rails must be installed on personnel routes. If the sorting area is at loading-bay floor level, chocks should be provided for parked vehicles.[4]

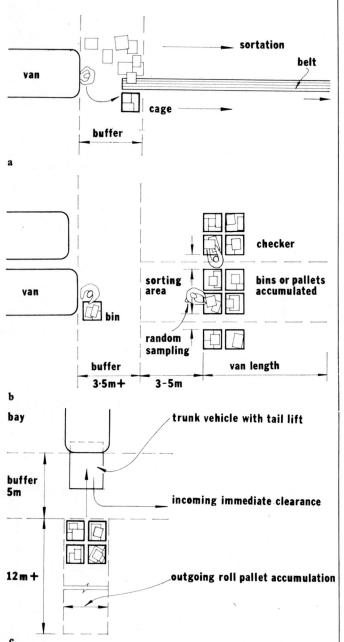

a

b

c

7 Layouts for handling in buffer zone. **a** Random unloading into buffer: goods are basically sorted by driver before being placed onto belt for routeing to secondary sortation. Buffer width 3·5 m. **b** Parcels in wheeled cages for dispatch, accumulated behind van. It is here that dispatch checking takes place. Buffer width 3·5 m+. **c** Bay for handling trunk vehicles: either raised or at ground level with a tail lift. Goods in roll pallets. Buffer width 5 m, ie, tail lift or dock leveller+ 2 roll pallets.

Table I		
Maximum desirable loads for personnel		
Age	**Men**	**Women**
16-18	20 kg (44lb)	11·8kg (26lb)
18-20	23 kg (51lb)	13·6kg (30lb)
20-35	25 kg (55lb)	15 kg (33lb)
35-50	21 kg (46lb)	12·7kg (28lb)
50+	15·9kg (35lb)	10 kg (22lb)

38 Circulation and parking

38.01 Personnel routes and fire exits are important in this type of storage facility. If reach trucks are combined with manual barrows, routes should be segregated wherever possible. The sorting and loading zone is complicated as two-way circulation conflicts with the inevitable cross-flow. If a raised area is used for trunk vehicles a ramp will be needed between this and the main floor (maximum slope 1 in 10), which can inhibit other areas and is space consuming. For manual handling, all pallet trucks should be fitted with brakes. If possible there should be segregation between flows to the vans and across the bay **7**. With manual operation circulation is less of a problem as men can organise their own routes in very constricted circumstances. Man is supremely adaptable, especially with financial incentives, but this is no excuse for thoughtless design. The designer's responsibility is to plan both a building and an integrated system of storage and manual handling that will be profitable to the owner and pleasant for the operatives.

References

1 Factory Act 1961. HMSO
2 Offices, Shops and Railway Premises Act 1963. HMSO
3 Sprinkler Rules for Automatic Sprinkler Installations, 29th edition, Fire Office Committee, Aldermary House, Queens Street, London EC4
4 Health and Safety at Work Act 1974 HMSO. This places particular responsibility on the designer.

Information sheet Manual storage 1

Tote boxes, drawers, and storage cabinets

The importance of efficient storage and handling of small goods and parts is often underestimated by designers, and can cost companies a great deal of money.

1 Tote boxes

1.01 A tote box is an intermodal container specifically designed for small parts storage and fast manual order picking. It is replacing the drawer or shelf unit for some applications, as it provides the additional flexibility of being able to be used as the transport and storage medium on the shop floor.

Materials

1.02 The standard type of tote box is made of metal, plastics or board and can be straight-sided or semi-open at the front for easy access. Steel tote boxes (or tote bins) are strong, durable and easy to stack, and do not deform under load **1**. They do however, corrode in certain conditions and impose much weight on racking and shelving. Aluminium is lighter, but expensive. Plastics boxes are increasingly popular, being corrosion-resistant, and can be moulded with an integral colour to any shape and size required. Colour coding is possible and has been used, both in the store and on the shop floor, by many companies. Plastics bins with small loads can be clipped on to louvred metal panels, thus eliminating shelving altogether **2**. Mobile louvre panel frames are increasingly used in such industries as electronics manufacture, where an operative's whole day's supply of parts is accommodated in tote boxes sized for the

1 *Stacked metal tote boxes*

part and colour-coded for the manufacturing stage **3**. Some paper products tote boxes are still available, but they are not very strong and are a considerable fire hazard. They are usually assembled at the store from printed sheets.

Size
1.03 Sizes vary from 76 mm × 100 mm × 50 mm, to 1·5 m × 750 mm × 500 mm. Bins with a large cubic capacity do not necessarily mean reduced costs in this type of storage. Large-capacity boxes, infrequently replenished, waste volume and may be overloaded, making them difficult to handle. For space requirements see **7**.

Shape
1.04 Tote boxes can be divided to suit the product. Special moulded plastic inserts are available for fragile goods. Considerable volume wastage is caused by the tolerance that has to be left above and between tote boxes for easy picking and placing. A simple method of increasing volume efficiency is to use mobile racking (see Information sheet Mechanical storage 2). In some cases, it has been found more economic to use the manufacturers' returnable special boxes and trays, which have been designed specifically to suit the product.

Method of storage
1.05 Most plastic tote boxes and several of the steel systems nest, and in certain circumstances dispense with shelving altogether. Louvre panels are suitable, and each 300 mm × 450 mm section of the panel can support 73 kg weight, with average end frame capacities of up to 408 kg **4**. Heavy duty panels with loads up to 1907 kg are available. As well as tote boxes, shelves, clips, hooks and tool holders can be clipped to louvre panels, giving additional flexibility for shop floor and spares depot. Cantilever shelving is also used for metal and paper tote boxes which cannot be clipped to louvre panels. This shelving is mounted on slotted angle uprights so that the shelves can be adjusted for bin height. Other systems for heavier steel tote bins include frames mounted in post pallets, so that the pallets nest to form a storage rack, and act as a dispense unit on the shop floor.

Shelving for tote boxes
1.06 Shelving for tote boxes is usually steel. Uniformly sized boxes can be stored on cantilever brackets with continuous shelving above, saving up to 25 per cent of normal shelf space, but this is best used for relatively slow-moving goods **5**. Most shelf systems adjust to suit bins, tote boxes and special rack components such as cable reels and tyre spindles. In small-goods operations, storage capacity can be increased by over 50 per cent by a two- or three-level mezzanine system **6** (but this may mean expensive multi-level sprinkler installations. See Information sheet Mechanised storage 1).

Packing and stock control
1.07 Tote boxes are ideal for spare parts storage, where the access problem is not so vital. Colour-coded boxes guide the picking personnel quickly and accurately. Open-ended boxes, with a set number of units stored in each, enable the picker to tell at a glance when stock needs replenishing. When goods are withdrawn, a pre-printed stock control card on the box can be altered to show how much stock remains. Stacking or nesting boxes using the cut-away front pattern avoid the need for shelving. The principal disadvantage of this is that if the base units have not been calculated to hold slow-moving or reserve stock, all the boxes above have to be removed to allow replenishment.

2 *Plastic tote boxes, attached to metal louvre panels, can be used in several different ways.*
3 *Supplies of parts in tote boxes, used in electronics industry.*
4 *Louvre panels used in high density storage.*

Potential
1.08 Tote boxes have generated an industry of their own and manufacturers should be contacted to find out their full flexibility. Very intensive tote box storage has been successfully operated in high-rack, narrow-aisle layouts, using fixed path order picking machinery.
1.09 A sophisticated tote box development is a fully automated highly intensive store by Roneo-Vickers called Conserve-a-trieve, of American origin, now available

5

6

in the UK. The machine, a scaled-down stacker crane, was originally designed for document handling; it works in a very narrow aisle with tote boxes in racking. Control can be by paper tape, punched card or from a console. The system of tote boxes ten high and ten deep on each side of the aisle has an 11-second average retrieval time.

2 Drawers

2.01 These are still used for small components such as tool heads. Drawer units are generally slow to operate, requiring the extra movements of opening and stepping back before identifying the goods, which can also inhibit aisle movement **7**. Special tray drawers often swing open on a pivot system, and are less space-consuming **8**. Tote boxes have largely replaced drawers throughout the greater part of industry.

Pigeon holes and small drawer units
2.02 These use the same type of steel sheet construction as long span shelving. A wide variety of pigeon hole and drawer sizes are available from several manufacturers, with various weight ratings. Drawers are space-consuming in comparison with tote boxes but are still useful for high-security small goods and valuable spares. An example of this is drill bits, where semi-precious stones are often used as the cutting head. For very small goods, such as nails and screws in bulk, metal drawers are obtainable with adjustable division plates; these are still used effectively in small scale operations. The development of the multi-sized plastics tote box and ironmongery products being shrink-wrapped in preset quantities will make this type of drawer less popular.

Special cabinets and heavy tool drawers
2.03 For tools and drill heads, which can be very heavy, these drawers are available in swing-out pivot form, allowing narrower aisles, as the picker stands parallel to the drawer instead of behind it **8**.

Mechanised small parts and tool cabinets
2.04 For tools, drill heads, spares etc, there are mechanised systems based on the vertical conveyor principle as used in document filing. The goods are stored in bins or on shelves at an output point. They circulate vertically on an endless chain. This type of installation is not cheap but provides dense, secure storage and quick access to a wide range of components.

3 Small goods handling

3.01 The handling of small goods in high-speed, high-density systems is a complex problem. There is a definite point where so many parts are handled so fast that drawers, mechanical cabinets and even tote boxes become redundant. In manufacturing units like the automobile industry, fast-moving parts in cage pallets, bins, and stillages are block-stacked. Small parts needed in large quantities can be used directly from the storage cage without the need for decanting into tote boxes. The need for replenishment can easily be seen, a reach truck brings a full stillage to floor level, removing the empty unit. This should not be confused with tote box operation, as too often boxes are seen piled on floors, constricting circulation. In some factories, where management is concerned about machine operators running out of parts, a pile of full and empty tote boxes accumulate round their plant, which quickly conflicts with the operation. This is unnecessary if the supply system has been correctly programmed from the outset of the store design.

5 *Simple steel shelving for metal tote boxes.*
6 *Mezzanine system increases storage capacity.*

7 *Space requirements for ordinary pull-out drawers. Tote box space requirements are similar, less 600 mm drawer depth.*

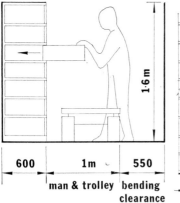

7

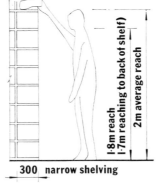

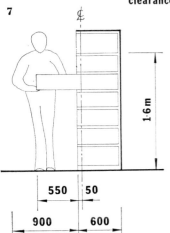

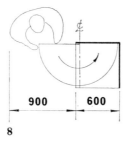

8

8a, b *Space requirements for swing-out drawers (operative picks at right angles to the drawer, **b**, rather than opposite as in **7**.*

Reducing multiple handling

3.02 Although a neat way of storing small parts, tote box systems involve multiple handling. Normally, goods arrive loose or on a pallet at the warehouse; they are off-loaded, checked, and sorted into tote boxes and stored; the original packaging material has to be collected and batched for disposal. It is likely that there will have been five or six movements by the time the goods are initially stored, before any selection or delivery process is operated. In this context, the use of drawers or tote boxes is questionable. A universal package should be developed, for transport, storage, picking and shop floor use. The designer should feed back data from pre-design studies to establish the best size of package for stacking on pallets, and order picking, or for direct transit and use as a container in the production zone. One computer-manufacturing company already works on this policy, and expects to start phasing out tote boxes soon.

4 Designers' checklist

4.01 The demands of stores for small goods for production or spare parts should be understood by the designer. Movements that do not seem particularly significant initially can have long-term, costly repercussions throughout the system. It is helpful to follow this pattern:
1 Predict daily/hourly throughput and flow per day for each outlet.
2 With this data, assess the optimum flow pattern for the goods, ensuring that critical supply routes do not converge at constrictions.
3 Calculate the best picking and replenishment pattern in the store, sorting the parts or goods into high-, medium- and low-use sections, allowing the most-used units priority access.
4 Design in flexibility so that a product or commodity change can be reflected quickly and cheaply within the store. This type of trade is changing increasingly quickly.

Design process

4.02 The handling and transport managers should be contacted throughout this design process, and the following questions checked:
● Has the product demand pattern been thoroughly studied? The intention is to minimise journeys from the store to production or load assembly areas, optimise the storage mode and minimise labour, time and cost.
● If there is a small-goods or parts store, is it operating at its highest potential? Is the new system to be a continuation of the old, and is the previous system suitable?
● How much space is under-utilised? Some is inevitable, but is it a minimum?
● Are personnel being used efficiently? Will picking staff follow carefully routed patterns?
● Why are tote boxes or drawers being used? Could a single package be used throughout the system instead?
● If it has been decided that tote boxes are the most effective storage medium, these units should be selected in the size, material and properties best suited to the product. It is the responsibility of production control personnel to decide whether one part has a unique box delivered frequently, or whether a group of parts are packed into a bigger box and delivered twice a day. These decisions are fundamental to a storage building and handling system design.
● Where should tote bins be grouped? Does the character of the parts change after the intermediate process and are they still suitable for tote box handling? Whatever happens, avoid situations that can generate heaps on the store or factory floor.

Information sheet Manual storage 2

Shelving

This sheet describes types of simple shelving.

1 Slotted angle shelving

1.01 Several manufacturers produce lightweight racking from slotted angle **1**. This is useful for small parts and spares stored on shelves. Adjustable shelving is important as spares operations change frequently and it can be expected that tote boxes will be changed to suit the product in that particular store location. This type of shelving is easy to adapt, with cross members quickly unbolted or unclipped; shelves can be adjusted to any level within 19 mm. Units can either be assembled from slotted angle lengths by the user, or purchased purpose made. A very wide range of shelf sizes and types is available; this includes open back shelving, closed back, long span with steel or chipboard shelving and with steel sides, back, and shelves with adjustable steel vertical dividers. Typical evenly distributed load per shelf:

  914 mm long: 457 mm wide: 158 kg
1828 mm long: 451 mm wide: 317 kg (18 mm chipboard)
  914 mm long: 610 mm wide: Open Back: 294 kg (with diagonal braces)

2 Boltless shelving

2.01 Performing an intermediate function between slotted angle and pallet racking, this is a steel clip-on system. Shelves are supported at the corners with adjuster clips which slot into uprights; alternatively, long spans can be achieved with horizontal beams with an added clip-on steel surface. This shelving is used for heavier parts, such as high density boxes of screws and fittings, and in open shelf form for storing comparatively heavy packs, of paper for example. Installations up to 6·1 m high have been used, but 2·1 m heights meet most hand-loaded shelf requirements. Frame loads exceeding 2034 kg can be met:
Open back: 914 mm long × 451 wide: 294 kg (using beams)
Braced back in place of beams 294 kg

3 Light duty cantilever shelving

3.01 This gives more storage space than conventional shelving and added product flexibility by presenting

1 *Simple slotted angle shelving using chipboard shelves.*

undivided lengths of shelving **2**. Shelving is supported on steel cantilever arms which pass through central steel uprights. Shelf levels are adjustable within 76 mm spacing in one system. They are useful for lightweight goods where most of the goods require manual handling and are similarly packaged with a fast stock rotation, the clear shelves allowing stock to be slid along to replace packages that have been removed. Usual height, 2·12 m with four shelves. Shelves up to 7·3 m long in 914 mm increments: typical maximum shelf loads: 5·5 m long, 457 mm wide shelving, 141 kg.

4 Long span adjustable shelving

4.01 Designed to meet span requirements exceeding 914 mm and loads up to 544 kg per shelf. Construction is a range of steel beams and panels, mounted on slotted steel vertical frames **3**. Steel panels are usually supported by integral ledges on the beams. A heavy duty version, with 3·04 m beam lengths is available; this is very useful for bulky light goods, where inspection is required on the shelving; maximum loading is 9070 kg per frame. A typical installation uses long span shelving for storing typewriters for inspection prior to dispatch.

5 Multi-tier slotted angle and lightweight clip-on shelving

5.01 When handling large numbers of small parts manually, the volumetric efficiency of the storage is low; this limitation can be overcome with multi-tier shelving **4**. This should not be compared with mezzanines; the upper tiers of shelving and the floor are an integral part of the slotted angle frame.

6 Mezzanine floors

6.01 For heavier manual operation; these can be in the form of a flat deck mounted on heavier duty shelf and drawer units, or as complete purpose-made structural steel frame, with one or two levels. The latter case can accept a floor loading with 15 mm plywood flooring of 688 kg/m² giving internal column loadings of 10·67 tonnes, versions with additional steel floor support beams can accept up to 1952 kg/m². These systems, offered by several manufacturers, are complete with handrails, stairs and, if required, steel framed and panelled offices.

7 Typical mezzanine installation

7.01 Drawer units at ground and first floor, and palletised goods too big for shelving on the top deck, supplied by a forklift truck running in an aisle at one end of the racking. Mezzanine storage must be designed with reference to demands by statutory authorities and the firm's insurance company. Note also the Health and Safety at Work Act regarding open mesh flooring and guard rails.

8 Live racking

8.01 For high throughput picking, such as cash-and-carry operations **5**. The goods flow by gravity on inclined roller conveyor tracks to the picking face. These store-and-dispense units are often used where the public are allowed to pick the goods, as they can be made to look like large display cabinets.

8.02 Live storage provides the best possible stock rotation by achieving a first-in, first-out cycle. This system is mainly suitable for applications involving comparatively few stock lines. Cartons or product packaging need to be of a high standard to avoid crushing.

2 *Light duty cantilever shelving.*
3 *Long span adjustable shelving.*
4 *Three levels of storage for different types of product.*

5

6

9 Mobile shelving

9.01 Useful where there is limited space available and permanent 100 per cent stock accessibility is not required. Mobile shelving can give up to 60 per cent more storage space than conventional shelving **6**. Construction is similar to clip-on steel shelving or slotted angle shelving, mounted on a mobile base. Some manufacturers offer their timber frame shelving on a mobile base. Typical loads are 3 tonnes on two tracks or 4 tonnes on three tracks. Mobile frames are suitable for drawers, shelves or tote boxes. Manual, electric, pneumatic, hydraulic and cable operation are available. The power system should be chosen on the potential damage to the product being stored. Some power systems have proved

unpredictable. A problem has been personnel who, becoming impatient with the slow operation of mobile racking, have tried to help by pushing, causing units to come off their tracks and jam. One system employs horizontal guide wheels as well, to prevent this contingency. If a power system is used, personnel safety is provided by a press bar at foot level that immediately cuts the power on impact.

9.02 There are two possible arrangements; the conventional method is lateral movement, with the shelves resting face to face **7b**. One manufacturer offers a longitudinal movement, arranged up to four racks deep **7a**. The latter allows a larger picking face to be exposed at any time, although marginally losing volume capacity over lateral moving units. A man can push four mobile units with adjustable shelving in steel or timber.

Fire risk
9.03 There is some controversy about the fire risk involved with mobile shelving. One manufacturer considers that there is less fire risk with timber construction, as any fire would be localised; steel shelving would transmit heat, causing spontaneous combustion, and could buckle the rack stopping movement and so eliminating the possibility of firemen reaching the seat of the fire in time to gain control. Intermediate level sprinkling is possible in mobile shelving and racks, using a jointed supply main.

10 Special lightweight racks, shelves

10.01 Single- and double-sided cantilever racking for light metal sections and bars. Distributed loads of up to 10 tonnes are possible, double-sided. Sheet metal racks for vertical or horizontal use can also carry 10 tonnes. Typical size for a horizontal sheet rack 2·5 m × 1·3 m × 1·2 m high. Other special racks include tyre racking, multi-rail open frames for clothing and many other types produced to special order.

11 Timber frame shelving

11.01 Similar to the steel systems, but with timber slotted frames. A high level of fire performance is claimed, with an improved storage environment. Shelves rest on steel clips, located into slots in the timber. Loads of up to 400 kg per shelf are permitted.

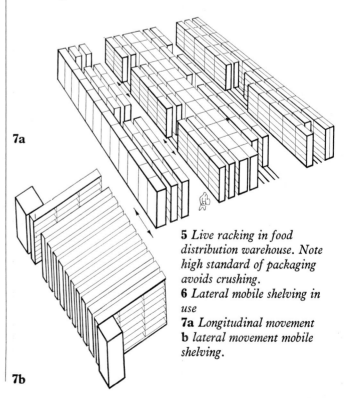

7a

5 *Live racking in food distribution warehouse. Note high standard of packaging avoids crushing.*
6 *Lateral mobile shelving in use*
7a *Longitudinal movement* **b** *lateral movement mobile shelving.*

7b

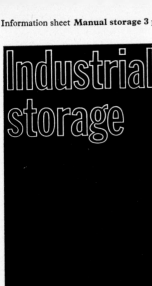

Information sheet Manual storage 3

General purpose handling aids

This sheet describes low technology ie non-specialised equipment, which can handle all types of goods.

1 Hoists and lifting devices

Uses
1.01 In manually operated stores, loading bays, repair workshops. Can easily be carried about on vehicles.

Capacity
1.02 Up to 500 kg.

Space requirements
1.03 Will turn in their own length. Space depends on whether used as stacker or hoist.

Equipment design
1.04 Can be converted to stacker or hoist. Very simple strong components. Some fold flat for storage in small spaces.

Building needs
1.05 Flat or smooth floors. Stowage space.

Prices
1.06 £200-£250 approximately.
1.07 Typical hoists and lifts are shown in **1** to **3**.

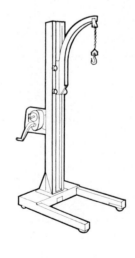

1

2

1 *Small hoist, which can be converted to a hand stacker.*
Size 740 × 840 *mm* ×
2·3 *m max height.*
2 *Floor crane; can be folded and stored flat.*

2 Pedestrian trucks and trolleys

Uses
2.01 Order build-up. Transfer within manually operated warehouse.

Sizes and shape
2.02 No standard size and shape, and can be made specially to order. 460 mm is minimum width for picking in narrow aisles. If used as dispatch cages, size should be commensurate with internal body dimensions of carriers' vehicles; this also applies to tail-lift sizes. One man can move 2·021 tonnes on steel wheels and 0·76 tonnes on soft rubber tyres.

Space requirements
2.03 Should be capable of turning in their own length, allow space for empty trolleys and damaged units.

Equipment design
2.04 A very wide variety of designs, within an equally wide range of weights. Choice depends on particular application. Most types of hand truck are available off the peg.

Building needs
2.05 Level floors.
2.06 Typical pedestrian trucks and trolleys are shown in **4** to **10**. See also information sheet Mechanised storage 4.

3 *Combined trolley and lift.*

4

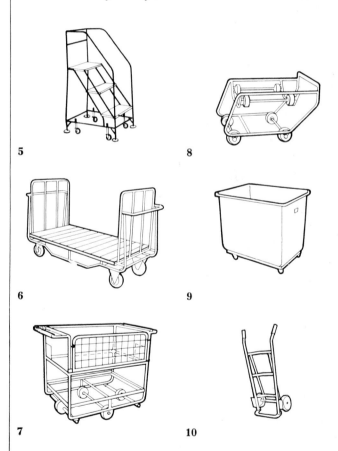

5

8

6

9

7

10

4 *All-purpose tug/lift unit comprising platform and handle. Length 1·15 m × 760 mm wide.*
5 *Mobile picking steps; when mounted the sprung castors retract, leaving a firm base.*
6 *General-purpose warehouse truck. 1·5 m long × 840 mm wide.*
7 *Parcels trolley 1·2 m long × 700 mm × 940 mm high.*
8 *Drum trolley. Upper wheels allow drum to roll for discharge. 900 mm × 500 mm × 380 mm high.*
9 *Mobile polythene bin 940 mm × 630 mm × 1·2 m high.*
10 *Sack truck. 400 mm × 150 mm × 1·2 m high.*

Information sheet Manual storage 4

Pedestrian controlled handling plant

This sheet gives information on types of pedestrian controlled plant used in storage buildings.

Table 1

Typical pedestrian controlled handling plant

Powered pallet truck

850mm

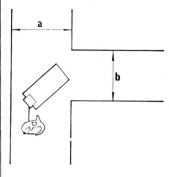

a

b

Uses and limitations
Internal transfer, loading vehicles on docks, order build-up, transporting roll pallets to load assembly position. For use with all types of pallet and cages. Some with long forks carry three roll pallets at once.

Sizes and capacity
1800 to 3000 kg capacity. Fork lengths 750 mm to 1·8 m. Speeds up to 3·6 km/h running light. Widths up to 850 mm, usually 760 mm.

Space requirements
Turns in its own length, but needs additional clearance for overhangs. Some have 200 degree turn on the single power steering wheel. Aisle width depends on fork length.
a (90° stacking aisle) = 1840 mm (truck + 1000 mm pallet)
b (intersecting aisle) = 1570 mm
Turning circle 1·78 m radius with 960 mm long forks.

Equipment design
Can be fitted with special forks for drums and paper rolls. Some of the large capacity units can also be ridden on, and can tow other non-powered pallet trucks behind if long distances are involved.

Building needs
Level floors. Single- or three-phase charging point. Can handle ramps to 1 in 10.

Price
Heavy-duty power pallet truck, approximately £1400; rider/walker control, approximately £1600

Platform truck

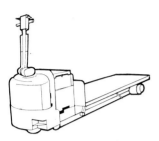

Sizes and capacity
Similar in design and capacity
to powered pallet trucks.
1500-3000 kg.
Overall length
1·7 m with 914 mm platform;
2·7 m with 1·829 m platform.
Longer platform lengths are
available to special order, with
787 mm width.
Travel speed 4·8 km/h unladen
3·2 km/h laden.

Space requirements
Turning radius, machine only,
1·37 m;
with platform 914 mm;
with 1·8 m platform 2·4 m.

Equipment design
Similar to a powered pallet
truck, this raises load platform
about 100 mm for travel. Some
pedestrian platform trucks have
a small folding platform at the
rear with a short arm so that
the machine can be ridden

Building needs
Level floors. Single or
three-phase recharging supply.
Typical wheel loading (unladen)
726 kg on drive wheels, 199 kg
on trailing wheels.

Price
£600 approximately.

Manual stacker truck

Usually manually powered for travel and lift using
hydraulic hand-pump for lift, so is restricted in lifting
ability in height and weight. Power and manual control.

Uses and limitations
Internal lifting. Best used as
secondary lifting device in
loading area. Ideal as portable
unit travelling on delivery
vehicle. Pallet and stillage
handling. Lift is restricted and
slow. Heavy loads can tire
operator. Can be fitted with
numerous small attachments for
lifting drums, rolls, sacks etc.

Size and capacity
Very varied with loads from
0·2 to 0·76 tonnes lifting up to

1·8 m. Width 763 mm on
standard straddle. Check that
lifting centres are suitable for
pallet handling.

Space requirements
Will turn in own length and
with 914 mm × 762 mm pallet
could be operated in 1·5 m
aisle.

Building needs
Level floors.

Prices
Approximately £175 to £350.

Powered and manual stillage truck

Powered or manually propelled for carrying stillage (see
Information sheet Mechanised storage). Often special
machines for special purpose stillages, eg pipes. Some can
swing stillage 90° manually to stack in narrow aisles.

Uses and limitations
Internal transfer of long loads
on special stillages. Cannot be
used for pallet handling.

Size and capacity
Length overall 1·68 m
(depending on type of stillage
used);
width 0·8 m;
height lowered 152 mm to
203 mm;
height lift 76 mm;
maximum width of load 0·6 m;
capacity 2·03 tonnes.

Space requirements
Will turn in its own length but
can carry a 3·6 long load for

which overhang must be
allowed.

Equipment design
Wheel material should be cast
iron but can be used with
polyurethane or rubber wheels
for lighter loads.

Building needs
Level floors.

Price
Approximately £60 for 7620 kg
capacity manual stillage truck,
£1150 for powered 1360 kg
type.

Pedestrian-controlled forklift truck

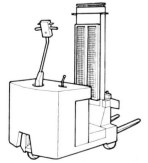

Powered travel and lift forklift machine of heavier duty than
stacker truck. Pedestrian control of forklift and reach truck
enables accurate manoeuvring in restricted areas, but are
slower than rider trucks. Range of sizes from small
machines to full size forklifts with pedestrian control.

Uses and limitations
Internal lifting under localised
conditions with relatively light
loads up to 3·6 m. Pallet
handling.
Can be fitted with most
attachments.

Sizes and capacity
Lift height up to 3·6 m.
Load up to 0·9 tonne.
Straddle width from 889 mm to
1·3 m. (Not less than 1·2 m
for maximum lift.)

Space requirements
Will turn in own length and
with 914 mm × 762 mm pallet
would work in 1·8 m to 1·9 m
aisle. (Needs more space for
maneouvring than manual lift
truck with power lift.)
Capacity—0·56 tonne load at
457 mm centres 3·6 m in
1·8 aisle.

Building needs
Level floors. Charging point
either single or three phase.

Price
£2860 for 1500 kg capacity.

Manual pallet truck

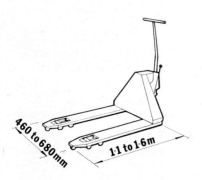

Uses and limitations
Internal transfer within warehouse for order build-up, loading vehicles on raised docks general pallet handling; with tail-lift vehicles. Increasingly used in retail premises for handling bulk goods, can be used as a stillage truck with adaptor fitted. Where loading ramps are used pallet trucks with brakes should be supplied.

Sizes and capacity
If over 1500 kg capacity and long distance travel is required, a powered truck is better, as operatives soon tire when pushing heavy loads.
Fork lengths available from 0·81 m to 1·62 m. Widths also vary from 460 mm to 680 mm. Where gangways are very narrow and stability is important, a heavy truck should be used with as much width between forks as possible.
Height lowered 83 mm; height raised 203 mm.
Pallet width should be 152 mm over fork (typical length is 1·06 m for a 1·21 m pallet).

Space requirements
Will turn in its own length. Additional clearance for overhangs.

Equipment design
Large wheels in nylon or with solid rubber tyres are required on uneven floors or for heavy loads; steel wheels are also available but are less popular nowadays.

Building needs
Level floors, articulating axles available for trucks to be used in old buildings, but a good chance of unstable loads.

Price
1500 kg £150 approximately; 2000 kg £200 approximately.

Shaped or angled fingers for drum, paper roll handling. Skid adaptor for stillages.

Pedestrian-controlled reach truck

A reach truck with pedestrian control. Gallows or pantograph type.

Uses and limitations
Used as a reach truck in confined spaces, where speed is less important or where infrequent use does not justify skilled personnel trained to operate a rider reach truck.

Size and capacity
680 kg-1360 kg at 600 mm load centres.
Overall length: 1168 mm (1360 kg capacity).
Overall width (without pallet) 915 mm.
Travel speed 6·3 km/h (unladen).
Lift speed laden: 15 m/sec.
Lift height 4·9 m.

Space requirements
Turning radius 1372 mm (machine only).
Minimum stacking aisle (90°) with 1000 × 1200 pallet; 2710 mm.

Equipment design
Can be purchased in either moving mast form (gallows type) or with extending forks from a fixed mast (pantograph type).

Building needs
Level floors; single or three-phase recharging supply.

Price
1360 kg model, £3100 approximately.

Power travel and lift pedestrian-controlled stacker truck

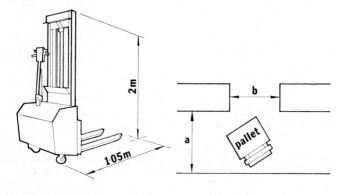

When travelling, the pallet rests on the stacker frame, which has travel wheels; power lifting is independent of the travel frame, and is directly into the rack. Only suitable for short travel distances.

Uses and limitations
Internal lifting under localised conditions with relatively light loads up to 3·6 m. Pallet handling. Not suitable for horizontal movement over anything but shortest distances. Would work well with pallet truck. Can be supplied with attachments.

Size and capacity
Capacities to 1500 kg at 600 mm centres.
Straddle with 864 mm to 1·3 m. Now available in more compact form.
Travel speeds to 4·8 kpm laden.

Space requirements
Will turn with full load in 2·2 m aisle.
Tyres tend to be polyurethane.
Lift height to 3·8 m (triple extension mast).

$a = 1300$ mm ($800 + 1200$ mm pallet)
$= 1500$ mm ($1000 + 1200$ mm pallet)
$b =$ width of largest load $+ 100$ mm
increase of b means a can be reduced.

Equipment design
Can be fitted with scissors mechanism to make it into a reach truck.
Batteries will now work full shift without recharging.

Building needs
Level floors; single or three-phase supply.

Price
From £450, simple self-propelled lift truck (500 kgs capacity) but can become more expensive as machine becomes more sophisticated; eg £1600 for 1500 kg capacity model.

Technical study Mechanised storage 1

Storage process

Mechanised storage ranges from simple forklift truck operation to complex integrated handling systems. It is becoming more difficult to distinguish between mechanisation and automation—some highly sophisticated mechanised handling plant is still controlled by an operator, but actions are planned by a computer. (Section 6 Automated storage covers full automation.) It is in this type of storage that architects and designers will be most involved.

1 Introduction

1.01 The users' aim is that goods should be stored, sorted and dispatched in the most efficient manner, for the lowest cost. To fulfil this brief, the mobile handling equipment should be treated as an integrated concept. Product and packaging affects the form of transport, the mechanical handling and storage medium to be employed. Mobile plant has a major effect on planning storage areas, type of storage, and the ultimate cubic efficiency of the racking. The requirement for maximum cubic storage is a reflection of the initial product and its packaging.

1.02 In manual storage, man's dimensions determined the scale of the operation; in mechanised storage, the determining factors are: using the maximum cubic capacity of the building and placing goods correctly in the shortest possible time. The initial design decisions will be determined by the economic policy of the user, for instance if he requires a quick return through rental, or if the store is part of a production process. There are many factors vital to the success of a mechanised storage installation outside the building designers' range of knowledge. Architects should not necessarily become mechanical handling engineers, but should appreciate these problems and should know why certain decisions are made, if all the other parties are to be successfully co-ordinated.

User specification

1.03 The term 'mechanised warehouse' is generic for a range of storage types and users. Basically it consists of four types of storage:
1 Stockholding warehouse
2 Transit warehouse
3 Accumulation warehouse
4 Repository

In fact, most mechanised warehouses are a compromise between several of these functions, so the characteristics of the company's trade should be carefully examined before any design decisions are made. Often, a company's present trading pattern is a result of an existing storage and distribution system; a user specification based on this situation may be obsolete before a new building is commissioned.

1.04 Organisation during the initial planning stage is based on the users' desire to make use of the maximum cubic capacity, the fastest method of handling goods, for the lowest cost. The economics of using handling plant are inevitably entwined with the warehouse building, and the system is ultimately a compromise between the building designer and the mechanical handling engineer.

1.05 To decide which system is best suited to the client's requirements, the cost, speed and cost-in-use of moving unit loads through the various types of warehouses will be compared. One of the major decisions that affect basic design is: to what level the warehouse will be mechanised. Mechanisation has advantages of accuracy, reduced personnel and the possibility of future developments towards automation, balanced against maintenance requirements and potential breakdown. Cost and efficiency of control systems should be equally considered, and the overall flexibility of the scheme in terms of pattern of trade, handling methods and the characteristics and potential of the site.

Types of mechanised warehouse
1.06 A warehouse that is not designed for change can quickly alter from being a cost benefit to a liability. The designer should be able to assess the factors for and against the types of storage available.

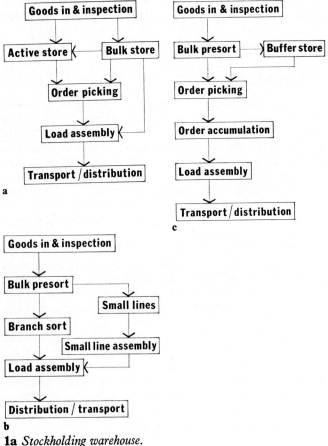

1a *Stockholding warehouse.*
b *Transit warehouse.*
c *Accumulation warehouse.*

Stockholding warehouse
1.07 A stockholding warehouse provides surge capacity to match consumer demand and peak requirements. Function is usually split between bulk and active stock sections. Order picking is from active stock, and is usually planned round unit loads. The bulk stock is used to replenish the active stock or to supply full unit loads. The reason for this type of store is logistic. It is usually impossible to supply a customer direct from a factory in the time available, or economically to gear the line to this type of production.

Transit warehouse
1.08 The transit warehouse is usually a stage in the distribution system of an operation involving bulk purchase and distribution to a number of outlets. Typical is a warehouse serving a chain of supermarkets, located in an optimum position for the sales area. The sortation function is similar to a stockholding warehouse, but more stock tends to be picked direct from the bulk store. Transit depots are an economic necessity in saving transport and distribution costs. The cost of 'trunk' hauling goods is half that of delivery.

Accumulation warehouses
1.09 Accumulation warehouses collect components required

for a particular operation, eg a pre-production parts store for a batch production line. All items should be immediately available when the manufacturing operation requires, and double handling and order picking should be avoided. The sortation process tends to be earlier, often with a primary sortation as the goods enter the store, with storage separated into fast moving bulk lines, and slower parts that are racked in their own areas of movement speed. 'Buffer' storage is often used to provide the exact order requirements for the production process: surge capacity is needed, as some parts are liable to be rejected, and others may build up a surplus. A high level of stock control is required in these stores.

Repository
1.10 A repository provides storage space, often for hire for long periods, for spare materials and equipment. The main difference between this and the three other categories is that the amount of usable space is more important than the speed of handling. A typical example is a furniture repository (see Section 9 Special storage).

2 Source of goods
2.01 Due to the varied range of storage functions, goods will be received from many sources. For example, a store for a retail organisation will receive goods from local sources within Britain, from Europe and from the Commonwealth. A warehouse for pre-process storage (in manufacturing) will receive goods from another factory of the company, another department of the same factory or, as with the motor industry, from a wide range of outside suppliers. All goods, except those produced on the spot, will arrive by road or rail packed in some form of intermodal container. Goods produced within the site pose a different set of conditions. Special storage applications such as steel stockholding impose different constraints and will be discussed in Section 9 Special storage.

3 Form of transport
3.01 Depending on where the goods originate and the method used to package them, a wide range of transport can be

2 *Articulated trailers parked at warehouse loading bay; from left to right: 40ft (12 m) container, two 20ft (6 m) containers, one 12 m tilt trailer. Approximately 3·5 m wide bays. Shows also canopy over loading zone, spotlight, and strip lights over circulation zone.*

expected. In a store big enough to justify substantial mechanisation, many different types of heavy lorries should be planned for. Most goods from the Commonwealth and the USA will arrive in ISO containers. From Europe, ISO containers, articulated and drawbar trailer TIR combinations should be expected 2. With a manufacturing industry, for a pre-production store, it is easier to predict the type of transport, as the number of suppliers is often less than for the retail trade. If large regular numbers of parts are involved and the site has suitable access, bulk consignments by rail can be economic. Container trains are a satisfactory and flexible solution.

3.02 Light vans and trucks will also be involved, especially where small-scale suppliers are used. Each industry generates a particular transport pattern, based on type of supplier, characteristics of the goods, distances involved, and the distribution system for the company. The transport manager should be contacted at an early stage if possible to ascertain if there is an existing pattern. Suppliers may not continue the same mode of transport; they will use whatever suits their economics best at the time, or place a surcharge on their delivery.

4 Control of transport

4.01 In this type of storage operation, most vehicles will be of the largest sizes. To avoid providing large buffer areas for vehicle arrival, or risking a queue tailing back to the public road, every effort should be made to spread delivery and dispatch peaks throughout the day. Often management does not realise the effects of vehicle peaks on the whole storage operation. Installations have been seen where, to clear a backlog of trucks, handling plant has been diverted from inside the store. This blocks the line further up, as the remaining plant cannot handle the greater influx of goods; soon all buffer space is full, goods waiting to be stored constrict the loading bay area and the whole storage cycle gets out of phase.

Delivery times
4.02 Often management is loath to dictate delivery times to suppliers, as accurate timing for long-distance trucking is unrealistic; however, 'block' allocation can help to control vehicles. The designer should point out how useful land is wasted if occupied only during peak periods, the overall effect on the handling and storage system, how extra handling plant is likely to stand idle for much of the day, and the added intangible factors of considerable peak strain on the facilities, and the greater chance of stealing and accidents. Management should be consulted about the predicted growth of seasonal peaks; often a new storage installation will generate its own trade.

Vehicle flow
4.03 The control of transport on the site is important in the efficient use of the warehouse. Vehicle flow should be one way wherever possible with routes, accumulation and parking zones clearly marked. A tannoy to call vehicles forward from a position well out of the manoeuvring and loading bay area prevents accumulating vehicles constricting circulation (see Technical study Loading 1). Light vehicles, if numerous, should be segregated from heavy traffic. They have a faster throughput, and constrict heavier vehicles.

4.04 Vehicle control is bound up with documentation, security, and the type of loading dock best suited to the application. Plan vehicle routes in a clockwise direction for Britain, with flexibility in mind, as there are fashions in vehicle operation. For large-scale operation, a control box at the gate with a document handling system to the traffic office is an advantage (see Technical study Loading 1, **5abc**). The office will then be a step ahead of incoming traffic, and can

plan movement to the most efficient bay for the part of the store involved. They can also control the vehicles more accurately by anticipating trucks' arrival and doing any 'shuffling' necessary before a jam occurs. For dispatch vehicles, a gatehouse linked with the traffic office helps security, and clears the dock area more quickly in that the drivers will collect their documents as they leave the site without blocking circulation in the loading area (see para 37). *Remember* that some buffer space is needed close to the gatehouse on the dispatch side, as document delivery is sometimes slow or the documents are inaccurate, requiring confirmation.

Traffic office siting
4.05 The traffic office should be in a commanding position, able to view accumulation and loading bay areas. A segregated dock system may have two traffic offices. In a segregated dock, two accumulation areas are also needed, and free circulation must be possible at all times to and past these areas. In the smaller-scale operations, drivers will bring their documents to the traffic office, and the route from the vehicle parking area should not cross the stream of circulating traffic. Serious accidents have occurred by pedestrians' vision being obscured by high sided vehicles.

4.06 The type of storage operation also affects the control of transport. For example, if the store is for components for machine production mainly arriving in cages and post pallets, for block stacking, side loading is often the quickest way to turn the vehicles round. As the vehicles need at least 4·9 m between them for forklift trucks **3**, it would be wasteful of space to place the accumulation area next to the loading zone. In a warehouse for the retail trade, the dock is mainly handling pre-grouped loads of roll pallets for rear loading; then the vehicles need to use a bay as near their next load as possible, and accumulation opposite the bay ensures a fast turnround.

4.07 In some large-scale mechanised installations, the designer has to integrate road haulage circulation with tractor trains or forklift trucks from another part of the works. Clearly marked priority signs and warnings should be provided where routes cross truck ways. Crossings after blind corners or areas of parked trucks should be avoided; this may sound obvious but it is often neglected. If hidden access is unavoidable, a mirror can be useful, but beware of glare and of high vehicles fouling it, as their roofs swing several inches off vertical on cambers or when turning.

3 *Forklift trucks side-loading crates on to flat-bed rigid trucks.*

4.08 Rail wagon arrival depends on British Rail's time-tabling. If wagons have to be shunted across major vehicle routes, these tracks should be carefully marked and a visual and audible warning installed. There is no point in planning fast circulation and efficient vehicle accumulation if they will be baulked for long periods at a rail crossing. Check with management and British Rail that the peaks will not conflict.

5 Receipt of goods

5.01 Buffer space is required after unloading. Goods have to be checked against documents; in some cases shrink wraps removed prior to sorting out for storage. Unless the form of packaging is specified in a supplier's contract, goods can arrive in old cartons, unsuitable for the storage process in operation and must be unpacked and repalletised. It is better to provide space to repack than risk a protracted stoppage in the warehouse or injury to operatives. The same applies to damaged pallets **4** and stillages of an unsuitable size for the storage plant or medium. Care should be taken to segregate incoming and preassembled goods for dispatch in single loading bay zones, and space should also be provided for pallet trucks and cutting gear. A strip of at least 6 m should be allowed inside the cross circulation zone for this buffer area.

4

4 *Space should be provided in the unloading area for the disposal of load strapping and packing material. Added* *tyre sections act as buffers, and chocks on chains prevent the truck from moving forward.*

6 Form of goods

6.01 Most goods received in mechanised storage installations are unit loads, in the form of pallets, post pallets and stillages, packed into ISO containers, trailers, box-vans or flat vehicles. As a rule, except in groupage operations and some cases of specialist component supply, large numbers of small packages loose-packed should not be expected. The exception to this are containers arriving from 'deep sea' routes that have been hand-stuffed for maximum use of volume.

7 Unloading

7.01 The type of unloading organisation depends on mode of transport, product and the type of storage operation. If all goods are palletised and arrive in 'tilt' or 'flat' trailers or side door containers and a high throughput is needed, then a finger dock is the most effective. Finger docks use more space but have faster handling speed, but with a normal 90° dock more vehicles can be handled at once in the same space, so turnround is nearly as fast, with less chance of a troublesome load constricting the whole system (see Information sheet

Loading 1). The designer should assess the relative merits carefully with the transport manager, considering possible future trading patterns and vehicle types.

7.02 The unloading of pallets in mechanised warehouses is normally achieved with forklift trucks. However, although ISO containers are capable of accepting 2-ton forklifts on their floors, most British flat trailers cannot, and require handling from ground level. In raised docks if light vans with loose loads are anticipated, it is worth providing a special bay with a ramp, so that a powered pallet truck can be used for unloading. Difficulty has been found in some cases with suppliers arriving at a store with a small van, with goods loaded on pallets placed at their premises by a forklift truck operating at ground level. The ramp could also be used for a forklift truck in this case, but ought not to exceed 1 in 10. If there is not the space, a scissor lift table can be provided for lowering the forklift or raising the van or specify an elevating dock leveller. (See Information sheet Loading 5.)

7.03 Space should be provided in the unloading area for storing or the disposal of load strapping and packing material **4**, especially if involved with 'deep sea' ISO containers.

7.04 In a warehouse for the retail trade there is a particular problem as, unless a segregated bay layout is planned, vehicles arrive with empty pallets and roll pallets from their delivery rounds. In several installations, peaks of returning vehicles restricted movement in loading area. In one dock, vehicles from the first delivery round to the nearer supermarkets arrive at approximately 9.30 to 10 am meeting the second phase being loaded. Large numbers of empty roll pallets accumulate in the dock area, although there is a towline system to remove them as fast as possible **5 abc**. Some roll pallets are inevitably damaged during retail distribution, and these are liable to accumulate, as they have to be sorted for damaged units. Once removed from the loading area, these roll pallets usually end up in a corner of the yard, or an empty loading bay. Space should be provided for this. However much space that can be spared in a loading bay area for pallets, it will never seem enough.

Unloading rail wagons

7.05 Unloading rail trucks is an over-the-side operation, and sliding door wagons and side access containers allow normal fork truck access. If the train carries ISO containers, standard pallet heights are applicable, but if normal wagons are used, clearances are lower. Travel distances are greater; economically a train can be counted as a long picking face (see Information sheet Loading 6).

8 Characteristics of goods

8.01 It is worth considering whether the goods concerned have any special characteristics, for example, are they easily damaged? It is at this point before they are sorted and mechanically handled into the store that any extra protection can be added.

9 Sorting

9.01 Prior to storage, the goods are recorded and labelled or coded for data feedback to the stock control section. Once recorded, goods can be either allocated a rack, or randomly stored and the driver records where they were placed (see Stock control para 14). In smaller low height installations, most of this area can be dispensed with, as the same forklift usually stores direct from unloading into the racking. This is only possible if the turnover is relatively slow, as the road vehicle turnround will be hindered due to the forklifts being away in the racks. For faster operation, the unloading unit meets the plant serving the racking at a point in the sorting area. This point can be a forklift-to-forklift or a forklift-to-reach truck interface, but in all cases these positions should be clearly marked. (See Technical study Loading 1 **15**). Note:

5a

5b

5c

5a *Numbers of empty roll pallets have accumulated, and heaps of broken units have developed round the edge. Pallets are also awaiting sorting to the rear. At peak times, these would overflow into the loading area.*
b *Damaged roll pallets have collected in a corner, and are beginning to encroach on circulation space.*
c *Damaged roll pallets have encroached from the left towards the towline track; reach trucks have to wait*

until the towcart has passed to get by. The roll pallets on the right are waiting for sorting.

1 If a high lift machine is used in the racking, take care that there is sufficient clearance at the interface point. Some turret trucks that lift to 10 m + are 3·9 m tall when operating at low level. Often there is a fire wall and this is convenient for use as a run for pipes and cables. Ideally the unloading forklift should just intrude into the rack zone, but some managements prefer all unsorted goods to be kept 'truckside'.
2 Container stuffing forklifts, although capable of being equipped with three-stage masts, are not very efficient in rack areas.
3 If a finger plan is used in the dock for three-sided access, and most of the vehicles can be side-loaded, it is possible to run a turret truck into the loading bay and use its side delivery characteristic to advantage; again this is only possible where throughput is low, but saves double handling.

9.02 In production buildings, where the store is too far away from the loading bay for a direct handling interface, 88 m is the break-even point between the choice of a tow train with eight pallets and a fork or reach truck with two[1]. In this case the sorting area will be used for loading tow carts, recording goods, directing the towcarts with their code and informing stock control so that the stacker truck can be ready to store the goods correctly when the tow train arrives.

9.03 Goods in this area are sorted for high, medium and low user stock. If the number of stock lines is small and the throughput is high enough for a block stack, the sorting area is purely for recording case numbers as the forklift truck passes through. The same applies in pre-production storage, where large loads of high user parts in post pallets can be block-stacked.

9.04 With mechanised parts storage, the sorting process can be more complex. Bulk loads may require splitting down into tote boxes prior to storage, and this is space consuming. It is likely that with industry's greater packaging awareness this process will disappear, and modular 'ready-to-use' packs will be introduced that can be stored on pallets in the normal way and withdrawn from bulk to access storage as required.

10 Volume calculations

10.01 Initial calculations should be made in a feasibility study at sketch design stage. Volume calculation is dependent on the storage system proposed, the characteristics of the commodity, and the speed of throughput predicted. Different storage methods produce various volume characteristics. Unless the designer is particularly skilled in accurately assessing warehouse volume, a mechanical-handling consultant should be included into the design team.

10.02 Store throughputs and build-up patterns can be simulated quickly and accurately with computer aid, and various aisle widths and handling plant work cycles compared against initial and long-term costs and the expected throughput and return. The designer's responsibility is to understand the implications of any form of storage suggested. Table I gives a rough estimate of the volume characteristics as a check.

Table I Volume characteristics of types of storage		
Type of storage	Cubic space utilisation	Effective use of medium
	per cent	per cent
Bulk stacking	100	75
Post pallets	90	75
Drive-in racking	65	75
Pallet racking	30–50	100
Gravity live storage	80	70
Powered mobile racks	80	100

10.03 At this point, site characteristics have increasing influence, with type of storage required, and the money and erection time available. For example, the site might be small when the area required for vehicle circulation has been subtracted, and thus demand a high rack installation in order to achieve the required capacity. This has to be balanced with the increased cost of turret trucks, of a double reinforced floor, and for stronger foundations.

6a

6a *Cosmetic warehouse in USA.*
6b *Interior view of a warehouse showing towline conveyor serving order picking racking.*

6b

11 Turnover calculations

11.01 Turnover calculations are based on the demands of the distribution or production systems. This will determine whether block or rack storage will be required, what mix of these and what scale of mechanisation will be required. This should also be considered at the sketch design stage. For example, in a warehouse serving the retail outlets of a region, planned demand from supermarkets and predicted seasonal peaks and growth of certain products, linked with the most economic distribution pattern, will dictate the throughput of the store. Further examination of the transport system in detail will illustrate the exact requirements day to day, with the addition of a built-in overload and expansion capacity. Data are available from manufacturers on forklift, reach truck and turret truck cycle times, although beware of these figures being optimum performances in ideal conditions. The possibility of meeting optimum throughput cycles should be balanced against the availability of volume and area, and the cost of the operation. The same applies for a pre- or inter-process store, but calculation is easier as production cycles can be accurately gauged.

12 Variety and flow

12.01 The wide variety of goods to be stored affects the level of mechanisation required. If the stock is a large number of different lines, the store organisation will have to be based on the relative speed of movement of goods so that mobile plant can work economically. If the flow of several commodities is very fast compared with a general medium level over the bulk of the stock, but not enough to justify block stacking, it is worth considering a live system on a first-in, first-out basis rather than keeping a forklift truck shuttling in and out of the racking. If, as in many retail and pre-production warehouses, there is a large variety of stock to be dispatched in small lots, the main store really backs up the primary function of order picking and dispatch. A hybrid solution will probably result.
12.02 Analyse the characteristics of the storage processes in terms of throughput per item. The typical product quantity curve is shown in **6a.** Stores can be classified into categories requiring different treatment: **6 bcd**.
High throughput, low variety. This requires block stacking, drive-in racking, or live racking.
Medium throughput, medium variety. This requires a mixture of bulk storage racking and active storage.
Low throughput, high variety. This is basically an access store; pallet racking and order picking divided by speed of throughput. This type will have more personnel involved.

13 Type of storage

13.01 The type of storage and handling system to be adopted will be determined by the requirements of the logistics of the situation rather than by those of the primary storage function. Any choice of mechanised storage system is therefore based on the best method of order picking. In brief, the parameters which affect the choice of the system are:

Stock characteristics
1 Degree of variety of items in stock.
2 Size, shape and weight of individual items.
3 Item dispatch rate and difference between items.
4 Ratio of stocks held to throughput.
5 Change in volume of goods in storage to volume of goods assembled for customer delivery.
6 The requirements to dispatch in quantities smaller than manufacturers' unit packs.
Customer order characteristics
1 Number of customers.
2 Number of items per order.
3 Volume or weight of orders.
4 Time between receipt of order and dispatch of goods.
5 Frequency of customer dispatches.
6 Significance of any 'special' order requirements.
13.02 Having examined the basis for the order picking system, and for the storage method most economic in terms of space and flow, next examine the type of handling plant required. Systems available include: block stacking, pallet racking, and live racking.

Block stacking
13.03 This is the stacking of unit loads one above the other in

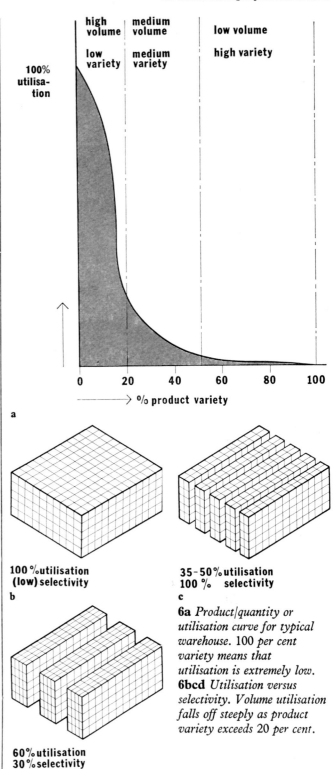

a

100%utilisation
(low) selectivity
b

35-50%utilisation
100% selectivity
c

6a *Product/quantity or utilisation curve for typical warehouse. 100 per cent variety means that utilisation is extremely low.*
6bcd *Utilisation versus selectivity. Volume utilisation falls off steeply as product variety exceeds 20 per cent.*

60%utilisation
30%selectivity
d

blocks several loads wide and deep. **7** Blocks are separated by a grid of aisles which provide access for each block. Advantages are: no special storage equipment is needed except for pallets. This is the cheapest form of storage as far as capital investment in equipment is concerned. If loads are crush-sensitive, use post pallets or drive-in racking (drive-in racking is really a type of block stacking). With post pallets in Britain, shoe-type legs are traditionally used, which wastes space. In USA for example, 1100 × 1200 mm stacking containers can accommodate 40 per cent more material by eliminating the stacking shoe. Typical cost savings in a large-scale American operation are 20 per cent on in-plant handling, 14 per cent transport, 13 per cent storage (using pallets nested with a conical peg and recessed cone). (See Information sheet Mechanised storage 3.)

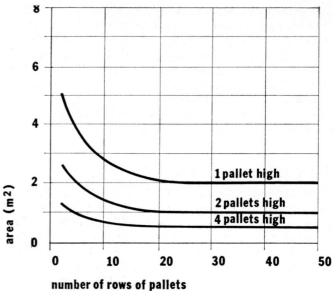

7

7 Block stacking pallet loads   Note stabilising straps.
of bottle crates.

13.04 Area required per pallet position for various block widths
and stacking heights is shown in **8, 9**. These show comparative
areas for pallet racking. Up to four pallets high, the floor area
requirements for block stacking are much lower. **8** also shows
that little advantage can be gained from having blocks larger
than 20 pallets square. One consultant calculated that where
material is block stacked two or three stacks deep from the
aisle and the store is bounded by normal factory service
aisles, 34 per cent can be added to the actual pallet area to
allow for internal aisles. If the block stack is isolated and
requires its own main aisles and marshalling area, a further
allowance should be made to increase the basic pallet area to
180 per cent. A designer or materials handling engineer
should of course develop his own factors according to the
peculiarities of the goods and unit loads.
13.05 Disadvantages of block stacking include the difficulty
of obtaining direct access to the block, except for top loads
at edges of aisles, and overall poor selectivity. This is a
drawback if several varieties of items are to be held in stock,
and in this case drive-in racking might be a better solution **10**.
13.06 The dispensing of part pallet loads is difficult unless
post pallets or drive-in racking are used. The need for stability
and prevention of load crushing limits most block stacks to
two to three pallets high. Again drive-in racking is the answer
to load crushing. Drive-in racking, with the pallets' edges
resting on rails and without cross members, allows up to
65 per cent cube utilisation, as loads can be nearly up to the
base of the unit above **10**. Some products in large post pallets
or stacking crates allow heights of up to 10 m block-stacked
by an overhead stacker crane.

8b

8 Rough calculations for
feasibility studies. To find the
area per pallet position
for block stacking a given
number of 1200 × 1100 mm
pallets.
1 Divide number of pallets by
four (ie, assume they are
stacked in rows four deep and
count the rows a). Ignore
aisle spaces (dotted). These are
included in graph calculation.
2 Decide how many pallets
high the block stack will be.
On graph b, reading
number of rows of pallets
along the bottom line, and
number of pallets high along

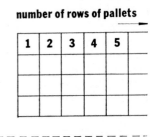

8a

the right hand vertical, area
in m² can be found. For
example: 200 pallets at
4 rows deep = 50 rows.
Stacked 2 high
Area required = 1 m²
per pallet position.

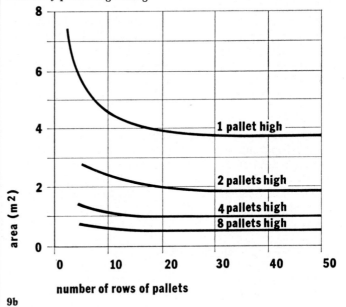

9b

9 To find area per pallet
position for pallet racks for a
given number of 1200 ×
1100 mm pallets.
1 Divide number of pallets by
two (ie, in rows two deep).
(Ignore dotted aisle spaces
included in graph calculation.)
2 Decide how many pallets
high the racking will be. On
graph b, correlating number

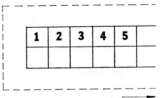

number of rows of pallets

9a

of rows and height stacked,
area in m² can be found.

10 *Drive-in racking. Forklifts drive right into the racking,* *placing pallets in front of each other on projecting rails.*

12 *Block-stacked kegs*

Block stacking

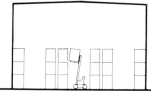

11a Fork lift trucks
Aisle width = 3·4 m
Stacking height = 6 m
Box pallets over width of building = 18
Total number of pallets = 396
Utilisation 100 per cent

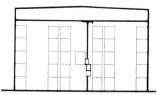

11b Normal stacker
Aisle width = 3·4 m
Stacking height = 10 m
Box pallets over width of building = 30
Total number of pallets = 660
Utilisation 166 per cent

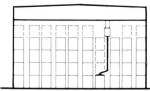

11c Stacker with grapple
Aisle width = 780 m
Stacking height = 8 m (10m)
Box pallets over width of building = 880 (1000)
Utilisation = 220 per cent
(250 per cent with large boxes)

11abc *Comparison of type of block stacking. Warehouse dimensions: Width 20·4 m; height 11·7 m; length 46 m. Box pallets 1600 × 1600 × 2000 mm, weighing 1200 kg.*

Pallet racking

11d All-purpose building with universal stacker crane
Utilisation = 35 to 50 per cent

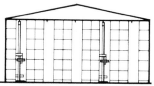

11e Warehouse with pallet rack and order picking machines
Utilisation = 65 per cent.

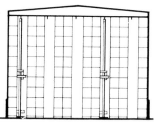

11f Pallet warehouse rack structure also serving as roof support.
(see Automated storage).

11def *Comparison of pallet racking and stacker cranes. Utilisation refers to pallet places available, not that achieved in a store turning over stock, which will vary according to stock and manpower.*

13.07 The poor selectivity afforded by block stacking will probably bias the type of storage against a random block system, and a system of allocated storage will probably have to be employed, ie areas in a warehouse set aside for particular items. Block stacking is best suited for the storage of palletised goods and inherent unit loads such as bales or drums, in buildings where available headroom limits storage height, and where variety is low and throughput is high **12**. Block stacking can be ideal where goods are stored in complete loads prior to removal to the active area for order picking, and in load marshalling areas before dispatch where random storage is acceptable because no order picking is involved.

Pallet racking

13.08 The limits of racking height are determined only by the height of the building and by the capability of the device used for placing and removing the unit loads. Advantages include: direct access to every single item held in the store; a great advantage in order picking when a large variety of items is involved. Direct access also gives 100 per cent selectivity, allowing the use of random storage with considerable savings in floor area requirements. Because racking supports pallets or unit loads, stability and crushing resistance are not important. Stacking heights of at least seven loads high are normally possible. The 100 per cent selectivity means that there can be a first-in, first-out system where necessary. High capital cost is the principal disadvantage. Pallet racking is most suitable for storage of palletised goods and other unit loads where there is a wide variety of lines in stock. It is particularly suitable as an active store for order picking.

Choice of racking and handling plant

13.09 Racking and handling plant should always be considered as one integrated system. Up to heights of about 6 m, normal forklift trucks can be used, but aisles need to be as wide as their swept turning circle and the tolerance of the swinging load. If floor area is at a premium, aisles can be narrowed by using reach trucks, whose turning circles are more compact, and which tend to be more stable **13**. If more volume capacity is required and a 50 per cent reduction in selectivity is acceptable, storage can be two loads deep in the racks **14**. (This is different from drive-in racking; the racks are normal pallet racking, and the reach truck has a pantograph action on the fork head so that the rear pallet can be placed without fouling the cross members.) If the area-to-volume ratio needs to be increased, keeping 100 per cent individual pallet selectivity, narrow aisle reach trucks can be specified, where the aisles need only be marginally wider than the widest pallet **15**. There are several forms of these trucks available, with lifts of 6 to 7·5 m. Usually these do not turn in the aisle, but are either side loaders with a mast that moves across the chassis on a carriage to push the pallet into the rack, or can rotate at the base of the mast to allow double-sided access without having to leave the aisle. Other forms have a conventional mast facing the direction of travel and a fork system that will extend either side. A third method uses a conventional forklift with a special three-way attachment, but this has to be aligned correctly before entering the racks. All these types are 'free path', in that they can also be used in the warehouse for general purposes.

13.10 For a higher cubic capacity with the minimum of floor area, free-standing racking can be built to over 12 m high. For 10 m work, free path turret trucks are available that can also be used for general duties **16**. One model allows the operator to rise with the load and so can use this as an order picker as well. (All dimensions of forklift trucks are in Information sheet Mechanised storage 1.) These machines require aisles only a little wider than the pallet length. When fitted with side guide wheels running in channels at the rack base for greater stability, these machines can lift to over 10 m. Obviously the amount of vertical rack divisions and lift height are governed by the average height and weight of the pallets handled, and the capacity of the turret trucks.

13.11 Most racking manufacturers offer adjustable systems that can be quickly altered to suit the maximum cubic potential with various pallet heights throughout the store (see Information sheet Mechanised storage 3). As a rule, beam pallet racking has a 35-50 per cent cubic space utilisation, and the height from the ground to the top of the highest load should not exceed six times the depth of the rack. Thus with back-to-back racking, the unrestrained height potential is greater; if exceeding the 1:6 rule, some form of restraint is needed, such as bolting to the floor. For higher cube utilisation, live storage and powered mobile racking can be used. Both these share a cube efficiency of approximately 80 per cent.

Live racking

13.12 Live racking means a number of sloped racks, into one end of which the pallets are inserted and through which they either flow under power or gravity to the other end for dispersal **17**. Gravity flow is not recommended, as jamming can occur, and impacts can be substantial. If this is required, a 1 in 36 gradient is adequate. Live racks which allow a mixture of gravity rollers and power accumulation brakes are more usual. It is most effective to use pallets in these racks, though drums are often stored free (see Section 8 Bulk storage). Advantages include high space utilisation, as only one aisle is needed at each end. However, much space can be lost in the racking if pallets are not loaded to full height. The system is compatible with mechanised sortation systems, such as automatic dispensing of cartons.

First-in first-out is automatic, and selectivity is good as long as each rack division is devoted to one product. Random storage is not feasible except in load marshalling. Effective applications include mechanised warehouses with low variety and high throughput where first-in and out operation is important, such as semi-perishable foodstuffs. Any items of regular shape, cartons, tote boxes, as well as pallets, are suitable, where throughputs are fast and varieties are low.

13.13 Powered mobile racking has proved successful for varied stock with a medium selectivity rating. It is expensive and slow to install. A reach truck driver can operate the movement controls until the correct aisle opens **18**. Although dense stock is possible, only one aisle can operate at a time.

13

14

15

13 *Typical reach truck.*
14 *Pantograph attachments allow forklift to stack loads two deep from one aisle.*
15 *Narrow aisle reach truck.*

16

17

19

High-bay mechanised warehouses

13.14 Above 10 m, installations begin to be classed structurally as high bay. (Heights above 7·5 m gain an extra hazard fire rating (see para 27).) Although most fall into Section 6 Automated storage, some high-bay warehouses are mechanised. These consist of stacker cranes with full driver control **19**. The majority of these run on tracks at the base, stabilised at the top. One crane is offered as a more stable unit with additional support two-thirds of the way up the rack. A further system, popular in stores for heavy stillages like engines in vehicle production, has a mast suspended from the roof structure or top of the racking, allowing free travel within the rack and a rotating fork head. One version available is mounted on a gantry crane beam for full cube block stacking with no need for aisles (see **11b**).

Structural racking

13.15 Once racking becomes semi-structural or structural,

18

costs rise considerably. Careful economic studies should be carried out to examine whether the increased cube and throughput benefits increase with the saving in site area, or are eliminated against the extra cost of structural racking, specialist fixed path handling plant, stronger foundations and building structure. In several recent installations, it is suspected that they will not prove economic in the long term, due to lack of racking flexibility.

Overhead cranes

13.16 Overhead cranes feature in special storage applications such as steel stockholding (see section 9 Special storage), and can be used for such commodities as rolls of newsprint. Overhead stacker cranes are limited in flexibility by the track and gantry, and are expensive to install. All these systems discussed have been used to great effect in some installations. It should be remembered that the successful choice is a result of many integrated factors; alternatives should be carefully assessed and costed.

14 Stock control

14.01 Stock control and distribution systems in mechanised storage buildings are so complex and need such fast and accurate stock appraisals that computers are now widely used for this purpose. The rack organisation has a bearing on how this is achieved and how successful the result will be.

16 *Transfer position between turret truck and forklift from loading bay.*
17 *Live racking.*
18 *Mobile racking.*
19 *Gantry slung stacker/order picker. Allows narrow aisles but only one crane per gantry.*

With a small, comparatively unsophisticated computer, stock can be randomly stored within the user-rated sections of the store, and its position recorded for data processing. Random storage should be specially programmed to prevent the rack spaces closest to entry and discharge points of the aisles gradually becoming filled up with slow-moving items, while fast-moving items have to travel further within the warehouse. This gradually reduces the utilisation of the handling plant.

14.02 A computer, if used, will work out the best picking pattern for the reach truck wherever the goods are stored. However, some installations that continue the order picking function within the bulk rack dictate a planned storage facility with allocated spaces for particular commodities (see section 6 Automated storage for fuller descriptions of computer-aided stock control).

15 Stock withdrawal

15.01 In mechanised storage, withdrawal follows a similar pattern to stacking except that often now the retrieval path is calculated for optimum handling plant travel by a computer. For easy identification from a moving reach truck, graphics for rack location should not be less than 75 mm high × 13 mm thick **20**. For bulk withdrawal with a set pattern, as in warehouses serving the retail trade, all rack spaces should be coded with a similar code in each aisle. Corresponding numbers help stacker truck drivers to remember where high user locations are, and the position of other frequently picked commodities.

16 Order picking

16.01 A wide range of order picking methods achieve the required speed and volume in a mechanised warehouse (for basic considerations see para 13). If handling more than 500 orders a day with more than two items per order, bulk order picking can prove more economic than sequential picking. Bulk order picking involves progressive movement, picking several orders at a time. The items are then sorted for individual orders. Bulk picking can save manpower; the picking operation is more efficient due to less travel per order and the increase in number picked at one time. If later order sortation is mechanised, there can be substantial savings in cost.

16.02 Sequential order picking involves progressive movement through the storage area, selecting the commodities to complete an individual order so that one circuit is travelled for each order.

16.03 In most warehouses, conventional methods of order picking involve excessive personnel movement or, if mechanised, repeated movement of the mechanical plant. The greater the area, the more walking has to be done by the staff. If instead of handling each order separately, several orders can be picked simultaneously, wastage is reduced. When the storage pattern is assessed at stock control stage into bulk, general, and small use lines, it is then more efficient for each class of goods to be held in a unique position and employ the method of order picking best suited to the scale of operation.

16.04 There is still no machine that can match man's efficiency of selection and single unit picking, but there are considerable aids to help the picker reach this position and inform him of the correct number of items to be picked. Many order picking systems are linked to the stock control computer; for complex picking operations, eg small components for batch production, the computer can predict the orders, and will calculate the shortest and easiest picking path. If the storage has allocated positions, based on order picking accessibility, personnel soon learn the principal sections of the warehouse and, with the aid of numbered aisles and rack positions, quickly identify the loads required.

16.05 The simplest method of order picking is along the bulk racks at floor level **21a**, but this usually does not present a large enough picking face for the collection speeds required

20 *This shows the main rack code, ZA, and the pallet position code ZA2/194. The rack behind is numbered ZA1/194; ie, transverse aisle pallets are numbered ....../194 for identification. Also illustrates adjustable pallet racking.*

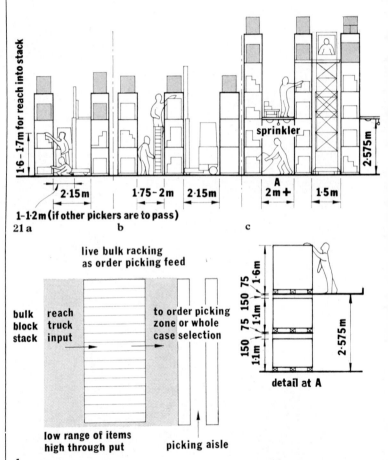

21a *Picking aisle (2·15 m) at floor level. Back-up stock (shaded) at high level is lowered to picking face by reach truck in same aisle.*
b *Picking aisle at floor level. This time reach truck is in separate aisle (2·15 m) so picking aisle can be narrower* (1·75 m min) (see **22**).
c *Picking aisle (2 m +) floor and mezzanine level, with turret truck in separate (1·5 m) aisle.*
*In plan **d**, goods pass from bulk block stack (left) to live bulk racking (centre) to picking aisle (right).*

in a mechanised warehouse, and it is preferable to have personnel grouped in one zone out of the way of mobile handling plant. As a rule, in medium-sized operations, the picking area is replenished from bulk stock; whenever the pallet from which the goods are being picked is nearly empty, it is replaced by a full pallet from reserve stock (often stored

c

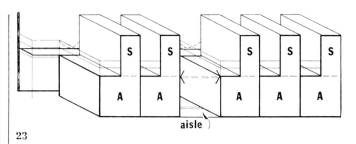

23

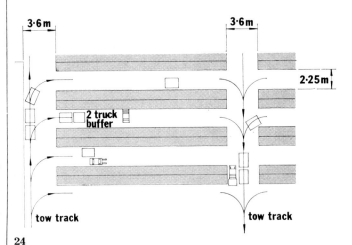

24

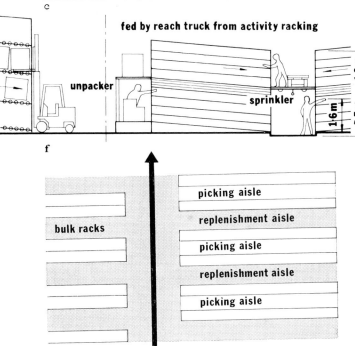

fed by reach truck from activity racking

unpacker

sprinkler

1·8 m

1·6 m

2·5 m

f

picking aisle

replenishment aisle

picking aisle

replenishment aisle

picking aisle

bulk racks

large range of items

22

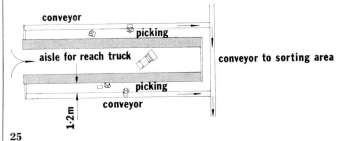

3·6 m

3·6 m

2·25 m

2 truck buffer

tow track

tow track

conveyor

picking

aisle for reach truck

conveyor to sorting area

picking

conveyor

1·2 m

25

21e, f *Multi-line live racking.*
Goods are picked onto the
belt **e, f,** *right, which takes*
them to the lower level for
assembly into roll pallet loads.
This type of racking is
hand-loaded and demands a

large area behind the input
face to accommodate pallet
loads of goods to replenish
the flow lines. The pallets are
raised to the mezzanine level
by a forklift truck.
22 *Enlarged plan of* **21b** *:*

(**22** *continued*)
reach trucks move stock from
bulk racks (left) to
replenishment aisles (right),
allowing plant-free picking
aisles. Shaded area is reach
truck path.
23 *Mobile racking, with*

pallet racking **A** *below,*
shelving **S** *above.*
24 *Order picking with tow*
trucks.
25 *Picking into tote boxes,*
sent by conveyor. Reach
truck aisle feeds racks (shaded).

above the picking positions). For larger and faster picking cycles, bulk stock is often moved to an active reserve stock area, and then is withdrawn by a machine allocated to feed the picking positions. This generates a section of racking backing up the picking face. If the number of lines to be picked is small, live storage can be effective and is efficient in volume; this can be designed to handle goods in full pallet form, **d,** or the unit loads can be unpacked at the upper end and the live racking used as a carton dispenser, **e, f.** The latter enables more lines to be picked, but involves additional labour.
16.06 Many fast picking operations are achieved by an alternate aisle system. Pickers work from two faces on as many levels as can be reached safely in an aisle unique to the picking operation. The aisles on the other side are used for replenishment and the upper levels of racking used for reserve stock **21b, 22.** Although this only reaches 50-65 per cent volume utilisation, it does allow for fast replenishment and uninterrupted picking, without plant interference. A development of this to double the effective picking area is to install a mezzanine in the aisle **21c,** but it should be remembered that this needs intermediate sprinkling and lighting, and a method has to be found to carry the goods to the sorting area.

16.07 Mobile racking can also be used for order picking on a two-tier system **23.** Bulk stock is carried at the lower levels, and picking takes place at the upper one, arranged in such a way that pickers do not get crushed. This system combines a high volume of bulk storage and medium selectivity with multi-face order picking. There are differing views whether the pickers should operate at ground or high level. At ground level, pickers can build orders direct into roll pallets for removal by pallet trucks or be towed in trains by forklift.
16.08 Another effective method in large installations is for picking to be done into towline trucks **24.** Goods can either be picked into roll pallets that are then placed in a towline frame, on to trolleys direct, or the roll pallets themselves can be converted for towline operation. A major advantage of a towline system is that orders can be dispatched at the end of a picking aisle and automatically routed to the load accumulation position. Empty trolleys or containers can be handled in this way and returned to the picking zone and stored automatically in a siding until required.
16.09 In larger-scale operations requiring the build-up of a lot of small loads, eg retail pharmaceuticals, conveyors are useful for transporting the picked goods to a load assembly position. In bulk order picking areas, operatives work in special picking aisles; goods can be picked into tote bins sized

to suit the average order, which are then coded and placed on the conveyor, positioned at the end of the rack or running down the aisle. In most cases, multi-level conveyor lines alternate with replenishment aisles **25**. Ground based or overhead conveyors severely inhibit the free movement of handling plant and are expensive to install and operate. Throughput must justify this type of installation. Conveyors are faster than towline trucks for load assembly purposes, but both allow automatic routeing and queuing.

16.10 In some installations, a more efficient and cheaper picking operation could have resulted from reassessing the speed of product movement and racking planning rather than accelerating movement between the picking and load accumulation area. The efficiency of the whole warehouse is most important, and the installation of special in-store transport systems can have side effects by creating constrictions at certain points and impairing the operation of other sections.

16.11 Order picking can be done at high level to free all the floor for reach trucks and remove personnel from the risk of damage by mobile plant. High level picking allows conveyors to be used freely. Roll pallets can be loaded at high level, and sent forward as required to the load accumulation zone on a goods lift or paternoster. One installation handling paper products saved half the designed floor area by placing the pickers on a floor right across the top of 6·4 m high racking. High level picking is suitable for bulk order picking with the ease of conveyor operation, or sequential picking with goods lifts.

Fixed path and free path order pickers

16.12 In order to minimise the number of aisles in large installations, and to reduce travel distances, fixed path order pickers and higher free path machines are now more frequently used **26**. (Automated versions are discussed in section 6.) With manually operated fixed path pickers, discomfort can be experienced with constant, rapid acceleration and deceleration forces. The limit is thought to be decelerations from 20-15 m/min. The space-to-speed ratio should be almost equal for horizontal and vertical movement; for rough assessment at sketch design stage, height and length of the racking can be found from assessing the figures of vertical travel speed and the horizontal travel speeds of any systems being examined with the planned height and length of rack bays.

16.13 Rack-mounted order pickers do not allow indiscriminate movement. Operating in the horizontal and vertical planes simultaneously the driver can always work at eye level. The volume utility is about 60 per cent. Fixed path order pickers combine pallet storage with order picking, useful for medium throughput operations or where the majority of withdrawals are full pallet loads. They are restricted by having to return to the end of an aisle to leave or collect each load, but can place the pallet on to a mezzanine for further picking or sortation. One of the advantages of using a free path special purpose turret truck is that they can stock the racks with pallets like a narrow aisle reach truck, the operator can rise with full load to the maximum height, pick full pallets or order pick in safety, and then carry the load directly to the assembly zone without double handling. They also enable a greater amount of flexibility in allocating machinery to racks. One machine has an additional useful feature for order picking, where the elevating cab works independently from the fork carriage, so that when a load is being built up, the operator can lower the forks a little at a time to keep the working surface conveniently at hand level.

16.14 Special purpose pickers can also be used to collect multiple orders at one time on the principle of 'gather and dispense'. One large pharmaceutical bulk warehouse works on this principle. Picking towers ('panelveyors') are used for general goods picking; these are really rack-height mobile frames of shelves with an operator's cage that can be raised or lowered on either side **26**. The operators serve about 230 stock

26

27

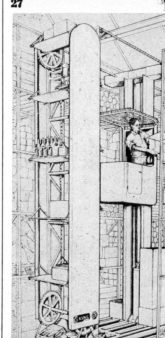

28

26 Mobile picking towers used in pharmaceutical warehouse.
27 Free path order picker picking from tote boxes.
28 Highly mechanised order picking system, consisting of mobile picking tower and lowerator, picking from pallets.

lines each (there are 2300), and pick from a summary prepared by the stock control computer. The operators collect the goods from their section for each shop served, and place the goods on one of the shelves. When an order is complete, the goods are placed into a tray and these are placed on to a take-away conveyor to the load assembly area. (More complex computer-controlled operations will be discussed in section 6.)
16.15 An intensive mechanical order picking system involves a high speed belt running at the base of the racking to the load assembly area **28**. The operator works in a mobile picking tower with an elevating platform. He picks goods into a tray from a computer written manifest. When a tray is full, it is placed with a coded-destination on to a circulating lowerator, which places the tray on to the removal belt, so that the operator can immediately start a new cycle. This machine can travel horizontally at 61 m/min and the lowerator moves at 18 m/min; full pallets are stacked conventionally from the opposite side of the picking face.
16.16 The planning of any order picking system depends on the type of goods stored, the speed of picking required, and the most economic compromise between picking plant, personnel, and rack height. Consider several alternatives at the sketch design stage, discuss these with the client, and plan for future flexibility; if the installation involves fixed path picking plant, future alteration can be very costly and time consuming.

17 Picking area

17.01 Order picking areas for personnel have been discussed in Technical study Manual storage, para 17. In mechanised installations safety is of prime importance on the operator/machine interface. Noise and vibration can also be a considerable problem. Discomfort reduces efficiency and leads to labour troubles. Warehouse environment characteristics that affect order picking are:
1 Space available for order picking related to the required throughput.
2 The predicted picking activity per metre run of order picking face.
3 Available headroom (several consultants have found that productivity rises in high, airy spaces).
4 Special environmental requirements (some chilled foodstuffs. See also section 8 Cold storage).
5 The ratio of order picking work effort involved in selecting quantities of one item for one order to the effort required in selecting quantities of one item for a group of orders.
A high level of lighting and ventilation helps efficiency.

18 Load build-up

18.01 Warehouses with bulk order picking require an area for orders to be consolidated into unit loads. Even small, simple operations, picking full pallet loads, cannot dispense with this, as a buffer and sorting area is useful for incoming as well as outgoing goods.

Conveyors
18.02 The sorting area in a mechanised warehouse can be complex, and space-consuming if not carefully handled. As described in para 16, bulk order picking at over 500 orders per day is likely to mean that goods will arrive from the picking zone by conveyor, partly sorted or unsorted for consolidation into unit loads for distribution; if sequentially picked, goods just have to be grouped. Areas with conveyor lines have to be carefully planned, as not only the layout of the conveyors themselves has to be considered, but also wheeled traffic circulation and future flexibility. In all but the smallest operations, the conveyor lines from the order picking area are split into accumulation lanes for mechanical sorting. More goods 'snarl-ups' can occur at positions of changing conveyor

29

30

29 *Lightweight overhead*   *store.*
track conveyor used in book   **30** *Tilt tray conveyor.*

lanes than anywhere else (see Information sheet Mechanised storage 8). The greater the diversity of package types in relation to the diverting method, the more complex will be the decision about what type and surface of conveyor will be chosen.

Choice of type of conveyor
18.04 Some order picking areas, where tote bins or small wire baskets are used, employ overhead conveyors to the sorting area. These can queue and be directed round various circuits **29**. They impose extension problems for reach trucks and there are especial clearance difficulties with turret trucks that can be approximately 4 m high when at their lowest position. Overhead tracks routed round the structure and building services may impair access and maintenance. The overhead conveyor can be used with its queuing ability as a multitrack accumulator, and can take the load right to the loading bay if no further sortation is required; in one large warehouse the return loop removes all empty distribution containers from the loading bay, pushing them out of the way above head level, the circuit acting as an empties store, passing an inspection area to remove any broken containers.

Tilt tray conveyors
18.05 Tilt tray conveyors are an instance of part automation in a mechanised warehouse. The tilt tray conveyor is useful for most turnover situations, as it combines the sorting and transport function. These units consist of closely spaced trays mounted between axially disposed pivots, on carriages that travel round a fixed track. The tray is tilted by a pneumatic roller or electric trip when it reaches the correct sortation point. These conveyors can be used in two ways; with the 'gather and dispense' principle of picking several orders together **30**, if a computer guides the picking personnel, and they are picking a small range of products for a series of similar orders, the computer can automatically sort the goods into the correct lanes (see section 6 Automated storage). With a more mixed situation, the pickers can stick on a label printed with the picking list; the tilt tray will pass an operator on its way to the sortation area, who will key-in the code of

each pack that passes. The tilt tray conveyor can have a simple mini-computer memory unit, programmed by the operator to divert all packages of a certain code to the correct destination. Operators can handle 80 packages per minute in this way. With a slightly more sophisticated peripheral computer linked to the stock control unit, the picker sticks on a photo-sensitive label which will activate the tilt diverter when it coincides with the correct photo-electric light cell. This performs the same function as an operator, but much faster. At the destination, the tray tips the goods down a chute. Length of package is unimportant as long as the receiving conveyor can handle it, as the machine can be quickly programmed to link rows of trays together for tipping and directing long and bulky objects (in some cases with sensitive light beams, this can be done automatically). A sorting process involving tipping means that goods can experience intense local shocks. Before deciding on a tilt tray, look at the fragility of the goods and the strength of their packaging.

Belt and roller conveyors
18.06 Belt and roller conveyors are suitable for dispatch sorting; they can have powered or unpowered rollers, and belts with a wide variety of surface textures for different applications (see Information sheet Mechanised storage 8). These types are floor-based, and sterilise an area on either side of them, the amount of space lost depending on their height above the ground, any turns, joints and inclines **31**. With high throughputs, the main supply conveyor will be high speed. This reduces the time available for control and recognition, so a deceleration and spacing mechanism is needed on the conveyor line, with high-speed diverters and multiple lanes. This is costly, and the deceleration and spacing controlled accumulation belts use up valuable floor space. Conveyors cannot be considered in isolation; there must be space for maintenance, and for work to diverters, which have pneumatic or electric operation, and room for personnel to clear blockages safely.

18.07 When planning these areas, conveyor manufacturers should be contacted from the outset, and all accessories—diverters, tilters and accumulators—should be designed into the initial scheme. Back-up facilities and maintenance planning is of prime importance, especially in high throughput areas. Consider at the initial planning stage:
1 How suitable are the goods for handling in this way.
2 How effectively can they be coded for identification during sorting, manually or mechanically.

18.08 The way some goods behave during conveying is crucial to sorting efficiency, and is influenced by shape, rigidity, and the interface of the conveyor's surface and the base of the package. Blockages can affect the operation of the whole warehouse system. Friction levels between some conveyor materials and packages and the effects of uneven weight distribution and humidity can all lead to diverters mis-timing and damaging goods, and causing blockages. If there are a large variety of goods and fast sorting speeds it can be cheaper and simpler for coding and handling to unitise items into a standard box, if this can be made compatible with the order picking system.

18.09 Less space consuming than flat accumulation conveyors are tiltable versions, with chute accumulation. Belt conveyors can run at an angle, and the doors open automatically to the correct channel, controlled in the same way as the tilt tray conveyor **32**. Various commodities and package types limit turning radii and acceptable slopes; tilt conveyor makers should be made aware of any space or height restrictions due to structure or other plant at an early stage.

Blow diverters
18.10 A recent development for light goods that is fast, simple in operation and nearly maintenance-free is the blow diverter. This puffs the package into the correct channel.

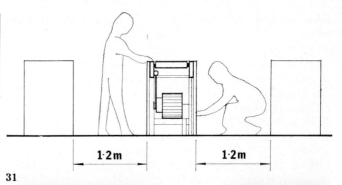

31

32

31 *Clearances required for accumulation conveyor.*

32 *Tilted band conveyor used for GPO sorting.*

Air film conveyors are effectively used for light goods. Requiring no moving parts, these combine lift with direction. Wide, long conveyors could lose a lot of air, requiring uneconomic compressor plant; to cope with this, various valve types have been developed, that are depressed by the package moving over them. One experimental system uses valves of low friction ptfe balls, which release a directional air jet when depressed to overcome friction. For air cushion systems, regularly shaped, flat bottomed packages are required.

Packaging equipment
18.11 More plant can be expected in dispatch sortation areas especially in post-manufacture storage. The development of unit loads and the rising cost of transport and handling have brought many improvements in packaging. Manufacturers and retail organisations expect goods to reach their customers in as good condition as they left the warehouse. Many loads are still manually assembled. An experienced team can assemble pallet loads from conveyors very fast, judging size and shape, rejecting unsuitable or damaged packages. But to reduce manpower, and with increasingly standard packaging, palletising machines are being specified for sorting areas **34**. Some will shuffle various sizes of goods into the most efficient pattern to be placed on the chosen pallet size. Many accumulation lines feeding different products to one machine can be accommodated by an integral accumulation conveyor. As each lane assembles the load, the information can be fed to a mini-computer attached to the palletiser. When the appropriate goods are released, sensors tell the 'brain' to choose the correct pattern. Up to 20 different patterns are a normal capacity for a palletiser. There are various types including totally mechanical, variations with vacuum heads, and simplified machines for small operators. These palletising machines normally require 220 volt and 440 volt 3-phase power sources, and a compressed air supply (see Information sheet Mechanised storage 1). Palletisers will form a constriction at the end of a number of load accumulation lines, and generate their own traffic in the form of an empty pallet supply to their magazine, and a further conveyor sortation system or a pallet truck route to the load assembly area. Work

cycles can be very fast, depending on the variable factors of package size, pallet size and the number of layers. These machines are space consuming; a typical high capacity palletiser requires an area 9·4 m × 3·35 m × 3·65 m high, requiring this area again surrounding it **35**.

33

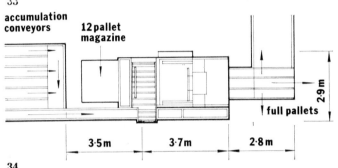

34

33 *Large palletiser for plastic cases of bottles.*
34 *Plan of typical palletising machine. Top right is buffer track required for slower*
shrink wrapper.
35 *Shrink wrapped palletised load emerging from shrink wrap tunnel.*
36 *Vertical banding machine.*

Shrink wrapping

18.12 The development of shrink wrapping pallet loads has resulted in more stable pallet units that are sealed against accidental exposure to the weather, and which dispense with the cardboard outer. This helps visual selection during order picking, but can lead to easier theft. For bulk dispatch, shrink wrap tunnels taking full pallet loads should be positioned at the end of the accumulation lines or at the output side of a palletiser **34**. These machines also constrict the handling system, but allow documentation to be added before dispatch assembly as they emerge from the tunnel. At present, palletisers work faster than shrink wrap machines, so some buffer conveyor track is required between them. The number of shrink wrap tunnels can be calculated from the desired speed of throughput, their speed of operation, and the amount of constriction that they will place on the system during peak periods, or in situations of breakdown and maintenance. Shrink wrap machines can give off substantial amounts of heat, and areas surrounding them need added ventilation in summer, which can be offset against the winter heat load, especially useful if near the loading bay zone. Some of the latest models claim very low heat gain characteristics.

18.13 A number of small goods-in-travel shrink wrappers are now available. Especially useful in storage operations that include a certain amount of load breakdown and repackaging, motor spares for example, these small machines operate fast on the conveyor line, but usually dictate primary sortation

(special narrow lightweight conveyors are available for packaging machine supplies). If a groupage production line for special packs is anticipated, this should be planned from the outset as it can affect the space allocation to the order picking zone, and can constrict the flow to the sorting and assembly area. Repacking operations should be removed by a spur conveyor away from the picking zone, so that personnel have a more pleasant environment, and a breakage will not affect the whole picking operation. This arrangement is also required in warehouses for supermarkets, where bulk cheese is cut up and repackaged.

Banding machines

18.14 In some ways in competition with shrink wrapping machines and in others complementary to them are banding machines. These can also be placed at the output side of a palletiser, and operate at the same speed (depending on the amount of bands that need to be applied, and whether the pallet requires turning for double direction banding) **36**. A

35

36

banding machine mechanically wraps a pallet load with retaining plastics bands, cuts the band and heat-seals the ends together. A binding machine does the same with wire or twine; this is intended for smaller unit loads like soft cartons that could still move within a shrink wrap. Both make necessarily accurate loading operations, as for 'deep sea' container services, much easier to plan and operate. Horizontal and vertical banders are marketed, and if the load is fragile an operator is required for placing paperboard angles to prevent corner crushing. Banders can be fully automatic; a 400 lux light level is suggested for this area.

19 Order and document check

19.01 In storage systems using full pallets, checking is often carried out before vehicle loading, in the load assembly area. However, with small goods accumulation and palletising into orders, a check is often required prior to the pallets or roll pallets being sent forward to the dispatch accumulation area. If palletising, shrink wrapping or banding machines are used, the documentation check can be made immediately after this, using the inherent circulation constriction to the best advantage and allowing a check on the routeing of goods to the correct dispatch bay. A duplicate copy of the print-out for the accumulation conveyor operator can be used for this, or special lists can be drawn up. Many loads are still hand assembled, and then checking is simultaneous.

19.02 The traffic control office is often used to issue checking and drivers' documents; check the distance involved to the sorting area, and whether any possibly dangerous routes have to be crossed; delay in the transit time for documents can delay checking. If the traffic office is too far away, some form of print-out or visual display terminal will be needed at the checking point. (On-line visual displays are discussed in section 6 Automated storage.) A buffer area should be provided for some pallets that will be returned to the accumulation area as incomplete or incorrect; one to two pallet spaces per checking line, for example. A minimum light level of 400 lux is suggested for this area also.

20 Loading and dispatch

20.01 In its most simple form, this is an area where roll pallets or normal pallets are assembled prior to loading, and where document checking can take place **37**. Layout depends on the organisation of the loading bay and lorry assembly area (see Technical study Loading 1). If there are few bays and fast turn-round the accumulation space should be large enough to pre-group a complete load before a vehicle's arrival **38**, and to be well into assembling the next one during the loading operation **39**. The space required should be sufficient for a load and a half of the most common size of vehicle anticipated. Vehicle sizes are growing, with swop bodies for easy trunk haulage-delivery cycle interchange (see Technical study External storage 1). Whether this space is to be provided in-line or transversely in several lanes depends on the shape of the building, the routeing of the fork trucks or tow train, and the position of the loading bay relative to the racking. The planning of the assembly area is made easier if the load pattern is similar day by day. For instance, in a large warehouse serving supermarkets, the detailed content of loads will differ, but basic load characteristics will be the same, whether deliveries are several times daily, daily or weekly. With stock control computers linked to retail ordering systems, a prediction pattern can quickly be calculated. In these situations, a daily order picking schedule can be fixed, based on predicted vehicle arrival patterns. Loading bays combining incoming and dispatch are possible here, sharing an incoming and outgoing sortation area. However, in peak situations, when the system is under pressure, the incoming empty roll pallets quickly constrict the operation of the load assembly

Table II How to calculate approximate numbers of roll pallets in dispatch assembly area.

	Load platform size		Number of roll pallets	Weight of load and vehicle
	Length m	Width m		Tonnes
Rigid vehicles	5·1	2·3	18	11
	6	2·3	21	13
	6·9	2·3	24 (28)	13-14 (30 gtw)
	7·5	2·3	27 (31)	15 (32 gtw)
Artic vehicles	10·2	2·3	36	21-23
	11	2·3	39	23-24
	11·75	2·3	42	29
	12·6	2·3	45	32

Note 1: Figures in brackets are roll pallets for drawbar trailers, and gross weight of vehicle with drawbar trailer.
Note 2: These 720 × 800 mm roll pallets are placed three abreast in the trucks. Other types are larger, and are packed two units across: adjust the numbers accordingly.

37

38

39

37 *Load assembly area of large food distribution warehouse. Congestion occurs when incoming roll pallets meet full units seen here awaiting dispatch.*
38 *Roll pallets are being* *accumulated into vehicle loads, in anticipation of being called forward to the loading bay: Lanes are clearly marked.*
39 *Partly-loaded trucks with a line of roll pallets behind their doors.*

40

41

42a

area. In theory, even with closely spaced van bays at 90° to the dock **40**, there is usually room for both activities (ie about 6 m buffer space before load assembly where empty pallets can be quickly handled to one side). What happens in practice is that vehicle arrival is staggered, so some trucks are being loaded when others arrive **41**, this means that the partly loaded trucks have a line of roll pallets behind their doors. The path for empty roll pallets is therefore already constricted and soon the buffer space becomes jammed with full pallets, empty ones, and broken units to be sorted out for repair. If a dual-purpose bay must be used, designers should plan the dispatch load assembly area so that there is always room to clear empties and broken pallets, and insist that a substantial buffer space is essential to keep flow running smoothly. Suppliers' vehicles will use the single bay, and these goods will have to be checked-in **42**. If there is room, it is preferable to remove the cross route out of the immediate loading bay zone, and clearly mark lanes for each direction on the floor, preferably in different colours. If incoming roll pallet tracks are marked 'No waiting' on the floor, there is a good chance of operation without blockage. If roll pallets are used during the order picking process, empty units should be stored as near to the order picking area as possible; some large installations have towline conveyors just to handle the empties, but one major user has found that even this is not fast enough to stop the jams, and wants to change to straddle trucks that can move eight roll pallets at a time at a greater speed.

21 Additional data

21.01 The growth of hypermarkets has introduced a new unit load device: the cage. This is a wire pallet with fold-down sides. By combining transport and retail display into one unit, a handling stage is eliminated. Although cost-effective for the retailer, the cage is bad for distribution efficiency. It must be handled by pallet trucks, both in warehouse and vehicles, and its volume efficiency is low. Its widespread adoption will demand a reassessment of transport and dispatch facilities.

References
1 Department of Employ-ment Bulletin 43, Safety in Mechanical Handling. 1970, 25.

42b

40 *Truck in position, filled with empty roll pallets.*
41 *Even at non-peak hours, incoming empty roll pallets are already clogging up dispatch assembly areas.*
42a *Suppliers' vehicles are often larger than the users',* *and may require a different unloading technique. Note tarpaulin on the dock, and broken roll pallet carrying a waste bin. No real provision has been made for debris disposal. This also applies* **b** *to external areas.*

43

43 *The roof structure of a warehouse can cause a pallet position to be lost throughout the length of a whole aisle at each turn position.*

44 *A big box structure allows both freedom in positioning racking and full height stacking.*

44

Technical study Mechanised storage 2

Building function

22 Structure

22.01 Mechanised storage buildings house sophisticated plant and large quantities of valuable goods. Maximum cubic capacity for the expenditure is important, and by using high lift, narrow aisle reach trucks and turret trucks, storage can be right up to roof level.

22.02 The structure and fabric of a mechanised warehouse is not only an enclosing shell, but also a frame to which mechanical handling plant is attached, eg, conveyor lines, and order-picking machinery. At the same time, the structure should provide as large column-free spaces as are economically possible, considering movement characteristics of handling plant, dimensions and tolerances dictated by rack spacing and future flexibility and bearing capacity of ground. Ideally, a mechanised warehouse should allow a clear span with no column intrusion into the storage space; 24 m bays have been built economically from steel. Although vertical expansion is cheaper than lateral, vertical travel speeds on handling plant are considerably slower; the cost of this should be carefully studied before any decisions are made.

22.03 With the requirement to store high, and for the frame to carry sprinkler lines, lighting, heating and ventilation services, the pitched roof, portal-framed warehouse can no longer be realistically considered as an economic solution in the long-term, except for bulk storage and small manually operated installations (see Technical studies Manual storage). What is required is a well-insulated big box. The pitch of a portal frame interferes with stacking space and, even if the racking is erected to maximum height at the apex of the pitch, there is considerable danger of forklifts fouling the structure, services or sheeting **1, 2**.

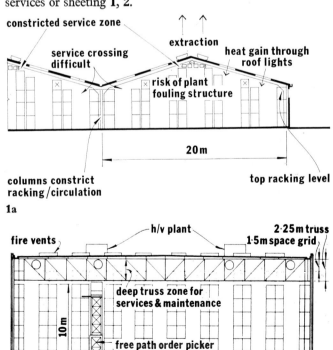

1b Comparison between **a** portal frame and **b** 'big box' structure

2a

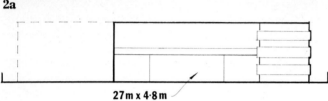

27m x 4·8m

lift truck cannot damage roof structure or services

all loading
inside

9·1 m

maximum utilization of height for racking & block storage

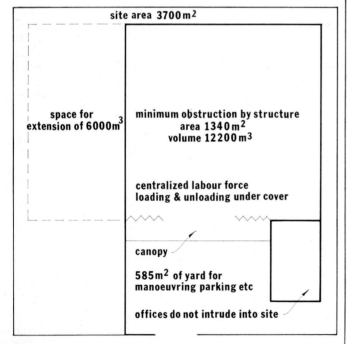

site area 3700 m²

space for
extension of 6000m³

minimum obstruction by structure
area 1340 m²
volume 12200 m³

centralized labour force
loading & unloading under cover

canopy

585m² of yard for
manoeuvring parking etc

offices do not intrude into site

2b

2c

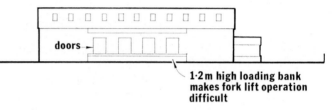

doors

1·2 m high loading bank
makes fork lift operation
difficult

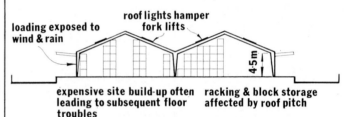

roof lights hamper
fork lifts

loading exposed to
wind & rain

4·5 m

expensive site build-up often
leading to subsequent floor
troubles

racking & block storage
affected by roof pitch

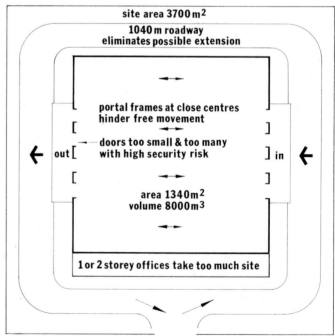

site area 3700 m²

1040 m roadway
eliminates possible extension

portal frames at close centres
hinder free movement

out [doors too small & too many
with high security risk   ] in

area 1340m²
volume 8000m³

1 or 2 storey offices take too much site

2d

*2 Detailed comparison between different types of structure
(**ab** big box, and **cd** portal frame structure). Good **b** and
bad **d** layouts are also compared.*

Materials

22.04 The relative performances of cladding and insulating
materials are discussed in AJ Handbook of Building enclosure
and AJ Handbook of Building environment, Section 8
Heating and ventilating. Initial expense on an efficiently
insulated sheet material can save considerable expenditure
on heating and ventilation plant in a large warehouse.
22.05 A big, insulated, wide span box with a deep, flat truss
roof structure allows stacking as near to the roof sheeting as
load and mast tolerances allow and enables building services
to be run in the roof void, unhindered by racking and possible
damage by plant. For example, roof water can be routed
through the truss without intruding into the floor zone.
A straightforward big box is remarkably cheap; the extra
cost of 10 m clear headroom against 4·5 m on a building area
of more than 1400 m² is about 7 per cent. If the extra volume

can be used effectively, the initial area could possibly be smaller. Space grids are also effective for wide, flat spans. A double layer grid such as Unibat can be economic for wide spans of over 30 m and can be much shallower overall than a truss. A space frame allows flexible positioning of sprinkler lines and other building services, and permits artificial lighting, roof lights, and ventilation plant to be clipped to the structure. The storage area layout can easily be changed as necessary—a warehouse not designed for change can soon turn into a liability. Arguments against space frames have been initial expense and number of members that require maintenance and repainting; the latter can be avoided by hot-dip galvanising, whose 15-year maintenance-free guarantee has long justified the additional expense.

22.06 A deep truss allows marginally greater volume utilisation, but clearance has still to be left for services and machine operation. A further advantage of the space frame is that there can be irregular perimeter column spacing, which is useful for loading-bay and sorting-area positioning **3**.

3 *Typical big box structure.*

22.07 The advantages of a wide span structure are:
1 Range of planning possibilities for general enclosed warehouse spaces is greatly increased by reduction in number of columns intruding into the storage area;
2 Potential use of the volume is improved;
3 A greater degree of servicing adaptability and quicker installation can be achieved. Pitched-roof design has led to difficult cross routes for pipes and awkward changes of level;
4 Prefabrication as a small number of large elements with fewer columns and bases makes for fast erection.
5 Free floor has great potential for adaptability of racking and choice of handling plant.

Cost comparisons
22.08 Compared merely with an off-the-peg short span steel structure, long span buildings are more expensive but their performance is much superior. If one could cost accurately:
1 The inhibiting influence of column and pitch intrusion on handling plant.
2 The effect of lack of flexibility upon the whole distribution system, and
3 The value of the lost volume, it is likely that the big box would prove to be substantially cheaper. The National Materials Handling Centre found[1] that the lower the pitch, the higher the initial cost, but the lower the maintenance and operating costs.
22.09 If a rack structure over 10 m high is used, large areas of unrelieved wall face the weather. Consider the effects of wind buffet and heat changes on the cladding. Both have been known to affect the tight tolerances required between stacker cranes, turret trucks, order pickers and racking. If there is continuity between the handling plant and racking and the roof or wall structure, extra bracing is often needed to combat

potential movement. Fixed-path order pickers and stackers may put stress on the structure by running against their stops. A 15-tonne machine with a 1-tonne pallet decelerating sharply from 140 m/min plus impact, can make solid-looking structures move alarmingly. The factory inspectorate are now insisting that fixed-path plant be tested to run against these stops, to prove that the structure will not be permanently deformed. These are a worse problem with highbay automated stores (see Technical study Automated storage 2).

23 Floor

23.01 The floor finish should be designed as carefully as the mechanical handling equipment that operates over it. Both designers and management tend to believe that a hardened granolithic screed is the most suitable for all purposes because it is cheap and requires no special treatment, but this can be a false economy, as it is quickly damaged by fats and oils as, for example in a cheese-cutting and packing line.

Floor loadings
23.02 The rule for flooring in a mechanised warehouse is to have a well-prepared base calculated to accept the wheel loadings of plant such as turret trucks and narrow aisle order pickers. As a guide, the ISO recommends that container floors shall withstand a wheel load of not less than 26·7 kN per wheel, assuming width of not less than 180 mm and centres of 760 mm. However, some forklift trucks and turret trucks exceed these loadings; eg, the Spacemaster narrow aisle stacker/order picker imposes a 36 kN front wheel load on the loadside when the pallet positioning attachment is extended laden. Check with the equipment manufacturer. However good the floor surface, it can only be as good as its base.

Important factors in floor design
23.03 *Wheel loadings* Forklifts have been known to break up floors very fast, not from insufficient reinforcement but because it was in the wrong position.
Rack weights Will special bases or double reinforcement be required for high racking? Turret trucks work to close tolerances in high racking; there is no room for settlement. Consider also the chance for future rack repositioning. Rack combinations with a height/depth ratio of more than 6:1 need either roof restraint or floor bolting. Bolt positions, if not specifically planned and reinforced from the outset, may lead to radial cracking and local surface failure.
Point and impact loads For example, post pallet feet, stacked post pallets and stillages and heavy set-downs.
Product characteristics What is the effect of accidental spillage?
Tyre scrub High speed turns and rapid deceleration by forklifts and tugs on major forklift or tow train routes can quickly bring up a faulty floor surface, especially if there is spillage as well.
Mobile plant. Straddle trucks and pallet trucks with small front rollers can be made dangerously unstable by bumping on expansion joints. A poor floor can dramatically increase tyre and castor bills.

Types of floor specification
23.04 *Granite screed* For general-purpose, high-use warehouses, a screed of granite chippings 12 mm thick, set in a mixture of cold bituminous mastic and Portland cement has proved effective and durable.
Concrete Another well-tried method is to lay the whole floor with 200 mm-thick road mix concrete with a road-paving machine, finishing with a 12 mm hardened granolithic screed. This method is fast and the paver can work to tight tolerances. The lack of expansion joints is a great advantage.
Jointed floors Although as efficient between the joints as

jointless flooring, these may break-up along the joint lines, where handling plant with polyurethane wheels and roll pallets with metal castors abrade the edges.

Epoxy jointless floor An accurate and long lasting finish is the epoxy-based jointless type. This is hard-wearing and can be laid to tight tolerances. Some can be laid with a non-skid finish at route crossing points, and are resilient enough to stand continuous heavy impacts from metal objects. It can handle heavy block stacks, and its jointless character makes it ideal for food processing areas or where oil or chemical spills may be expected (see Technical studies Bulk storage, Cold storage, para 23). The extra cost should be offset against the maintenance costs of conventional granolithic screed, replacement costs for forklift tyres, castors for pallet trucks and roll pallets, and stoppages due to joint break-up.

Always use a specialist flooring contractor who guarantees not to sublet any of the work; the method of laying and care over curing is critical to success.

24 Building services

24.01 In this type of warehouse building services are usually 10-30 per cent of the total warehouse cost. Using a 'big box' and a well-insulated outer skin, large warehouses may show only small variation in temperature and other environmental conditions. Two or three air changes are sufficient per day except in order-picking areas, where more ventilation is needed. (This figure is for handling plant powered by electric traction; if any internal combustion machinery is used, localised extraction is required). For order-picking areas, airchanges can be minimised by ensuring a constant circulation; air movement gives a feeling of freshness. With big box buildings, summer heat build-up can be dissipated at night by pumping cool air in from high level **4**. This should ensure a normal summer variation of less than 5°C. A light-coloured roof surface will combat insolation.

only vents if internal temperature reaches 21°C

draws in cool evening air

direct oil or gas-fired boiler mounted in roof

heat   heat

4 *Services in 'big box'.*

24.02 For winter heating, blown hot air is effective; the volume and insulation characteristics of the building and the added heat gain from lighting and handling plant keep the building at a comfortable temperature. With a deep truss flat roof or a space grid, combined heater and ventilation units can be mounted either within the truss depth, or on top of the roof surface, so as not to intrude on the storage space. The external road/loading bay interface may prove to be troublesome in winter, but dock shelters and air curtains help combat this (See Technical study Loading 1) **5**. Shrink-wrapping plant in the load assembly area can add to the heat, especially if there are several units; this should be considered when planning summer ventilation. If shrink wrappers are close to the order-picking area, extra extraction should be provided, as they give off an unpleasant smell of hot polythene film. (Some machines have built-in extraction equipment.)

The increased cost of fuel since the autumn of 1973 makes the reclamation of heat, where it is available, a possible source of heat for space heating of warehouses.

The heat requirement of a warehouse can be diminished by heavy insulation in roof and walls and exclusion of draughts from the main doors by the use of internal walls and small self-closing or air barrier doorways. Where there is a manufacturing process the process heat may be put through a heat exchanger, such as a Munters wheel, through which the warehouse air may be recirculated or the warehouse topped up with warm air.

There are many possible heat sources, such as the cooling side of the refrigeration system, the heat from electrical transformers, lighting systems, and where goods are warm from the manufacturing process, early storage within the warehouse will provide extra heat when required.

Because warehouses often need no deliberate air changes and when full of goods have their own inbuilt heat balance it is possible to provide some of the heat by solar radiation, just as it is possible to keep warehouses cool by the use of the cool night air drawn from some feet above the ground. It may be common practice within the next 10 years to heat warehouses entirely with heat tubes drawing their heat from process or extract systems, cooling systems, effluent, rubbish disposal and sewage systems. Heat pumps can be used to draw the heat from all these sources but are more costly to operate because of the electrical power required.

5 *Structure continued over totally enclosed loading bay.*

Natural lighting

24.03 In big box warehouses, the use of natural lighting is questionable, especially for perishables. Structures 10 m high with full racks and narrow aisles usually require permanent, supplementary artificial lighting to 200 lux minimum level. Natural light from rooflights increases heat variation adding to the cost of ventilation and heating plant, and may produce glare within the racking by intense light and shade contrasts. Infra-red and ultra-violet rays can also damage packaging and fade printed labels and cartons. Successful naturally lit installations have been built, and it is suggested that model studies be made to investigate the effects of sunlight on the orientation of the building and the racks within it. Glare can be dangerous with forklift trucks, resulting in racking damage and possible injury by misplacing pallets on upper levels.

Artificial lighting

24.04 *Long-term storage areas* Where storage is long-term or picking infrequent, lights may be turned off for long periods in certain areas.

Mixed storage Where there is mixed storage and goods have to be identified by markings on boxes or cases for movement or stocktaking, an intensity of between 200 and 300 lux is required.

Picking areas: Where lights must be kept on at all times for picking purposes or security, running costs are important and overall intensities of less than 200 lux should be considered.

Intensive picking areas In areas such as dispense units and intensive picking, lighting intensities may have to be as high as 500 lux.

Block stacking: Where block stacking is restricted to a depth of 18 m, continuous rows of twin fluorescent tubes with angled reflectors, mounted in the lanes, will give adequate lighting and easy maintenance. An intensity of between 200 and 300 lux is required.

Special problems of lighting mechanised storage buildings

24.05 *Vertical lighting* In mechanised storage buildings, unlike most other buildings, light is required primarily on vertical surfaces, ie, racks. No light sources should be obstructed by stores or their racking. This may be particularly difficult where the layout is changed in accordance with the stock position. When racking is moved often and a lower intensity of lighting is acceptable, continuous fluorescent tubes at right angles to the aisles are effective.

24.06 *Glare* Lighting into deep bins or racks from a relatively narrow access space may cause shadows of the tops of the bins or shelving **6**. If the equipment is lowered to give maximum penetration to the bins, it becomes an obstruction. In multi-level spaces, it is extremely difficult to prevent glare from all angles of view. The problem is accentuated if the operators are on mechanically operated platforms (eg, free-path order pickers) which can move up and down. In high-bay storage, glare from ceiling lights may prevent easy identification of goods. Some storage buildings are fitted with overhead travelling cranes, which complicate the lighting problem, since the crane driver must have a good view of the floor and his vision must at no time be impaired by glare. Specialist advice should always be sought.

Methods of lighting

24.07 Some methods applicable to particular cases are now described. In all cases a well-maintained white ceiling and walls improves distribution of lighting.

24.08 *Lighting from gangways only* Where the building is laid out so that positions of gangways are well-defined and unlikely to change, lighting can be concentrated over the gangways and directed outwards and downwards. Where the ceiling and walls are of high reflectance (and likely to remain so during the life of the building), diffusers may be sufficient. The effectiveness of this method depends on the gangways being long in relation to the width of the building, and on the horizontal distribution of lighting being relatively unobstructed. Bare tubes are preferable, and louvres should not be used.

24.09 *Lighting in racked areas* It is usually satisfactory to provide a single line of fluorescent tubes along the centre of the gangway **7a**. Where aisles are narrow, and racking high, an effective solution may be **7b**. The driver switches on light **B** when working on rack **A**, and light **A** when working on rack **B**. This cuts down glare and gives a better quality of light on the picking face.

24.10 *Lighting from side walls only* Where the building is relatively narrow in relation to its length, fittings mounted in the angle between the wall and the roof can sometimes cover the whole area. But drivers will tend to have the light facing them when they are moving among objects stored, so that the near side of what they wish to see may be shadow **8**.

6 *Lighting into narrow aisles causes shadows.*
7 *Single line of tubes* **A,** *along centre of aisle, or double line*
B *on each side.*
8 *Nearside of object onto which driver is loading may be in shadow.*

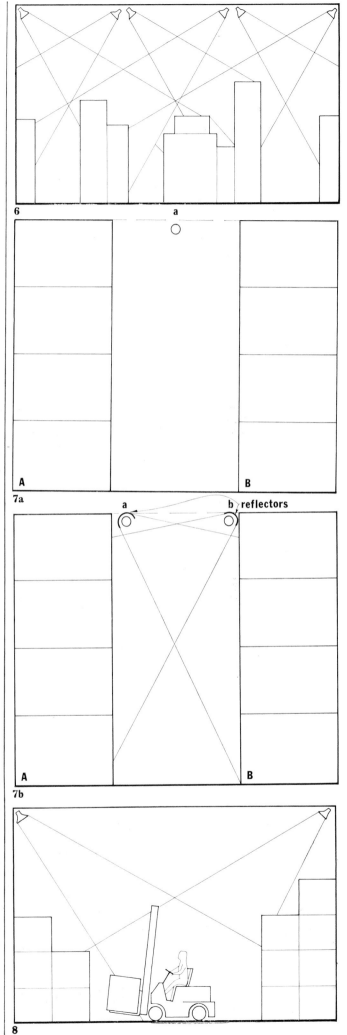

24.11 *Overhead trunking* Where goods are stored in racks, it is usually desirable to ensure that the lines of lighting coincide with the gangways between racks, but where racks may be moved about this is impossible.

There are many lighting trunking systems which can be suspended over the rack areas, and permit the layout of fittings to be changed as the racks are moved.

24.12 *Lighting on mobile plant* Lights on fork trucks operated by the driver are best for detailed operation, although a lighting scheme is still required for personnel, stocktaking, etc.

Lighting sources

24.13 Two broad categories can be distinguished. Where linear sources are required, fluorescent tubes are the obvious choice, and in most cases the high efficiency types such as white and warm white are good enough.

24.14 In very tall buildings, general diffusing fittings will waste too much light on the upper walls and the most economical solution is likely to be a limited number of high power sources giving narrow beams of light downwards. In these cases, mercury discharge lamps or other point sources with an integral reflector (corresponding to the incandescent reflector spotlight) have been used successfully (but drivers looking up to see 10 m above themselves may find point sources troublesome, if not carefully diffused).

24.15 High pressure mercury lamps give a very bluish light, but they can be obtained with fluorescent envelopes which give a better colour. All the reflector types are colour-corrected in this way. Alternatively, mixed fittings are available in which a mercury discharge lamp and an incandescent lamp are enclosed in one housing: another alternative is the tungsten halogen tubular lamp. High-pressure sodium lamps may also be useful, especially in high racks. Precise guidance as to which of these alternatives is likely to be the best in any given circumstances should be sought from a specialist. 'Kolorarc' and 'Kolorsun' give a much higher lumen output for the same rating and very good colour rendering. They usually save on installation and running costs.

Service routeing

24.16 The path of building services should not affect handling plant and inhibit the use of racking. One architect was taken to court for installing rainwater down pipes on the 'wrong' side of the stanchions through a misunderstanding, making work more difficult for forklifts and reducing the store capacity by a complete rack space at each column position. In another case, a sprinkler main was positioned so that the whole top length of a rack was useless for normal loads, as the tolerance was too tight for the reach truck to lift the pallet in. Service routeing is critical round doors or breaks in the structure. Beware of conflicts with overhead conveyor lines and overhead tracks for stacker cranes, order pickers, and if mobile racking is used.

25 Special services

25.01 Fixed path stacker cranes and order pickers require an electric source, either on a reeled cable or on a busbar system. Machines such as palletisers, shrink wrappers, and diverters for conveyors require compressed air services. Loading bay equipment, eg, banders, binders and nail guns also operate on compressed air. A vacuum source may be needed for certain types of palletiser, and for vacuum tube document carriage systems. Special service routeing should be flexible, as machines are moved to suit changes of the storage pattern.

9 The scuff marks at high level occur where forklifts have scraped by with their forks high to clear the drivers' *vision. Note also the new plates covering badly scored brickwork, marked even before they could be painted.*

26 Building fabric

26.01 The increased use of forklift trucks has reduced in-store product damage by five times; the damage to static storage plant, racking and the building fabric has risen accordingly. Where there are many forklift trucks, crash barriers should be installed to lessen serious damage to the structure and cladding. If a forklift route runs round the perimeter the fabric may be damaged by impact and abrasion. Most damage occurs when forklifts turn out of aisles with their loads in travel position, and when the truck is lifting its load as it places itself to enter the racks. Ground level damage can be reduced if enough clearance is provided in the aisles (using 'swept' turning circle data), and by a hard composition-rubber bumper strip up to 1·5 m high running along susceptible wall surfaces, painted in bright alternating stripes. Columns, door openings and rack ends should also be guarded in this way on movement routes. A sheet cladding material easy to remove and replace will also save later expense. Deeply scored and cracked brickwork produces dust and may let the weather in.

Damage to racking

26.02 Racking is damaged both by impact and abrasion. Most is easy to replace in sections. Vertical and horizontal members are painted in contrasting colours to help drivers to identify and position accurately. Adjustable member-retaining clips prevent horizontal members from being lifted out of place by accident from underneath. (See Information sheet Mechanised storage 1).

26.03 High racks over 10 m in mechanised warehouses offer very large faces to the weather. Consider the effects of differential heating of the south face of the building on structure and plant. Roof-hung stacker cranes or order pickers, or racking with links to roof or wall structure have been known to jam where one face exposed to direct sunlight has expanded, and this has been reflected through movement in the structure. (See also High bay problems in Technical study Automated storage 2 para 26.)

27 Fire control

27.01 Fire control in mechanised warehouses is an increasing problem. Plastics packaging materials and shrink-wrapping, although flame-proofed, have added to the danger to personnel by producing noxious fumes when hot, by spreading the fire,

9

by dripping onto such combustible material as cardboard cases, and by diverting water from sprinklers. Immediate detection is therefore of prime importance. (Fire control in high-bay warehouses will be discussed at length in the section on Automated storage).

27.02 It is likely that insurance companies will insist on sprinklers and break-glass fire alarms in all warehouses in the future, and multi-level sprinklers in buildings over 7·5 m high. It is very important to consult the client's insurers at the sketch design stage, as some large store owners have been forced to pay 35 per cent premiums because corners were cut on fire control.

27.03 The principal aim of a detection system in a warehouse is to catch the fire before it can spread. The fire should be detected quickly, and checked and extinguished in the cell or rack space of origin. The system should be capable of operating those sprinklers needed to achieve this, and the rate of water delivery from the sprinklers must be high enough to ensure success. Install hose reels and hydrant points as well. The system should be robust, simple and easy to reset after a fire. This approach necessitates a separate detection system for each rack bay, capable of operating selected zoned sprinklers. An effective method, developed by the Joint Fire Research Organisation, uses a line detector **10**. This should cost little more than a standard system, owing to reduced water storage and pumping requirements, and possibly lower insurance premiums. (See AJ 30.8.72 p472.)

27.04 Full-scale fire tests have confirmed that solid masses of stock burn with greater intensity as the amount of horizontal channel ways is increased, and as stacks become higher, simulating vertical flues. The speed of fire-spread can be exceptionally fast in high racks. This is serious in pallet racking, since the pallets are exposed to air on all sides **11**. The necessary density of discharge to extinguish the fire is in direct relation to both the stack height and the degree of combustibility of the stock. Smoke is a further problem. Smoke in a food warehouse may taint a large amount of stock; some materials smoulder without activating sprinklers—coffee beans, for example. There are arguments for and against smoke vents in high rack arrangements. One argument against is that it spreads the fire more quickly up the rack. However, it is generally thought preferable to burn out one insured rack and prevent the fire jumping from rack to rack across the underside of the roof owing to great stack pressure and no venting; immediate large-area venting clears the smoke and makes fire-fighting easier. Vents operated by fusible links should operate at 71°C.

27.05 From the user's angle of cubic capacity, intermediate sprinkling is a waste of space. The sprinkler mains are difficult to handle in adjustable racking, virtually reducing adaptability to nil. Some do not like the idea of wet system sprinklers overhead at all, as stock damage from leakage is possible. (This can be insured against.) For these reasons, foams and gases have been considered. It is thought that gas is not effective in a large volume warehouse for long-term extinction. CO_2 has often been mentioned, but this is dangerous to personnel. CO_2 is fatal with 10 per cent in the atmosphere; 28 per cent is often quoted as the level required to extinguish a rack fire. BCF and BTM gases are considered to be the most effective for closed-cell storage.

27.06 The arguments about the use of high-expansion foam continue; experiments with foam have shown that foam generation stirs up the air and so causes better combustion, the foam level chasing the fire up the racking and the flames spreading more quickly than normal from the increased turbulence. A foam installation can be designed to fill one million cubic feet volume in one minute. However, there can still be stock damage through overall dampness, and to ensure extinction, foam has to be topped up every half hour. Unlike water, foam has to be left for some time to ensure that smouldering has been extinguished. Some tests illustrated

that directly the foam deteriorated, some smouldering pallets started to flame again. (See also 6.3.6. Automated stores.) It should be remembered that if the warehouse is artificially lit, emergency lighting off batteries or separate generation will have to be installed. Pedestrian escape routes, often tortuous in warehouses at the best of times, should be especially well indicated and lit.

27.07 The efficiency of ordinary-hazard sprinkler systems may diminish with rack heights over 7·5 m in the three lowest categories of combustible stock, and 4·4 m in the fourth and most hazardous category, unless intermediate sprinkling is provided. The limit for ceiling-based sprinklers is 7·5 m. Intermediate sprinkling is well-advised as it may contain a fire that would otherwise run very fast up the stack. Almost inevitably, it will be necessary to have pump supplies—few town mains can produce 2·3 m³/min at a pressure necessary to maintain the density of discharge at the highest and most remote part of the warehouse. Insurers require two pump sets, one of which must be diesel-driven, and two separate reservoirs. On the basis of a 45-minute discharge, the minimum capacity of a reservoir is liable to be 11 300 litres (112·5 m³). It is suggested that warehouses should be sufficiently heated to ensure that a constantly charged sprinkler system can be used without any risk of freezing. If there is any

10 *Line detector.*
11 *Fire test on high rack storage.*

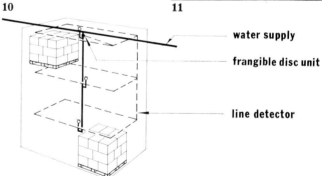

10   11

water supply

frangible disc unit

line detector

doubt about this, the sprinklers should be installed on a wet-and-dry pipe system. However, there is a problem of time-lag; when a system is charged with compressed air, there is bound to be a time-lag of as much as three minutes. Remember that where sprinkler protection is provided only at ceiling or roof level, the requirement is for the design area of sprinkler operation to be increased by 25 per cent, requiring also larger-capacity pumps and reservoirs. The basic fact to remember is that the extra cost of intermediate sprinkling over 4·5 m can be considered well spent in the light of insurance premiums. The insurer and local fire officer should also be contacted early in the design process concerning fire stop walls and zone segregation. The maximum volume without segregation allowed is normally 1080 m³. These can fundamentally alter a warehouse's operation if they have to be installed as an afterthought. Problems have been experienced with providing openings through fire walls large enough for handling plant, for instance between a sortation area and the loading bay. These rules are recommendations; they are negotiable with the insurers and the fire officer.

27.08 Intermediate sprinkling requires a minimum of 150 mm clearance for the sprinkler head above the highest unit load to be effective, but must also be clear to avoid damage from handling plant. This affects volume utilisation. Room must also be allowed for sprinkler down-pipes in the racking. For intermediate systems, sprinkler heads 3·5 m apart in alternate rack positions are considered sufficient for ordinary hazards. The heads should alternate, as fire spreads sideways first, and then rapidly upwards.

27.09 Live storage racking is a major problem, owing to the density of stock. Sprinklers can also be staggered effectively up to six pallets deep, but for greater runs, full individual sprinkling for each channel is required. Drive-in racking has the same problem, but standard intermediate sprinkling, mounted between the cantilever rails, is possible. Mobile racking is difficult for intermediate sprinkling, but swivel joints work effectively.

28 Security

28.01 There are two types of security in mechanised warehouses.
1 Safety for people from machinery;
2 Security of goods from theft.

Safety for people
28.02 The safety aspect of mobile handling plant is largely one of common sense and circulation planning.
To prevent accidents,
1 Avoid blind corners, or give adequate warning.
2 Design carefully against glare.
3 Ensure that mobile racking and fixed-path handling plant has a fail-safe pedestrian cut-out.
4 Guard ramps against accidental misalignment.
5 Guard all sorting plant.
Most safety aspects are covered by the Factory Inspectorate and DOE publications (see Index 1, Bibliography).

Security of goods
28.03 Security from theft is an ever-present problem. In large-scale warehouses, especially where a large order picking staff is employed, losses can be considerable. Most warehouses holding consumer goods lose between 1 and 5 per cent of their stock annually in this way. Shrink-wrapping and modern packaging techniques have not helped. On the whole, a deterrent is more effective than prosecution after the act. Designers can help by placing control points (eg, documentation issue offices) in order-picking areas and traffic offices in load-assembly and incoming check areas, in positions that dominate these zones. Amenity areas and lavatory and wash zones must not be a 'through' route between inside and outside without a measure of supervision. If a policy of spot searches is instigated, which has been proved to work without alienating labour, the search rooms should be carefully designed to give a sense of security so that operatives do not feel harassed. Closed-circuit television is useful for store security, safety and for keeping track of handling plant in extensive rack areas. Television is only as vigilant as the security officer watching the battery of screens. Also care is needed to place cameras where they cannot be damaged by passing handling plant.

External security
28.04 Ensure that forklift and truck parking areas cannot be used as a convenient step-ladder for intruders. A strong boundary fence helps; also avoid placing rainwater down pipes near possible entry positions, running up past flat roofs with roof lights. If an intruder is really determined, it has been shown that he will gain access somehow, and remember that it is thought that the majority of warehouse robberies are 'inside' jobs.

29 External works

29.01 For detailed planning of external areas, see Technical studies Loading 1 and External storage 1. Mechanised storage installations, especially those handling pre-production parts, often require extensive external storage. Many goods are not worth using up valuable space in a building, eg, post pallets of rough castings, and empty stillages. Areas for these should be marked out for block stacking, and should be well-lit for winter, and well-drained; with castings and stillages from a production line, oil interceptors may be required on the drains. British Rail should be contacted for any external works with railway tracks.

30 Structure-based plant

30.01 This includes goods lifts, paternosters, pallet elevator and lowerators, stacker cranes and order-picking machinery.

30.02 *Goods lifts, paternoster lifts and pallet elevators* These were widely used in old multi-storey warehouses, but are now only used for mezzanine handling, for example, when an order-picking area is mounted on top of the rack structure. Goods lifts can be made flame-proof with electro-hydraulic and pneumatic controls for dangerous areas, eg, where there are chemicals or paints. Some goods lifts, for use where head room is at a premium, have a fully hydraulic motion from a ram under the base of the platform. Scissor lifts can be effective for single-stage lifts and need no shaft or counter weights. Some can lift a maximum weight vehicle; large scissor lifts are often used for difficult level changes between new and existing buildings, where a ramp would be too space consuming. The scissor lift should have a safety 'skirt' and guarded sides.

12 *Manually operated vacuum palletiser.*   **13** *Free-path order picker.*

30.03 *Pallet elevators.* These have continuous action and integrate well with accumulation conveyors. They work on the paternoster principle, but return to the thickness of a belt on the return side. A typical use is from a mezzanine order-picking area, with pallets being moved automatically down the lowerator, through a shrink-wrap tunnel, and then on to the load assembly position to be palletised **12**. (A lift or elevating device will cause a circulation constriction here.)

Mobile structure-based plant

30.04 *Fixed path, manually controlled stacker cranes and order pickers.* These are floor, rack or roof supported, depending on type of machinery or rack chosen. The effects of acceleration and deceleration on structure, floor and racking should be considered. Double reinforcement of the slab is sometimes necessary against 'rippling', especially where heavy stackers impose 'hunting' loads. Fixed path plant must be removed for major repairs, either along cross tracks to the maintenance bay or by a conventional gantry crane. A gantry crane in the sorting area is also useful for handling parts of shrink-wrap machines, palletisers etc; a one-ton lift is normally enough for general purposes, but before lifting out stacker cranes, check with the manufacturers first.

31 Mobile plant

31.01 This includes plant for lifting and plant for horizontal travel. All mobile plant should be considered as an integral part of the storage system, as the turning and lifting characteristics affect the positioning and height of the racking.

Lifting plant

31.02 Typical sizes, turning circles, weights and applications of forklift trucks **15** are given in Information sheet Mechanised storage 3. Reach trucks are basically the same as forklifts, but designed specifically for narrow-aisle operation **14**. Whereas forklifts are designed for both inside and outside, on a variety of surfaces, reach trucks are designed for operation in racks on flat floors. There is a wide range of accessories and fittings (see Information sheet Mechanised storage 3). To save stacker and reach truck drivers from spending time reversing, several manufacturers have placed the operator at 90° to the direction of travel. The logical development from reach trucks, for higher, narrower aisles was the turret truck. In some makes, the operator still has to sit at ground level and crane his neck, but he is aided by push-button rack height selection. Other makes allow the operator to rise with the fork carriage.

15 *4500 kg capacity forklift working in assembly plant buffer store.*

Horizontal travel plant

31.03 Horizontal-movement vehicles include tractor-drawn trains, overhead and ground-based conveyors and towline trucks. Forklift trucks are not considered economic for horizontal transport over distances of 70 to 80 m; they are designed primarily as stacking machinery. If goods are small and unpalletised, conveyors are useful: if unit loads are to be handled, towline trucks or tractor trains are effective.

31.04 *Conveyors* have been described in Technical study Mechanised storage 1 para 18. There are many speeds, and special surface textures for slopes and accumulation. If roller conveyors are involved, check that roller pitch is correct for the product handled, especially on bends **16, 17**. Linear induction, motor-powered conveyors with very low maintenance costs and trouble-free, high speeds (see Information sheet Mechanised storage 9) are being developed. Plate conveyors perform a similar function to tow trains. Capable of running flush with the floor surface, and of tight loops and turns, these conveyors are useful in sorting and dispatch accumulation areas, for instance, in parcel grouping. Plate conveyors are

14 *Reach truck.*

16 *Accumulation conveyor.*

17 *Manual packaging with overhead conveyor.*

slow, but can be strong enough to be crossed by forklifts. Plate conveyors can be routed round any number of loops and picking positions, but their length is limited by the required speed of the package.

31.05 *Towline truck systems* are similar in theory of operation to plate conveyors, with the added benefit of automatic routeing, queueing, and sidings for temporary holding. These trucks can be drawn from a drag chain in the floor (or a cable), or from an overhead conveyor system. The same barrows can be used for order-picking, transport to the packing area, or returning goods and empty pallets to the storage area. Direction is gained by simple pin codes on the trollies. Parked barrows may block loading bay and goods assembly areas if these are not carefully planned keeping in mind other plant and that as the barrows are dragged by a pin at the front, they cut in on corners. Clearance should be left for personnel to pass safely, especially where there is cut-in near stanchions or in two-way tracks. However, a towline may act as a useful buffer during meal-breaks, and can accumulate empty barrows and carry them round until required. (See Information sheet Mechanised storage 8.)

18 *Tow tractor pulling roll pallets to sorting area.*

19 *Heavy duty tow tractor.*

31.06 *Tractor trailer trains* are most economic for long distances, eg, between pre-production parts store and production line in a large factory **18, 19**. Electric and internal combustion tractors are available, which are capable of towing trains of up to 10 tonnes at speeds of 24 kph. Above this weight, special

industrial tractors can take gradients of 1 in 10, and some versions can be used externally or in fireproof areas. Tractor trains are much faster than towlines. The former tend to steer on a close radius with little cut-in, owing to the castor action or steering on the trailers. Greater clearance is needed with two-way operation, as trailers have been known to 'hunt' at speed. If any internal combustion tractors are used in store, this must be taken into account when planning extraction.

32 Integration of building and plant

See paras 26, 30 and 31. Integration of building and plant is considered in detail in Technical study Automated storage para 32. Warehouses must be built for change; planned life spans continue to get shorter.

33 Maintenance

33.01 Building maintenance in mechanised warehouses should be kept to a minimum. Low-maintenance materials help, but maintenance is also required for the impact, abrasion and vibration caused by handling plant. There is a direct correlation between structural damage by mobile handling machinery and the productivity bonus incentives offered to operatives. For example, in one large warehouse operatives carry roll pallets two at a time on a rider pallet truck to the assembly area. To get a higher bonus, they all manage to secure a third roll pallet with one hand and a knee, and occasionally a fourth one. Not surprisingly, racking and roll pallets are often damaged. The designers must mount bumper bars and guards on the structure and rack ends, and ensure that main circulation routes do not coincide with unprotected columns or cladding. The sight of deeply gouged and cracked brickwork and scratched forklift trucks is common. At what point does maintenance cost outweigh gain from increased productivity? **33.02** In a 'big box' type of warehouse, roof-slung heating and ventilation plant, lighting and sprinkler lines all need access for maintenance. Deep roof trusses allow catwalks, which, if positioned near the tops of the racks, can also be used for lighting and sprinkler repairs. Free-path order picking plant can be used for general maintenance as long as the correct guards and fail-safe devices are fitted. To keep a warehouse running smoothly, good housekeeping is important. Mobile ride-on sweepers and floor cleaners should be provided. These run on batteries similar to a forklift or are powered by LPG. A rubbish compactor can be very useful in the loading bay area where baled waste is put into a skip. (See Information sheet Loading 3.) With the use of integrally coloured cladding internally, a waiver can be obtained against the frequent

20 *Mobile sweeper.*

repainting often required by the Local Authority.
33.03 The external appearance of large warehouses may act as beneficial publicity for their operators, but can also have the reverse effect if unsuitably treated. Sheet steel insulated panels are not only easily replaceable after impact damage.

but can be integrally faced with a coloured plastic finish.

Lighting maintenance

33.04 For maintenance, access from above by walkway or from below by mobile platform is essential. Turret trucks and freepath order pickers can sometimes be used for this function, but consult the Factory Inspectorate, as there are regulations concerning special guards and fail-safe devices. Every effort should be made to encourage the maintenance of good reflecting surfaces.

33.05 Where access for lamp replacement is difficult, ordinary incandescent lamps are unlikely to be economical, despite their small size and low initial cost. This is because their life at 1000 hours is much less than that of the other sources available. Discharge lamps, including fluorescent tubes, have lives from 2500 hours to 7500 hours.

34 Management

34.01 The continued operation of the project team during commissioning is of prime importance: see Introduction.

35 Personnel accommodation

35.01 The number of personnel in a mechanised warehouse is falling. However, small goods order picking requires more personnel. Most members of the staff of a mechanised warehouse are highly skilled, either as order pickers or turret truck drivers. The environment of tall racks is not pleasant, and some form of amenity accommodation should be provided. Companies with order-picking staff have found that order picking productivity has been improved by high airy spaces and by the inclusion of windows in one of the walls. This is for visual relief from the picking face and so that weather conditions can be seen; industrial psychologists say that this is a basic psychological need.

Office accommodation

35.02 With computer-operated stock control, documentation can be minimised. Therefore office accommodation is not likely to grow as fast as storage; check carefully the number of clerical personnel needed and what documentation systems imply, considering future expansion, a change towards automation, and a different distribution pattern **21**. One of the

21 'Big Box' warehouse showing adjoining office accommodation.

present drawbacks with computer operation is the growth of white-collar staff to process the software. As offices tend to be placed on a perimeter so as not to encroach on valuable storage volume, the office should be insulated against noise, vibration, fumes and dirt from heavy traffic passing nearby on its way to and from loading bay and assembly areas. Other offices required are the traffic manager's, which should have optimum visual range, and those for non-management staff such as shop foremen, shift foremen, shop stewards and security staff. These offices are best located where foremen have most contact with the staff they supervise, but, in large installations, should be equipped with a document link to the main office.

36 Amenities

36.01 Heated locker and changing rooms should be provided for operatives. They should be able to dry wet clothes and store personal effects securely. Many large warehouses that operate smoothly have strategically placed beverage machines so that forklift truck drivers can stop for a quick drink when they like as long as they fulfil their quota of work. This usually operates with a bonus scheme. If management prefer set tea-break periods, then an amenity area away from the racks should be provided, which can also be used by the order-picking and loading bay staff. In this case, parking for mobile handling machinery is necessary. The Factories Act demands a room for operatives' meals segregated from the storage zone. Smoking is obviously forbidden in the warehouse, so the amenity room is useful for this also.

36.02 Lavatory and washing accommodation should be separately provided for warehouse staff and lorry drivers, as joint access can lead to valuable stock 'walking out'. If order-picking staff are involved, accommodation for women and clerical staff should also be provided and some managements insist on segregating clerical staff washrooms from those for general personnel.

37 Personnel safety

37.01 Personnel safety precautions are very important. There is a great deal of fast-moving machinery and heavy weights are being raised and lowered. Unit loads are often unstable when delivered, so space should be allocated in the incoming check area for repacking; this is also useful for changing broken or non-standard pallets before storing.

37.02 Accidents are inevitable. A first-aid room with equipment for handling broken bones, fractures, electrocution and crush injuries should be provided in the amenity zone. If possible, the first-aid room should be near to a loading bay that can take an ambulance. This room should be equipped with 600 lux lighting, hot and cold running water, and a high level of ventilation; in one installation, air inlets were positioned over lorry-parking areas and sucked in diesel fumes.

37.03 All ramps, catwalks and pedestrian routes shared with mobile plant should have a strong dividing rail in a bright colour, and floor markings. If blind corners are inevitable, a carefully placed mirror can be useful, but beware of glare, and consider load tolerances and fork lift mast heights, as they tend to lift on the move.

37.04 Security against theft has been discussed in para 28. For bonded goods, such as spirits, highly sophisticated security systems are available. (See AJ Handbook Building services and circulation: section 13.)

38 Circulation and parking

38.01 There are several traffic systems to be considered, some of which conflict:
1 External heavy vehicles.
2 External light goods traffic.
3 External passenger traffic.
4 External pedestrian circulation.
5 External inter-store transport.
6 Internal main storage traffic; input.
7 Internal main traffic; output.
8 Internal sub-systems.
9 Internal pedestrian routes.
All these have to work together to be successful, but safety must not be sacrificed for expediency.
1 and 2 have been discussed in Technical study Mechanised storage 1 para 4. External passenger traffic is directly related to office and warehouse staff numbers, and ideally should be segregated from heavy traffic. Some visitors' parking should also be provided since maintenance staff and suppliers often

require access to the premises. If a shift system is operated, extra space as a parking buffer is required. Warehouse personnel parking should not be in a position where staff can shift goods into their vehicles unseen. Also consider office and warehouse expansion.

38.02 External pedestrian routeing should be segregated from heavy traffic, since heavy lorries have blind spots in rearward vision, and pedestrians can be hidden until too late by parked vans. If pedestrians have to use the same gate, a heavy duty crush barrier, painted in 'dayglow', should be erected between the routes.

38.03 Internal routes depend on the type of plant and the store arrangement. For block stacking, the theoretically ideal route is a 'cartwheel' **22**. Routes should therefore be as direct as possible. With racking, the installation may be large enough to require primary and distributor routes before reaching the aisles. Treat this circulation as a normal road system with priorities and passing clearances. If towline trucks or conveyors are used, the cross routes with other plant must be carefully planned. Towcarts are slow-moving, and if the circuit is busy it is often difficult for a forklift to get across; an interruptor can be fitted, so that a forklift driver can make his own gap. Pedestrian escape routes must be especially carefully handled, as unrestricted egress is essential. These routes should be clearly identifiable with illuminated wall signs and floor markings. Zebra crossings should be marked where escape routes cross principal, internal circulation routes.

38.04 If vehicle routes are needed to an external area, impact-opening hard rubber doors are cheap and effective in reducing draughts and providing weather protection. Some operators prefer a more expensive type of door that slides under pneumatic control, activated from compression pads **23**. If there is two-way traffic through the doors, it is advisable to fit a warning system, and separate pedestrian access should be provided. Compression pads that give adequate warning by light and siren to any approaching vehicles or personnel can be placed at an adequate distance calculated from the average operating speed. If there is frequent use, a hot air curtain may be required to prevent intense local heat loss; check the orientation of the door to the area's prevailing wind. A drain grating to squeeze water from forklift tyres is advantageous, saving on floor wear and lessening chance of skidding. Where a large number of order-picking staff are involved, the personnel should be segregated from the main plant routes. If their routes to the amenity and lavatory areas have to pass through the active zone, the path should be clearly marked and protected where possible.

22 *Block stacking of eight different varieties of goods (numbered 1 to 8) by 'cartwheel' method. All goods are unloaded into central area; forklifts can then move radially, taking the shortest possible distance from centre to each block stack.*
23 *Door zone for high throughput. Plan **a** and section **b** show major forklift or tractor train route out. If impact doors are used, omit opening pads. Dimension **a** = time lag required to operate doors × speed of plant in m/sec. Dimension **b** = number of seconds warning × average speed of plant in m/sec.*

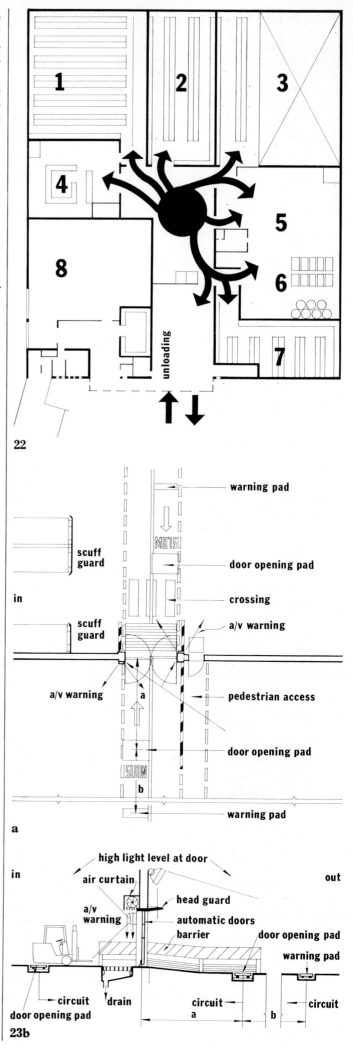

Information sheet Mechanised storage 1

Racking

Racking is the most important storage element in a warehouse. This sheet describes types of free-standing racking—adjustable, static, live and mobile. Structural racking is discussed in Section 6 Automated storage.

1 Introduction

1.01 Racking can be structural or free-standing. Structural racking is an engineering problem, and because it forms a rigid chassis for the building fabric and handling equipment, it cannot be adaptable. (See Section 6 Automated storage).

Free standing racking
1.02 Before choosing the type of racking, consider:
● The crushability of the goods. If live racking is required, will braking be needed?
● Whether goods will be palletised or cartons loaded directly onto shelves (see tables III and IV)
● The loadings involved
● The required rate of stock rotation. If the goods are crushable, and a rotation more suited to block-stacking is

1 *Simple shelving.*

Table I Mechanical handling

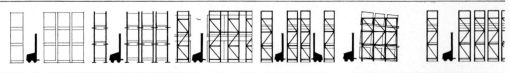

	Block stacking	Post pallets	Drive-in racking	Beam pallet racking	Gravity live storage	Powered mobile racking
Cubic space utilisation %	100	90	65	35-50	80	80
Effective use of installation capacity %	75	75	75	100	70	100
Accessibility of unit load %	10	10	30	100	30	100
Order picking %	1	30	30	100	30	100
Speed of throughput	Fastest	Good	Poor	Good	Good	Quite good
Load crushing	Bad	Nil	Nil	Nil	Some	Nil
Stability of load	Poor	Fair	Good	Good	Fair	Good
Ease of relocation	Not applicable	Not applicable	Fair	Good	Difficult	Difficult
Speed of installation	Not applicable	Not applicable	Good	Fastest	Fair	Slowest
Rotation of stock	Poor	Poor	Poor	Good	Excellent	Good

Table II Manual handling

	Long span shelving	Tiered shelving	Raised storage area	Cantilever shelving	Lightweight live storage	Fir tree racking
Cubic space utilisation %	45	45	80	50	65	25
Effective use in installation capacity %	95	95	50	100	70	70
Accessibility of goods	Good	Good	Poor	Good	Excellent	Good
Ease of relocation	Good	Fair	Difficult	Fair	Very difficult	Best
Load range kN/m²	2-9·5	2-9·5	2·8-11	2-4·7	Up to 0·2 kN per m run of track	2·6-4·4 kN per arm
Speed of picking	Good	Fair	Poor	Good	Very good	Good
Speed of installation	Very good	Good	Fair	Fair	Slowest	Fastest
Rotation of stock	Very good	Good	Poor	Very good	Excellent	Very good

Table III Load mounting

Load mounting	Type of load Heavy unstable load	Flat cards/ sheets	Sacked/ bagged loads	Small unit loads	Drums Reels Barrels	Coils	Casks	Bales	Textile Raw materials
Special cradle with/ without pallet	*								
Standard pallet		*	*	*	*	*	*	*	
Flat board pallet + decking supports		*	*			*		*	
Direct mounting on timber panels		*	*	*		*	*	*	*
Drum supports					*				
Post pallets—cage/bin			*	*		*	*		*
Coil supports					*	*			
Skips/skeps with skids									*

Table IV Classification of materials for handling and storage as unit loads

Description	Examples	Storage method	Description	Examples	Storage method
Materials not strong enough to withstand crushing—not suitable for unit loads	Automobile components, made-up textiles, electrical appliance components, manufacturing chemists' sundries, light engineering products, glassware	On pallet in rack	Large irregular loose materials	Moulded plastics; sheet metal pressings	On post pallets and stacked
			Small irregular loose materials	Machined and moulded parts, pressings, forgings	In cage pallets and stacked
Materials strong enough to withstand crushing—suitable for unit loads	Casks and drums, sawn and machined timber, sheet materials	On pallet, or self-palletised and block stowed	Materials hot from production processes	Castings and forgings	On post pallets and stacked
Irregular shaped materials, strong in themselves suitably packed into unit loads	Goods in cases, crates or cartons	On post pallets and stacked, on pallets in rack or self-palletised	Materials too long to be handled other than by side loader or boom	Steel sections, tubes, timber	Horizontally in tube or bar racks
Bagged materials which form a flat surface under load	Grain, powder, and similar	On pallet and block stowed	Materials strong enough to withstand crushing but subject to damage	Partly machined automotive parts, painted finished materials, books	Steel box pallets with special partitions
Bagged materials which do not form a flat surface under load or will not take pressure	Forgings, moulded or machined parts, nuts and bolts	On pallet in rack	Perishable goods	Frozen meat, vegetables, drink	Cartons, soft packs pallets, box pallets etc

predicted, drive-in racking should be installed
● Degree of accessibility required
● Volume of building available to the volume of goods
● The amount of order picking. Certain types of racking are better suited for this
● Is racking needed at all? Could post pallets be block-stacked to achieve the same throughout for less cost? For example, if the goods must be highly accessible and have a high turnover, live racking may be required. Or, a large volume of goods stored in a tight area, which must also be highly accessible may require mobile racking. (See Technical study Mechanised storage 1, paras 13 and 16).
1.03 Tables I and II compare different types of racking.

Shelving
1.04 Static or adjustable **1**. Available with steel aluminium or timber frames. See Information sheet Manual storage 2.

2 Standard adjustable racking or shelving

Shelving
2.01 This is suitable for light and medium duty work. Mostly used as shelving, adjustable units can be assembled rapidly and adapt to change and expansion. Each shelf can be adjusted independently; used efficiently, this allows the storage space to be used to the full. Most adjustable shelving can be altered without tools. Many companies buy adjustable racking and never use this potential; the additional investment must be justified.

Slotted angle
2.02 This is popular in smaller installations and in factory stores. Built from rolled steel angle, with slots cut into it **2**, any rack size or shape can be quickly bolted together. This Meccano-like system is very adaptable, and inexpensive.

3 Pallet racking

Tubular racking
3.01 Early installations often employed tubing with 19 to 51 mm bores. These were adjustable along rack lengths but not for individual positions. The basic construction is much like scaffolding **3**.

Boltless, adjustable pallet racking
3.02 The most widely used form of racking today **4, 5**. The choice of the racking is closely linked with the choice of pallet, or chance of pallet size being sent in by suppliers, as shown in table III. The size and weight of pallet or stillage determines whether double pallet-spacing can be allowed. (See Information sheet Mechanised storage 2.)

Tolerances and clearances
3.03 Two-way entry pallets require 75 mm minimum overhang at the front and rear of the rack. Four-way pallets require special consideration; with non-reversible four-way pallets, the corner blocks must be positioned directly over the supporting beams, otherwise the pallets may be damaged. With this type, corner blocks are often too small to ensure safe pallet location. If post/skid pallets are used, the support legs should be directly over supporting beams. Cartons or skips should also overhang 75 mm front and rear.
3.04 The following clearances are required to permit easy location and retrieval of pallets:
1 Lateral spacing. Allow 50 to 80 mm between adjacent pallets and between outermost pallets and vertical members.
2 Vertical clearance. Allow 50 to 80 mm measured from top of load to underside of support beam at next level.

2 Slotted angle.

3 Tubular racking.

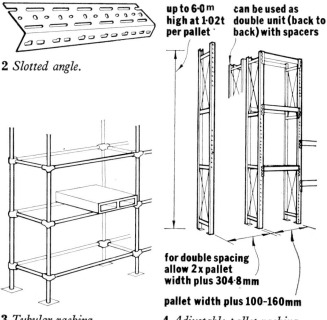

up to 6·0 m high at 1·02t per pallet

can be used as double unit (back to back) with spacers

for double spacing allow 2 x pallet width plus 304·8mm

pallet width plus 100-160mm

4 Adjustable pallet racking.

5 Adjustable pallet racking in use.

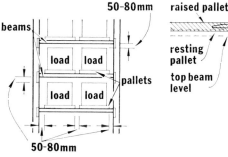

beams
50-80mm
load load
load load
pallets
50-80mm

6 Pallet clearances.

raised pallet
required reach height
resting pallet
top beam level

7 Forklift position in top rack.

Table V Types of standard pallet racking

Trade name	Series 88	Major Rack	Boltless systems	Speedlock	Gripsafe	Intastruc	Structorak	Beamlock
Method of fixing beam to upright								
Profile of upright								
Maximum capacity of frames with beams at 1·5 m centres. Kg	(Type 288) 14 000	11 300	9500 to 17 600	9000 to 16 300	12 000 & 16 000	16 000	3100 (type M65)	10 800
Accessories	Skid supports, wall ties, fork spacers, supports, cradles, foot plates, drop-in decks, drive-in arms, back ties.	Mobile bases, post pallet skid channels, barrel chocks, coil support bars.	Drum supports, coil supports, row/wall spacers, skid support, drive-in racking arms, decking supports, lightweight shelving, fork spacer.	Post pallet and skid channels, fork entry pallet and coil support bars, barrel chocks, shelf panels, rack protection guard, truck guide rails, pallet pick-up and set-down stations, portal system for high rise applications.	Drum chocks, foot supports, shelf panels, fork spacers, pallet back stops, aisle ties, coil chocks.	Back stops, top ties, row spacers, safety panels, supports, slats, spacer bars, drum chocks, coil cradles.	Fork spacers, flush pallet supports, skid channels, drum cradles, drive-in arms, drum or coil supports, row spacers, wall ties.	All
Supplier	Acrow (Automation) Ltd	Bar Productions	Boltless Systems	Dexion Ltd	Finspa Engineering Ltd	Integrated Handling Ltd	PLC Engineer Co Ltd	Steel Equipment Ltd

3.05 When the full lift height of a forklift truck is to be used, ensure that the true required height of lift is calculated **7**. The required height for the topmost row of pallets is from floor level to loaded pallet platform, when the pallet is raised sufficiently to permit easy withdrawal, accounting for the depth of pallet stringers and clearance. This may well be 150 to 180 mm above the level of the topmost beam. (See Information sheet Mechanised storage 3, concerning free lift masts.)

3.06 Several racking manufacturers paint vertical and horizontal members in contrasting colours to help forklift drivers locate levels accurately; this should reduce racking damage. With high lift racking using turret trucks, guides are placed at the base to keep trucks in line.

3.07 Modern modular adaptable racking systems can be tailored precisely to the varying load conditions within a structure and are able to extend in the vertical and horizontal planes **8**. Economically modular racking is best, as the base unit takes the most weight; savings can be achieved by using different steel section for the frames to take the weight of various components. The frame looks the same throughout its height, but the steel is of different sections.

One example, Boltless Systems frames, are self-stacking and can be joined in heights up to 18·23 m. Several strengths of frame are employed for each frame size, so that tie structural level can be maintained to the corresponding load requirement, ensuring the right size of component for the job. Bearer beams are supplied in a range of lengths and capacities to suit the load. Typical fixing is a pair of connectors that lock positively into vertical members, with a lock to prevent accidental lifting out by forklift trucks **9 a b.**

3.08 Pallet racking has become a standard product. Many similar systems provide a racking system that is easy to erect and adaptable (see Table V). At present standard data is not

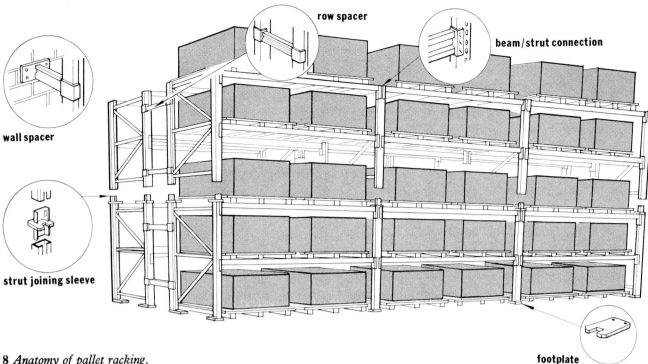

wall spacer

strut joining sleeve

row spacer

beam/strut connection

footplate

8 *Anatomy of pallet racking.*

produced by the racking manufacturers, so that designers find it difficult to compare safety, strength and adaptability. The Storage and Equipment Manufacturers Association (SEMA) is working on standards for these specifications.

3.09 The vertical spacing of the beams affects the loading capacity of the end-frames. The wider the spacing, the lower the frame-loading capacity. When calculating load potential, consider the distribution of the load over the whole racking structure. There should be a uniform load distribution throughout the rack. Always consult the racking manufacturers about working stresses **11**.

3.10 The choice of method of clipping horizontal bearers to vertical frames is important. Accidental displacement by handling plant must be prevented while retaining adaptability. Various interlocks are offered by the racking manufacturers. There is controversy about whether frames should be bolted or welded. Manufacturers who still use bolted construction do so to simplify transport and make replacement easier. It is claimed that bolting is as safe as welding.

3.11 The important design parameters are the yield strength of the members and their ultimate tensile

strength. Beam-loading figures incorporate a 2:1 safety factor, based on collapse or deflection, whichever is the greater. With hot-rolled steel frames, a safety factor of 1·65:1 is used. With cold-rolled frames, the safe load is calculated on 0·2 per cent of the proof stress. Some manufacturers quote a 3:1 ultimate safety factor; this does not hold to the point where the racks begin to deteriorate.

3.12 Most manufacturers recommend a height/depth ratio of 6:1 for free-standing racking; over this height, racking should be bolted to the floor. If they are bolted, the floor finish need not be so precisely laid. Point loads from the vertical members must be within the limits of the floor.

3.13 Special purpose bearer beams for drums, coils or skid-mounted cartons can be supplied **12**. Drive-in racking has double-sided cross frames, with stronger central bracing and skid plates welded or bolted to the frames instead of the conventional bearers **10**. The pallet rests on its edge on the skid; this enables pallets to be stacked several deep. Pallet racks are available for two-deep pallet storage; the forklift is equipped with pantograph fork carriage. (See Information sheet Mechanised storage 3.)

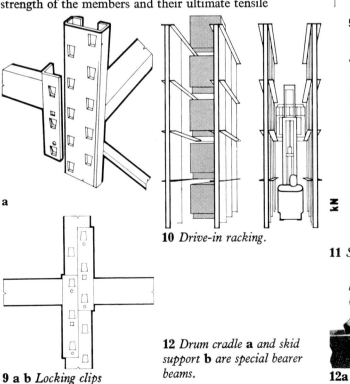

a

10 *Drive-in racking.*

9 a b *Locking clips*

12 *Drum cradle **a** and skid support **b** are special bearer beams.*

11 *Shelf beam loading graph (per pair of beams).*

12a

b

4 Special racking

4.01 This includes fir tree racks for steel coils, racks for plate glass **13**, long racks for rolled fabrics and carpets **16**, and drum racking or cantilever bearers for tubes or sheet materials. Special racking should be matched to the characteristics of the product to be stored **14, 15**. Most of these applications are one-off jobs, tailored to a particular product. Careful studies should be made of how the handling plant, also requiring special attachments, will interact with the racking. One installation handling steel coils employs a gantry slung stacker crane, incorporating 360° rotation for the coil bearer. At the tip of the crane's bearer is a closed-circuit tv camera, so that the operator can position accurately and quickly. The racking here is interesting too, as to gain maximum use of volume, the bearers for the coils are staggered. (See Section 9 Special storage, Steel stockholding.)

13

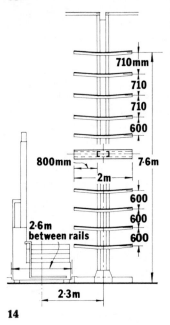

14

13 *Special rack for glass.*
14 *Typical fir tree racking for high-lift narrow-aisle sideloader.*
15 *Fir tree racking is suitable for long narrow objects.*
16 *Racking for rolled fabrics made up from standard units.*

15

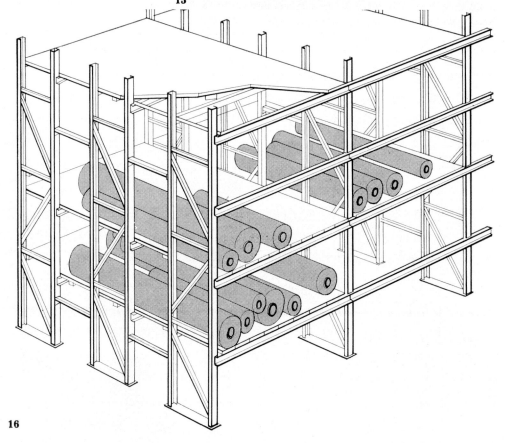

16

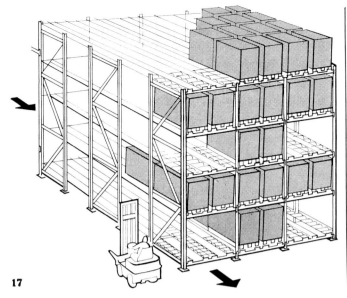

17

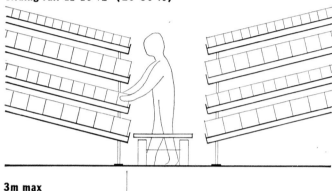

sliding rail 11-16$\frac{1}{2}$° (20-30%)

3m max

a

wheeled rail picking 2-3$\frac{1}{2}$° (3-6%)

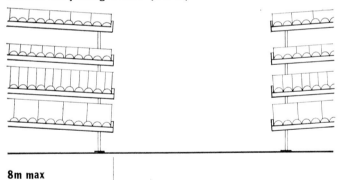

8m max

over 4m guides usually needed

b

18ab

19

5 Live racking

5.01 See Technical study Mechanised storage 1, paras 13 and 16.

Gravity live racking

5.02 The lateral and vertical tolerances apply as in adjustable pallet racking. Wheels are used for light loads, and rollers for the heavier units **17, 18**. A fall of 1 in 75 has been found to operate effectively for gravity storage but trial and error is often the best way to achieve the correct gradient. Drums simply roll down guides. The high capital and maintenance costs can be justified with high stock throughput and first-in-first-out applications. For pallet loads, braking should be specified; the shock of each pallet moving down the tracks may cause instability and a fouled pallet load is difficult and time-consuming to extricate. Braking should be specified for weights above 50 kg; lightweight centrifugal brakes are available. For full pallet loads, use powered live storage, so that heavy loads can be completely controlled. Greater speeds of throughput are possible if the load is completely stable.

5.03 Powered live racking uses roller chains, with location dogs, widely spaced slats to coincide with pallet dimensions, and powered rollers to carry goods. Powered live storage racks can cost more than £50 per pallet position. Transporter systems can also be used in this way. (See Technical study Automated storage 2 para 31 and Information sheet Automated storage 2.)

6 Mobile racking

Manual mobile racking

6.01 Manually operated mobile shelving and racking has long been popular in spares stores, libraries, and stores for a wide range of cartoned stock requiring 100 per cent selectivity **20, 21.**

6.02 Two systems are available; the most popular moves face-to-face and parallel **21ab**; the other slides laterally, offering more picking faces simultaneously. A man can push four units loaded with 900 kg without difficulty. Some manufacturers offer adjustable shelving in steel or timber, mounted on a mobile carriage; others manufacture integrally based shelving, specially designed for mobile use.

6.03 There is some controversy about the fire risk of mobile shelving. One manufacturer considers that there is less fire risk with timber construction, as fire would be localised; steel shelving would transmit heat, causing spontaneous combustion, and could buckle, stopping rack movement and so preventing firemen reaching the seat of the fire in time to gain control. Intermediate-level sprinkling is possible in mobile shelving and racks, using a jointed supply main.

Power-operated racking

6.04 Manual racking is limited by a maximum 6-8 tonne loading. Power-operated racking overcomes this and ensures that the racks move together. Lighter manually operated racking caused operators to become impatient, and to push eccentrically, moving the racks off their tracks and jamming them. Mobile racking is basically adjustable pallet racking on a powered base (see table VI), and the same tolerances and pallet clearances apply (see **3.03** to **3.05**). These racks allow compact storage and 100 per cent selectivity, once the aisle is opened. The controls can be place at a height for operation by forklift drivers (approximately 1·6m). Racks

17 *Gravity live racking for full pallets.*
18ab *Manual picking from live racking.*
19 *Foot-operated brake release on manual carton dispenser.*

are moved by cable and dog clutches; when a lever is pressed, the rack on which it is mounted and all those behind it moves, opening a space for the forklift to enter. One system, 'Cubestore', is operated hydraulically by vertically mounted cylinders driving bars buried in floor tracks via cables **23**. The bars lock onto a selected rack, and the cylinder action allows the drive bars to return automatically to move the next rack. If the cable snaps, the whole system stops. To eliminate this, individual rack power (electric or pneumatic) is offered by some manufacturers. Typical horse-power requirements to overcome initial inertia are $\frac{1}{8}$ hp for 8 to 10 tonne loads and 10 hp for 1000 tonne loads.

6.05 Safety devices are usually in the form of kick bars, at floor or breast height, that immediately cut all power when depressed. Photoelectric sensors and interlocks are used for heavier installations. In case of power cuts, even heavy racks can be manually handled without much effort.

6.06 Check that foundation and floor finish are suitable for mobile racking. The stresses are different, as some racks are loaded more heavily than others. Floor dusting has occurred adjacent to rails and channels. The surface finish should accept vibration. Epoxy finishes are sufficiently flexible for this.

20a

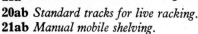

b

b

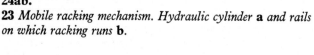

21a   b

22

20ab *Standard tracks for live racking.*
21ab *Manual mobile shelving.*
22 *In many cases, nearly as much space can be gained by using narrow aisles and high lift machines as by more expensive mobile racking and general purpose reach trucks. Compare with* **24ab.**
23 *Mobile racking mechanism. Hydraulic cylinder* **a** *and rails on which racking runs* **b**.

b

6.07 A typical operating time cycle is a rack-opening speed of 76·2 mm/sec with stacking aisle width of 2·743 m to accept a 1800 kg capacity forklift truck, plus load; it would therefore take 36 seconds to open the aisle fully, although the machine could start to move before **24**. Radio control can decrease this time lag; a central controller opens the appropriate aisle and directs the forklift driver to the rack bay, so that aisles are always open by the time the forklift arrives. A possible future development, providing high volume utility and automated storage, would be the use of a wire-guided free-path stacker working in 12 m-high mobile racking. This could also operate with a gantry-slung stacker crane.

6.08 Combined storage and order-picking on an upper level of mobile racking has been operated successfully in a warehouse handling light fittings **25**. Order-picking from free-path, elevating cab machines is also possible with mobile racking; one installation uses custom-built machines with elevating cabs, and rotating masts to pick from either side. This last feature reduces rack movement and could be calculated for maximum picker efficiency by the stock control computer.

24 *In* **a**, *rack opening mechanism is operated, causing racks to open* **b**.

Table VI Comparison of powered mobile racking with other systems

	Block stacking	Post pallets	Drive-in racking	Beam pallet racking	Gravity live storage	Mobile racking
Cubic space utilisation*	100%	90%	65%	35%-50%	80%	80%
Effective use of installation	75%	75%	75%	100%	70%	100%
Accessibility of load	10%	10%	30%	100%	30%	100%
Order picking	1%	30%	30%	100%	30%	100%
Load crushing	Bad	Nil	Nil	Nil	Some	Nil
Stability of load	Poor	Fair	Good	Good	Fair	Good
Ease of store relocation	n/a	n/a	Fair	Good	Difficult	Difficult
Cost per unit stored including pallets (1970)	£2 per tonne pallet	£12 per tonne unit	£8 per tonne pallet	£6 per tonne pallet	£18 per ½ tonne unit	£18 per 1 tonne pallet
Speed of installation	n/a	n/a	Good	Fastest	Fair	Slowest

* Access gangway area is not included, but working gangways are.

25 *Back-up stock is placed below, and order picking above on mezzanine. Forklifts either transfer loads between levels, or replenish loads in adjacent racks.*

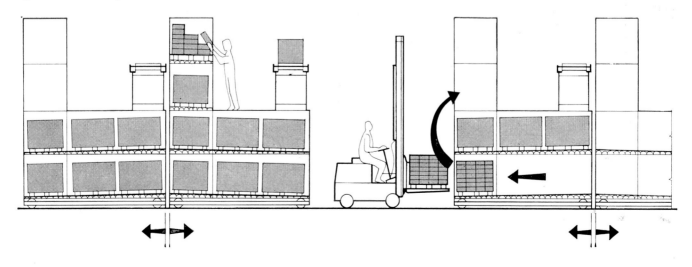

26

26 *Macy's San Bruno distribution building, San Francisco, showing full-width loading bay.*

27 *Note combination of display on the warehouse floor and order picking racking in the background, with a tow cart system. The wide spans and height make this building flexible for future development.*

27

Information sheet Mechanised storage 2

Pallets

The pallet is universally recognised as the basis for unit loads. This sheet gives dimensions, types, materials of pallets, and pallet converters, post and roll pallets.

1 Pallet types

1.01 A pallet is a portable platform, with or without superstructure, for assembling a quantity of goods to form a unit load for handling and storage by mechanical appliances **3**. It consists of a deck on bearers constructed for transport and stacking and with the overall height reduced to a minimum which can be handled by forklift and pallet trucks. It was thought that unit loads would dispense with pallets, especially with shrink wrap and banding techniques, but this has not happened, as the pallet gives stability, and is quicker to handle than 'squashy' cardboard wraps; indeed, the number of pallets is constantly rising.

1.02 The two basic types of pallet are the two-way entry and four-way entry timber pallets **2ab**. In both, decks can be single- or double-sided, ie reversible. Low profile versions popular in the USA are available in both, with heights of $2\frac{5}{8}$in (66·7) or 3in (76.2) depending on whether single or double ply top boards are used **21**. With 6-high stacking 1ft³ (0·03 m³) is claimed to be saved for every ft² (0·09 m²) of floor area. But handling low profile pallets calls for greater driver accuracy, and can lead to slower work cycles. These pallets are more expensive than the standard types, but would be cheaper if there was a greater demand.

Pallet converters

1.03 A pallet converter **4** is a device attached to a timber pallet to secure the load and to provide a method of stacking unit loads without conventional racking. Recently pallet converters have begun to be increasingly used, especially in the retail trade. Previously, they had been used principally in cold stores for hanging meat, and as a stacking method. However, pallet converters can greatly increase the utility of a pallet in block stacking; a converter overcomes the problem of loads that are too weak to be block stacked normally unless equipped with post pallets or drive-in racking. This is particularly attractive to the small operator, and where a temporary stack is required without recourse to racking, but the load is not suitable for stacking. As a racking system, converters are not economic, as they

1 *Contrast between palletised and non-palletised goods.*

are more expensive per position than racking, but they can be used as such in certain situations up to six pallets high, with loads limited normally to 1 tonne per pallet, although one manufacturer offers stacking six-high with 2 tonne loads.

1.04 There are two types of converter: one uses the structure of the converter to withstand the weight of the pallets above, and the other ultimately lets the bottom pallet take all the weight (not a disadvantage as the load is transmitted through the strongest part of the pallet, the corners). Pallet converter structure is normally tubular steel or angle. Some converters are simply four corner posts and a bridging structure across the top. More sophisticated units can be equipped with side panels, turning a timber pallet into a box pallet. Some converters can be totally dismantled, so that when not in use they have a dissembled stacking ratio of 10:1.

Pallet collars

1.05 These work on the principle of converters, in that they adapt a normal pallet to an instant bin **2h**. They can be in timber or steel mesh, and are largely self-locating. They can be block stacked. Pallet collars are useful for small part order picking, as they can be removed layer by layer for convenience as the load is picked.

Post pallets

1.06 Post pallets are used for components, spare parts and materials more suitable for bins. Most post pallets, cage pallets, box pallets and demountable side pallets are made from steel. These can be block stacked 10 m high; UK post pallets use a shoe-type leg **1, 2e**, but they tend to waste volume. In the USA a rail and conical peg stacking system is used, saving a considerable amount of space (possibly 13 per cent volume saving) **2f**. Most post pallets are 40in × 48in (1016 × 1219 mm), but some use metric sizes for containers. 1016 × 2200 mm units have been used for body panels in a vehicle factory and component store. Some post and cage pallets can be folded, so that up to seven can be returned empty in one pallet. Post pallets with hinged fronts are useful for order picking, as goods can be seen **2g**.

Roll pallets

1.07 A roll pallet is a castored container, used as a link between a warehouse and a distributor **6**; loading and turnround times are claimed to be cut by up to 80 per cent. Many sizes and types are available; most can be dismantled and nest for storage (eg two roll pallets can hold ten dismantled units, one all the bases, the other the sides). A typical size popular in the UK is 800 × 700 × 1500 mm, with a working load of 508 kg. In Germany, two sizes are used, 720 × 800 × 1500 mm and 640 × 800 × 1500 mm. Many types of sides are available for various products, eg packaged foods, textiles, sides of bacon. Castors are usually 102 mm, in nylon or other plastics, and usually only two wheels steer, for towing ability in warehouses and stability in vans. Special versions can be specified for chilled use or high security.

Stillage

1.08 A stillage is a load board which may be very similar to some forms of pallet, but stillages are not normally intended for stacking.

Platten

1.09 A platten is a special pallet for 'captive' use, ie in-store only. They are often specifically designed to work with an automated stacker crane system, where tolerances are critical and differences in pallet size or shape could be disastrous.

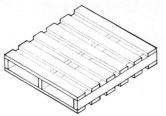

a *Two way entry pallet.*

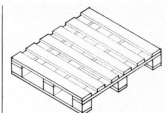

b *Four way entry pallet.*

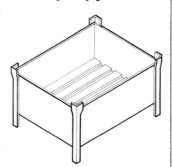

c *Steel box pallet.*

d *Steel post pallet.*

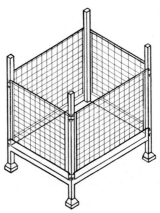

e *Standard post pallet with feet (waste volume) (used in* **1**).

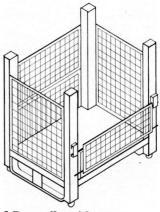

f *Post pallet with cones (greater capacity possible than* **e**).

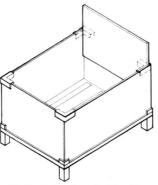

g *Pallet with detachable side.*

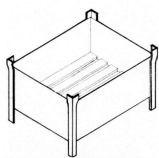

h *Collapsible timber pallet with collar converters.*

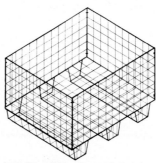

j *Collapsible wiremesh box cage. Direct order picking to retail distributors.*

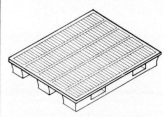

k *High quality plastic pallet.*

2

2 Size standards

2.01 Although the advantages of palletisation are very clear **1**, as yet it has been impossible to achieve a final set of dimensional standards. There are three basic groups.

ISO container module

2.02 The first group, sea-based operators, argue that the 8ft (2·4 m) ISO container is here to stay, and that investment in equipment is so great that it would be unrealistic to change. 1100 mm width pallets with lengths of 800 mm, 900 mm, 1100 mm, 1400 mm can be used in ISO containers; 1100 mm × 1100 mm pallets are the most economic for maximum volume utilisation (so important for 'deep sea' containers), allow more variety of carton dimensions than any other pallet, are ideal for carrying drums on road vehicles, and offer greatest flexibility between transport modes.

Packaging module

2.03 The second group base the pallet dimension on the packages to be stacked on them. It has been suggested that an international packaging module should be based on 400 mm × 600 mm (recognised as the standard ISO TC 122). This is compatible with the 800 mm × 1200 mm European standard pool pallet, sized for railway interchangeability. There are between 60 and 70 million European pool pallets in use and 30 million 1000 mm × 1200 mm pallets. This group argues that these sizes are already standard in many countries, and that equally high investment has been made in automated warehouses and other storage areas based on this size as on ISO container areas. To base a standard on a module of a container size ignores the vast number of products that never travel in containers and need the best pallet size for general use. Also, although 2 × 1100 mm pallets will fit across a standard ISO container, there may not be sufficient clearance in an insulated unit. 800 mm × 1200 mm is uneconomic for container use, but the 400 mm × 600 mm package size would suit both European pallets; it has been suggested that the 1100 × 1200 mm pallet would be the most economic for all methods of transport.

2.04 A third group states that any standard is unrealistic, with such a wide variety of goods. Pallets should always be chosen for the greatest economy, for the particular transport and storage mode, and product characteristics. So much investment has been tied up on both sides that it is unrealistic to standardise on one particular size, or base a pallet size on a package dimension, which is sized for display and ease of distribution, ie one product with several different sized packs. The standards should be a minimum number of sizes, but flexible and not a rigid single one.

2.05 The basic differences are between nations with land-based and maritime economies, between road and rail traffic and the 'deep sea' container trade. Now there is no agreement between nations, and little within countries. Standards committees have tried to fix a majority view, but large multinational companies are unlikely to accept standards that conflict with their economic interests. So warehouse and distribution system designers are left with metric and imperial pallet types, which look similar in operation, until, for example, it is found that sufficient tolerance has not been left in the racking for the larger unit. For this reason, it is inevitable that some waste of storage volume will occur, as installations are planned to accept the larger sizes of pallets used by a particular industry, unless substantial repacking is accepted.

Actual sizes

2.06 The pallet size for which the storage is being designed must be fixed at the initial sketch design stage; this is vital

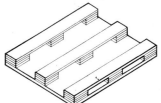

1 *Low profile pallet.*

m *Disposable corrugated board pallet with cone legs.*

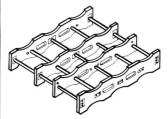

2 *Key spacer pallet.*

o *Special drum pallet (see* **7.***)*

3 *Bins to modular pallet dimensions loaded into container by forklift.*

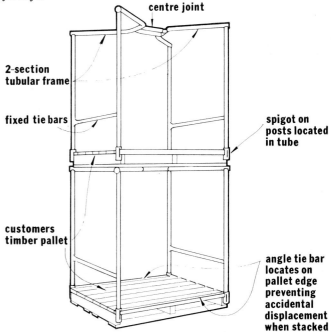

centre joint

2-section tubular frame

fixed tie bars

customers timber pallet

spigot on posts located in tube

angle tie bar locates on pallet edge preventing accidental displacement when stacked

4 *Pallet converter.*

to racking and handling plant alike. Table I gives the range of actual sizes.

Table I Pallet sizes

Pallets for materials handling[1]

Imperial in	Metric (exact values) mm	Metric (ISO/BSI rounded up[1]) mm
32 × 48	812·8 × 1219·2	800 × 1200
40 × 48	1016 × 1219·2	1000 × 1200
48 × 48	1219·2 × 1219·2	1200 × 1200
48 × 72	1219·2 × 1828·8	1200 × 1800

Pallets suitable for ISO containers[2]

		1100 × 800
		1100 × 900
		1100 × 1100
		1100 × 1400
40 × 48	1016 × 1219·2	1000 × 1200

ISO Types R198 and R329

32 × 48	812·8 × 1219·2	800 × 1200
32 × 40	812·8 × 1016	800 × 1000
40 × 48	1016 × 1219·2	1000 × 1200
48 × 64	1219·2 × 1625·6	1200 × 1600
48 × 72	1219·2 × 1828·8	1200 × 1800
		1100 × 800

Insulated ISO container internal sizes

	2235 (ACT Line)
	2235 (OCL Line)
	2254 (BEN Line: refrigerated)
	2178 (Insulated)

Pallet heights (ground to underside of deck)

5	127 (max)
5½ (USA[3])	140 (1200 × 1600, 1200 × 1800 pallets and International average)
2⅝	(66·7)
3 (USA[3])	(76·2)

[1] BS 2629: 1960 Part I Pallets for materials handling
[2] BS 2629: Part II: 1960.
[3] New type of low profile pallet developed in the USA; these are 2⅝in high for single deck, and 3in for a multiple deck. These offer considerable volume savings with high racks, eg, a saving of 362 mm in a typical six-high block stack 0·45 m³ approx.

3 Materials

3.01 Pallets are traditionally made of timber or steel, but recently of plastic, and expendable paper plastics have been developed **2a-n**. Timber pallets are still virtually the cheapest and strongest type available **2ab**. Plastics as yet share only a very small sector of the total market **2k**. But timber pallet prices are likely to increase by between 10 and 15 per cent, while plastic pallet prices will probably stay static (present (1973) cost is approximately £5 each for a rigid, high strength unit). Tests have shown that a life of six to eight years can be expected with plastic, but operators are waiting for a guarantee of this before making large-scale changes.

Plastics compared to timber

3.02 The advantages of plastic over timber are:
Weight: plastic is only half the weight of timber.
Cleanliness: they are being adopted by the food industries. The more complex plastic pallets need mechanical cleaning, as they have dust-catching crevices.
Colour coding: operator's name can be moulded in for return.
Durability: plastic withstands impact damage better.
3.03 Disadvantages of plastic pallets are: they are more costly; they can deform under load, making fork entry difficult and, when wet, can slide off forks. At present plastics pallets' applications tend to be specialised, and timber is likely to continue popular for some time.

Disposable pallets

3.04 These create a rubbish problem, and like 'prefabs' are used long after they should have been replaced, often resulting in the need for repackaging before entering the storage system. Because of expendability, prices need to be very low; for this reason one-piece mouldings from plastic, foams and vacuum-moulded polyethylene, have been produced, as well as cardboard and plastic composites. These pallets tend to suffer from lack of strength and

resilience in use. Cardboard sheet pallets supported on nine plastic 'cups' have been used effectively and are cheap (about 65p each 1973 prices), but stacking is a problem, as the cup legs are not strong enough for block stacking **2m**.
3.05 *Cellular material pallets.* These are made from cardboard sheets filled with a cardboard honeycomb. These are very rigid and strong for their light weight; the cardboard can be impregnated with a flame-retardant compound. This pallet type is mostly seen as the base to a full cube pack, as for a computer component.

Cages

3.06 The growth of hypermarkets and super-stores in Europe and the UK has introduced the cage pallet into distribution. This combines order picking, transport and retail display into one unit, eliminating a complete handling stage. Cages have four feet of open wire construction: although some fold flat when empty, cages are bulky to store, and produce poor volume utilisation, especially in transport. Having been developed in France, there are still no firm dimensional standards, although two sizes are most likely:

Length	width	height
1150 mm	850 mm	1000mm
600 mm	850 mm	670 mm

Although only a small part of the distributive industry will be affected, it is predicted that 250 000 cages will be in UK circulation by the end of 1976.

Reference
1 BS 2629: 1960
Pallets for materials handling.
HMSO (Aa8).

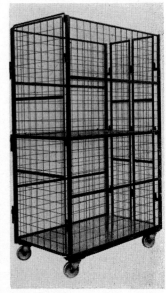

5 *Special pallet for radioactive material* **6** *Roll pallet.*

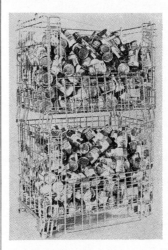

7 *A special trolley for conveying stacked cages so that they can be transported as a roll pallet.*

Information sheet Mechanised storage 3

The forklift family

The family includes forklift trucks, reach trucks, turret trucks, side loaders, and free-path order pickers. The principles of their use have been described in Technical study Mechanised storage 1. This information sheet gives most common sizes, capacities, and types of mobile lifting equipment based on forklift technology, so that performances, aisle widths, clearances and turning requirements can be roughly assessed at sketch design stage. At no time should these typical dimensions be used for a final design scheme. The manufacturer of the plant to be used should be contacted at the earliest possible stage.

1 Counter-balanced forklift trucks

1.01 Maids-of-all-work in a warehouse. They can lift all warehouse loads and are available from $\frac{1}{2}$ tonne capacity to 5000 kg for normal use. Much larger trucks are available for handling stillages and ISO containers. Forklifts take up more space in stacking areas than reach trucks or turret trucks **1a, b, c.**

1.02 Developments include more accurate control for electric trucks, hydrostatic steering and automatic height selection for high lift machines. A future development, especially for turret trucks and order pickers, is likely to be wire guides in aisles, freeing operators to pick goods, or allowing full automation for stacking yet keeping freepath characteristics. The ranges of forklift types are polarising into two groups within each capacity; internal use compact machines with solid tyres and electric power, and i/c[1] engined trucks for general purpose and external use, of more rigid construction, oscillating rear axles and pneumatic tyres. Table I illustrates dimensional implications of internal and external forklift trucks of similar capacity.

1.03 Forklifts can be fitted with electric traction from batteries, or diesel, petrol or lpg[2] i/c engines. Care should be taken in designing installations when using internal-combustion-powered trucks, as fumes may build up. At present 60 per cent of the UK market is for electric trucks, but this is likely to drop to 55 per cent if the present trend towards internal combustion power for certain applications continues. The largest growth area is in the distribution field and now many operators are hiring or leasing their forklifts. It has been estimated that 8200 trucks are available for hire in the UK, which helps small operators with little working capital. Designers should plan racking clearances to allow for different leased plant to be used with flexibility of plant operation in mind.

Mast types

1.04 Many attachments and several mast types are available for varied lift heights and performances: All trucks derate as lift increases; eg, a 3·2 tonnes lift derates to approximately 0·9 tonne at 8·5 m. The following mast types are available as standard:

[1] i/c: internal combustion
[2] lpg: liquid petroleum gas
[3] CO: carbon monoxide

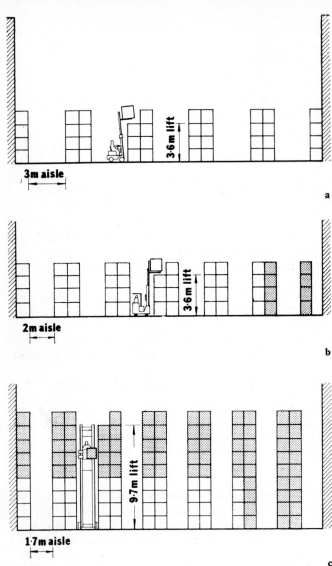

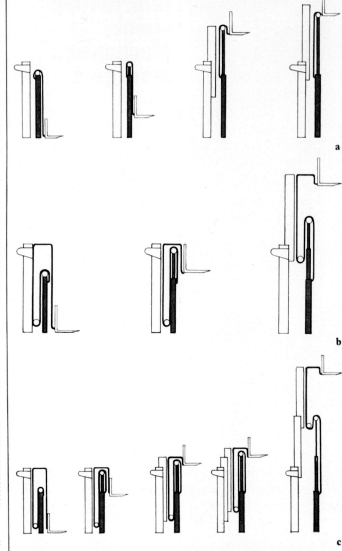

1a *Aisle and storage layout using* 1 *tonne capacity forklift with* 1200 × 1200 *mm pallets.*
1b *Layout using* 1 *tonne reach truck increases storage*

capacity by 20 *per cent over* **a**.
1c *Layout using* 1 *tonne capacity stacker/order picker increases storage capacity by* 192 *per cent over* **a**.

2 *Types of mast (rising from left to right). Outlines of basic mast on left, inner upright (shaded) on right, on top of which hoist cylinder (shaded) rises.* **a** *Two stage*

mast with little freelift.
b *Two stage mast with full free lift.* **c** *Three stage mast.*

Non telescopic single-stage Usually found only on the simplest low-cost stacking machines.
Two stage mast without free-lift An outer upright and an inner upright, to the top of which is mounted the hoist cylinder. As the hoist cylinder moves up, this pulls chains over a block, lifting the fork carriage. In practice, a few inches of freelift are usually possible **2a**. (Duplex mast).
Two stage mast with free-lift. These can be with partial free lift giving free travel, or full free fork lift at any mast position. The latter is the most common and should be capable of stacking goods in any position within the lifting range **2b**. Hydraulic rams and lift chains tend to be complicated.
Three stage mast. Permits high stacking without suffering the penalty of height when the mast is retracted. Capable of low-headroom operation, eg, inside ISO containers. Hydraulics and chain routeing become complex. Because of the extra components on three-stage masts, some loss of load centre has been experienced, and these cost 30-50 per cent more than two-stage types. Full freelift is possible **2c**. (Triplex mast).
Four stage mast. The main advantage is low collapsed height. Used for exceptionally high stacking, sometimes on reach trucks. Even more complex chains and hydraulics cause further loss of load centre and increases in cost.

Exhaust emissions
1.05 These are especially important in food storage, as they may contaminate it. Liquid petroleum gas engines produce carbon monoxide emissions as high as petrol units **3**. Some operators in very confined spaces such as ships' holds, where recharging is impracticable, use exhaust 'scrubbers'. CO output of a new lpg unit should be half that of a petrol engine, but it increases with engine wear and poor engine tuning.
1.06 There are no regulations governing exhaust emissions in enclosed spaces in the UK to date; in the US, it is suggested that the level should not exceed 50 ppm CO, 0·005 per cent exposure on the basis of an 8-hour shift, 5 days per week. Design extraction facilities on this basis. For nitrogen oxides, 5 ppm is reasonable. (Note that catalytic converters only convert CO to CO_2, and nitrogen oxides are still emitted.) Electric trucks are still really the only answer in cold stores and the food-processing industry.

Building needs
1.07 Level floors and ramps not to exceed 1:10 for intermittent working. Charging points are required for electric trucks, either in the loading bay or special maintenance area. (See Information sheet Mechanised storage 5). Table I shows typical sizes and properties.

Forklift attachments

1.08 There are many attachments available to enable forklifts to handle various shapes and sizes **4** to **8**. Some may need increased hydraulics. The maintenance area should be able to cater for hydraulic repairs (see Information sheet Mechanised storage 5).

3 *Histogram showing emission of carbon dioxide from diesel, petrol and liquid petroleum gas vehicle engines in good tune.*
4 *Turning fork attachment with arms set in palletised load carrying position.*
5 *Turning fork attachment with arms set in load clamping position.*
6 *Push/pull attachment in extended position with load on slip sheet about to be withdrawn onto platten arms.*
7 *Rotating paper reel clamp with short and swinging arms.*
8 *Forklift with high mast and clamps for paper reels.*

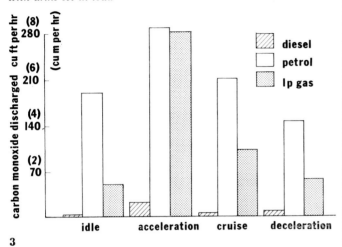

3

6

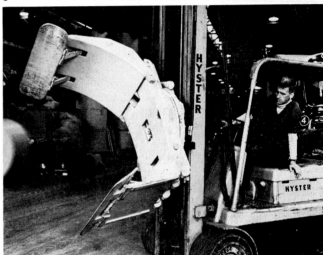

7

4

5

8

2 Rider controlled reach trucks

2.01 Suitable for narrow aisles where lifts are not to exceed 6 m. Some models can be driven from the elevating fork carriage, giving them an order-picking facility. If travel distances of over 45 m are expected to be frequent, check battery capacity, as some reach trucks have smaller storage capacity than forklifts of the same size. Flat floors are required. There are two basic types:

Gallows type: the mast moves forward with the carriage.
Scissors type: the mast stays in-board, and the fork carriage moves forward with pantograph action. Slightly more stable with heavy loads.

Typical applications have been discussed in Technical study Mechanised storage 1.

Table II shows sizes and properties of typical reach trucks.

3 Free-path order pickers/stackers and turret trucks

3.01 For use in very narrow aisles and high racking. See Technical study Mechanised storage 1 for applications. Turret truck operators do not usually rise with the fork carriage. These machines are very versatile, being able to operate in aisles between 25 mm and 150 mm wider than the widest load, with side-guidance wheels, and can be used for general warehouse and loading work as well **10**. Developments include wire guidance and, in future, fully automated on-line control. (See Technical study Automated storage 1.) Table IV shows sizes and properties of free-path order pickers, stackers and turret trucks.

4 Side loaders

4.01 There are two types:
Single side loaders
Dual side loaders

Single side loaders

4.02 A very useful type for general use in lifting long and awkward loads such as steel sections and textiles into racking. Can be fitted with many special fork attachments, such as outrigger forks for springy loads. They are able to work in aisles 150 mm greater than their width, or only 25 mm wider with in-rack guide wheels. Some models are fitted with four-wheel steering to alleviate cut-in on tight turns. They can have adjustable ground clearance of 125 mm. They are available in a wide range of capacities, up to the container handling giants illustrated in Technical study External storage 1.

Dual side loaders

4.03 For very narrow-aisle work, allowing double-sided access without having to leave the rack to reposition. Some can be used as order pickers with an elevating operator's cabin.

4.04 Always check with manufacturers for turning and clearance dimensions. Side loaders for use in racks should not need to be jacked when lifting. Flat floors are required. Table III shows sizes and properties of side loaders.

9

10

9 *Stacker truck with spindle for lifting carpets.*
10 *Turret truck in narrow aisle.*

racks

Table I Sizes, weights and turning circles of forklift trucks and reach trucks
Diagrams show limits of dimensions contained in the table

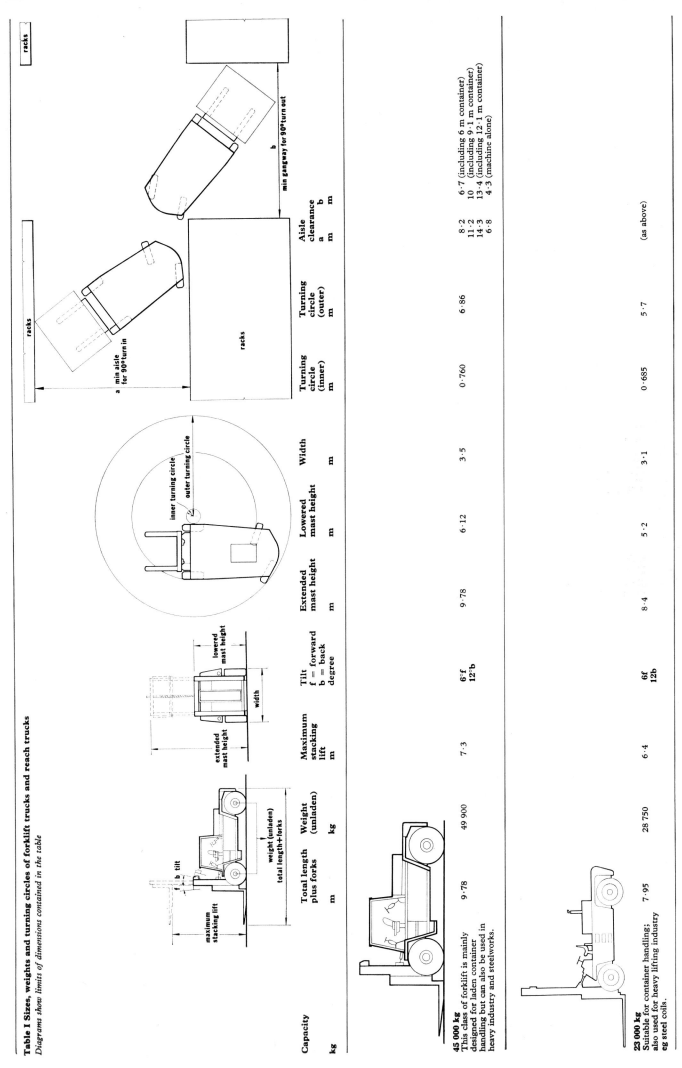

Capacity	Total length plus forks	Weight (unladen)	Maximum stacking lift	Tilt f = forward b = back	Extended mast height	Lowered mast height	Width	Turning circle (inner)	Turning circle (outer)	Aisle clearance a	b	
kg	m	kg	m	degree	m	m	m	m	m	m	m	
45 000 kg This class of forklift is mainly designed for laden container handling but can also be used in heavy industry and steelworks.	9·78	49 900	7·3	6°f 12°b	9·78	6·12	3·5	0·760	6·86	8·2 11·2 14·3 6·8	6·7 (including 6 m container) 10 (including 9·1 m container) 13·4 (including 12·1 m container) 4·3 (machine alone)	
23 000 kg Suitable for container handling; also used for heavy lifting industry eg steel coils.	7·95	28 750	6·4	6f 12b	8·4	5·2	3·1	0·685	5·7	(as above)		

min gangway for 90° turn out b

a min aisle for 90° turn in

inner turning circle
outer turning circle

Capacity kg	Total length plus forks m	Weight (unladen) kg	Maximum stacking lift m	Tilt f = forward b = back degree	Extended mast height m	Lowered mast height m	Width m	Turning circle (inner) m	Turning circle (outer) m	Aisle clearance a m	b m
9000 kg Popular large capacity forklift in industry for heavy loads eg steel work and cable drums.	5·29	12 065	4·6	6f 12b	5·69	3·4	2·49	0·430	4·06	4·7*	3·7*
5450 kg Developed specially for handling empty containers and stacking them up to 3 high.	4·85	15 440	8·3	6f 12b	9·6	5·05	2·4 3·6 (spreader)	0·635	4·6	10·9 12·6 14·3	6·7 (including 6 m container) 10 (including 9·1 m container) 13·4 (including 12·1 m container)
5450 kg Useful general purpose forklift for external use for 5–6 tonne unit loads.	4·5	7530	3·65	6f 12b	4·6	2·6	1·8	0·121	3·03	3·6	2·9
2700 kg Popular size of heavier standard forklift. Integral combustion engined truck with pneumatic tyres for mainly external use.	3·9	5307	4·3	3f 10b	5·03	2·6	1·66	0·09	2·3	4·06	2·17
Cushion-tyred electric truck for internal use.	3·5	4990	4·3	3f 10b	5·04	2·6	1·12	0·127	2·1	3·7	2·06
1300 to 2200 kg A popular category seen in many warehouses and factories. Internal combustion engine (diesel, petrol/lpg) and pneumatic tyres.	3·6	3630	4·27	5f 10b	4·85	2·62	1·14	0·127	2·1	3·86	2·05
Electric unit with solid tyres. Dimensions within each i/c engined and electric range do not alter significantly.	2·7	2680	3·66	2½f 10b	4·2	2·3	0·96	0·127	2·1	3·5	2·05
900–1300 kg Popular size for the smaller operator or for light pallets.	2·79	2132	3·66	2½f 10b	4·2	2·26	0·91	0·05	1·7	3·15	1·7

*Aisle clearance for truck only (ie without 1200 × 1100 pallet)

Capacity kg	Total length plus forks m	Weight (unladen) kg	Maximum stacking lift m	Tilt f = forward b = back degree	Extended mast height m	Lowered mast height m	Width m	Turning circle (inner) m	Turning circle (outer) m	Aisle clearance a m	b m
Under 900 kg Small rider forklift useful for unloading and light duty work in confined spaces eg on factory floor	2·65	2730	3·5	3f 8b	4·04	2·3	0·92	inner wheel reverses on full lock	1·34	3·05* (including 200 mm operating clearance)	
Three-wheeled stacker truck 2600 kg Intermediate model between forklifts and reach trucks. Exploits narrow aisle capabilities, but has fixed mast and conventional fork attachment. For over 3·5 m lift, hydraulic extension stabilisers are often fitted, that retract to allow the narrow width for tight turning.	2·01	3050	6	—	6·8	2·5	0·87 (1·01 with stabilisers)	not applicable	1·64	1·9	1·78
Scissor or pantograph reach truck 2040 kg	1·97	2490	5·5	3f 5b	6·39	3·4	1·24	not applicable	1·6	2·34	1·72
Gallows or moving mast reach truck 2040 kg	1·92	—	8·3	2f 5b	9·05	2·1	1·01	not applicable	1·77	2·39	—
Four-way reach truck 2040 kg Combination of reach truck and sideloader. Uses the scissor principle as a reach truck. Steering turns through 180° to allow instant 90° changes of direction. The frame can take extensions for handling long bars and tubes. Aisles need only be a few mm wider than reach truck in sideways travel position plus load.	1·85	2980	6·03	—	6·9	3·7	1·96	Four way steering		2·26	2·0

Table II Free path handling equipment

	Free path, narrow aisle stacker/order picker	Free path stacker/order picker with elevating cab, fixed mast and rotating fork

Elevation

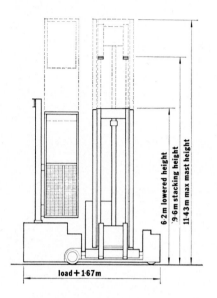

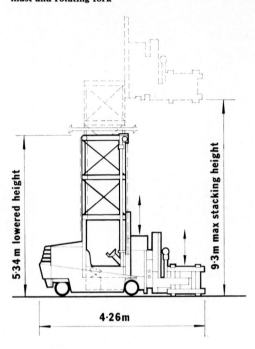

Plan

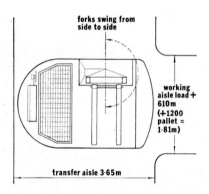

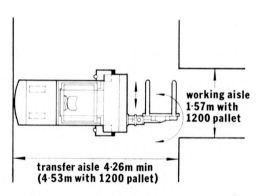

Description   This model is custom-built. It incorporates a separate order picking cabin and fork attachment mounted on independent masts. The advantage of this is that as the pallet load of goods is picked the relationship between the pickers' hand level and the top of the accumulating load can be adjusted to save operator fatigue.

The four-post mast gives extra stability. This type can be used out of the aisle as a forklift truck. The free lift on the fork carriage also allows differential movement between the pallet and the picking platform.
Maximum mast height: 10·03 m

Capacity   1 to 3 tonnes   1520 kg

Trade name   Gala   Spacemaster

Manufacturer   Cleco Electric Industries Ltd, Riverside, Market Harborough, Leics.   Integrated Handling Ltd, Brierley Hills, Staffs

Table II Free path handling equipment

Turret truck	Fixed/free path order picker	Free path order picker

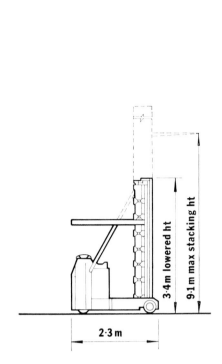

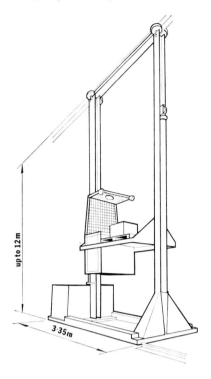

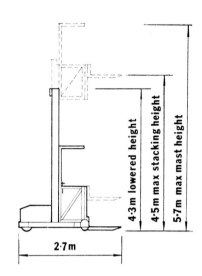

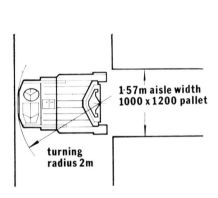

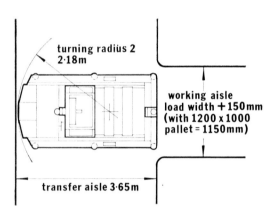

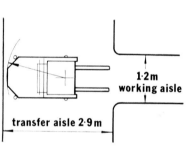

Turret truck operators do not rise with the fork carriage. In high racks they work to close tolerances, so level floors are required. Revolving and sliding fork carriages allow access to racks on each side without the need to turn the machine.

When in the picking aisle the machine is guided by rails at base of racking and is further stabilised by a rail over the aisle centre. This type can be higher than others, and when travelling between aisles it can be driven like a manual free path machine.

This type is a simpler machine than the others. The pallet on to which the goods will be picked rest on the fixed forks in front of the operators' cabin. Some machines incorporate a small amount of lift for the forks to relieve the picker of stooping and reaching. These are increasingly popular for the smaller warehouse operator.

1000 to 1500 kg

Faer 5-1

Lansing Bagnall, Basingstoke, Hants

1100 or 2200 kg

Maestro/Eye-rise

Cleco Electric Industries Ltd.

500 to 1000 kg

Cleco Electric Industries Ltd.

Table III: Sizes, weights and properties of sideloaders

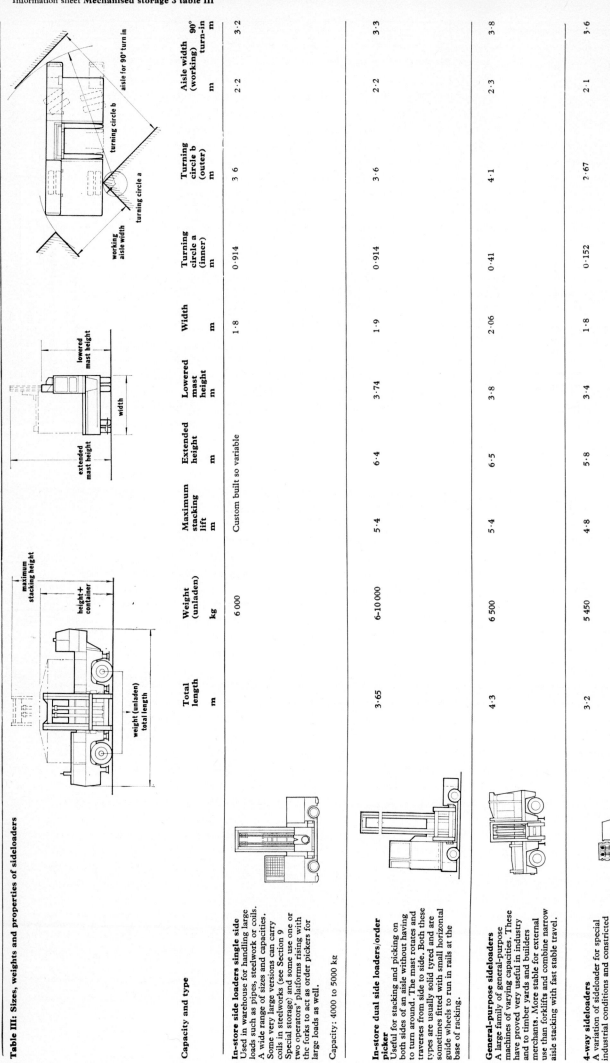

Capacity and type	Total length m	Weight (unladen) kg	Maximum stacking lift m	Extended height m	Lowered mast height m	Width m	Turning circle a (inner) m	Turning circle b (outer) m	Aisle width (working) m	90° turn-in m
In-store side loaders single side Used in warehouse for handling large loads such as pipes, steelwork or coils. A wide range of sizes and capacities. Some very large versions can carry coils in steelworks (see Section 9 Special storage) and some use one or two operators' platforms rising with the forks to act as order pickers for large loads as well. Capacity: 4000 to 5000 kg		6 000	Custom built so variable			1·8	0·914	3·6	2·2	3·2
In-store dual side loaders/order picker Useful for stacking and picking on both sides of an aisle without having to turn around. The mast rotates and traverses from side to side. Both these types are usually solid tyred and are sometimes fitted with small horizontal guide wheels to run in rails at the base of racking.	3·65	6–10 000	5·4	6·4	3·74	1·9	0·914	3·6	2·2	3·3
General-purpose sideloaders A large family of general-purpose machines of varying capacities. These have proved very useful in industry and to timber yards and builders merchants. More stable for external use than forklifts and combine narrow aisle stacking with fast stable travel.	4·3	6 500	5·4	6·5	3·8	2·06	0·41	4·1	2·3	3·8
4-way sideloaders A variation of sideloader for special industrial conditions and constricted conditions. These machines have wheels that all turn through 180° allowing instant 90° direction changes and 'crabbing'. The machine can thus act as a reach truck side-on. Machines of this type have been used successfully in glass works for handling large sheets of plate glass.	3·2	5 450	4·8	5·8	3·4	1·8	0·152	2·67	2·1	3·6

External heavy duty sideloaders
Heavy duty sideloaders have been used in industry for some time. They are scaled-up general-purpose models; they usually use integral hydraulic stabilisers for heavy lifts; steel fabricators, handling whole trees in saw mills, coil carrying (See Section 9 Special storage).

5·6 · 3·2 · 5·4 · 0·84 · 2·6 · 4·5 · 7·57 · 6·1 · 12 610 · 5·54

Container handling and heavy lift sideloaders
A special type of sideloader developed as the container trade grew. Various ratings are available, for 20ft (6·1 m) and 40ft (12·1 m) containers. These are big machines designed for rugged use, fast work cycles and rapid travel fully laden. (See Section 4 External storage).

(see below) · 9·1 · 0·76 · 3·7 · 4·7 · 5·5 · 7·7 · 47 000 · 9·5

Aisle widths of container-carrying sideloaders

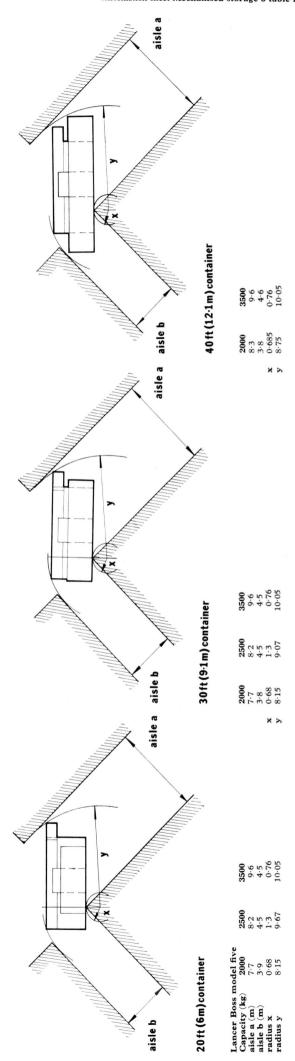

20 ft (6 m) container

Lancer Boss model five			
Capacity (kg)	2000	2500	3500
aisle a (m)	7·7	8·2	9·6
aisle b (m)	3·9	4·5	4·5
radius x	0·68	1·3	0·76
radius y	8·15	9·67	10·05

30 ft (9·1 m) container

	2000	2500	3500
	7·7	8·2	9·6
	3·8	4·5	4·5
x	0·68	1·3	0·76
y	8·15	9·07	10·05

40 ft (12·1 m) container

	2000	3500
	8·3	9·6
	3·8	4·6
x	0·685	0·76
y	8·75	10·05

11

12

11 *Free-path order picker truck with operator at picking level.*
12 *Turret truck entering aisles. Note guide rails at base of racking, and use of post pallets in racking.*
13 *Reach truck, illustrating narrow aisle, and how load is carried within wheelbase. Mast moves forward to place load.*
14 *Narrow aisle stacker truck: a forklift with no reach action, relying on mast angle and short dimensions to reduce aisle space; often used in smaller stores.*
15 *A narrow-aisle adaptation of a conventional forklift: note tilting forks and sliding central pivot, and stabiliser wheels at top of mast.*

13

14

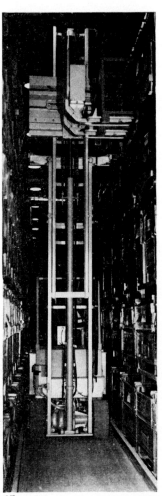

15

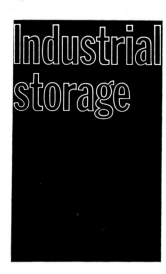

Industrial storage

Information sheet Mechanised storage 4

Packaging plant

This sheet gives information on properties of plant used for packaging.

1 Use

1.01 Use of plant is discussed in Technical study Mechanised storage 1, para 18.11 to 18.14. Packaging plant includes palletisers, depalletisers, shrink wrappers, banders and pneumatic nail guns.

Palletisers
1.02 Mechanical or vacuum-mechanical operation, depending on size. Up to 50 pallets per hour can be palletised by a high capacity unit, with regularly shaped cases. Normally, where the machine must arrange combinations of packages, it averages 30-40 pallets per hour **1, 2**. Transistorised controls form the 'brain' that holds the range of stacking patterns for the product. Twin-headed versions are available.

Depalletisers
1.03 Used to unpack regular loads from pallets. A typical use is unloading empty bottles or crates for filling and repacking. Typical machines unload 400-600 bottles per minute. Mechanical and vacuum versions are available, **4**.

Shrink-wrappers
1.04 Used for placing polythene film over pallet loads of goods, and heat-sealing the film and shrinking it by passing it through an oven, **3**. Capacities vary, depending on size of pallet, thickness of film, and whether a straight-through or single entry is used. Units weigh about

1 *Automatic palletiser, showing palletised load emerging on conveyor.*

1000 to 2000 kg, depending on size and performance. Shrink-wrap tunnels can be linked, so that large objects such as machine components can be wrapped in one operation. In order to shrink the film tightly, air is extracted, and this is the main source of heat build-up in the surrounding area. The machine casings are usually well insulated.

Banding machines
1.05 To stabilise unit loads. These may be used after shrink-wrapping with very difficult loads, or in place of shrink-wrapping where a seal is not required. Available in vertical or horizontal form, these machines can handle strapping automatically or may be manually controlled.

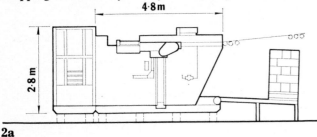

2a

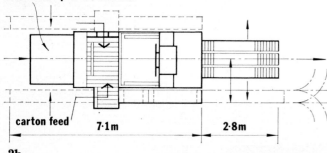

2b

3a

3b

Horizontal banding load cycles tend to be in the region of 10 seconds each for one band, 25 for two bands and 40 seconds for three bands; operation can be activated by a pre-programmed banding pattern and sensors on the approach conveyor. Vertical banding cycles are faster, strapping up to 400 cartons per hour. Heat-seal heads are incorporated into the winding mechanism **5**.

Pneumatic nailer/stapler
1.06 A wide variety of these machines is marketed. They are used for making and sealing crates in the packaging area, and for assembling abnormal size cartons. Hand tools are mostly used, so only an air line is needed.

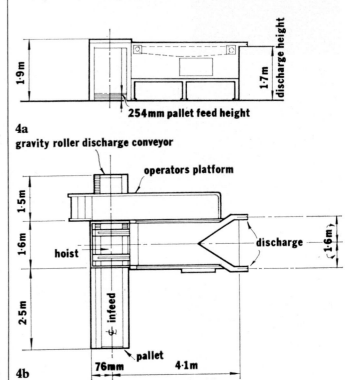

4a
gravity roller discharge conveyor

4b

2 *Dimensions of typical automatic palletiser* **a** *elevation,* **b** *plan (alternative carton feed positions are dotted).* 3 *Views of shrink* *wrapper,* **a** *exterior,* **b** *interior view.* 4 *Dimensions of typical depalletiser,* **a** *section,* **b** *plan* 5 *Dimensions of horizontal bander.*

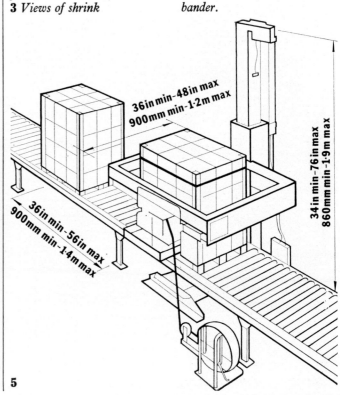

5

Information sheet Mechanised storage 5

Battery charging and maintenance areas

This sheet gives information required for designing charging and maintenance areas.

1 Battery charging areas

1.01 Free path mobile mechanical handling plant which is electrically powered requires an area for battery charging. Traction is still by lead acid battery. Batteries are designed to give a high discharge rate over periods up to eight hours. Common practice is to charge lead acid batteries over an 8- to 12-hour period, but shorter charges are possible with new types of equipment. Battery-powered forklift trucks are either plugged into a charger direct 1, or (for continuous truck use), batteries are slid or lifted out and replaced by fully charged units. Traction batteries are heavy; some operators slide the batteries out on to trolleys fitted with roller beds. A two-tonne capacity chain hoist is useful in these areas, as counter weights sometimes require removal for battery access. If a spare battery pattern is used, a container is required to hold batteries over the charging process, to protect them from damage from other plant.

Types of charge
1.02 It is common to charge batteries for eight hours, but some large organisations use boost charging to put 65-75 per cent of the charge into the batteries in about an hour. Charging systems are available that will charge batteries fully in five hours. Boost charging is the application of high currents to batteries discharged to about 10 per cent and lifting them to about 80 per cent of full charge in very short periods. It is popular, but is not recommended by battery manufacturers. A widely used charger is the taper charger, named so due to the manner in which the current is applied. There are two types; the single stage taper charger is mainly for slow charges and battery balancing over 10 to 12 hours. The double stage charger is for higher ratings, charging in eight hours.
1.03 Whether batteries are charged in-situ, or away from their vehicles, a special area should be provided. It should be well ventilated, and forced circulation is often required in areas of high ambient temperatures; batteries give off heat when charging. Fire protection is also important, and there should be provision for neutralising any spilt electrolyte. With large installations, equipment for dispensing distilled water can be installed, converting mains water.

Floor
1.04 The floor of a charging area can be damaged by spills, and wheel abrasion. Ideally, a strip of heavy duty epoxy-based jointless finish should be laid, which is impervious to acids, alkalis and which can withstand heavy impacts from batteries without permanent deformation or cracking. The area of special floor should extend further than the actual charging zone, as acids can be transferred by tyres; constant truck movement could indent a conventional floor finish, if softened by long-term acid exposure.
1.05 All charging plant, distilled water tanks, and spare batteries should be guarded against accidental impact damage.

1 *Typical battery charging area.*

1.06 Battery chargers are sometimes supplied as a package with the forklift trucks, but usually are produced by special manufacturers; contact the charger manufacturer of the client's choice early in the design process, as some installations require special conditions and safety features.

Typical sequence of activities of battery charging and maintenance areas
1.07 *Every day.* Inspection of battery cells and topping up.
Every 40 hours of forklift operation. (As truck maintenance is staggered, most of these functions will take place at the same time.) Check electrolyte levels in batteries. Check speed controller timings. General maintenance on tyres, brakes, power steering and hydraulic pumps will also be required.
Every 160 hours of operation. Give batteries an equalising charge, clean pump motor, blow carbon dust out of motors. Grease all round truck, checking hydraulic hoses and connections, and electrical connections.
Longer term maintenance involves the 'taking down' of traction motors, and general dismantling for repair. Substantial oil spillage can occur during maintenance, and certain hydraulic oils are very corrosive to normal concrete flooring.

2 Maintenance areas

2.01 The long-term maintenance zone should be part of the charging area, but should be separated to prevent interference to normal charging movement by components and 'dead' trucks. The maintenance area should also have 2 tonne hoist provision; this could be shared with charging activities if the installation is small. A hydraulic lift and a pit are often specified, and should be well guarded.
2.02 Lighting levels of 400 lux minimum are suggested for these areas. There should be space for spares storage; plastic tote bins mounted on an expanded metal sheet are useful for small parts, and larger parts, eg wheels and tyres, can be placed in racks. Space should also be planned for keeping jacks, grease guns, and all the dirty paraphernalia that maintenance bays generate. A lorry-loading access door is an advantage, with the chain hoist able to extend over the truck bed. Forklift trucks tend to be delivered two or three at a time on special articulated low loaders; plan external access for a 15 m articulated vehicle.

3 The use of internal combustion engine powered forklifts and tractors

3.01 In place of battery charging, a fuel dispensing area is required; check from the outset with the fire officer, insurance company and officer responsible for petroleum regulations about any special measures that might be required. These can be especially stringent with lpg replenishment; removable gas bottles are used usually, and the bottles filled from a bulk tank outside the building or by a special contractor. Diesel filling areas are dirty, and solid and cushion tyres can transfer the fuel over a wide area of floor if a special surface is not provided in the maintenance zone. Diesel can quickly corrode a concrete floor, increase wear on tyres and cause dangerously slippery areas. These activities should be in a separate part of the warehouse building, as far from stock as possible. If any i/c engine test facilities are included, these should extract directly to the outside, with a high level of ventilation. Take care not to extract fumes near other higher intakes.

4 Services required in forklift charging and maintenance areas

4.01 *Compressed air* for tyre inflation, cleaning.

Cold water, hose and tap (for floor swilling, hand cleaning).
Hot water. Pressure hose cleaning, hand washing.

Distilled water; battery areas only.

Grease; centralised pressure greasing in large installations.

Hydraulic oil; centralised hydraulic oil reservoir in large installations.

Power; special three-phase supply for battery chargers. Check with charger manufacturer.

Mains power for power tools used in maintenance area.
Drills, grinders, power for pump for hydraulic lift.

Steam; special for diesel trucks, especially if operating often externally. Steam cleaning is effective for degreasing, and is cleaner than water jets.

Information sheet Mechanised storage 6 Tractor trains

This sheet gives dimensions of typical tractor trains.

1 Use

1.01 Tractor trains are useful for long inter-store runs requiring faster speeds and more flexibility than tow carts. The lighter types of tractor, for towing up to two tonnes, are usually battery powered, and cannot keep travelling up ramps without recharging. Heavier tugs for between 7 and 20 tonne train loads may be electric, petrol, diesel or lpg powered. Speeds of electric vehicles decrease considerably with heavy loads, and frequent gradients can drain the battery. Some tractors have load platforms of their own. They require a recharging bay. Table I gives properties and dimensions.

Table I Sizes, weights and capacities of tractor trains

Key diagrams

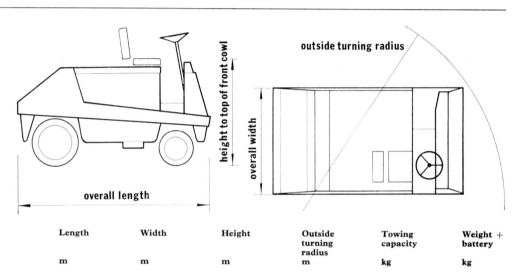

Type	Length	Width	Height	Outside turning radius	Towing capacity	Weight + battery
	m	m	m	m	kg	kg
 Typical high power electric tractor	2·5	1·3	1·4	3·5	20 000	4090
 Typical medium weight tractor	1·8	0·93	1·1	1·7	7000	1120
 Typical lightweight tractor	1·6	1·01	0·86	1·1	2000	680
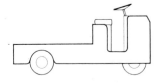 Platform truck/tug	2·64	1·07	1·0	2·1	2268	884

Industrial storage

Information sheet Mechanised storage 7

Static vertical movement plant

This sheet gives information about lifts, elevators and lowerators, spiral conveyors, vertical belt conveyors and scissor lifts.

1 Properties

Uses and limitations
1.01 Used where mezzanine sorting is necessary, where lack of space eliminates ramps or normal conveyors, and for over-rack order picking. Also useful in joining new buildings to old units at different levels, where space is restricted. These methods are slower than belt conveyors, more expensive and complicated, but can carry large unit loads.

Sizes and capacities
1.02 A very wide variety of sizes is available, from carrying individual cans to a packaging area, to elevators for full pallets, and scissor lifts capable of lifting a full 32 tonne truck.

Space requirements
1.03 The great attraction of this type of equipment is the small amount of space used in comparison with other plant for inter-floor movement. Space should be allowed for queueing on either side, and for maintenance access.

Equipment design
1.04 Most plant can be automatically fed and discharged, with accumulation conveyors and spacer stops. Special types of lift with pneumatic/electro-hydraulic control instead of exposed electrics are available for use in areas of high fire risk.

Building needs
1.05 Lifts of this type usually have their own independent shafts, thus requiring only a foundation. Some pallet elevators require a pit for belt clearance. All machines should be well guarded, and any shafts clearly marked and protected. Most of this equipment can suffer considerable abuse unless safety interlocks are specified.

Prices
1.06 Prices can range from £1500 for a small scissor lift, to £20 000 plus for sophisticated elevator/lowerator systems.

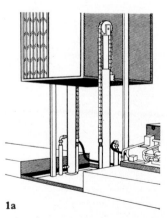

1a *Electro-hydraulic lift.*   **1a**

2 Lifts

2.01 Available as four-post or single-post, cable or hydraulically operated units, or can work on the scissor lift principle, **1, 2**. Other types are available with combinations of these features (eg for explosive atmospheres, a lift elevated with rams pulling chains on the forklift principle).
Cable lifts need overhead clearance for motors, and space for counter weights
Hydraulic lifts work in confined headrooms, but require a pit for the retracted lifting gear. With hydraulic lifts, the motor/pump units can be isolated up to 30 m away, useful in confined areas.

3 Pallet elevators and lowerators

3.01 A modification of the paternoster. The load platforms are made of slats that are rigid with load in the horizontal position, but which bend over rollers to return flat to save space, **3**. Normal operating speed: 8-16 pallets per minute, depending on the pallet size and weight. With 2000 kg pallets, speed tends to reduce to 6-8 pallets per minute. Normal belt speeds are 12-18 m/min, but 20 m/min available for certain high throughput, lightweight operations. Most modern elevators are automatically fed. Various protective devices are available. Variations of load platform are available for barrels, casks and paper rolls. The units have integral supporting frames, incorporating motors and pulleys.

4 Spiral conveyors

4.01 These range from the vibration type, used for light, small packages and powders (see Section 8 Bulk storage) to single bottle or can units employing a screw conveyor in a vertical configuration, **4**, and to larger spirals of powered rollers for large cartons. Useful for the fast transport between levels of small, regularly sized products. Speeds of between 600 and 1200 units/minute are possible. Working with a filling line and palletiser, very fast cycles can be achieved.

5 Vertical belt conveyors

5.01 A comparatively new method, originally designed for mailbags and baggage in airports. Basically, they sandwich a package between a drag belt and another flexible belt, **5a**, partly supported on an airbag, so that the belts deform to the shape of the package. This form of vertical conveyor offers fast handling of individual packages of very varied sizes. They are only used for elevation; down travel is provided by a spiral chute **5b**. Sizes can be supplied to suit the range of commodities handled.

6 Scissor lifts

6.01 A well-tried and simple method of raising a variety of unit loads, **6**. The lift tables can be equipped with rollers, so that pallets can be automatically accumulated on a roller conveyor, and released in single or multiple units on to the lift to suit its work cycle. Scissor lifts can be single- or multi-stage; as a rule no special foundations are needed, all the spread being in the lifts' own structure. Most types are supplied with full guards and safety features. This form of lift is comparatively slow, and is especially useful for lifting in infrequent situations, such as a forklift truck and load between a new warehouse and an old factory, where a 1 in 10 ramp would not be accommodated.

1b

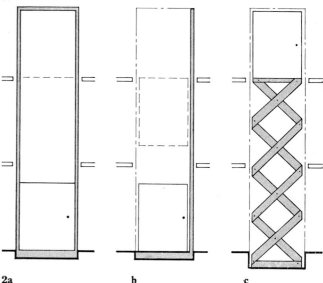

2a   **b**   **c**

1b *Free standing lift.*
2a *Four post lift.*
2b *Single mast lift.*
2c *Multiple scissor lift.*

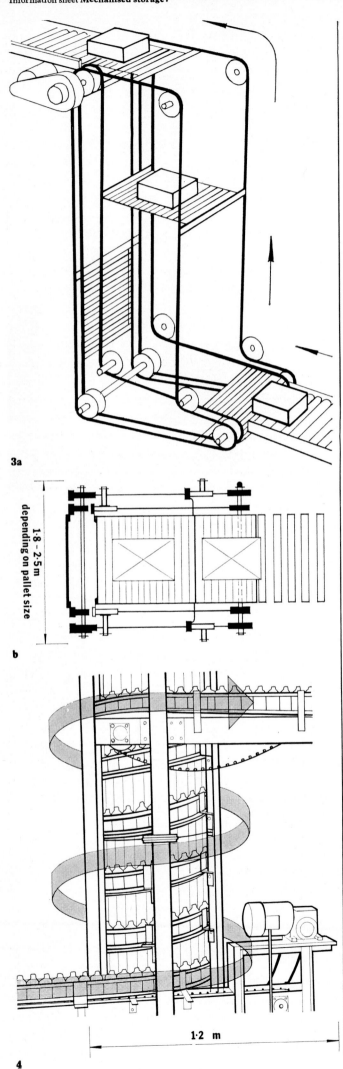

3a

1·8 – 2·5 m
depending on pallet size

b

1·2 m

4

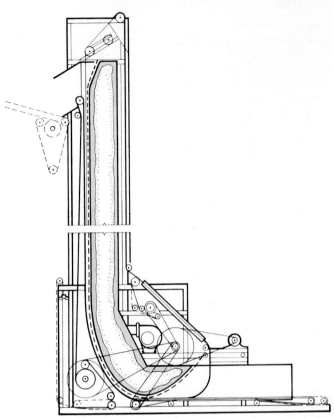

5a

b

3 *Pallet elevator/lowerator*
a *in action* **b** *plan.*
4 *Vertical spiral screw*
conveyor for small products.
5 *Vertical belt conveyor*
a *for upward movement. This*
is designed for soft packages

and lifts them against an
inflated air bag in the centre.
It can be made to any height
to order, and **b** *spiral chute*
for downward movement.
6 *Scissor lift on ship handles*
cargo between decks.

6

Information Sheet Mechanised Storage 8

Fixed path handling plant

These include manually controlled stacker cranes, gantry cranes and order pickers. Versions which are automated are described in Section 6 Automated storage. This sheet gives designers typical dimensions and performances of equipment, for use at sketch design stage only. Manufacturers should always be consulted.

1 Uses

1.01 Fixed-path manually controlled plant is useful for block-stacking and in high racks above 12 m. Below 12 m, new types of free-path stacker/order pickers are more flexible. Fixed-path equipment uses very narrow aisles and roof suspension, does not need aisles for block stacks, and can place loads not acceptable to forklifts on to lorries.

Systems

1.02 Various systems are available for medium-rise warehouses where the manufacturer supplies both racking and stacker cranes. Stacker cranes work to tight tolerances within racks. Accurate construction is important.

1.03 There are many varieties of fixed-path handling plant particularly for specialised uses like steel stockholding, and sheet board stores. Both the machine and the supporting structure are costly and they lack flexibility. Within racks, stacker cranes are limited to one machine per aisle, or a transfer carriage is necessary; this can be extremely complicated as rails have to be correctly aligned, and need electrically operated locks and side-travel devices. Operators of fixed-path order pickers and stackers experience discomfort in high, narrow aisles, with fast acceleration rates, and substantial deceleration stresses are imposed on structure and racking.

1 *Gantry hung stacker crane.*

a

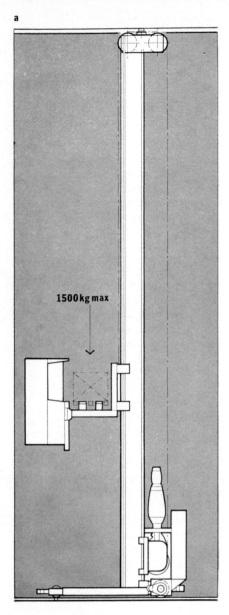

1500 kg max

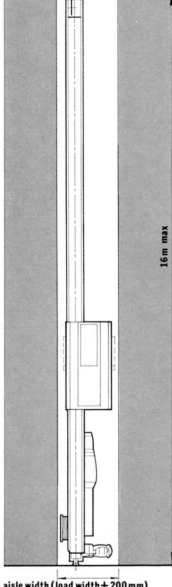

16 m max

aisle width (load width + 200 mm)
view across aisle

side elevation
2

b

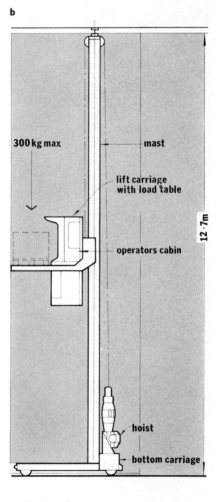

300 kg max

mast

lift carriage
with load table

operators cabin

12·7 m

hoist

bottom carriage

b side elevation

Stacker cranes
Uses and limitations
Lifts and carries pallets or long loads in narrow aisles and stacks
up to 30 m plus with twin masts (**2a** shows typical single mast).
Mechanical faults have caused difficulties, but latest units are more
reliable. Lacks flexibility and restricts change of use.
Types of stacker crane are shown in **1, 2a, 3**
Sizes
To order
Space requirements
Aisles 1·37 m to 1·67 m. For roof-mounted units, clear height is
required over racking for carriage. 1 m is usually enough, but
sprinkler clearance is also required.
Equipment design
Racking, if integrally structured, must be strong enough to support
crane. If floor mounted, it must have close tolerance finish or
self-levelling jacks; if roof mounted, it needs rigid support, taking
into account tolerances and summer expansion.
Building needs
3-phase power. Bus bar or winding cable.
Prices
Generally expensive.

2a *Typical single mast*
stacker crane viewed (left)
parallel to aisle and (right)
across aisle (racks shaded).
b *Order picker viewed*

parallel to aisle.
3 *Gantry hung stacker crane.*

3

Order pickers
Uses and limitations
Very useful for high density stocks of small parts and components, or bulk picking. Dimensions are similar to stacker crane. The fixed path is an advantage in this case, as accuracy is important, and the machine will be continuously used; it can also deliver loads to mezzanine sorting areas.

Fixed path order pickers are becoming more popular; several ranges are offered with standard components and performance limits.
Sizes
To order
Space requirements
Aisles 1·37 m to 1·67 m. For roof-mounted units, clear height is required over racking for carriage. 1 m is usually enough, but sprinkler clearance is also required.
Equipment design
Racking, if integrally structured, must be strong enough to support crane. If floor mounted, it must have close tolerance finish or self-levelling jacks; if roof mounted, it needs rigid support, taking into account tolerances and summer expansion.
Building needs
3-phase power. Bus bar or winding cable.
Prices
Generally expensive.

4 *Fixed path order picker in 950 mm wide aisle used here with tote boxes.*

4

Gantry cranes
Uses and limitations
Lifting and carrying of non-palletised loads or containers. Allows dense use of floor space. Lacks flexibility; cannot pass or store in racks without transfer carriage. Can be remote-controlled, or controlled by cable, as well as from integral cab. Can be used for pallets with special fork attachment but is not as effective as a forklift. This is a useful piece of plant in a large loading bay, especially if there are non-standard loads, such as large crates too big for standard fork trucks.
Size and capacity
Depending on application. Small, low-cost versions are available for loading and maintenance bays.
Space requirements
Clear height required over stacking height for beam and lift carriage and hoist machinery. Types are offered with over- or underslung hoist and carriage equipment.
Building needs
3-phase supply. Support is needed from building structure.
Prices
Vary considerably, based on size and capacity. Typical 15 m span/2 tonne with pendant control would cost £3000 plus.

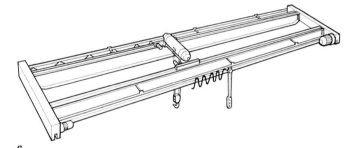

6

5 *Gantry crane using special stillages for storing pipes on fir tree racking.*
6 *Double girder overhead gantry crane.*
7 *Gantry crane showing transfer mechanism and stacked carriage with forks.*

5

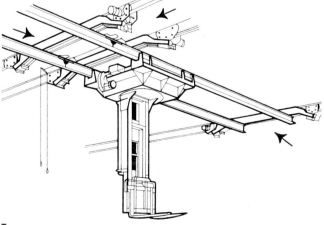

7

8 *Fixed path order pickers used for a spares storage/picking system.*

Industrial storage

Information sheet Mechanised storage 9

Towline conveyors

This sheet describes components of towline conveyors.

1 Use

1.01 Conveyors are described in Technical study, Mechanised storage 1, para **18.02** to **18.10**.

Definition

A towline conveyor is an endless chain running in an overhead track or channel in the floor with means for towing floor supported trucks, dollies or carts. These units can provide both a transport and linear sorting function.

1.02 Towline carts are ideal for large groupage depots and parcels sorting. A new use is 'U'-framed tow carts which each carry up to four roll-pallets between racking and load-accumulation zone. They also carry nested empty roll pallets out of the loading bay area.

2 Components

Towline carts

2.01 There are three main types:
Pushing cart; most frequently used, non-powered spurs ie, sidings, rigid steel bumpers **1**.
Cart fitted with accumulation bumpers. When pressed, the

1 *Simple pushing cart.*
2 *Cart fitted with accumulation bumper, and selective route control (shown ABCD).*

1

2

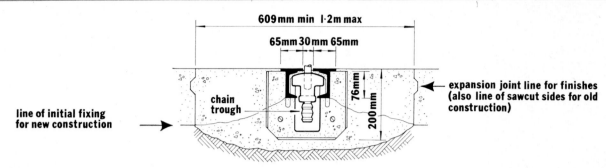

3 *Typical construction for installation of towline track.*

4 *Section through floor showing cart attached to chain.*

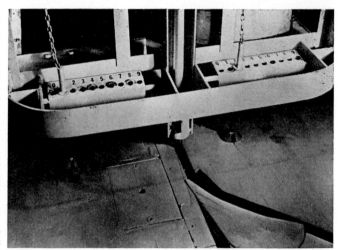

5 *Close-up of typical junction.*

bumper raises the pin, releasing it from the chain **2**.
Carts with dual push and accumulation bumpers. This is the
most sophisticated form. Sliding bumpers lock a dog on the
chain so that other carts cannot approach **4**.
Carts should have a minimum length-to-width ratio of
1·25:1, preferably 1·5:1 for stability when being pushed off
into spurs. 203 × 51 mm castors in a low friction material
are best for towline operation.
2.02 Carts are seldom used for loads of more than 1400 kg,
but 3000 kg are possible. Speeds of over 24 m/min are
seldom required. With tow chains, fast speeds lead to
accelerated wear and increased maintenance. A typical high
speed, heavy-weight cart system, 2700 kg carts moving at
36 m/min at 3·6 m centres, requires substantial deceleration
cushioning (2700 kg at 36 m/min generates 230 kg kinetic
energy).

Conveyor chain
2.03 The most common chain is the low profile type, with a
forged chain sliding in steel trough section **4**. Drive chains
work on the caterpillar principle; special chains are used for
contaminated and very dirty areas.

Straight track
2.04 The most common type has a track in floor which is
usually 75 mm deep formed from mild steel channel **3**.
There are several installation procedures; the general
contractor can leave an open trench in the floor surface, the
specialist installation subcontractor fixes the channels, and
the contractor then grouts round. Tracks are usually fixed at
1·5 m centres. Care must be taken with floor finishes, as
break-up round joints is possible. A possibly more acceptable
method is to have a base slab laid by the general contractor,
and the channels then aligned and fixed with shot bolts. The
final 90 to 115 mm finish can thus be laid monolithically,
but care should be taken over vibration. For installation in
previously jointless floor finishes, the trench can be saw-cut
and the channels fixed by epoxy-cement two-part glue.
This applies only to straight track, and is useful in not
disturbing previously laid jointless finishes.

Overhead tracks are vulnerable to forklift damage, and trucks
are less stable than with floor chains. Drag method is by
chain sling and rigid hook, tow ring, or two-piece nylon
strap and adapter; the most sophisticated method is a rigid
mast fixed to the towing shoe, with a shock absorbing
bumper/stop. If products are likely to be damaged by falling
lubricating oil, a guard should be fitted.

Drive units
2.05 Separate drives for loops are preferred, because if there
is a jam on a spur it only stalls one small motor, not the
whole system. For big chains, 11 kW is a typical motor size.
Motors should be positioned at least 6 m away from
bends; on multiple drive systems, motors should be located
so that they will share identical loads if possible, unless
deliberately of different powers, for example owing to a
space constriction for the motor size. Motors can be
positioned plus or minus 30 m from each other, as the chain
helps to equalise the power. Drives should be placed at the
base of ramps, minimising chain pull, and lengthening chain
life. A powered spur drive should be placed at the end of a
spur. A transfer drive is always located at the merge end of
the conveyor. For power calculations, add up the working
load; 25 per cent is chain friction, 2 per cent is cart rolling
resistance. Divide the total load by the working load to find
the number of drive units.

Horizontal turns
2.06 Direction is changed by running the chain over rollers;
the rollers, with ball bearings top and bottom, can be
sealed for life. A 1·8 m radius is usual, but 1·5 m is
possible in certain situations.

Vertical turns
2.07 30·4 m radius bends are the maximum for normal
chain operation.

Chain removal and cleaning section
2.08 These should be placed approximately 6 m beyond
each main line drive unit. Maximum intervals should be at

90 to 150 m throughout the system, also at the top and bottom of ramps.

Track expansion joints

2.09 These should only be run at 90° to the direction of the floor expansion joint. If not at 90°, there is a chance of chain pinching.

Non-powered spurs

2.10 Load speed is critical. Unpowered spurs should not generally exceed five carts deep with 450 kg loads; larger spurs are possible if speeds are 18 m/min or slower, of if carts are empty. With gravity spurs, involving gentle slopes, a good standard of concreting is essential. In warehousing, carts are generally pulled off these spurs for order picking, **6**. Non-powered spur intersections should not be positioned less than a cart length plus a cart width apart, in order that one cart will not push two others into two spurs at once. After a bend, a spur should not start less than 4 cart lengths beyond the tangent line of 90° bend, or 4½ times after 180° bend.

Powered spurs

2.11 Carts should never be planned to accumulate on powered spurs. Powered spurs are generally used with accumulator carts, where shunt shocks cannot be tolerated. 30 m/min should not be exceeded for powered spurs.

Ramps

2.12 All ramps involve custom engineering; rises should be a maximum of 17·6 per cent, preferably 10 per cent. Vertical bends have removable cover plates, where flat runs have welded plates. Great care should be exercised with towline ramps, as a runaway cart can do a great deal of damage, and injure personnel; warning signs should be placed at top and bottom. At the top of 'down' ramps, a pushed-cart detector is required with a limit switch at about 10 m from the start of the ramp, based on speed and gap between carts. If a cart shunts another on the slope, the fault will show on a panel, and the circuit will shut down.

Automatic accumulation stops

2.13 Blocks rise out of the floor to catch the cart's bumper and so slip the pin from the drag dog. These can be automatically controlled, or by a switch operated by a forklift driver, for example, who wants to cross a busy track. When a spur is full, the leading cart will trip a switch, protecting the entrance to the spur, diverting other carts away. There are four ways to accumulate carts the tow pin can be moved up or sideways, or the tow chain can be moved across or down with overhead drag units, pin withdrawal or trip is effective. Carts can congest if planned to accumulate on bends of more than 10°.

Direction controls

2.14 *Pins* with simple 10-unit selection, which meets a tab in the floor, releasing the drag pin, or also dropping an auxiliary pin into a spur slot (see **2**, **4** and **5**).
Sensing fingers that are activated by the cart's draw pin, coinciding with sensing pins on the cart that operate a power switch or slip the dog, resetting when the cart has passed.
Carts can be electrically diverted, by photo-electric sensors reading a bar code, or radio control. Towlines can also work with automatic car lifts.

6a

6b

6a *Switchcart loops feeding reach truck (left) Another switchcart is waiting to be unloaded in loop.*
6b *90° spur (right) joining a main route.*

7 *Pallet racking and block stacking in a warehouse. The racking is used for high selectivity, the block stacks for fast turnover goods: the reach truck is lifting in two pallets at a time. Note the narrow aisle suitable for reach trucks, and the use of the full height of a flat-roofed building.*

8 *Stacking and order picking aisles arranged alternately at a warehouse in Holland, with turret truck and pallet transporter working in combination. Note how flat trusses allow maximum cube stacking, and the racking on a plinth which guides the turret truck's wheels.*

7

8

181

Information sheet **Mechanised storage 10 para 1.01 to 2.02**

Industrial storage

Information sheet Mechanised storage 10

Conveyors for warehouse use

These include roller, belt, plate, overhead, pneumatic and sorting conveyors.

1 Use

1.01 Conveyors are ideal for transport and sorting of many goods. They are not cheap, but in overall cost for order picking, interzone transport and sorting, load assembly and packing, they are economic for heavier and faster duties. Small, low-cost, portable conveyors are very useful in loading bays, especially for groupage operations. (See Technical study Manual storage 1).

Limitations

1.02 All conveyors form a barrier to other movement, although they can be routed over obstructions and combined with elevator/lowerators for major level changes.

1.03 Conveyors can also feed palletising plant, shrink-wrap tunnels and banding machines. The possibility of automatic accumulation, diversion and sorting makes a conveyor system more attractive than several forklifts shuttling at high speed, or towline trains which load and unload mechanically. However, the scale, speed and flexibility of the operation should be carefully assessed before deciding to fit a large conveyor system. In some installations, a great deal of money has been spent on complex conveyor sorting and transport systems which are working to only a third of their capacity even in peak periods. £280 per metre run is a high price to pay for idle plant.

2 Roller conveyors

2.01 Roller conveyors are the most widely used for warehouse duties. Powered **1** or gravity operated, they are the cheapest form of conveyor, and can be obtained in a wide range of configurations to suit the type of goods being handled, from full pallets to small cartons.

2.02 Before deciding on a roller type, the characteristics of the package should be examined. Rollers are not suitable for goods that deform easily. Roller pitch should be calculated to support the package smoothly at all times, without risk of snagging and continuous vibration.

1 *Powered roller conveyor*

Table I Roller diameters and curves for parallel rollers

Roller diameter	Radius of curve
mm	mm
25·4	630/800
38·0	630/800
51·0	800/1000
63·5	800/1000
76·1	800/1000
88·9	1250

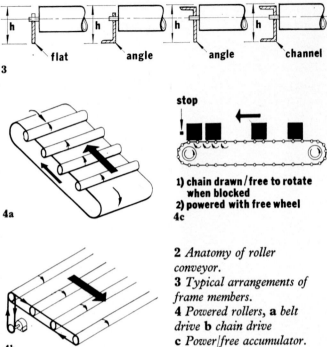

3

4a

stop

1) chain drawn / free to rotate when blocked
2) powered with free wheel
4c

2 *Anatomy of roller conveyor.*
3 *Typical arrangements of frame members.*
4 *Powered rollers,* **a** *belt drive* **b** *chain drive* **c** *Power/free accumulator.*

4b

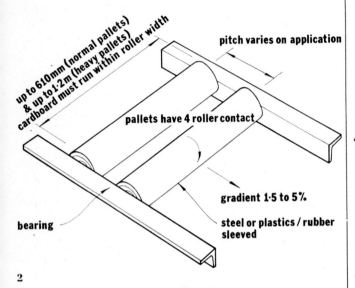

pitch varies on application

up to 610mm (normal pallets) & up to 1·2m (heavy pallets) cardboard must run within roller width

pallets have 4 roller contact

gradient 1·5 to 5%

steel or plastics / rubber sleeved

bearing

2

BS 2567:1972 provides useful guidelines for non-powered roller conveyors. It suggests that under any rigid, flat-based object there should be a minimum of three-roller contact. Flexible loads, such as thin cardboard cartons, may need a reduced roller pitch, or require a wheeled conveyor to prevent sagging. Rigid, flat-based loads can be carried on rollers narrower than the load, but flexible packages require rollers to be wider than the load. The possible distortion of loads on bends often determines the minimum roller width. The minimum pitch on straight track depends on the diameter of the roller used; six pitches are suggested by BS 2567; 38, 50, 75, 100, 150 and 200 mm. Pitch may be reduced at loading points to accommodate shock loads. Curved track is available in multiples of 30°, 45°, 60°, and 90°. The radius of the curve is measured to the inside face of the inner frame rail, and table I shows roller diameters and curves for parallel rollers.

2.03 *Special sections*, (see **5**) include switch sections, butterfly junctions, turnovers and turntables, hinged gates and transfer cars. Some accessories require manual assistance or a mechanical diverter.

Size and capacity
2.04 Roller conveyors are usually formed in standard 2·43 m sections, with a range of widths including 304, 308, 460, 700, 760, 970 mm, 1120 and 1270 mm (the last three suitable for pallets). Allow 75 mm minimum over dimension of rollers for total width (more if powered) **2**.
2.05 The following data should be considered when choosing roller type, surface and bearings:
1 Maximum and minimum size of load.
2 Maximum and minimum weights.
3 Particulars of package surface if not rigid or flat.
4 Special operating conditions, eg from chilled storage.
5 Whether fixed or adjustable supports are required.
6 Maximum accumulating load per 2·5 or 3 m run.
7 Conditions of loading: batching or single units.
8 Whether there will be impact shocks (locally or continuously).
9 Clearance heights and design restrictions.

Equipment design
2.06 Rollers can be steel or plastic, depending on required performance. Surface textures can be used for slopes with powered rollers. The frames are normally of angle or channel sections, **3** supported at centres to suit conveyor weight and load, and the floor surface. Roller bearings are normally semi-precision ballraces or nylon bushes. Flexible supports can increase the slope of gravity rollers or alter the height of a flat section to help manual picking. Wheeled supports with retracting conveyor sections are useful in loading bays. Flexible versions that can follow a variable, curved path round obstacles are also marketed.
2.07 For non-powered rollers, gradients of 2-5 per cent are normal, but can be as low as $1\frac{1}{2}$ per cent depending on load, roller surface and bearing, and length of travel. Powered rollers can move goods up gradients and allow selective accumulation. Sometimes this is cheaper with short sections of belt conveyor (which can also boost long unpowered roller sections). In most large warehouses, powered rollers achieve a measure of individual section control (only possible with belts by using over-belt equipment, whereas with roller systems, diverter gear and accumulation sensors can be mounted within the pitch).
2.08 Rollers are driven by a flat belt, or a vee belt running beneath the rollers and tensioned to press against them; this method is considered best for long runs, **4a**. More expensive are chain and shaft drives, which (linked with dog clutches and sensors) allow accumulation and sorting, **4b**. Special chain and shaft drives are used for powered curves. Other variations include roller sections with power brakes with progressive deceleration for fragile loads.
2.09 There are two types of accumulator roller conveyors.
1 A combination of chain and roller conveyor. A continuous set of rollers are chain drawn, yet are free to rotate under a load when it comes up against a spacer bar, **4c**.
2 Powered rollers with sensor devices that automatically remove the drive from the rollers. A typical system drops the roller that tensions the belt under the carriage rollers pneumatically, and this can be arranged for as many pallet lengths as the accumulation requires. This is the most usual type of accumulator.

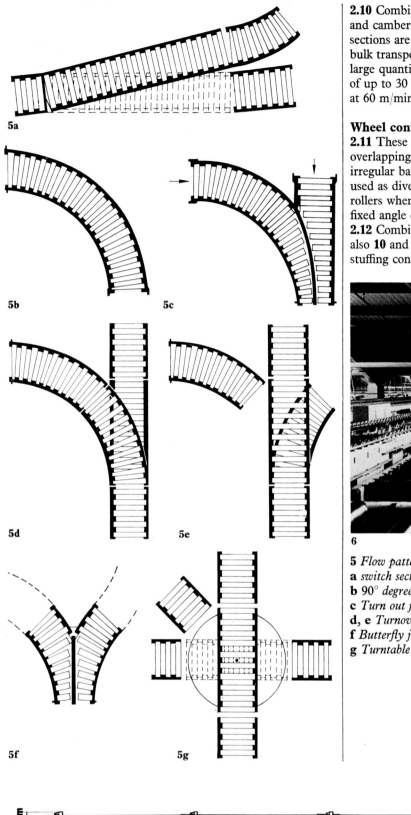

2.10 Combinations of powered and free rollers, with spurs and cambered curves, down-grade brakes and accumulation sections are a versatile method of high speed sorting and bulk transport in warehouses and groupage areas handling large quantities of cartons. Curve and accumulator speeds of up to 30 m/min are normal, with the ability to move at 60 m/min on long, straight sections.

Wheel conveyors

2.11 These are a variation of roller conveyors, with overlapping wheels to support packages with soft or irregular bases. They can be curved, powered, and are often used as diverters, being pushed up between the pitch of rollers when the package activates a sensor. Free castor or fixed angle diverter actions are available.

2.12 Combinations of roller and belt conveyors are available also **10** and **12**. Extendible portable conveyors are useful for stuffing containers, **8, 12**.

6

5 *Flow patterns*
a *switch section*
b *90° degree bend*
c *Turn out junction*
d, e *Turnover junction*
f *Butterfly junction*
g *Turntable*

6 *Combinations of powered and free conveyors in factory.*
7 *Free standing telescopic conveyor* **a** *extended plan* **b** *section folded up.*

4·2 m

7b

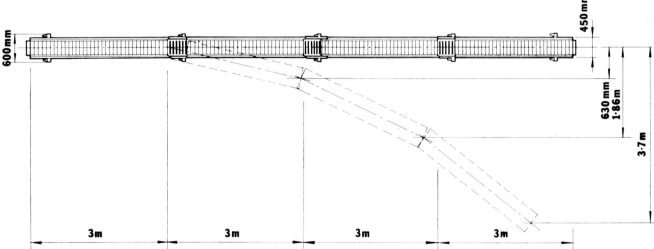

7a

8

3 Belt conveyors

3.01 See also Information sheet Bulk storage 2, on belt and slat conveyors, and Technical study Mechanised storage 1 para 16.

Uses and limitations

3.02 Belt conveyors are normally used in warehouses, for long straight inclines and flat sections **9a**, **b**, **c**, **d**, where roller accumulation is not required, and where layout requires movement by power rather than gravity. Suitable for high throughputs, belt conveyors are often part of a larger conveyor system of rollers and accumulation equipment **10**, **11**. Belt conveyors are particularly suited for use with small packages, and for loads with uneven or soft bases. Belts are capable of close radius bends at a wide range of angles **9e**, and are efficient for incline work for general goods. A wide range of covers are available including plastic, eg, neoprene for food stuffs, ptfe for easy tilt sorting, and rough surfaces for steep inclines. Check the friction characteristics of goods to be carried before choosing the incline surface, as some covers are ideally suited to certain loads. On normal belts, inclines are limited to 18°, but this can be increased to 35° by using a cleated belt, to 40° with rough rubber or a chevron pattern, and for certain products up to 70°with integral cross bars. Check whether the type of package to be handled will stay stable on certain slopes and not roll back. The biggest drawback of any conveyor in warehouses is that it can form a barrier for other movement.

Size and capacity

3.03 Length of runs is limitless with booster motors, and direct transfer is possible (usually at right angles) to another belt. Selective sorting can be effected by tilt or inclined belts. Belt widths of 304 mm to 760 mm are usually available from stock, in 75 mm increments. Fully metric belting has been available for some time. Speeds of up to 60 m/min are standard, but 36·5 m/min is more usual. Reversible motors can be fitted for loading bay use, or for sorting return and unblocking. Simple belt units, some with powered extensions, are available at low cost, as are portable versions for container 'stuffing' **12**, **14**. (See Loading Bays and External Storage Information sheets.)

Equipment design

3.04 *Steel band conveyors*, widely used in cold store and food processing operations, are also useful for general warehouse duties. A recent development is an integral system of magnetic sorting. The inherent magnetic qualities of steel banding enable a magnetic message to travel with the goods, that is rubbed off when the diverting mechanism has been activated.

8 *Extendible roller conveyor 'stuffing' truck.*
9a *Belt change from upper level. Link section lessens abrupt incline.*
b *Belt change from flat to inclined run (adjustable)*
c *Belt drive and tension units*
d *Types of belt cross-section*
e *Belt twin dimensions for 609 mm wide belt (bracketed figures for 1·06 m wide belt).*

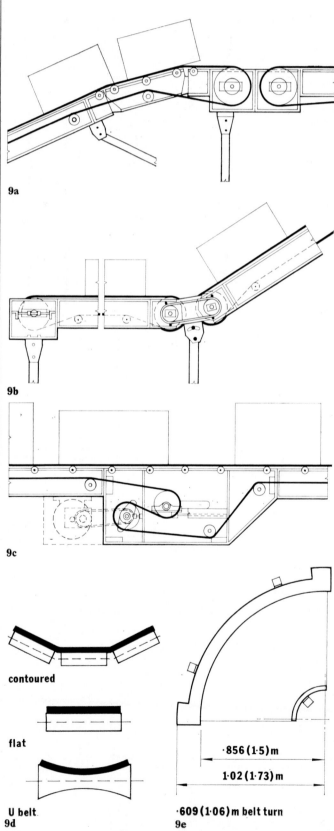

9a

9b

9c

contoured

flat

U belt.
9d

·856 (1·5) m

1·02 (1·73) m

·609 (1·06) m belt turn
9e

10

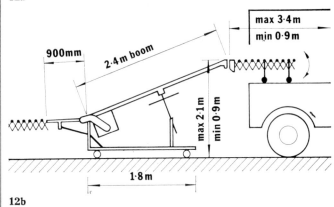

12a

12b

11a

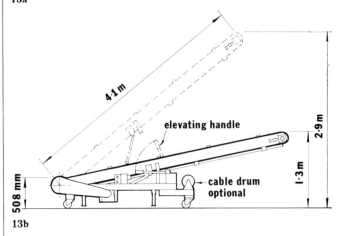

13a

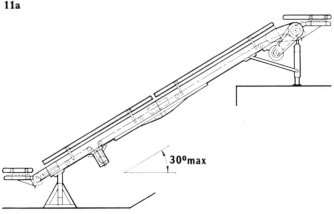

11b

13b

10 *Combination of belt and roller conveyor.*
11ab *Typical inclined belt conveyors.*
12ab *Mobile motorised belt.*
13a *Dock belt conveyor,*

which extends, rotates and elevates for loading sacks.
13b *Mobile slat conveyor.*

3.05 *Slat conveyors* operate on the belt principle, and are normally used for heavy duty work. Some accept wheeled plant over them; slat inclines are limited to 15-18° angles, unless back rest plates are fitted. Slat conveyors can carry full pallets, where their advantages of rigidity and of a solid surface between idler and power rollers and the load is best used **13b**.

3.06 *Plate link belting* is increasingly used for the approach lines to packaging and small scale shrink wrap machines.

They are also used for example, in repackaging after order picking to place the goods in a different 'outer', and in shrink wrapping small parts into more convenient retail units. Available in plastic or metal, plate link belting can be obtained in most sizes, from 25 mm for pharmaceuticles, to 1250 mm for full pallets.

Building needs
3.07 Overall belt widths are normally 102 mm to 150 mm

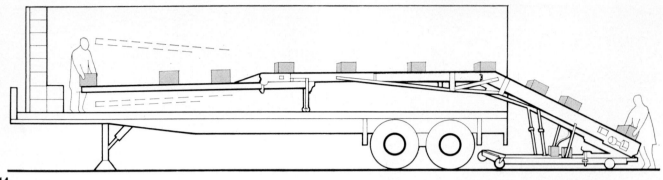

14

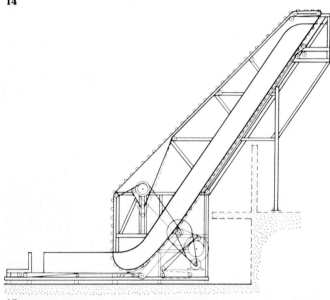

15

16a

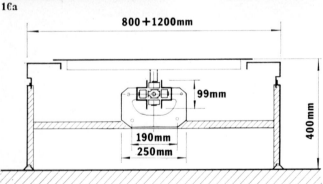

16b

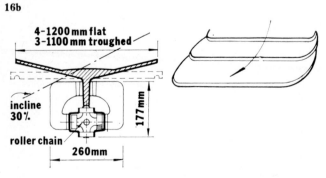

16c   **16d**

greater than the moving surface itself. Motors are usually placed underneath, running on a standard three-phase power supply. Space should be provided for motor access. At least 1·2 m should be left between parallel belt runs. On some models designed for manual picking, the supporting legs are adjustable for operators' convenience. Prices: these vary considerably, depending on duty, size, belt materials, frame and motors.

4 Plate conveyors.

Uses and limitations
4.01 These are for heavy duty use, often flush with the floor. They could be considered as a combination of conveyor belt and tow carts, being made of continuous overlapping plates, but are mounted on a track with rails and roller guides. Plate conveyors are less limiting to circulation than normal conveyors, and can be driven over by wheeled plant (check with the manufacturer what wheel loadings are acceptable). Plate conveyors need not be set in the floor, but can be mounted in the conventional manner. Normal uses include parcels and baggage sorting, **16, 17,** but they are also used for heavy-duty goods such as paper reels and steel coils.

Sizes and capacity
4.02 Typical widths range from 400, 500, 600, 800, 1000, to 1200 mm. For standard use, loads of up to 14 kN/m run are acceptable, but heavier duty versions are available for casks, barrels and heavy components. Maximum speeds are up to 100 m/min, although for use flush with the floor, they tend to be slower.

Equipment design
4.03 Plate conveyors are powered by a drag chain, with metal or plastic rollers set in a channel. A typical chain is 5 mm thick, with links at 203 mm pitch. One system employs guide wheels on all four faces of the chain for reduced wear and increased stability. Horizontal bends are available at 5°, 10°, 20°, 30°, 45°, 60°, 90°, and 180°, with standard radii of 750 and 1200 mm. Vertical ramp bends are available at 5°, 10°, 15°, 20°, 30°, 45°, with 750 mm and 1200 mm radii. The plates or scales are bolted to the drag chain, overlapping each other. Plate material is steel, plastic or rubber, depending on the duty required, and can be supplied with a non-skid surface for inclines and plant crossings. Motors are underneath the belt for raised

14 *Extendible portable belt unit loading a container.*
15 *Steep incline conveyor Packages are sandwiched between lower and upper corrugated and weighted belt.*
16a *Plate conveyor in use, with diverter (right).*
b *Section* **c** *detailed section*

d *overlapping scales.*
Loads: 150 kg/m.
Speed: 100 m/min
Incline: 30° standard scales.
Horizontal/vertical bends:
750 mm/1200 mm radius.
Limitless length.
Weight/m 19 kg.

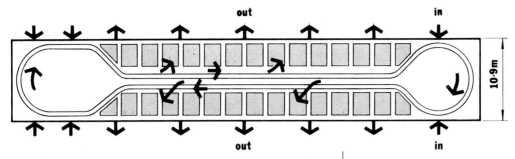

17 Plate conveyor circuit in loading bay, sorting parcels from trunk vehicles to local delivery vehicles.

operation, or in pits as with towline conveyors, when a sunken unit is installed. Some plate conveyors can be supplied with tipping plates, so that they can act as a tilt tray sorting unit as well, or can be tilted *en masse*, as in tilt belt operation.

Building needs
4.04 If set in the floor, a special pit must be cast with the floor to accept conveyor and motors. Steel edge plates are cast in, and concrete must be laid to fine tolerances. Over the floor, standard supports are used. Typical chain and track weigh about 18·5 kg/m run, although heavier duty models weigh more and require a heavier support structure. Check with the manufacturer what the point loads on the floor are likely to be. Power is by a three-phase electrical supply. This machine can be very flexible, being able to change direction quickly through its track and carriage design in either the horizontal or vertical planes. If set in the floor, this becomes less easy.

5 Pneumatic conveyors

Uses and limitations
5.01 *Airfilm conveyors* are a specialised form of warehouse transport, but may be increasingly used in the future. The hovercraft principle is used in reverse, in that the package rides on the air blast, and the conveyor itself has no moving parts. Present airfilm conveyors are mainly for light, small packages, where there are straight runs, and comparatively narrow tracks. They are basically long air tables, with surface openings that give direction as well as lift, **19, 22**. Large numbers of packages can move fast and easily, but air wastage is a serious limitation.
5.02 One system **21** has been suggested which incorporates an air conveyor and plastic (ptfe) ball valves with a very low coefficient of friction, which contain the air until the pallet depresses the ball valve, liberating a directional air jet supplying lift, and sufficient forward motion to overcome any friction from the valves. Pallets used in the system must have flat, single piece floors or base boards (plastic pallets would work well).
5.03 *Air-supported tracked conveyors* are based on articulated hollow plates with air fed vertically and horizontally through shaped outlets, **20, 23**. With nozzles of the correct shape, efficiencies of 80 per cent are possible. Friction is negligible, and speed control is by adjusting air pressure. The only moving parts on the conveyor bed are idler wheels at the turn points. Air pallets work on similar principles, **18**. A great deal of work has been done on air cushion handling technology recently, and full scale commercial systems will soon be available.
Building needs
50.4 These are limited to the air compressor requirements and a standard conveyor base.
5.05 *Helical conveyors* are used to transport containers such as bottles and aerosols at high speeds with stability. Triple helical worms can handle such inherently unstable units as plastics containers and are very useful for supplying palletisers. The worms are often machined from plastic, matched exactly to the shape of the containers to be handled.

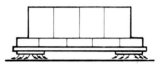

18 Air pallet
Must have flat floor. Pallet rests on hollow pad with perforated membrane. Air escapes through membrane perforations, round the circumference of disc and supplies lift.
Air supply is either flexible line or integral blower.

19 Air table
The package moves over the surface of a hollow chamber full of compressed air.
Air escapes through holes in surface. Goods can be moved with 1/1000th of power required to lift them. Can take several hundred kgs distributed weight.

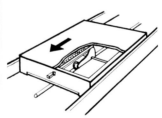

20 Air cushion
For use in live storage racking or buffer storage. Seal increases directional air supply to pallet if load increased, and is cut off when pallet stops. Speed controlled by degrees of pressure of wheel on seal.

21 Air in the floor
Same as 'air table' except that holes in surface equipped with ballcheck valves, so that air only escapes when load is over area. Load also partly supported on balls. The system is more economical for large surface areas and heavy loads.

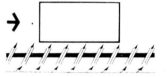

22 Air conveyor
Basically a long and narrow air table. Angled air flow mean that goods are propelled as well as lifted. Used to transport high volume/low weight goods at high speeds.
Very suitable for packages on the way to palletiser from order picker.

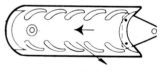

air flow from iink providing second thrust

23 Air supported/tracked conveyor
Plan view of undersurface of one link.
Articulated hollow units linked together at each end, with air fed vertically and horizontally into the linked units to give lift and direction. Shape of escape outlets gives extra thrust.

6 Overhead conveyors

Uses and limitations
6.01 These conveyors keep goods off the floor, clearing it for the use of wheeled plant. But overhead tracks can constrict fork lift trucks. Overhead conveyors cannot be altered or moved easily if requirements change. Where headroom is limited, this conveyor will obstruct wheeled plant and personnel unless the chain speed is slow. With their ability to queue, rise vertically as lifts, and be routed around structural obstructions, these conveyors can be used very successfully in warehouse operations.

Sizes and capacities
6.02 Chain lengths are limitless, with booster motors. Standard bends **25** are usually 700, 1000 and 1700 mm, with the capability of 900 mm vertical radii. Carriage loads vary from 150 to 1000 kg per hanger; hangers can be connected for heavier loads. Speeds range to 0·45 m/sec.

Space requirements
6.03 This depends on the width of the carrier, but overhead conveyors sterilise an area at a fixed height above the floor. The system can be elevated locally to cross aisles and door positions. In some installations, an overhead conveyor is used for order picking; the gangway should be 1·5 m-1·8 m plus the width of the carrier to leave adequate clearance for the swing-in.

Equipment design
6.04 Overhead conveyors are similar to underfloor towlines in operation. They can be mechanically directed by a pin system, **24** and be used as an accumulation conveyor or moving buffer store for full and empty containers. There are many variations of drag head, carriage and table, designed for specific speeds and duties.

25

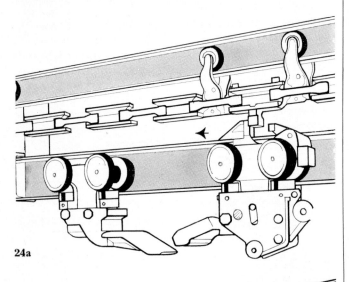

24a

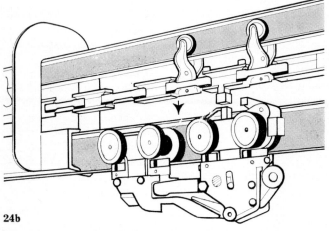

24b

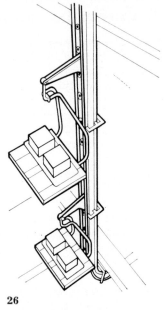

24a *Overhead support carriage approaching already accumulated carriage.*
b *The lug of the support carriage locks into the accumulated carriage ramp, releasing the pin from the chain.*
25 *Typical overhead conveyor showing drive sprocket and curve.*
26 *Chain conveyor used as vertical lift.*

26

6.05 Extra equipment includes automatic chain switching, controlling carriers in and out of the main line, vertical hoists that convert the track and carriage into a lift **26**, full queueing ability, free track turntables, and it can be adapted to full on-line computer control.

Building needs
6.06 Provision is needed for track suspension from the roof, or floor. Allow for the load in structural calculations. The system should be integrated with services and sprinkler lines. Power is usually three phase, to several motor points. If an overhead system is planned, the manufacturers should supply the dead and operating weights to the structural engineer at the earliest instance.

Price
6.07 Allow approximately £150/metre run for complete installation. This is a rough estimate, as there are so many accessories that prices are variable.

7 Sorting conveyors

7.01 These include drive-off and push-off diverters, slide-slat and tilt-tray sorters and tilt-belt conveyors.

Drive-off and push-off diverters
7.02 Drive-off diverters are faster than push-off methods. Many are designed for high speed sorting, and are costly as they have to be engineered as part of the conveyor.
7.03 *Deflectors* are the least expensive type of diverting mechanism. There are two types. Fixed position or stationary arms are the least expensive, physically brushing the goods off to one side. Pivoting arms, powered by air cylinders, motors or solenoids move back and forth across the conveyor surface. Other movable arms do not swing, but move across for the package to touch, the momentum pushing it off the conveyor surface. Both types can be powered by adding a short belt to boost the deflected item, and prevent any jams at the turn point. Pop-up deflectors can only be used with roller conveyors, either gravity rollers or powered rollers and wheels.
7.04 *Drive-off diverters* protrude slightly above roller or wheel conveyor beds to engage the bottom of the package and carry it off the conveyor. Belts can be used if short drive-off sections are inserted between belt runs. Both push-off and drive-off diverters may be blocked by damaged packages. As a rule, speed is usually responsible for blockage. If high speed sorting of small goods is anticipated, an inclined belt is less prone to jam. The belt is laterally inclined and, as parcels move along the lower face of the conveyor, flaps open, releasing the package onto the accumulation line. Control can be manual or 'on-line'.

Slide slat conveyors
7.05 These slide physically to divert packages to the correct channel. Typical speeds are 5500 packets per hour if 300 mm long, and 2000 per hour if 1·2 m long. Slide slat sections can be easily integrated with belt or slat conveyors. Typical slide slats move at 49 m/minute **27**.

Tilt tray sorters
7.06 A combination of sorter and conveyor **28**. Unlike other systems, the carriage unit actually does the sorting at the required point on the circuit. Mechanically a tilt tray is a series of closely spaced trays, mounted between axially disposed pivots on carriages that travel around a fixed track. Each tray is held in the horizontal position by a cam plate, which locates onto a peg mounted on the carriage. The cam plate is lifted clear of the peg for tilting. Controlled either manually (with a limited memory unit) or automatically (by package codes and sensors) the movement carriage tilts at the discharge point by pneumatic or hydraulic activation. Loads of up to 70 kgs can be carried, with trays at 300 mm or 460 mm centres. If longer loads are handled, the trays can be programmed to tilt in series. Speeds of 91·44 m/minute are possible (100 trays per minute with 915 mm length trays). The drag chain that pulls the carriages around the track is powered by a three-phase motor, from a 3·66 m diameter combined sprocket/tensioner. Motors are from 2·2-22 kW to suit the application.
7.07 Although the number of discharge stations is only limited in theory by the length of the conveyor, costs rise steeply over 125 sorting positions. Tilt trays are very efficient for high speed sorting in warehouses involved in bulk order picking. Bulk orders can be withdrawn from live racking direct onto the tilt tray conveyor, either under manual control or fully 'on line'.

Tilt belt conveyors
7.08 These are flat belts, where the supporting rollers are mounted on a hinged axle. When a package is to be diverted, the section usually drops sharply on one side. Control and throughput tend to be similar to tilt tray units. Operation is usually single sided as roller tilting is complex if double sided discharge was installed. These diverters rely on regular based packages, and a combination of belt and package material that allows immediate sliding: if friction is not quickly overcome, package and belt damage can occur.

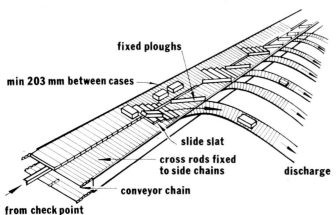

fixed ploughs
min 203 mm between cases
slide slat
cross rods fixed to side chains
discharge
conveyor chain
from check point

27 Slide slat conveyor
A computer controlled console unit is situated next to the conveyor infeed and recognises the number of carrying slats, and remembers their destination. As each case approaches destination, slats slide automatically to fixed plough. Slats 760 mm wide. Unit 1·5 m wide. Up to 91 m long. Minimum floor to top height = 760 mm.

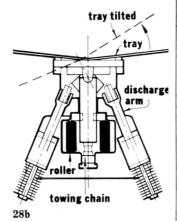

tray tilted
tray
discharge arm
roller
towing chain
28b

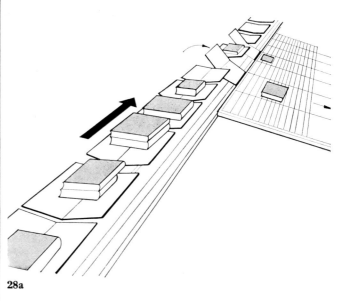

28a

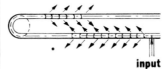

input
28c

28a *Tilt tray sorter carrying books.*
b *section* **c** *typical sorting pattern.*

29

29 *A conveyor system serving a three level mezzanine storage system leading to the dispatch sorting area.*
30 *Manually-propelled system that both transports and acts as inter-process storage medium. By depressing a foot pedal units can change direction of travel from one set of rails to another at 90°.*

30

Technical study Automated storage 1

Storage process

Automated storage, in which plant is planned and controlled by computer and automation, is the most sophisticated storage type.

1 Introduction

1.01 In theory, automated storage offers fast and accurate mechanical handling and stock control, operated by a computer. In practice, this is difficult to achieve. In spite of improved handling and control methods, several companies found that overall costs soon overtook predicted savings. What has been lacking is a broad-based approach to design, and a full understanding in designers of the impact and implications of automation on the distribution system.

1.02 Computer-manipulated stock control has been used for some time to decrease the lead time for orders, reduce stock levels and calculate the positions in the racking best suited for moving stock quickly. It seemed logical to expand this function and link the handling machinery directly to data-processing equipment. This limited the design of the early installations.

The development of automated warehouses

1.03 The first automated warehouse to attract widespread attention was that of the Brunswig Drug Company in Los Angeles. It was built in 1960 but, although successful in technical operation, was put out of action by a company policy change (an example of the importance of forward planning). The next major development was for the kitchens of Sara Lee, Chicago, a warehouse whose complexity and sophistication of control systems and handling plant blazed the trail for development all over the world. It was a cooled store for perishable cakes, handling over 100 product types 'on-line'.

1.04 In Europe, development started in countries with limited land and expensive labour, such as Sweden and Switzerland. By the mid '60s, several high-bay automated warehouses had been built for the retail and pharmaceutical trades and for parts storage for the manufacturing industry (eg, Oehler's warehouses for Suchard Chocolate in France, **1**, West Germany and Switzerland, for the Dr Maag pharmaceutical company in Dielsdorf, and the warehouse in Lausanne for the Baumgartner Papiers, SA). The Dr Maag warehouse, **2**, was constructed with vertical precast concrete rack elements, and in the paper warehouse the steel racks were an integral part of the building structure, **3**. These installations were 'on-line' controlled.

1.05 The Volvo Company in Sweden had built an automated store for parts and spares that used standard pallets as the storage medium, and their competitor Saab-Scania also built a high-bay store at that time. In Lucerne, Demag built Viscose Suisse **4**, a 29 m-high warehouse of concrete, but with pallet supports made of steel and bolted to the cross walls.

1.06 In the US, automated stores developed quickly, but fewer were high bay as there was less pressure on industrial land. Installations with live storage and automated cranes were developed, such as the Ford Motor Company's parts store at Plymouth, Michigan, which was only 12 m high. Complex horizontally oriented systems, ie not high bay were designed, as at the US Navy's Oakland warehouse, handling over 15 000 lines. This relatively simple warehouse broke even in under three years. Most automated warehouses in the US were for goods with very high flow rates with small or large variety of product lines.

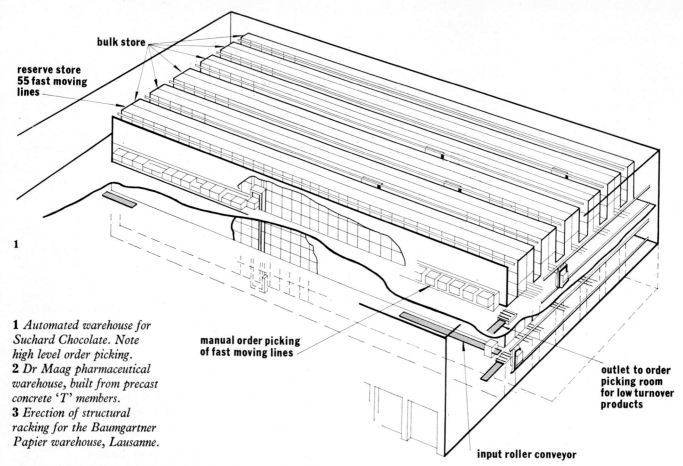

bulk store

reserve store
55 fast moving
lines

manual order picking
of fast moving lines

outlet to order
picking room
for low turnover
products

input roller conveyor

1 *Automated warehouse for Suchard Chocolate. Note high level order picking.*
2 *Dr Maag pharmaceutical warehouse, built from precast concrete 'T' members.*
3 *Erection of structural racking for the Baumgartner Papier warehouse, Lausanne.*

2

3

1.07 In the UK, the CWS warehouse at Birtley, Co Durham incorporated many novel features, including 'on-line' control structural racking and an order-picking system that brought the goods to the pickers, called 'carousels'. Unfortunately, this installation suffered from a protracted and complicated commissioning period so that only recently has it become fully operational.

1.08 Other British automated warehouses of the late '60s included Boots at Nottingham, **6** (which used a peripheral mini-computer for real-time control and a central computer for process documentation) and the stores for Perkins Engines at Peterborough and for car bodies at Pressed Steel Fisher, West Bromwich. The former store was controlled by consoles at the end of each aisle, the latter by punched cards. The PSF warehouse incorporated air-conditioning with humidity-control in 20 m-high aisles so that unpainted car bodies did not have to be treated before storage.

1.09 A survey of automated stores in the UK in 1971 found that, out of 50 installations, 25 had directly computer-operated stock control, 16 out of these 25 had direct computer control for the stacker cranes, but only four were fully 'on-line'. Out

of these four, three used stacker cranes and one used a transporter system; only one was fully operational at the time.

1.10 European automated warehouses have worked more successfully than UK ones. Sometimes a highly mechanised, and not automated warehouse, would have been the solution.

1.11 Other reasons for the lack of success of UK automated warehouses included one or more of the following:

1 The company was a step behind its competitors and wanted to be two steps ahead at one leap.

2 The company had already been sold a stock control computer too big for their requirements by a hardware-oriented industry, and it seemed economic to use the spare capacity for 'on-line' control of handling plant.

3 Rationalisation of a diversity of interests, possibly of merged companies, by streamlining every stage of the distribution system, assumed an automated warehouse to be the panacea.

1.12 The results have been warehouses that required considerable expenditure in the automation of redundant functions, and which so greatly affected the total distribution system that more had to be spent to bring this into line.

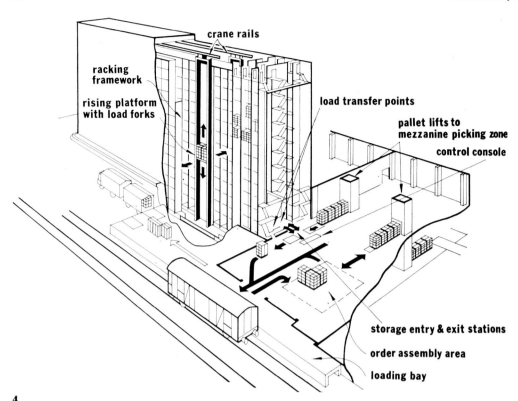

crane rails

racking framework

rising platform with load forks

load transfer points

pallet lifts to mezzanine picking zone

control console

storage entry & exit stations

order assembly area

loading bay

4

4 Warehouse for Viscose Suisse: steel pallet supports bolted to concrete cross walls.
5 Economies of scale in conventional and high-bay warehouses.

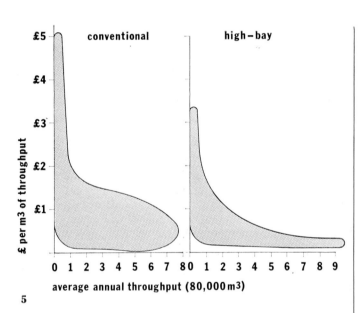

5

Planning
1.13 In planning an automated warehouse, the fundamental issues have to be identified from the outset. Techniques often alien to designers and operators in the warehousing field are needed to predict throughput and future trade.

The team
1.14 More than in any other section of the storage industry it is important that designers fully understand the potential and operation of all the systems involved. The project leader chosen should have the expertise and the skill to integrate the diversity of parts and systems that compose an automated warehouse. It should be the co-ordinating designer's responsibility to inform the client of the suitability of the brief (which is often inaccurate). Adaptation of an automated system after construction affects every element, and is both difficult and expensive.

Total system approach
1.15 When automation has been selected as a realistic and economic concept, the control system should be developed in parallel with the handling system and building design.

Consultants
1.16 A consultant should be appointed at the inception of the project. The consultancy organisation must be able to appraise production and distribution plans, assess throughput requirements, develop the 'software' and integrate computer control with machinery. Some of the larger equipment manufacturers, especially the European ones, offer integrated consultancy services (which, unless run as a totally separate professional organisation, will inevitably be partisan).

Client/designer relationships
1.17 Packaged deals by consortia of equipment manufacturers and control specialists may lead to the client being subjected to pressures in design, resulting in over-automation and complicated 'hard-wired' data transfer.

Implications of automation
1.18 In assessing the brief, the designer should consider the following:
1 Is the need to reduce distribution costs best achieved in this case by automation? There are hidden costs such as the creation of 'software', the increase in data-processing staff, and possible losses due to system breakdown.
2 Does improvement of customer service depend on improved warehouse function or is it the transport and distribution system that is at fault? To answer these questions, designers should understand the implications of automation.
1.19 Automation means replacing a man by a machine, with advantages of accuracy, reduced personnel, and standardisation of equipment and control systems.

How much automation?
1.20 The following questions should be asked:
1 Are all functions still relevant? Briefs tend to be based on client's existing operations and it is wasteful to automate redundant functions.
2 Is there an existing data-processing system that could be used more effectively?
3 Will the cost of mechanising some particular functions limit the capital resources for the rest of the warehouse system, so that other areas cannot be brought up to a commensurate standard? If so, the overall potential will be restricted.

4 Should on- or off-line control be used? The present trend is towards both on- and off-line mini-computers, as slaves to a central master control. One consultant visualises these machines being plugged into a large, central, data-processing machine on a time-sharing basis, as easily as plugging a power tool into a ring main.

1.21 The biggest problem with automation is that people have to play a new role.

1.22 Despite the application of sophisticated data processing techniques, and the use of more reliable handling plant, there has been little overall reduction in the cost of distribution.

Summary

1.23 In automated warehouse projects:

1 Overall project control by one person or team is essential.

2 The user does not always know accurately what is required. He may be under pressure from several sources, and be trying to tighten up the wrong part of the system. A full reappraisal should be made.

3 It is important to choose a consultant suitable for the type of warehouse involved.

4 If computer-controlled systems are to be used, the 'software' should be designed in parallel with the handling and building systems from the outset.

5 A total-system approach to design is necessary.

User specification

1.24 *Definition* An automated high bay warehouse is a pallet silo, equipped with high racking to cover a minimum site area, capable of fast turnover and automated materials handling, with simultaneous stock control.

1.25 Before the user finally decides on an automated warehouse he must accept a 5-10 year commitment for the following:

1 *The maximum weight of the unit load* for dispatch. This will affect the transport and distribution system and possibly the type of goods acceptable by the warehouse.

2 *The size and type of pallet.* The pallet best suited to the system may prove too dear or unsuitable to leave the warehouse. Although checking equipment is available, one broken pallet can jam an automated system, so is the use of standard road pallets justified? Will the acceptance of a narrow range of sizes conform to the metric pallets used throughout the EEC, or will the size conflict with pallets arriving from suppliers or for dispatch in ISO containers? (see Information sheet Mechanised storage 1 Pallets.) The user should decide the strategy to be followed. An automated warehouse for contemporary market conditions should be capable of adaptability and expansion.

1.26 Users who want to reduce distribution costs per unit (as distinct from having low-capital-cost distribution facilities) may find automated distribution an economic necessity. Machine-intensive distribution systems will become more attractive as labour costs increase faster than those of mechanical plant. The need for more accurate dispatch to save expense on vehicle journeys and wasted sorting will also make automation attractive, as the reduction of dispatch error saves on total distribution cost.

1.27 Performance specifications have been widely used as user-specifications for automated warehouse design, especially by packaged deal consortia. This is a dangerous practice as the way which performance is achieved is left to the judgment of the equipment supplier. The elements of automated operation need to be precisely stated and to cover all possible development patterns that the client may take during the period for which he is committed. By describing the parts in detail, and relating these to the whole, a detailed skeleton should emerge as a base which the project team can work from and which can be reassessed at various stages in the design

process to ensure that the original strategy will not be lost during operational planning.

2 Source of goods

2.01 Sources of goods for automated storage are the same as for mechanised storage warehouses and are described in TS Mechanised storage 1 para 2.

3 Form of transport

3.01 This is also the same as for mechanised storage warehouses and is described in TS Mechanised storage 1 para 3.

4 Control of transport

4.01 See also TS Mechanised storage 1 para 4.

4.02 Automated handling and control systems are uneconomic if calculated to accept large throughputs of goods for only a short period of the working day. Some peaks are inevitable due to drivers' hours limits, the distance of travel and local road conditions; seasonal peaks should be taken into account when calculating storage capacity (see para 9). Stacker crane movement patterns require incoming and outgoing pallets to be handled from the same end of the aisle, which means a single loading bay and sorting area. Automated handling systems offer fast load build-up, so that truck turn-round times can be reduced. The collection documents must be received early enough for crane cycles to be calculated by the computer.

4.03 Automated traffic control reduces the peak build-up of vehicles and system-imposed queueing allows the stock control computer to plan the best stacking and picking patterns to avoid goods accumulating and jamming the sorting area. A block-allocated delivery policy for principal suppliers also reduces vehicle peaks, and the set pattern allows the computer to clear any backlog before predicted arrivals.

4.04 To allow a computer enough time to assemble return loads, collection papers should be handed in with those accompanying the incoming load at the checking office or gatehouse. The truck then moves into an accumulation park to await a bay allocation. The documents are sent to the programming area by a document conveyor, eg, a pneumatic tube, and the goods identified. Data for both incoming goods and the return load are then fed into a stock control computer, which can assess the existing loading bay position and allocate a bay to the awaiting truck. This information then passes to a subsidiary loading bay computer and is printed out for a traffic controller. An optimum picking cycle can then be calculated in relation to other loads being assembled simultaneously. So, as the truck is waiting in the accumulation park, the return load is already being assembled. Turn-round times can thus be as fast as it takes for the truck to be called forward, to position and to discharge its incoming load, and for the preassembled goods to be loaded. This can be 8-10 minutes, or less if total roll-on/roll-off systems (eg, Joloda or Berthelat) are used. Fast turn-round speeds reduce the requirement for space taken up by vehicles, but this should not be reduced drastically compared with the accommodation for a similar mechanised warehouse, as unexpected peaks and transport problems do occur.

The use of optical scanners

4.05 Traffic control automation can be taken a stage further by eliminating the traffic office and the document function of the gatehouse (leaving the latter as a security check). Optical scanners now available can read clearly typed documents. A driver at the gatehouse would place the documents for incoming cargo (and collection, if applicable) face down on a reader table, which scans them and sends on-line impulses to the stock control computer. The computer selects an accumulation

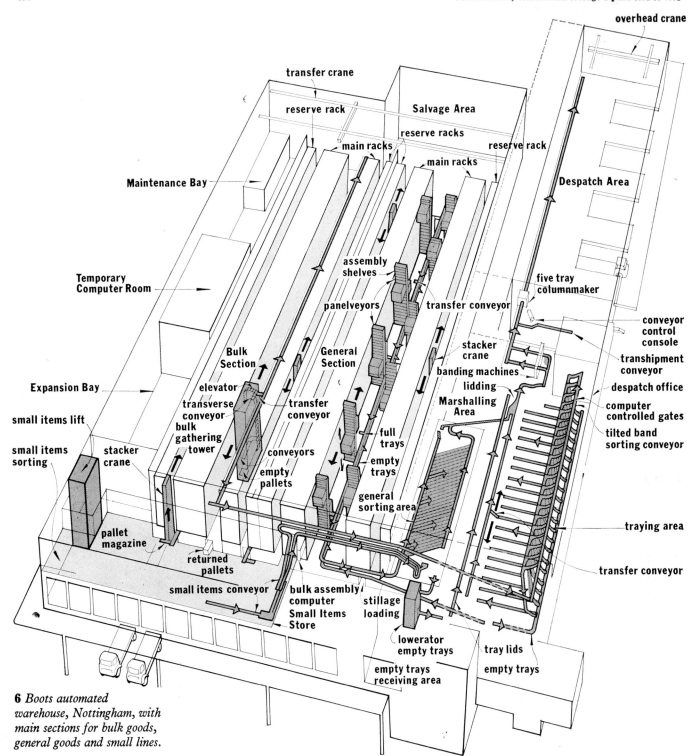

overhead crane

transfer crane

reserve rack

Salvage Area

reserve racks

main racks

main racks

reserve rack

Despatch Area

Maintenance Bay

assembly shelves

Temporary Computer Room

panelveyors

transfer conveyor

five tray columnmaker

conveyor control console

transhipment conveyor

despatch office

computer controlled gates

tilted band sorting conveyor

stacker crane

banding machines

Bulk Section

General Section

Expansion Bay

elevator

transverse conveyor

bulk gathering tower

transfer conveyor

lidding

Marshalling Area

small items lift

small items sorting

stacker crane

conveyors

full trays

empty trays

general sorting area

traying area

empty pallets

transfer conveyor

pallet magazine

returned pallets

small items conveyor

bulk assembly computer Small Items Store

stillage loading

lowerator empty trays

tray lids

empty trays

empty trays receiving area

6 *Boots automated warehouse, Nottingham, with main sections for bulk goods, general goods and small lines.*

lane opposite the loading bay and indicates this on a gantry-hung visual display screen on the approach road. The process can be very fast; order picking operates as before, the return load accumulating as the previous vehicle is being handled. When the vehicle has been loaded, either the loading forklift driver activates the traffic control periphery, or the leaving vehicle can activate a sensor. The control periphery would call forward the waiting truck by visual display or pre-recorded voice message. This is not a complicated program, and it is likely that this type of automated traffic control will be used increasingly in high throughput installations.

5 Receipt of goods

5.01 After trucks have been automatically called forward, the operation is as for mechanised storage (see Technical study Mechanised storage 1, para 5).

6 Form of goods

6.01 Goods for handling in automated warehouses should be palletised. Some pallets are unsuitable for the automated storage system (see Information sheet Mechanised storage 1, para **1.01**). The user is committing himself to a pallet type when he invests in an automated system. A certain amount of tolerance can be allowed economically, eg, the difference between 1100 and 1200 mm pallets. The size chosen should be the one most likely to arrive according to the trade involved. Sweden already operates a national pallet pool to alleviate this problem, and this might also be done in the EEC. Shrink-wrapping and banding help load stability, important in auto-mated warehouses. Some users like to remove the plastic film at the loading bay to lessen the fire risk, however, and others puncture it to avoid condensation.

7 Unloading

7.01 An intermediate unloading method is required between the transport and the automated system. If conventional loads are involved, a forklift system is usually operated. Special transport for steel coils requires an overhead gantry

7 *Loading bay serving both incoming and dispatch functions. Pallets are handled automatically once on the roller conveyors.*
8 *For fast vehicle handling the conveyors are double decked, mounted as lifts. Driver documents at gate house inform the computer of the incoming load, starting*

preparation of the dispatch. The truck enters the bay allocated while the dispatch load is accumulating on the upper level. The incoming load fills the conveyor at truck level, which then drops a level, allowing the conveyor above to lower to the truck bed and load the dispatch goods. Label check is completed simultaneously.

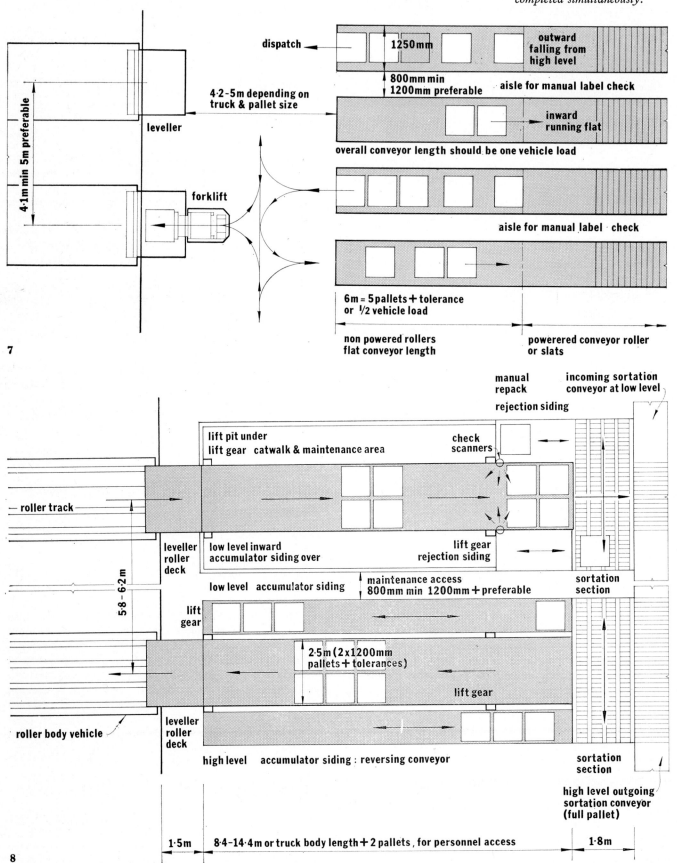

dispatch

1250mm

outward falling from high level

aisle for manual label check

800mm min
1200mm preferable

4·2-5m depending on truck & pallet size

inward running flat

overall conveyor length should be one vehicle load

leveller

aisle for manual label check

4·1m min 5m preferable

forklift

6m = 5pallets + tolerance
or ½ vehicle load

non powered rollers
flat conveyor length

powerered conveyor roller
or slats

7

manual repack

incoming sortation conveyor at low level

rejection siding

lift pit under
lift gear catwalk & maintenance area

check scanners

roller track

leveller roller deck

low level inward accumulator siding over

lift gear rejection siding

sortation section

5·8 – 6·2m

maintenance access
800mm min 1200mm + preferable

low level accumulator siding

lift gear

2·5m (2 x 1200mm pallets + tolerances)

lift gear

roller body vehicle

leveller roller deck

high level   accumulator siding : reversing conveyor

sortation section

high level outgoing sortation conveyor (full pallet)

1·5m   8·4-14·4m or truck body length + 2 pallets , for personnel access   1·8m

8

crane or a roll-in system (see Section 9 Special storage). With forklifts in the loading bay of an automated warehouse, the stuffer truck usually shuttles between the vehicle and a check-in area. The same loading bay and buffer zone dimensions apply as in Technical study Mechanised storage 1, para 6; a load and a half, with space for segregation and personnel access bay should be provided for both incoming and dispatch loads. Incoming pallets still have to be checked in automated stores and code labels added for correct routing.

8 Characteristics of goods

8.01 Any goods are suitable for automated storage, as long as they are properly packaged. The characteristics of the goods and their packaging should be carefully examined during the design of the system. Package strength is important, as packages have to accept acceleration and deceleration stresses with automated sorting systems. Some space has to be allocated in the loading bay area for repalletising; the depalletising/repalletising unit **10** is another machine which may break down. One firm dictates to suppliers a strict packaging specification, and accepts the 3 per cent additional cost to each contract as well-spent. Goods should be assessed for maximum cube potential of the pallet loads; it is worth dictating to suppliers the maximum and minimum pallet-stacking heights, as well as the pallet type itself, and also the lateral loading tolerances acceptable by the load centering and checking devices, which are necessary before acceptance into automated storage areas.

9 Sorting

9.01 The choice of sorting method depends on the stock control system used, the level of automation, the type of supplier and the method of unloading. Some buffer space for manual checking is always required in case of system breakdown or for random system checks. Automated sorting relies on the code attached to the pallet load. With a few suppliers (eg, parts for machine production) the code labels can be fixed at the suppliers' premises; sorting can be automatic from the immediate unloading position and any unlabelled goods can be ejected into a buffer line.

9.02 If conveyors run directly into the loading bay, space

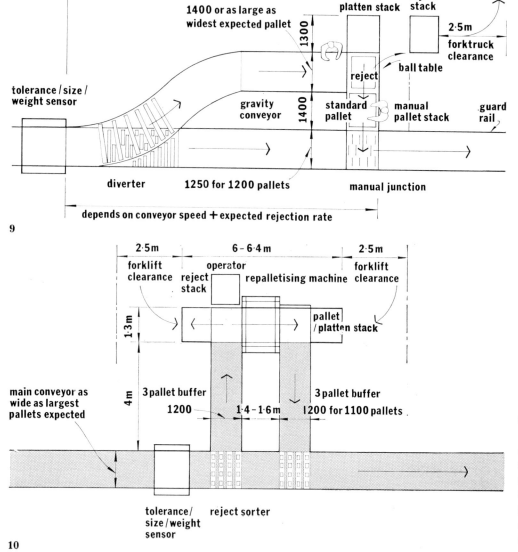

9

10

9 Manual pallet repacking.
10 Automated repalletising and plattenising machines are important, if road pallets are used in an automated warehouse, to avoid broken pallets passing to jam the automated equipment in the racking zone.

should be allocated for manual loading and code check. This can be done by cut-out sections on the powered roller conveyor, as in an accumulation unit. Some systems weigh pallets in motion, check their size and load tolerances, check their codes, and, if unsuitable, reject them into a siding. Sensors, switches and stop-start devices are required for this automatic operation, adding to the chance of breakdown;

loading bays and buffer areas serving both inward and dispatch goods must be kept clear and operational.

Coding methods
9.03 These include optical mark reading, bar codes and dot codes. Scanners can also read normal clear type, a useful function for use in manual override situations. Magnetic codes on special cards are also used. Optical scanners can read codes as the pallet passes, **11**, and one form, spray scanners, can read labels out of true, so the pallets need not be straight, **12**.
9.04 With multiple suppliers, as at a grocery warehouse, automated sorting is more complicated; the diversity of goods handled and the different speeds of throughput require a buffer area for pallets to wait while the stock control computer clears any backlog in the user sections. If the incoming goods' data has been processed while the truck is waiting for the loading bay to be freed, the buffer area can be minimised.
9.05 With many suppliers, goods are checked off against a recorded manifest, so that when passed as correct, the central data processing computer can draw up the suppliers' accounts. But in some operators' experience, many suppliers cannot be guaranteed to label pallets correctly and the diversity of pallets requires a careful check anyway. Some operators prefer to code all incoming pallets themselves, so that they have full control in case of system breakdown.

Pallets and platens
9.06 The CWS warehouse at Birtley was planned to dispense with road pallets as it was felt that there was enough chance of a broken or non-standard pallet jamming the system to justify plattenising machines. These machines tip the pallet upside down, remove the road pallet, and place the load on a platen, right-way-up again, **13**. In contrast, the Volvo warehouse uses standard pallets successfully, but the Swedish pallet pool keeps pallet standards high. A manual repacking position is provided also at CWS, as some loads are not well enough packed even for the plateniser. The choice of using plattens or pallets in an automated warehouse is a major policy decision. If a very varied range of pallet types and sizes are to be handled, plattenising is probably economic. If there are few suppliers who will accept a packaging specification, much money can be saved by using a standard pallet.

Feeding the storage area
9.07 Powered roller conveyors are used for transport to the storage area, as they offer greater scope for automated sorting. Overhead systems have also been used successfully and, if transporter systems are used for the storage medium, these can run under line control to the loading bay and sorting area. Towline carts have also been used, with roller platforms for automatic loading and discharging at the transfer positions.

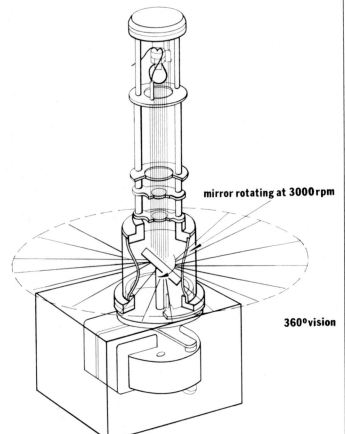

large fixed mirror
photoelectric sensor
returning reflected beam
laser beam generator
small mirror (hole for outgoing beam)
rapidly rotating mirror
area swept by beam
scanner
bin
belt

11

mirror rotating at 3000 rpm

360° vision

12

13

11 *Spray beam scanner.*
12 *Detail of spray scanner with 360° vision.*
13 *Automatic plattenising machine at CWS, Birtley. Loads on road pallets are turned upside down on to platens and the timber pallets withdrawn.*
14 *This pallet has a broken corner. Timber resin leaves a deposit on the rollers that may drop off and affect the mechanical equipment.*
15 *A platten being transferred into a stacker crane.*
16 *Off-line control.*

Robotug trains are another well-tried method, operating on a push-button code, punched cards or fully on line, following a wire buried 4 mm in the floor surface. A variation of this is a wire-guided train of pallet trucks, but these have to be un-hooked and discharged manually. Tractor trains are not as fast as conveyors for transport or sorting, but leave floor areas clear, and do not require substructures, special services or the considerable maintenance required by conveyor lines. (But tractor trains have jerky movements which may cause loads to become unstable.)

10 Volume calculations

10.01 These will determine whether the store has to be 'high bay' and to what level it should be automated, if at all. A consultant is of great importance, as volume and turnover calculations are linked with software development and the type of plant. However, the designer should be able to understand the processes that led the consultant to his conclusions. Computer techniques can be of great benefit here, as peak and system break-down situations can be simulated for various flow and turnover speeds, and the most likely constriction points and the resulting need for buffer zones, quickly observed. This can be programmed to printout graphically for easy interpretation by the designer.

10.02 Daily, weekly and seasonal peaks should be calculated to decide to what peak level the store should be designed. Seasonal and daily peaks can quickly push an automated storage system out of sequence. In some installations, stacker cranes cannot keep up with increased input, even when the store is part empty. If the decision is incorrect, the warehouse will be either mostly empty, or rapidly choked in loading bay and checking zones. Searching questions should be asked of the equipment and control systems' suppliers and salesmen about peak capacities and expansion potential.

10.03 One way to avoid the daily peak situation is to allocate block delivery times to suppliers. Otherwise, trucks have to be ranked to keep pace with the store, or buffer space should be provided between the loading bay and the racking, with the stacker cranes programmed on a priority basis. This tends to be clumsy; as a rule, pallets should be kept 'off the floor'.

10.04 The design of an automated distribution centre is influenced by methods chosen for order picking and outward load assembly, which are dictated by volume and throughput to be handled. There can be no standard solution for distribution warehouses, as there is such a variation in stock throughput over the range of products, from the fastest to the slowest movers. A formula to a check for cost comparisons of various throughput rates and systems is $C = T + NS$, where C is the cost of unit output, expressed in terms of T, the cost of handling a unit load; N is the number of weeks stock to be held for a product line; S is the cost of storage per position per week. T and S are functions of the method of handling and storage chosen, and T can be greater or lesser than S, depending on the system chosen. N can vary by 20:1 or more, so optimisation is not easy.

10.05 Although racking is now normally organised into notional divisions of goods with similar stock delay times, the most important area to invest for lost effectiveness remains the load assembly zone. Other parameters to consider include the likelihood of unpredicted peaks caused by new ranges of product or multi-shift operation, for instance the increasing chance of night deliveries to city shops. Flexibility carries a heavy cost penalty.

11 Turnover calculations

11.01 These are inseparable from volume calculations above.

14

15

12 Variety and flow

12.01 This depends on the type of trade that the warehouse is to serve, ie, whether it is performing a stockholding or transit function (see Technical study Mechanised storage 1, para 1). This affects the stock control system and the method chosen for order picking (see para 14 and 16).

13 Type of storage

13.01 This complex decision should be based on a systematic evaluation of data. Many variables are involved.
1 Should the handling plant be controlled by a computer on- or off-line?
2 How high should the store be?
3 Should a stacker crane or transporter type system or wire-guided, free-path machines be used?
4 Should the building be integral with the racking?
5 Should the associated sortation and handling activities be fully automated?
All these questions are closely related to the volume and turnover requirements (para 10), and to how much the user is prepared to spend on the plant and the control system in relation to the potential of his future business.

Off-line control

13.02 Off-line control involves an intermediate data carriage medium. A computer produces punched cards (or tape containing instructions) for the handling plant's work cycle, and this is placed into the peripheral machine. This system is flexible, as either several machines can receive instructions from a central reader or (more usual in a decentralised layout) each machine can be equipped with its own reader. Plastic punched cards survive over three years of intensive use. Off-line involves batch processing of data; all the data for a day or week is fed into the central control computer, which checks it against current stock-holding figures and isolates product lines for re-ordering. These programs can be a ready-made package or custom built to generate order-picking lists, dispatch documents, forecasts, trends and turnover analyses.

13.03 Standard package programs by computer manufacturers and software houses have helped the designer reduce the costs of computer control. But their weakness lies in the fact that data for one process might not be in a suitable language for printing out data from another. Computer languages for large data-processing units tend to be specialised for the work they have to do; but can be linked quickly with off-line peripherals by punched cards or tape.

On-line control

13.04 On-line control means that stacker cranes and sorting plant are directly connected to the electronic data processing machine, without a data carrier medium. On-line 'real-time' stock control and plant movement can use the client's own large commercial data processing computer, but it is necessary to have a multi-programming facility, often a language conversion unit, and a set of separate peripheral machines, **16**. These early systems, with complex 'hard wiring' have tended to be troublesome. Real-time, on-line stock control giving instant stock level information for any product line is very useful; data is either printed out or displayed on a cathode screen. (This is different from real-time machine control which controls simple movements, and is unsuitable for a large data processing unit.) With the early on-line installations, the problems can be simplified to the fact that computers can 'think' in under 1/50 000th of a second, and the machinery trundled down the aisle and back in over a minute; it was the incompatibility between system elements that gave trouble.

17 *Stacker crane.*

13.05 Real-time working with mini-computers has most inbuilt flexibility. 'Real time' is data handling of a function that is actually happening, not prediction or retrospective stock evaluation work. Process control units (or mini computers) can be used singly or in groups, they are easily programmed, and adapted, and can be linked on-line to the main data processing unit to receive work cycle instructions and pass back updated stock information. Mini-computers are safer in shutdowns, ie if one unit fails, the whole system does not suffer as with full on-line working. Quite sophisticated machines can cost as little as £5000.

13.06 There is a master-slave relationship between the central data processing unit and the peripheral mini-computers. At present most mini-computers work off-line from the central unit, with cards or a tape between them. But soon the mini-computers may plug into the central data processing unit to receive orders and feedback information as easily and reliably as an electric plug into a power circuit.

13.07 On-line control is extremely costly but involves minimum manpower.

Choice of storage plant

13.08 The height of the store will be decided by the volume of stock to be held in relation to the site area available, including space for truck assembly and loading bays, and the possibility of expansion. Whether the structure should be integral with the racks depends on the height of racking required, the type of handling plant to be used, and the requirement for later adaptability. One manufacturer claims that, if over 15·2 m high, integral racking can save over 30 per cent of the building cost over a comparable conventional building (see para 22). Having chosen control methods, and store height, the storage plant should be chosen. It could be either:
1 The stacker crane type of in-aisle, fixed path machine.
2 Free path, wire guided machinery.
3 Fixed path transporter types.
4 Combinations of these with live storage racking.

Stacker cranes

13.09 The most commonly used storage and retrieval method in high bay automated stores is the stacker crane, **17**. This can be hung from the top of the racking, floor supported with a roof-slung guide rail, or completely supported from a roof rail. They can be distributed one to an aisle, or equipped with a transfer carriage to serve the low user aisles. If the racking is not integral, the stacker can be mounted on a gantry carriage for multi-aisle operation.

13.10 Stacker cranes move slower vertically than horizontally, so that the optimum length to height ratio can be gained from typical operating speeds and work cycles. Stacker cranes can be operated on-line to the central computer or mini-computer, or off-line by an operator placing punched cards or tape into a terminal at the end of each aisle (or groups of aisles). Some installations work by cards, or an operator keys a code into a console mounted on the crane itself, which will perform its cycle and return to the operator for instructions. All stacker cranes should be able to be manually controlled in case of system failure.

13.11 Stacker crane operations need load transfer and buffer positions at the end of the aisles. Because of the economics of stacker work cycles (unless separate cranes are used for input and dispatch) cranes always return to one end of the aisle. The transfer position therefore handles both inward and dispatch goods. Transfer positions are normally the ends of powered roller conveyors, or tables for forklifts to place the pallets. (With the throughputs required to justify stacker cranes, forklift operation has to be intense and tends to be clumsy). Conveyors are often at two levels; incoming pallets pass through a centring device, **18**, to ensure that the pallets are not too big, and are stable and evenly stacked. (It is essential to eliminate damaged pallets in the racking.) If the loads have been platenised, centring is still necessary to line up the load with the crane's forks. Often several checking and centring machines are used between the loading bay/sorting area for

18

20

18 *Centring device to line pallet up for stacker crane's forks.*

19 *Height sensor relays data to the computer so that pallet location can be sized as near the load height as possible. This increases warehouse*

volume efficiency with varied height loads.

20 *Input roller conveyor sorts pallets to crane input tracks: note the sensors and limit switches to right.*

21 *Free-path, narrow-aisle stacker.*

19

21

22 Transporter: this runs to an elevator at the end of each aisle.

immediate rejection, others for in-travel stability checks, and a final check before the stacker pick-up position.

13.12 Output for full pallet loads is often to an upper level and the conveyor then falls to the dispatch sorting area. Stacker cranes work on a wave pattern for economy of movement, they pick up the load from the lower position, store it, retrieve the outgoing unit and return this to the upper level.

Conveyors, with right angle transfer devices and centring machinery can increase costs and may jam the system in case of breakdown. If each aisle has notional high, medium and low user sections, sorting conveyors are required at the input point. The central data processing unit or mini-computer will calculate the optimum movement cycle for the crane, considering the priority of the goods involved; and will pass over slow moving goods until there is a free cycle to store them. This arrangement needs two conveyors in parallel with right angle transfer. It is usually simpler for the cranes to store the pallets in the order that they arrive, providing a buffer for three waiting units. If high peaks are anticipated, buffer capacity should be provided between the sorting area and the transfer points, to avoid choking in the loading bay area; this can be simulated on a computer.

Free path automated plant

13.13 The stacker crane is likely to remain the basic pallet handling unit in large stores, and will continue to grow in height.

Free path automated machines, **21**, may be more suitable for the smaller operator with medium height warehouses, about 12 m stacking height. Developments in accuracy of wire guidance, and free path stacker-order pickers, means that these machines can be used as general handling aids out of the aisles and wireguided in racking with free positioning. Such plant would not be as fast as fixed path stacker cranes, and has tolerance problems at high level, but could be used with mini computers. A wire guidance network could be built in with the floor finish, and certain tracks brought into operation as the store develops. Transfer positions are unnecessary as the free path machines either leave the racks in slack periods to carry goods into the sorting area, or load directly on to trailer trains hauled by wire-guided robotugs. Although this type of system would be highly adaptable and cheap, some operators and equipment manufacturers have doubts about high level stability and achieving the accuracy demanded for high pallet positioning (eg floors laid to 3 mm tolerance).

Transporter systems

13.14 Transporter systems, **22**, sophisticated mini-railways, are suitable for lower throughputs than stacker cranes. They do not offer 100 per cent immediate selectivity, but can be flexible in operation. The system consists of principal distribution tracks at many levels which move vertically by using a special transporter carriage. This supplies subsidiary storage tracks at 90 degrees to the distributor. Withdrawal of goods tends to require a certain amount of shuffling, but this can be controlled by the computer. Transporters are suitable for a limited number of lines of stock, requiring medium speed throughput. Benefits are simplicity of control and mechanics and high use of volume. Transporters can also act as conveyors and sorters between loading bay and racking.

Live storage

13.15 Automated live storage is used successfully by operators with high throughputs and a limited number of lines. It is suitable for full pallet and carton loads, and for supplying order picking stations. A stacker crane or transporter carries the incoming goods to the input position of that product line's particular channel. The goods then flow on a first-in, first-out principal. With loaded pallets, live storage should be powered, or at least power braked, as local shocks can be intense with gravity operation. At the output position, the pallets are picked by a stacker crane or transporter for dispatch, or transfer to an order picking station. The crane can be used as a bridge between the live racks and a sorting conveyor, with on or off-line control.

14 Stock control

14.01 There is still little understanding of stock control in industry, it goes far deeper into the running of a company than many operators imagine.

14.02 The stock control system chosen for an automated warehouse will decide how the handling plant moves within the racks. This depends on the type of goods being stored, the throughput and volume characteristics, and the order picking requirements. The consultant should examine stock control at an early stage, as it is fundamental to the choice of control system, the complexity of soft-ware, and the height and length ratio of the aisles. Stock control was the first commercial computer application in warehousing and is still the most important.

14.03 Stock control is a method of solving the supply and demand problem within a storage system, such as:

1 How long commodity lines should be stored.

2 How long incoming goods take to be processed and what happens to them when they enter the storage zone.

3 How long it takes to locate the goods, and pass them for sorting and dispatch assembly.

4 Where the various parts of the storage offer the highest and slowest speed potential.

14.04 Computerised stock control allows random storage, as the computer 'thinks' so fast, that goods can be stored in the best position for stacker crane efficiency. The computer (by on or off-line control) informs the crane of any free slots in the sections relevant to the goods' movement speed. When the goods have been placed, the slot code is stored on tape or cards, or is fed back direct to the central data processing machine. Real time stock control enables stock levels of any product line to be called up at any time.

14.05 If there is a high throughput and a wide range of goods with varying flow speeds, it is often economic to divide each rack into three or more sections, **23**, so that the fastest movers are at the input/delivery end. Such positions are flexible, and can be altered for seasonal variations by reprogramming the computer. With high throughput and a smaller range of goods, and clearly defined limits between product speeds (eg some stock frequently moved to an order picking area, and other goods that might not move for months), the user speed differentiation can be by rack, using stacker cranes in the high and medium user areas, with a transfer carriage to place

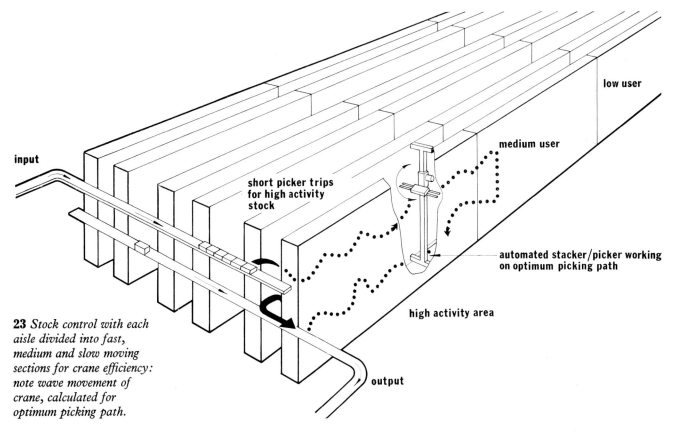

23 *Stock control with each aisle divided into fast, medium and slow moving sections for crane efficiency: note wave movement of crane, calculated for optimum picking path.*

the stacker crane in the low user aisles when required. Some installations have complete high user aisles, **24**, so that the stacker cranes can feed the order picking face by cross-aisle transfer. These control decisions can have a major effect on the distribution of the building on the site.

14.06 Stock control is affected by transport operations, seasonal peaks, the development of trade (automated warehouses tend to develop their own), and by the policy of the company concerned, ie whether the warehouse is one of several regional distribution centres, or the main centralised post production store. Flexibility should be built into the stock control system, as company policies change, and a profitable building can soon become an expensive liability. Care should also be taken concerning expansion, predicted or not, as mergers and a change of policy to absorb other unprofitable warehouses often cannot be foreseen.

15 Stock withdrawal

15.01 With stacker cranes this is the same as for input, but when transporter systems are used the operation is more difficult; some shuffling usually occurs, requiring spaces to be left free on either side of the aisle.

16 Order picking

16.01 One function can still not be economically automated, the final picking of discrete articles has to be done manually. Everything else can be automated to the point of taking the picker by computer controlled stacker crane to the picking position, **25**, informing the operator by visual display of what to pick, checking by a scanner on the takeaway conveyor that the right number of articles has been selected, and reversing the conveyor and reprocessing the order if incorrect. This degree of

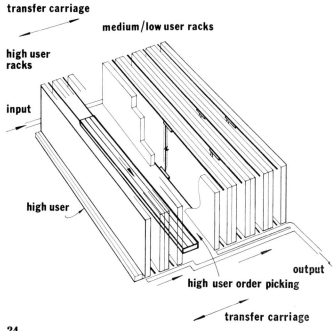

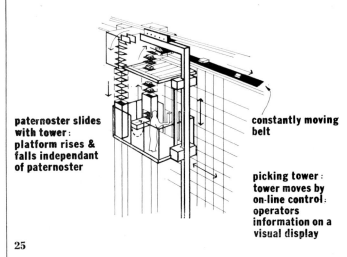

25

24 *Stock control organised into complete warehouse areas for different speeds of goods movement. This allows all stacker cranes to work in the fast section: a transfer carriage takes a stacker crane to an aisle in the slow area* *when required. This system is suitable for seasonal goods with predictable popularity peaks.*

25 *Order-picking tower for continuous discrete item-picking: tower movement is automated.*

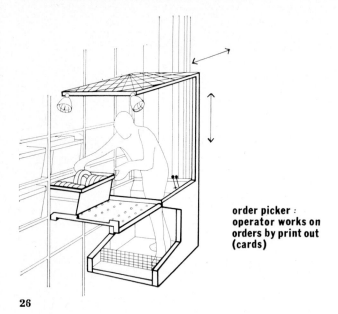

order picker :
operator works on
orders by print out
(cards)

26

automation has been used in the US, and it has been reported that operators performing a mechanical picking operation, **26**, and moved at speed in narrow aisles, constantly in a simultaneous vertical and horizontal pattern, soon begin to suffer psychological disorders. High speed picking in high bays should be removed from personnel altogether. Several stacker crane manufacturers offer machines with order picking cabins, with on or off-line control to the bay. Various arrangements of jointed takeaway conveyors have been suggested, but in-aisle sequential systems usually involve filling a bin and taking it to an output position.

26 *Order-picking from tote bins: the crane has located the picker automatically.*
27 *Free-path machines like this are now being automated*

by wire guidance or light beams.
28 *Fixed path order-picking crane at transfer points. This picks whole plattens at a time.*

16.02 Large scale order picking functions are inevitably manual. Several automated warehouses operate multi-level mezzanine picking systems, fed by automated cranes. A 'real time' periphery is required here, for immediate requests for replacement goods, when pallets have been emptied.
The order picking process is labour intensive; there are two basic methods:
1 Taking the operator to the goods.
2 Bringing the goods to the picker.

Free-path plant for order picking
16.03 There is scope for free path plant, with the possibility of wire guidance in medium sized installations. Costs of automating free path machines have been suggested at about £5000. One manufacturer already supplies machines for conversion, employing punched cards for aisle to aisle transfer and on-line control within the aisle itself. The operator is informed about which side to pick from by a light code.

Fixed path plant for order picking
16.04 Fixed path order pickers give quick aisle to aisle transfer (45 second cycles are possible) **28**. Consider also the picking personnel's environment of continuous vertical and lateral acceleration and deceleration forces in fixed path machines, especially if they are to be automatically guided to the picking position. Entry into the EEC implies that British equipment is now subject to the stringent FEM regulations concerning operator conditions with mechanical handling plant.

16.05 As automated warehouses involve high throughput operations, fast order picking of discrete items and less than full pallet loads can prove a problem. Space can be used more effectively for intensive storage if the pickers are kept out of the racks and the goods are brought to them. Pickers operate faster if movement and walking distances are minimised. Line produced picking lists linked with a gather and dispense principal can enable high speeds and accuracy to be achieved. The planning of gather and dispense cycles involves the programming of sorting machinery. The consultant should consider this at an early stage.

27

28

29 *Cartrac transporters being used as both transport and as order-picking carousel.*
30 *High user carousel brings pallets to the order-picker at CWS warehouse, Birtley.*

29

Transporter systems

16.06 Transporter systems can be used for order picking, bringing the goods to the picker and automatically returning part loads to the racking. The 90 degree direction changes possible with one of these systems, **29**, could save space in the picking zone. Queueing and accumulation characteristics can be built into the program, and priorities can be arranged so that if a picking zone is full, transporters can circulate a buffer track to keep the junctions clear.

Carousels

16.07 The much-publicised CWS warehouse at Birtley employs an order-picking system based on 'carousels', double deck conveyors that circulate platten loads of goods to present them sequentially to the pickers, **30**. In the zone for high throughput goods, each picker serves four carousels. There is a picking position related to the elevators at the end of each double deck conveyor, the picker visiting each position as instructed by the computer; and while this happens, other carousels are positioning for the next picking sequence. The potential of the carousels has been hindered by load instability, due to the height that the goods are stacked on the plattens, and the stop-start nature of the system.

16.08 Completely automated picking can be implemented with a limited number of lines in live racking. Opinions differ whether order picking of discrete items can ever be fully automated economically. Techniques in robotics have improved considerably recently, due to handling requirements in the aerospace and nuclear industries. However, even if the machinery is made cheap enough, it requires precise packaging and very stable loads to operate successfully.

16.09 If pallets or plattens are used in the picking zone, an empty return conveyor is required, feeding a magazine at the input side of the store. Care should be taken that this does not conflict with other conveyors. Some installations pile pallets at the end of the stacker crane aisle, so that groups can be treated as dispatch freight when the crane has a free cycle; the pallets are sorted automatically into a storage area.

17 Picking area

17.01 Picking areas should be treated as for Technical study Mechanised storage 1, para 17, with a minimum level of 400 lux light, and sufficient ventilation to provide comfort conditions for the pickers. If a picking tower is used in racks,

it should be made as comfortable as possible; comfort and safety go hand in hand. Lighting can be integral with the tower.

17.02 Picking from transporter systems can be isolated from the plant, as the transporter will stop at the correct bay and remain until the correct number of packages have been recorded by a sensor on a take-away conveyor. The picker can be protected by a screen from all moving parts. Noise can be a problem with so much machinery, but various silencing methods are available; contact the equipment manufacturers.

18 Load build-up

18.01 In automated systems, load build-up requires tilt tray, tilt belt, slide slat or various combinations of belt or roller

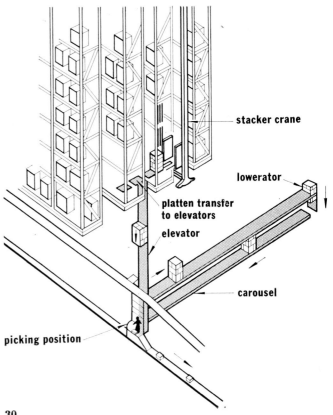

stacker crane

lowerator

platten transfer
to elevators

elevator

carousel

picking position

30

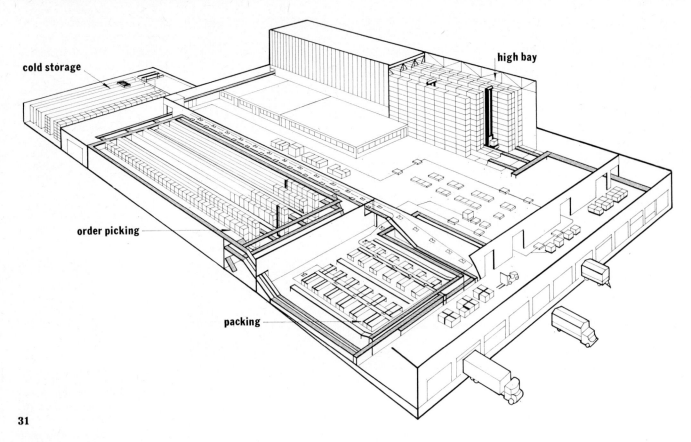

cold storage

high bay

order picking

packing

31

conveyors. These have been discussed in Technical study Mechanised storage, para 17, and Information sheet Mechanised storage 10.

18.02 The basic difference is in the control system. The greater the number of orders being assembled at one time, and the number of lines involved, the more complicated will be the software. Automation enables much higher sorting speeds, compared with manual operation. Some installations have got out of phase between the picking and sorting operations, and it has taken considerable time to restore the situation. The problem is again that computers work very fast, and machinery comparatively slowly.

18.03 Some automated sorting systems involve tipping goods down chutes. Check that the packaging is sufficient for the shock environment that is experienced; impacts of 140 g have been recorded on steel chutes on the first bounce, and 200 g on the second; test packages have shown that shocks are greater if the angle is steep enough to force packages to bounce on their apices.

18.04 Automated dispatch sorting areas are space consuming. Tilt tray and tilt belt chute accumulators are linear, they can be looped to save space, but this may affect the intermediate transport between sorting and the loading bay (linear systems are often most economic in the long run). Accumulation conveyors are a parallel function, fed from a high speed supply and sorting cross conveyor. Both the GPO parcel sorting office at Peterborough and the bulk picking area at Boots, Nottingham, use computer controlled tilted belt conveyors successfully.

18.05 One of the benefits of a transporter system is that it can be used for sorting full pallet loads direct to the loading bay, and accumulate the goods, without further handling **32**.

18.06 Palletisers, banders and shrink wrappers, if under fully automated control, require buffer conveyors at input (especially if goods are shrink wrapped after palletising, as the latter machines operate faster). If high peak throughput is necessary, more shrink wrappers should be provided than palletising machines, with a sorting mechanism between them, and at the

31 *A typical retail distribution warehouse: note the small area occupied by the automated warehouse in comparison with the order-picking, packing and load-accumulation zones.*
32 *Transporter serving load-accumulation conveyors: note elevator to racking at the end of the aisle.*

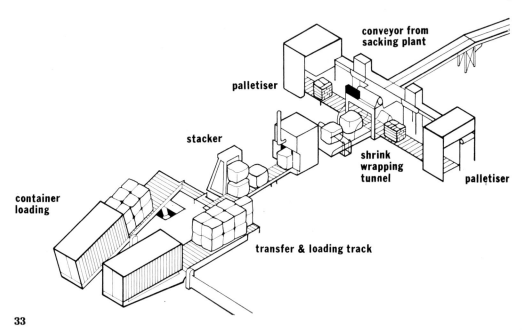

33 *Automatic palletising, shrink-wrapping and container-loading. Designed here for sacks, this could be used for pallets from high bay racking.*

33

shrink wrap tunnel output to redirect the pallet to the correct loading bay. This can all be on-line, but the software can be complex. Buffer space and diverting mechanisms should be provided in case of breakdowns; this too can be simulated at the design stage.

18.07 Clearance should be left for the maintenance of the large number of switches and sensors used in automated accumulation and sorting conveyors. One of the major problems experienced with this type of operation has been access for quick repair in case of breakdown.

19 Order and documentation check

19.01 An automated system performs this check prior to sorting for palletising. Once palletised, the correct routing to the load accumulation point can be checked manually or automatically. Manual checking is a question of pallets moving past an operator in a console, who checks them off a print-out or on a visual display. This can be automated by a code label being printed-out and applied at the palletiser, the pallets then passing an optical code scanner. It is at this point that full pallet loads selected from the store join those that have been built-up by order picking. Buffer track is needed for the rejection of incorrectly coded pallets, and mistakes in routing.

20 Dispatch collection and loading

20.01 Load assembly is a fast moving function in an automated warehouse. Preassembly can operate with the computer always working one load ahead, described in para 4, by scanning collection documents before the incoming trucks have entered the accumulation lanes; a suitable loading bay can be allocated, and the return load assembled. If only full pallet loads are involved, this can be achieved as fast as it takes the previous truck to load, clear the bay, and the incoming vehicle to unload, ie, 8-10 minutes.

20.02 Load accumulation is affected by the distribution of goods in the racks. If the required pallets are high user goods in several aisles, the picking will be fast, but if mostly low user material in few racks, and other orders are being assembled simultaneously, the operation will be slower. As shown in TS Mechanised storage 1, many load assemblies can be predicted day by day, and small goods order picking and pallet build-up can be instigated by the computer daily to be ready for the truck to arrive.

20.03 Accurate vehicle arrival can never be a foregone conclusion, due to traffic conditions or breakdown. 'Sidings'

should be provided so that pallets can be rerouted to allow the load to be accumulated without disrupting the picking cycle or the operation of the loading bay. This can also act as a peak buffer, when several vehicles are accumulating for each bay, and fast turnround is critical.

20.04 In peak conditions, the computer may have to operate different picking and storage cycles from normal speed working. Pressure can be taken off the loading zone by routing easily fulfilled orders involving full pallets to one area of loading bays for fast turnround. More complicated orders should be allocated a larger number of bays for slower turn-round cycles. If the collection documents have been processed when the vehicle enters the site, the trucks can be assembled randomly, and the central computer left to allocate bays based on updated data on loading bay and order assembly progress.

20.05 Both software and sorting plant can be complicated, as several loads will be accumulated at a time; in case of failure manual over-ride is necessary. An elevating double deck conveyor would segregate incoming and outgoing goods, and allow immediate loading after discharge for vehicles with tracked floors. Catwalks should be installed with this system, to provide access to the conveyor surface in case of blockage.

20.06 The amount of automation involved in dispatch sorting depends on the throughput, and how critical peak service is to the user. Lower key operations are used with combinations of on and off-line control, with forklift trucks and towline trains for accumulation, which although slower, are less prone to break-down.

20.07 An integrated system for automatically palletising goods and loading ISO containers has recently been proposed; this could be useful in high turnover operations, especially those involved in export such as groupage warehouses, **33**.

20.08 At present it is often the slow issue of documentation that inhibits the speed of loading. To accelerate document handling, a print-out terminal could be positioned in the loading bay zone, eg in the traffic office. With automated preassembly, manual load checks should eventually be eliminated, so that documents need not be issued until the gatehouse. Turnround can be fast, as the driver would pull out of the loading bay directly the operation were completed, to a buffer park, to shut the container's doors or 'sheet' the load, so not hindering incoming traffic. The documents, printed-out with the vehicles' registration numbers, would be issued as the trucks left the site; this system is advantageous as it provides additional speed and security checks.

34 *Not all automated warehouses involve pallet racking and lifting to great heights: this installation in France uses an automated transporter system as controlled roll-through storage for pallets of drums. Note the smoothness of movement implied by a stack of two pallets being handled together.*

35 *A low rise automated storage building in France: van bodies are stored before final assembly. Note the Transrobot storage machine on the bottom track and a similar unit carrying a van body overhead.*

Technical Study

Automated storage 2

Building function

Technical study 1 (paras 1 to 21) dealt with automated storage; this second study (paras 22 to 38) covers the design of the building.

22 Structure

22.01 Automated warehouses need not be high bay but high land prices in Europe have encouraged them to be so. Over 30 m is now possible and even higher buildings are planned. They impose special structural conditions and the basic question is whether to choose a structure integral with the racking or to have racking separate for flexibility. A factor here is whether fixed or free-path automated handling plant is to be used, and if fixed path, how will it be supported and guided. In using structural racking the intention is to exploit the racking's potential stiffness, thus minimising the peripheral support structure, and eliminating wasteful columns. One manufacturer claims that cost savings of over 30 per cent are possible with integral structures over 15 m, **1**. High racking has to be stiff to accept pallet loads on the upper levels, and it is therefore logical to hang cladding on the exterior of the racks and just stiffen the building across aisles which have already been made quite stiff by crane rail supports.

22.02 Although integrally structured high bay warehouses have operated successfully, there have been problems. High automated stacker cranes work in racking to tight tolerances, which must be achieved in their manufacture and erection. Allow for this in the design of structure and control systems. One Swedish company experienced considerable commissioning trouble with their high bay store. The stacker cranes were not stopping in a precise enough position for immediate engagement of the forks, causing them to retract in a way that did not retrieve the pallet cleanly. To ensure the correct alignment of crane forks, often based on an optical reflective system which can account for structural tolerance, it has been found necessary to use separate fine positioning systems. Accurate site welding becomes increasingly difficult at heights over 30 m. Inaccuracies in the support rails will make a stacker crane operate out of the vertical. The cranes themselves are subject to manufacturing tolerances; the problem arises where these crane and rack tolerances interact.

1 *Structural racking under construction*

22.03 Care should be taken over structural design: several loaded stacker cranes decelerating simultaneously in parallel aisles have made one installation sway alarmingly. Another user found that somehow a transfer carriage had allowed two cranes to operate in one aisle. Factory inspectors now tend to insist on 'running cranes against their stops' during commissioning to check that no permanent deformation occurs. Torsional forces can also be generated in stacker cranes when the loaded forks retract from a rack bay to the centre of the carriage.

22.04 Buffeting by wind in high bay warehouses has proved troublesome, especially where steel cladding has been hung directly from racking, **2**. High buildings with large wall areas are subject to high wind loadings, and if the buffeting coincides with the vibration wavelength of the racking considerable movement can occur; a crane may cause serious damage to rails and motors. One warehouse was designed with a special space frame between cladding and racks to absorb the buffet. Expansion of racks caused by insolation can also affect operation of stacker cranes. Long high walls catching direct sunlight tend to act as radiant heaters but this is less of a problem with insulated sandwich steel sheet. Concrete cladding transferring heat to racking has caused cranes to jam in at least one European warehouse—the tolerances between plant and racking must have been very tight.

22.05 The type of roof decking is important; steel sheet is often bolted or welded to a sub-frame sprung from rack heads, and is either welded and laid to falls, or covered with a lightweight foamed screed. Dark surfaces such as asphalt with chippings soak up heat and cause a cumulative effect down a rack range; end frames bow outwards at the ceiling position, complicating accurate control of cranes. A reflective finish or insulated roof decking can minimise the effect of insolation.

22.06 Automated warehouses generate large areas of peripheral equipment housed in buildings of conventional height. It is therefore important to detail the joint between high and low bay carefully to accept different expansions and to dispose of run-off from the large area of cladding above.

22.07 Care should also be taken in integrating services with structure, ensuring that movement of racks will not break pipe or cable mountings, and that services will not encroach on tolerances already reduced by structural movement.

22.08 If free-path machinery is to be increasingly used for medium-sized installations (see Mechanised storage), there will be a requirement for adaptable racking, quite independent of the 'big box' building enclosing it.

22.09 A further question is whether high bay integral rack structures should be steel, concrete, or composite. For fire control, concrete is an attractive proposition (see para 27.00), but it is not easy to adapt and is initially expensive. However, the 17 m high Dr Maag warehouse in Dielsdorf was easily erected from cruciform precast concrete sections from which metal pallet rails are cantilevered. Outer racks are T-shaped, providing an integral cladding function also. Stacker cranes run on top rails, fixed to cross-beams that stiffen the concrete sections laterally, and on base rails cast into the floor. A survey in a German materials handling journal *Fordern und Heben*, 1970, listed some 16 reinforced concrete warehouses, mostly high bay, constructed or under construction at that time in Switzerland, Germany and Italy.

22.10 Foundations for automated warehouses are complicated, since racking and vertical members can impose high point loads, and deceleration of heavy stacker cranes produced high forces. Structural consultants should be involved from the outset, as the condition of the land might preclude economic high bay development. With the tight tolerances required, only minimum settlement can be accepted. Manufacturers of equipment can handle this problem, but if the warehouse has been in use for some while, adjustment can be expensive both in lost time and in reprogramming and commissioning the

2

3

2 *Cladding hung directly onto racking.*

3 *Low rise peripheral building round high bay pallet silo.*

plant for accurate final positioning. Some international warehouse construction companies offer a complete structural service with their warehouse and control package, backed by considerable operating experience in countries such as Switzerland where seasonal temperature variations can make ground conditions difficult.

Summary: integrated structures

22.11

Steel: advantages
Adjustable to varied loadings.
Short preparation period for fabrication.
Little problem with transport and assembly.
Easily adaptable.

Steel: disadvantages:
Danger of distortion or collapse in case of fire.
Relatively high maintenance costs (these have been reduced in some modern finishes).
Danger of corrosion if aggressive materials are stored.
High elasticity for critical tolerances; in certain conditions this can be advantageous.

Concrete: advantages
Fire resistant.

Cheaper maintenance.
High inherent stability and little deformation.
Corrosion resistant.
Large dimensions are economic.
Concrete: disadvantages
High investment in building.
High investment in site equipment.
Lengthy preparation of site, unless precast is used.
Can cause transport and assembly problems.
Not easily adaptable.
Up to 18 m racking can be constructed from cold rolled steel section, but above that height hot rolled is required, which increases the price by about 25 per cent. Precast concrete tends to cost 15 per cent to 20 per cent more than steel up to 30 m high, and 40 per cent to 50 per cent more over that height, **4**.

23 Floor

23.01 The floor of a high bay warehouse can be critical to the tolerance of racking and stacker cranes. Stacker cranes are subject to oscillation caused by acceleration and deceleration in the aisle and irregularities in the floor rail. Slight irregularities in a running rail, which can be magnified by crane suspension systems, produce additional oscillations in the mast. These can be of approximately the same magnitude as the stresses caused by acceleration and deceleration and when in phase can cause high oscillation peaks. A damper may have to be fitted at the top of the mast, often in the form of an auxiliary drive to the upper rail.

23.02 The floor of an automated warehouse does not have the same function as that of a mechanised unit, where adjustable racking rests on the floor surface, and free-path plant relies on the overall floor finish for the tightness of tolerance in high stacking 5. Free-path machinery becomes uneconomic compared with fixed path stacker cranes at about 10 m; although manufacturers claim up to 12 m heights are possible, existing designs all suffer considerable mast sway beyond this point. Already manufacturers ask for unrealistic floor tolerances.

23.03 In high bay automated units with fixed path stacker cranes the floor is an integral part of the foundation and a base for crane rails, that are shimmed and grouted accurately into place. Racks tend to be bolted through to the slab, bolt mountings having been accurately cast with the final finish. The early problems of rail fixing and bogie oscillation have mostly been resolved, but the manufacturer's installation specification should be checked at an early stage in the project.

24 Building services

24.01 Environment should be carefully tailored to the requirements of the stored products. The large cubic capacity of automated high bay warehouses, and their insulation to prevent rack expansion caused by insolation, mean that the buildings can have virtually steady state thermal characteristics. As stacker cranes accelerate and brake rapidly, there is considerable heat gain from the motors. In high summer in the UK some cooling is necessary; in buildings over 15 m high this can usually be achieved naturally by drawing in cool air from high level at night. Some background heating may be needed in winter—although this has been disputed on the ground that comfort conditions for personnel are unnecessary except in order-picking and peripheral areas, and heat generated by crane motors combined with insulated cladding should keep the temperature above freezing—but this again depends on the temperature of the goods when they enter the warehouse. Goods from refrigerated lorries can lower the overall temperature by some degrees. Background heating to keep temperatures at approximately 10°C would reduce the possibility of condensation which can damage goods and electronic equipment, allow a wet charged sprinkler system to be used, and keep packaging materials in good condition.

4

5

4 *Structural racking in an automated high bay warehouse, made of welded hollow section tube.*

5 *Free path, high rise machine (here semi-automatic). Floors have to be constructed to very tight tolerances.*

Keeping the building near steady state will minimise rack and track movement. Owing to the height of these buildings, radiant panels have little effect; blown air is more useful. The blower units, which can also be used for extraction and for circulating fresh air in summer, and for some humidity control, can be mounted as packages on the rack structure on the roof far away from expensive electronic equipment, thus freeing the floor area for handling plant.

24.02 There is also argument about whether light should be provided in high bay stores except for maintenance purposes. As personnel are involved only in order-picking areas, general lighting is unnecessary. In-aisle order-picking by picking tower is a closed system in that operators are not aware of any of the aisle excepting the bay they are picking from, so lighting can be local. An argument for lighting high rack areas has been that it might be needed in emergency. But in the event of fire, power would be cut at once, and if a crane breaks down, portable emergency lighting can quickly be positioned by maintenance staff. The need for lighting is psychological; warehouse users seem to need to walk into the high bay area to see that everything is operating correctly—but this is dangerous, and in any case malfunction is obvious from the control boards and printouts.

24.03 Daylight should definitely be excluded except in order-picking zones. An interesting case occurred in the high bay automated warehouse for a Swedish company where cranes were stopping seemingly at random and restarting by the time maintenance engineers arrived. The fault was finally traced with the aid of a diary. The first stoppage was a few days before the winter solstice and the next a few days after it. It was found that on these two days a sunbeam had managed to activate a photo-electric sensor cell.

24.04 Rainwater downpipes can be a problem. Users are loath to allow these into the storage area for fear of leakage onto stock or electronic equipment, and so they are usually run outside the cladding. It has been suggested that rainwater be allowed to stand on the roof, as the roof sheeting is supported by strong racking and the water acts as an additional insulator. In this case overflows would be placed round the perimeter.

25 Special services

25.01 Automated warehouses involve quantities of wiring and electrical supply services. This is one area where money should not be saved. Wiring includes the power supply for handling plant, primary and final positioning sensors, limit switch controls, and heat and smoke sensors at each bay. Return wiring for data feedback to the peripheral or central computer is also run from each rack bay, and from the main position switches. With mini-computer control, transistorised circuitry reduces the amount of wiring needed. In the use of local logic control units, each periphery has its own cabinet equipped with basic power handling devices and full system interlocks and sequence controls. An alternative is to return all primary signals to the central computer which then calculates control decisions, but wiring in these 'hard wire' systems is complex; festoons of cable are a common sight, and finding a fault is laborious.

25.02 Control wiring and electrical supply has to integrate with other services when running up racks and in ducts. Care should be taken to prevent interference with control signals—a fault in some early installations. In order to keep floors clear for control cabling, wet services for environmental control units should be taken up to roof level, and fitted with drip trays. There they are adaptable. Sortation conveyors also require control and supply wiring, and compressed air supply is often required for sortation machinery **6**.

25.03 Computers tend to require special air-conditioned environments, although some mini-computers work successfully in normal 'office' atmospheres. Check with the computer

6

6 *Cartrac transporter used as a sorting machine: note pneumatic controls.*

manufacturer as to what is required and whether segregated compartments are necessary.

26 Building fabric

26.01 The high bay zone of the warehouse can be clad in several ways:
Cladding attached directly to racking.
Cladding attached to a subframe on the racking.
Cladding attached to a separate subframe.
Concrete integrated racking (as described in para 22.01).
The choice is governed by height of building, prevailing wind, exposure and type of cladding used. In conditions of extreme exposure, cladding can be attached to an independent subframe, restrained from the roof and the ground and incorporating the intermediate stiffening and wind bracing.

26.02 In order to achieve steady state environment internally, cladding with an efficient insulator should be employed.

26.03 Both steel and proprietary sheeting have been used effectively. Fire regulations concerning hazards from, and fire resistance of, walls close to boundaries can result in a heavy cladding being required, involving an expensive, heavy-duty subframe.

26.04 Fire vents should be provided in the roof cladding (see para 27.04); if packaged heater/ventilation units are roof-mounted then access hatches should be included. Catwalks are needed over rack runs, for maintenance of upper crane rails and access to sprinkler mains, wiring and heater units. With integral rack structures, the rack frames are extended up 2 m+ as roof support and accommodate the crane guide rails and services, so that there is adequate room for a catwalk without encroaching on storage space. Catwalks and escape stairs, should be well marked and lit, and provided with emergency lighting. Contact also the local fire officer and factory inspector.

27 Fire control

27.01 The choice of fire prevention, detection and control equipment plays an important part in initial costing, as equipment sufficient for all contingencies is expensive but affects the present weighting of insurance premiums against this building type. Little is known of fire characteristics apart from tests carried out by US insurers and the US Joint Fire Research Organisation. Those involved in the design of automated warehouses feel that the Fire Officers' Committee's recommendations need revision; some of the provisions of the 29th edition for automatic sprinklers are too severe, involving companies in unnecessary capital expenditure that is difficult to justify despite tax allowances. The lack of data on high bay fire characteristics, especially in the use of foams and inert gases, makes insurance companies weight these buildings heavily enough to impair seriously their cost-saving potential. The FOC is revising these aspects and intends to provide a firm set of recommendations on fire protection and detection systems for use by insurers and designers alike.

27.02 Regulations for means of escape are given in the Factories Act 1961; the Building Regulations 1972 gives rules for structural fire precautions in paragraphs E2, E5 and E7. The FOC *Rules for automatic sprinkler installations, Amendment* 2 gives guidance on in-rack sprinkler clearances for high bay stores. The complexity of detection and control equipment is based on the fire hazard rating of the goods stored; consult 'Classification of occupancies', in the 29th edition of the FOC rules. As insurance costs vary according to the type of product stored, the choice of the correct detection method can save the user a great deal in premiums. Consult the insurer from the outset.

27.03 High bay buildings can usually be classed under the Building Regulations E2, group VIII 'Single storey storage and general purpose', and so are not subject to limits in compartment size. Some might fall into group VI for factories. When peripheral sortation areas such as galleries and mezzanines are involved as elements of the structure, they can be required to have minimum periods of fire resistance. Between high bay and sorting and order picking areas there can be the requirement for a fire resisting compartment wall with four hours' duration, ie for floor areas over 3000 m² (see table A to regulation E5, part 2). Regulation E8 also affects high bay stores that are not freestanding. Insurers also tend to ask that the warehouse be divided into compartments. This is often impracticable with high bay stores but to date there is no firm policy.

27.04 Fire problems in high warehouses have been discussed (see Mechanised storage para 27). In a high bay warehouse, the stack effect becomes even more pronounced. Arguments about venting continue, but it is suggested the loss of one rack load by fast vertical flame spread is preferable to ignition of the top of several racks by flames being forced across under the roof sheeting. The problems are those of conventional 'big box' buildings, but magnified. Pressure build up can reach near-thunderstorm conditions; one warehouse in the US had a large section of its roof blown off by the internal pressure. The problem with venting is primarily expense. The true effect of venting on sprinkler operation is not known; there is a chance that if the vents open too soon, the sprinklers might not operate in time, and if too late, too many might open, damaging the goods. But it is unlikely that many sprinkler problems would occur with the new detection system produced recently by the Joint Fire Research Organisation (see Technical Study Mechanised storage 2 para 27). Another group has advocated shutting the warehouse off, and letting oxygen starvation contain the fire—but smoke would prevent firemen from finding the seat of the fire, and the pressure build-up would be dangerous.

27.05 Whatever measures are suggested for extinguishing a fire, there is no substitute for immediate detection. If an extinguishing agent were applied one to one and a half minutes after ignition, with substantial control after three to five minutes and total extinction in eight to ten minutes, damage by fire, smoke and water would be minimised. It is especially relevant in an automated warehouse, that although water is still considered by insurers to be the most effective extinguisher, if applied with enough pressure and in sufficient quantities, it can severely damage stored goods and, more important, electronic components. Users also fear that water-charged sprinklers could leak onto stock. Shrink wraps produce further complications, in that they deflect water and contain heat. When the wrap shrinks off allowing the heat to activate the sprinkler, the fire may already have taken a firm hold.

27.06 Because of these various arguments against water, other methods have been examined. One uses a stacker crane; fire control packs are placed in strategic positions in racking and fire is sensed by a linear sensor that follows the rack contours. The stacker crane is immediately put onto an emergency cycle, dumping its normal load, returning to pick up the extinguishing pack, and moving fast to the burning bay where it releases the contents of the pack. This might not be realistic in operating conditions; the first thing that is likely to happen in an area full of electronic equipment, especially as some fires are electrical in origin, is for the power to be cut.

27.07 Various extinguishing agents have been tried, high expansion foam with a 1000:1 water expansion ratio has been discussed. In high bay operations, the volume to fill is even larger, and there is a greater chance through increased stack effect for the foam to chase the fire up the racks. Foam can still damage stock by damp. The 1 million cu ft/min foam figure implies that a medium-sized high bay installation would take five to six minutes to fill. It has been found that the fire tends to reignite unless the foam is topped up about every half-hour.

27.08 CO_2 requires high concentrations to do an efficient job, but automated stores housing no permanent staff virtually eliminate the risk of people becoming trapped. To extinguish a fire with CO_2, the oxygen content would have to be reduced to between 12 per cent and 16 per cent for solids smouldering on the surface. For deep-seated smouldering oxygen content would have to be reduced further to 1 per cent to 2 per cent, in a 5 million cu ft warehouse, and this is a lot of CO_2. There is also a risk of pressure damage to the building fabric because, to be effective, no fire vents would have been installed, hence a blow-off valve should be fitted.

27.09 A more promising gas is BCF (bromochlorodi-fluoro-methane). A 5 per cent to 10 per cent by volume concentration is sufficient for inhibiting combustion but this has to be directed at the seat of the flame, requiring a sprinkler type gas outlet in each rack supplied from a central pressure source. A zoned system has been suggested, whereby a multi-shot application of BCF would operate in the applicable racking zone with possibility of extending the operation to other areas as required. Total flooding capacity would have to be provided. BCF would discharge on detection, and stop when the flame disappeared; injection being repeated until the fire brigade arrived. It is said that these gases would not damage goods, but check that stock will not be contaminated by gas.

27.10 The fire brigade is not enamoured of high bay warehouses, for the following reasons:

1 Height of racks and risk of burning goods falling on fireman.

2 In automated stores there are usually too few means of escape for firemen and routes to them are often tortuous.

3 Inadequate access for fire engines except through the loading bay.

4 Insufficient water supplies for the size of the job involved.

5 The amount of electrical equipment and cabling, some of which might still be live and have had its insulation burned away.

6 Density of storage in automated warehouses and height of racks in relation to width of aisles makes water penetration from hoses difficult. This is another attractive idea for using the stacker crane if emergency power can be brought into action fast enough.

7 With integral rack-building structures, the fire problem is further increased by the risk of racks buckling and jeopardising the whole structure. Crane rails will warp, and it is possible that a whole section of the warehouse would have to be cut out and rebuilt. It is likely that overall instability, especially under crane deceleration loading, would force a total shutdown during the work which, with rewiring and commissioning, would take well over a year. If the warehouse were a centralised distribution depot for a chain of supermarkets, a serious fire could quickly lead a company to near bankruptcy.

27.11 One suggestion to counter structural fire damage with integral racks is to use hollow, square section steelwork permanently filled with a water/glycol/rust inhibitor solution. Under-aisle piping would link the racks, when a fire is sensed, the solution would be circulated by natural convection, perhaps pump assisted, so keeping the steel below the temperature at which buckling takes place.

27.12 A high efficiency zoned detection and sprinkler extinguishing system as developed by the Building Research Establishment, UK, on a sufficient scale would be expensive, but worth while compared with the typical losses described above.

27.13 Fire prevention in automated stores hinges basically on good design of the electronic and electrical supply systems, and on designers taking care to keep flammable sources out of the high bay zone. Examples of excluded functions include battery charging, and repair of stacker cranes (often involving welding). A policy of good housekeeping should be instilled into the user, and planned maintenance and inspection cycles for the plant and all electrical apparatus built into the design proposal.

28 Security

28.01 In automated warehouses this is mostly concerned with malicious damage and pilfering of electronic equipment and copper wiring. There is little chance of thieves scaling high bay racks. One of the attractive features of fully automated control is the high security offered. However computers can be tampered with, and if wholesale theft is involved it is likely to have been carefully programmed. Agencies exist for checking programmes for such 'bugs'.

28.02 For peripheral areas and loading bay security, see Mechanised storage 28. With automated sorting, there is again little risk of pilfering, as the check scanner will record discrepancies at once on the stock print-outs. Order-picking areas still require supervision, but again with bulk picking, discrepancies would quickly show up on the documentation. Closed-circuit television has been installed successfully in some large order-picking areas.

8 *Twin mast stacker crane.*

29 External works

29.01 High bay warehouses are large enough to produce surrounding micro-climates. Careful siting is required: some installations generate dangerously high wind speeds. There was a case in the US where a high bay store was placed close to another large building in such a way as to form a high funnel, **7**. Wind already gusting near gale force, picked up a medium weight forklift truck, load and driver, and pushed them through the cladding of an adjoining building. One of the facts later admitted by several of the package-deal high bay constructors was that they were not concerned with external environmental conditions outside their immediate contract. High winds can have a slowing effect on truck marshalling areas, especially where high-sided vehicles are involved. Gusts are liable to blow dust back into the loading bay, shortening the life of sortation conveyors. Wind tunnel tests should be carried out on scale models to measure the effects of the warehouse orientation on surrounding buildings, considering local topography and the prevailing wind.

30 Structure based plant

30.01 Conveyors and sorting systems have been covered in Information sheet Mechanised storage 10, p181.
A carousel is a slow conveyor for platten or pallet circulation used in order picking.

30.02 Transporter systems involve special elevators. These can have speeds up to 100 m/min and can take the form of conventional lifts or paternosters. Automatic interlocks are provided in the queueing mechanism, so that transporters can flow smoothly onto the elevator as the plattens arrive.

31 Mobile plant

31.01 All plant can be fully on-line; this includes stacker cranes, order pickers or transporters. High bay stacker cranes are heavy pieces of equipment. Single-masted types operate to heights of 20 m, and twin-masted units to over 30 m **8**. Tracks run at both high and low level. Order pickers follow a pattern similar to that of stacker cranes.

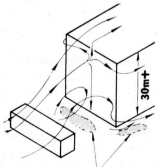

7 *Typical wind patterns round high buildings derived from tests performed on models by BRS.*

30m+

areas of very high wind speeds often 110 kph

31.02 The trend in fixed path automated equipment is away from one-off plant, ie towards ranges of standard equipment, adaptable for special purposes and sharing common parts to simplify the problem of spares.

31.03 Transporter systems are sophisticated interzone railways, with the added function of providing live storage. In general they offer reduced aisle areas, but do not provide immediate 100 per cent selectivity. One system employs a single type of transporter for all actions; another offers a basic carrier for live storage and in-aisle movement **9** and a larger 'mother' transporter for interzone movement.

31.04 Robot tractor trains have been operated successfully for horizontal travel. Although not as fast as conveyors, and requiring individual loading of trucks, these tug trains can provide flexible transport to a large number of sortation stations. Robotugs are battery powered tractors, guided by wires buried 2 mm to 4 mm under the floor surfaces, using solid state controls; they can have off- or on-line control. A further useful feature is their ability to send out feedback signals that can automatically open doors and turn traffic lights on cross-routes in their favour. More than 50 stations can be programmed with off-line control. Speeds vary from $3 \cdot 2$ to $1 \cdot 8$ km/h, depending on the pulled load. The control system prevents collisions at junctions and head-on accidents, and can be set so that the tug always takes the shortest clear route to the discharge point.

31.05 The development of automated storage has been impeded by a history of premature failure of handling equipment. Most manufacturers cannot afford to perform reliability trials at their factory before installing the plant, a problem aggravated by lack of testing with the integrated automatic control. In the past, handling plant tended to be overcomplicated, but this is no longer realistic in the present competitive market. Designers should write durability into the user specification and ensure that manufacturers have tested their equipment with the control medium. This may increase prices but will probably reduce overall costs in the long run.

32 Integration of building and plant

32.01 This problem is especially severe in automated warehouses, where racking is an integral part of the structure, and stacker cranes are mounted on rails attached to racks or the roof and floor. Tolerances have been discussed in paras 22.01-22.11.

32.02 Care should be taken in planning supply and takeaway conveyor lines between high bay store and sorting area. They will probably have to pass through fire compartment zones requiring fire shutters and possibly automatic swing-away sections on the zone line.

33 Maintenance

33.01 The fabric of a high bay warehouse should be designed to be maintenance-free: cladding materials such as plastic-faced steel sandwich panels ensure that the surface will be self-cleaning. With electronic equipment, it is essential to check for water leakage, and planned inspection cycles for roof and sprinkler lines should be treated as part of the building design. In a steady state environment racking maintenance should be minimal, except for repairing damage by handling plant.

Maintenance of handling and control plant
33.02 This is more of a problem. The maintenance zone for stacker cranes should preferably be out of the high bay area, in a segregated fire compartment. Hence the transfer carriage would have to pass through 30 m high fire stop doors, which would be costly. It is more realistic for maintenance contractors to dismantle the parts concerned in the warehouse and provision should be made for operation of a hydraulic

maintenance platform and a mobile crane. Access should also be possible to the accumulation conveyors in the high bay area. Electronic sensors and limit switches require maintenance in the racks themselves. Full safety interlocks should be built into the control system. Some unpleasant accidents have occurred where maintenance staff have been surprised by stacker cranes in narrow aisles, with little chance of escape.

Maintenance area for stacker cranes
33.03 This should have a vehicle entrance outside and should be equipped with a 5 tonne hoist or mobile crane. It is costly and disruptive to move components through the loading bay and sorting area: if restricted access makes this unavoidable, a maintenance gantry crane should be provided with unlimited access over the sorting plant to the maintenance zone. This can conflict with fire compartmentation.

33.04 As a rule, electronic equipment is taken off-site for major maintenance and the contractors normally supply moving plant. Check with computer manufacturers that areas where units are positioned have adequate access.

For maintenance of sortation plant, see Technical studies Mechanised storage 2, para 33.

34 Management

34.01 The project management of an automated warehouse is critical. The requirement for interaction between the handling plant and the racking, itself integral, and the factor of computer control, results in numbers of specialist design and installation teams being involved. The team should include staff from the existing facility, as management are seldom the users.

34.02 Contractors are loath to accept overall responsibility: this has been a danger of the 'green field to handshake' packaged deals. But these large projects cannot be successfully commissioned without the active co-operation of all the sub-contractors, with the general contractor taking overall control. The choice of electrical contractor is especially important; well planned and carefully installed wiring is essential. Operators' experience of recent installations points to the value of employing the same contractor for electronic control and equipment wiring, so that the various integrating systems can be co-ordinated. It is virtually impossible to budget accurately for electrical work until the control system's design has been finalised. Wiring is so important that this area should never be considered for financial savings.

34.03 The maintenance aspect is again important: with such complicated electrical work, protracted negotiation in an attempt to reduce costs is likely to be disadvantageous in that certain elements are liable to be skimped.

Building process
34.04 The building process of high bay warehouses has to be carefully programmed. So many specialists are involved that the construction and commissioning programme can be as important as the design itself. The main difficulties experi-

9 *Automated transport (foreground) holding van*   *bodies in an inter-process store in France.*

enced are where the programmes of various key groups, such as installation engineers and electronics personnel, conflict. Logical and clear responsibilities should be established between subcontractors at an early stage. A strong co-ordinator able to visualise the total system continuously is vital. During the construction phase, comprehensive operation and maintenance manuals should be prepared so that they are available some time before commissioning begins. These will be the basis for training clients' operational and maintenance staff. Designers should take care not to be forced into unrealistic construction and commissioning programmes by eager clients; this would cost both parties dearly later on.

When arranging the programmes from specialist subcontractors assume that the installation of complex wiring and heavy cranes is bound to run into some difficulties. New systems will have to be tried and modified: the difficulty of commissioning computer systems to bring them on-line and connect integrated sorting systems should not be underestimated.

35 Personnel accommodation

35.01 In automated warehouses the general labourers and plant operators are of course reduced in number and replaced by a smaller number of supervisory and maintenance staff, many of whom are highly skilled and require high standards of accommodation; their union has proved particularly militant recently. The amount of office space required can be calculated from the staff generated by the control function, and for document processing. A separate traffic office is still required with the possibility of print-out facilities for dispatch documentation. The offices which house data processing machinery usually require air-conditioning, though minicomputers have been developed to work in normal environments.

36 Amenity

36.01 Personnel fall into three categories:
1 Maintenance staff and loading bay operatives, including forklift drivers and general machine supervisors.
2 Order-picking staff.
3 Control system clerical staff, management, and 'white collar' staff concerned with proprietary systems and plant.
It is the user's responsibility to choose whether segregated or integrated amenity facilities are required. Whatever the decision, a high standard throughout leads to an attitude of 'good housekeeping'.
36.02 The washing and wc facilities for maintenance staff should provide for degreasing, and secure lockers for personal tools and equipment. Facilities should be bright, as psychological relief is necessary after working in high bay areas with only maintenance lighting. Order-picking staff become dusty from handling plastics and cardboard packs and will also require visual relief after long shifts at the picking face. Fire precautions in high bay warehouses, naturally preclude smoking or rest accommodation near storage. These activities are restricted to a segregated fire zone. Vending or beverage-making facilities should be provided: also washing, wc and restroom facilities with a tea machine for truck drivers. This area should not have direct access into the warehouse.
36.03 With the quantity of electrical equipment and fast-moving automatic plant, accidents are inevitable. Staff will break safety regulations, however stringent, for their convenience; this a fact of industrial life. A first-aid room should be provided with facilities for emergency treatment of electric shocks, burns and other injuries. The lighting system there should be capable of 600 lux at certain times, and a high level of ventilation should be provided. If the offices are air-conditioned, the system should be extended to the first-aid room. Ambulances should have easy and unhindered access to a loading bay or to vehicle access to office area.

37 Security and safety

37.01 The major problem is sabotage. With a centralised distribution facility serving a large chain of supermarkets or acting as a post-production store for a company's whole distribution system, a protracted breakdown could put the company out of business.
37.02 The sabotage of control equipment or tampering with the software would wreck the store's operation; although manual control should be built-in, the warehouse would have been designed for high throughputs and the simultaneous handling of multiple orders. Manual control would not allow orders to be processed fast enough for the installation to operate economically. Access should therefore be strictly controlled. As sortation is automated, the loading bay zone can be segregated from the rest of the warehouse, with openings to allow pallets through, and personnel access closely supervised; this segregation will be necessary for fire control as well. The only other required accesses to the warehouse are to offices, the order-picking zone and maintenance area. The only common link between these areas is the amenity zone, so access between them can be segregated from the warehouse itself and this is also likely to be a fire requirement. The only personnel requiring access to the high bay area are maintenance staff.
37.03 The grouping of control equipment into one area not only reduces the cost of environmental plant and services, but also allows supervision to prevent unauthorised access and simplified collection of software. The argument against placing all peripheral units together is that the whole system would be affected in case of fire. Mini-computers can be dispersed into the zones that they serve, and so only part of the system would be affected at one time.
37.04 Safety of personnel is not a difficult problem, as nobody except maintenance staff should have access to the high bay or sortation areas. If a supervisor is required for palletising and shrink wrapping plant, the operating position should be well guarded. The route through the machinery to the operator's console should be clearly marked, and guarded along its length. Fail safe stop devices should be positioned in high bay areas to protect maintenance staff; these positions should be lit, and routes to them clearly marked. The position of cut-offs should be linked back to a mimic diagram on the main control board, also with an audible alarm.

38 Circulation and parking

38.01 Parking should be provided for the external maintenance staff, and access allowed for heavy vehicles bringing replacement components.
38.02 Provision should be made in peripheral zones of an automated warehouse for circulation of maintenance equipment such as hydraulic platforms and mobile cranes. These routes should be lit and clearly marked. Cat walks should also be well lit, with guards and safety rails and attachment points for safety harness—maintenance of high racks closely resembles mountaineering. Lifts and access stairs to catwalks should also be clearly marked. Emergency lighting should be provided on all these high level routes, in case of central electrical failure.

Fire fighting and escape
38.03 Access routes should be provided for fire fighting personnel and equipment. Planned escape routes are important, as there is a possibility of fires in high bay stores getting out of control, with normal routes blocked by fallen burning pallets. Escape access could be in the form of cut-out panels placed at intervals along the base of the cladding, clearly marked on each side and equipped with an emergency light on the interior face.

Industrial storage

Information sheet Automated storage 1

Automated handling plant

The operation of automated handling plant has been described in Technical study Automated storage 1; para 13 describes stacker cranes, and para 16 describes order pickers. This sheet gives properties of a typical stacker crane and order picker, for use at sketch design stage, but plant is usually custom-built, and manufacturers should be contacted.

Order pickers

1.01 Order picking for discrete items must still be manual. In automated storage systems, mechanical control is limited to transporting the human picker automatically to the appropriate rack position, and showing on display system how many of which product are to be picked, **2a**.
1.02 Multi-person picking towers (as used at Boots warehouse, Nottingham) are partially computer-controlled; they take the pickers to the correct bay, and the pickers then bulk pick from a print-out or from a visual display.
1.03 The Owen Thorn tier picker is the nearest approach to a fully automatic order picker to date, **3**. A vacuum head picks a whole layer of cartons from a pallet and lowers it on to the carriage pallet.

Stacker cranes

2.01 Stacker cranes automatically lift and position pallets in narrow aisles up to 30 m high, **2b**. Cab is included, but only for emergency and breakdown use. Bottom rail supported cranes, rather than top hung, are becoming more popular. Typical speeds are 120 to 140 m/min horizontally, and 32 m/min vertically for single-masted types, and 200 m/min horizontally with 40 m/min vertical lift for the bigger units, usually to order. Movement motors are equipped with special controls for inching and final positioning. Electric pick-up can be from bus-bars at high or low level, or by a festoon cable. Aisle clearance is 100 mm plus width of widest pallet.

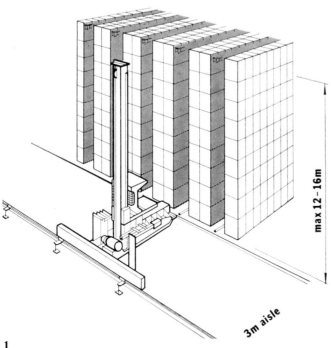

3m aisle

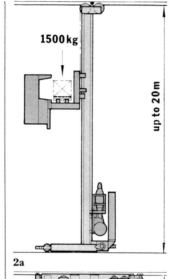

1500 kg

up to 20 m

2a

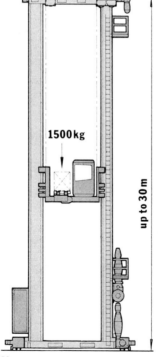

1500 kg

up to 30 m

max 12 – 16 m

2b
1 *Stacker cranes and order pickers can move from one aisle to another with a transfer carriage.*
2 *Dimensions of **a** order picker, **b** stacker crane.*
3 *Automated tier picker.*

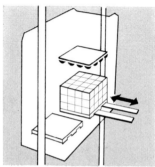

3 *Forks extend from carriage.*

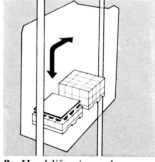

3b *Vacuum head is lowered onto top tier of boxes.*

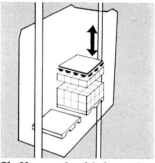

3c *Head lifts tier and lowers it on to pallet.*

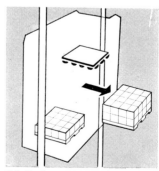

3d *Forks return rack pallet.*

4 *In this automated warehouse
there are three access levels:
this is the top one, showing
the stacker cranes and the
pick-up point. Note roof
support structure integral
with racking.*

5 *Central control room of
fully automated sorting
system.*

Information sheet Automated storage 2

Automated horizontal transport systems

This sheet describes how fixed and free-path horizontal transport systems can in some cases replace a system of stacker cranes and conveyors.

1 Free path systems

Robotugs

1.01 The Robotug driverless vehicle system has been used successfully in warehouses and factories throughout the world, and in some cases has superseded towline systems.

1.02 The Robotug is a battery-powered tractor fitted with an electronic control system, enabling it to be guided along a route from signals supplied by a mini-computer through a wire buried 2 mm to 4 mm below the floor surface. Control can be integrated with stacker crane cycles for automatic loading and discharge, and with other materials handling equipment. The tug's control mechanism can supply feed-back signals through the guide wire to open doors automatically, change traffic lights in its favour if crossing other vehicle routes, activate unloading devices, or to calculate the quickest unobstructed route to the destination at the time. Up to 50 predetermined stations can be selected with a standard programme, but more permutations are possible if the control system is custom built. Contact the manufacturer as early in the project as possible.

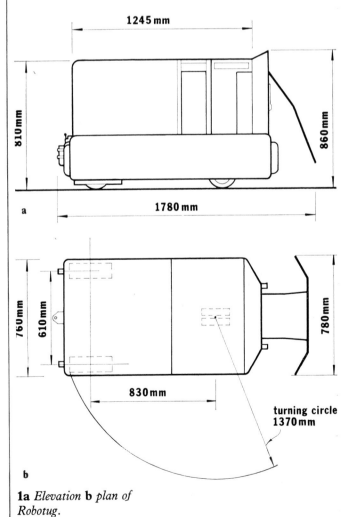

1a *Elevation* **b** *plan of Robotug.*

Size and capacity

1.03 *Towing capacity* The tug will tow a gross load of 8500 kg assuming a trailer rolling resistance of 23 kg/1000 kg over a smooth level surface.
Speed: 3 km/h maximum.
Size: See **1a, b.**

Space requirements

1.04 Turning circle fixed by track layout and determined by width of load and trailers **2, 3.** Aisle should be not less than 3·6 m wide at intersections.

Building needs

1.05 Tugs need level floors, and will negotiate only slight ramps under full load. Usually an off-track three phase recharging point is required (trucks are driven to this point by a manual control handle). Maintenance facilities are also needed.

2 Fixed path systems

Cartrac system: Uses and limitations
2.01 The Cartrac system uses one transporter for all actions. It can turn through 90 degrees without stopping or changing the axis of the load, and so acts as an efficient live storage module, and can be used in ovens and freezing tunnels. For order picking the Cartrac can act as a 'carousel' or pick whole pallets for immediate routing to the load accumulation zone.
2.02 Stopping is precise, with 0·8 mm tolerance in each direction. Queuing programmes can be supplied. The Cartrac can also be programmed to eject loads automatically at picking stations, or to phase in with stacker cranes, replacing roller conveyors at the transfer station.

Size and capacity
2.03 *Capacity.* Light duty model will carry up to 500 kg, heavy duty up to 1500 kg.
Speed. 60 m/minute average but faster on long runs.

Space requirements
2.04 Cartrac can turn through 90 degrees. Inside track widths are 500 mm (light duty) and 750 mm (heavy duty), but 100 mm building clearance and 25 mm machine clearance is required on each side, **4.**

Transrobot system: Uses and limitations
2.05 The Transrobot system consists of a basic carrier for use in aisles and live storage (the Transrobot) and a second transporter for interzone movement, the Transferobot, **5.** The Transrobot system is integral with the structure. Both steel and concrete frames are available, with rail supports doubling as structure for storage of pallets.

Size and capacity
2.06 *Capacity:* 1000 or 2000 kg
Speed: Transrobots move at 20 m/minute, Transferobots at 90 m/minute. Faster speeds are possible for long distances.

2 *Robotug in use in warehouse.*
3 *Typical layout for Robotug system with collection from production lines and delivery into storage and transfer to parking area. Routing from* **M**
direct to **13** *would be through stations* **1** *and* **2** *or through any free line.*
4 *Cartrac rails and transporter with pallet.*
5 *Transrobot meeting Transferobot.*

2

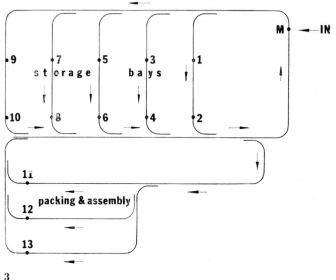

3

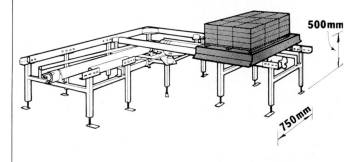

4

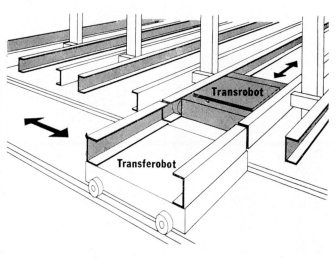

5

Traditional bulk storage: Flour warehouse at Poole, Dorset.

Technical study Bulk storage 1

Storage process

Bulk handling and storage involves the science of liquid and solids materials flow and pneumatic technology. This section gives sufficient knowledge to designers to co-ordinate specialist installation teams, and integrate other building functions with bulk systems.

1 Introduction

Sources

1.01 Research organisations, such as the Warren Spring Laboratory, and Loughborough and Birmingham Universities, specialise in the science of bulk handling. They offer material classification and simulation procedures for finding the most effective size and shape for hoppers, and for planning pipe runs. Scientific analysis affects the initial planning decisions through the layout of plant.

1.02 Experts are also available in explosion hazards, hopper design, special powders and many other areas. The Powder Advisory Centre in London acts as a data clearing house for the bulk handling industry. It offers an advisory service to designers, giving names of consultants and equipment manufacturers in the bulk handling industry.

User specification

1.03 This should not be confused with a performance specification for bulk handling plant. The user specification should consider all functions of the bulk storage process, tonnages, volume throughput, peak planning and expansion potential.

2 Source of goods

2.01 Bulk materials arrive
1 Direct from a quarry by conveyor, direct from a refinery by pipe.
2 By sea in very large shipments.
3 By rail in 1000 tonne trainloads (2000 tonnes on primary routes).
4 By road in loads of approximately 20 tonnes.

3 Form of transport

3.01 The transport interface for bulk materials is complicated. Handling installations for material direct from a quarry or for bulk vessels are outside the scope of this Handbook.

Barge transport

3.02 Architects may be required to design for barge handling. In Europe barges are widely used for bulk transport of liquids, powders and sacks, **1**. The new LASH (Lighter

1a *BACAT (barge aboard catamaran) a cross-Channel mother ship/barge system to serve the European canal system and smaller ports where larger LASH barges cannot gain access.*

1a

1b *Seabee 'mother' ship contains loaded barges which are hoisted onto the rear of the ship by an elevator.*

Aboard Ship) and Seabee barge carrier services have great potential for transporting unit loads of bulk materials from overseas. Large bulk carriers are limited to the major deep water ports and their loads have to be transhipped to barge or train for delivery to the consumer. The LASH system consists of a mother ship which transports a number of large barges across an ocean. The mothership anchors in a convenient estuary, and lowers the lighters over the stern to waiting tugs. These lighters are ideal for the European river-canal system which allows bulk materials to be handled door to door.

Rail transport

3.03 Rail transport is widely used for the delivery of bulk materials. 100 tonne hopper wagons, **2**, are specified for granular materials, and 100 tonne tankers are used for liquids. The trend towards bigger vehicles for both road and rail has influenced the type of handling chosen for certain materials.

Road transport

3.04 Before ISO containers were used for bulk haulage, pressure tank and bottom dump semi-trailers were the norm, **3**. These are still widely used, and are designed specially for the product being carried. Tank containers for liquids and powders are popular for international transport, **4**. For certain materials, eg granular types, ISO containers with plastic liners are used, **20**. Tank cleaning facilities are not required and, after the skin has been removed, the container can be used for conventional dry goods.

4 Control of transport

4 01 Railway sidings, points and curves are space consuming. Contact British Rail concerning train control.

4.02 A useful and adaptable machine for wagon marshalling is the Mercedes Unimog Road-railer, **5**. This small tractor performs the work of a shunting engine, but can retract its rail wheels and be used as a prime mover for many in-plant activities, such as yard sweeping, trailer towing and recovering broken-down forklifts. Several bulk handling installations in Europe use these machines for controlling rail trucks; when one line of trucks has been shunted, this tractor can drive off one track position onto another.

4.03 Rail wagon trailers save long conveyor lines and double handling. They allow the largest bulk trucks to be hauled off their track on to a tracked bed, and hauled by road tractor directly to the point where the load can be transhipped most economically. As all trailer wheels steer they are very manoeuvrable in restricted sites.

4.04 Major road routes should not coincide with feeder rail lines. As, for economic reasons, the largest trains possible will arrive, roads could remain blocked for some time. Clear warnings, markings and alarms should be fitted at all road-rail crossing points.

4.05 If several bulk materials are to be delivered, lanes should be clearly marked to segregate tankers before they enter the site. This process can be automated. In some petrol terminals, the tanker driver inserts an identification card into a scanner and is directed to the correct bay by visual display, where he loads his own tanker.

5 Receipt of goods

5.01 This operation is as for mechanised storage (see Technical study Mechanised storage 1, para 5).

6 Form of goods

6.01 Bulk materials are liquid or solid, but have very different characteristics. Some solids behave like liquids and vice-versa.

2

3

4

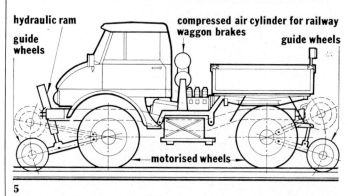

5

2 100 *tonne gravel hopper wagon.*
3 *Tank semi-trailer.*
4 6·1 *m ISO tank container*
5 *Mercedes Road-railer.*

Intermediate bulk containers

6.02 Intermediate bulk containers have recently been accepted as integral parts of warehouse handling systems, **6**. Their advantages are:

No need for hopper and tank storage and pumps for loading and discharge.

Can be carried directly from production to user feed position. In a store they can be block stacked, or place on plattens and stored in an automated warehouse.

They stack like pallets on road or rail vehicles.

Full volume storage is possible.

There is no need to provide extra hopper capacity for future build-up of materials.

They do not require cleaning unless used for a different material.

6.03 Typical materials carried are grease, oil, petroleum products, food concentrates, powders and granules. In some industries intermediate bulk containers have replaced 55 US gallon drums; drums can be used for approximately seven round trips, whereas bulk containers can be kept in usable condition for over 10 years. Other forms of intermediate bulk container are big plastic bags mounted in steel carrier frames that collapse (see Information sheet Bulk storage).

Drums

6.04 Drums can be palletised, or can be bulk handled by a forklift truck with a special drum clamp. (See Information sheet Mechanised storage 3).

Sacks

6.05 Most sacks are tailored to the material carried, and to the conditions likely during transport and storage. Designers should ascertain the size of sack used in relation to the pallet or skid board size, the loading pattern on the pallet, and the height of the load. Sacks are usually palletised, although ISO 'deep sea' containers need filling by hand for full volume utilisation.

7 Unloading

7.01 The interface between transport and storage depends on the characteristics of the material and the type of transport used. Palletised sacks and drums can be unloaded as for conventional palletised goods (see Technical study Mechanised storage 1, para 7). Access should be provided for sweeper machines in loading bays handling bagged foods.

Sacks

7.02 Sacks unloaded from ISO containers and rail wagons must be manhandled, though the process can be somewhat mechanised by using plastic skid sheets that can be drawn out of the container on to a pallet by a forklift truck.

7.03 *Unloading rail wagons.* Extendible conveyors can unload box vans and containers. Swivelling mobile conveyors can unload side door ISO containers and rail trucks. Some have capacities of up to 1600 sacks per hour with a two man final handling team. Mobile unloading belts avoid rail trucks having to be moved each time. They feed on to a fixed take-away conveyor running the length of the platform. Choice between a dock-length belt, **7**, or a Unimog-type shunter will depend on throughput and frequency of train arrival.

7.04 *Unloading trucks* Swivelling and extendible conveyors handle flat trucks and non-palletised loads. Hydraulic lift conveyors mounted on the dock are suitable for high throughputs of sacks, **8**.

7.05 *Unloading barges* Twin belt, arch, or spiral elevators are used for unloading sacks from barges, **9**. Belt elevators usually have one powered band, the other adding pressure against the sack to hold it in position. They are articulated or mounted on a wheeled gantry. Spiral conveyors (used for continuous unloading of LASH barges), move on carriages like dock cranes,

6

7

8

9

6 *Liquid intermediate bulk containers stacked by forklift truck.*

7 *Mobile railway wagon loading point, fed from high level cross belt.*

8 *Hydraulic bag loading belt for lorries. The end section pivots, and the whole can move up and down.*

9 *Barge unloading by arch conveyor.*

and feed to fixed take-away conveyors. Most handle over 2000 sacks per hour. For unloading barges and rail wagons, the arched conveyor is most commonly used, **9**. These are belt conveyors with an extendible section that can cover the hold of the barge, can elevate independently from the take-away section (to cope with varied tides) or dispatch to different floors of the storage building. The central movement section can be mounted on a rail carriage, and incorporate road wheels to enable the conveyor to be folded and wheeled out of the way when not in use. A 650 mm arched chevron-patterned belt can handle 600 sacks per hour at 0·8 m/sec.

Intermediate bulk containers
7.05 Intermediate bulk containers are handled as post pallets, over the back of the truck from a raised dock, or over the side from ground level or a finger dock. Post pallet type legs and location cones are used. Gantry crane overhead unloading can be used, linked with an overhead monorail system that block stacks the containers, or takes them directly over the process machinery for tipping.

Drums
7.06 Non-palletised drums can be unloaded on a conventional raised dock with a standard forklift and drum clamp.

Bulk liquids and solids
7.07 Bulk tankers or liquid and solid materials require special loading bays. Rail wagons are inherently fixed path unless a special trailer is used. They require linear unloading or continual train movements. Rail wagons for bulk liquids are usually handled in groups, plugged into line-side meterage and pump points with flexible sections. Absolute positioning is difficult due to buffer tolerance. Plug positions should have a high level of lighting, at least 400 lux, weather protection, and equipment to counteract any specific hazard. Flammable and explosive liquids loading bays should be segregated from production buildings, and allow natural air circulation to disperse the fumes that occur as tanks are emptied. Contact British Rail and the Factory Inspectorate. A separate track should be available for carrying special products, and for tankers which require cleaning (see para **7.11**).
7.08 Many granular and powdered materials are transported by rail pressure tanker, and discharged by air pressure or vacuum. Hopper wagons have side or bottom discharge, depending on the product. The wagons move slowly forward over a long pit with a screw or belt conveyor at the base. Discharge pits should have weather protection (see Information sheet Loading 6 for dimensions).

Road trailer tank discharge points
7.09 Methods of discharge of materials from road vehicles are shown in Table I and **11-15**. Most road tankers carry their own discharge pipes. For planning of accumulation zones and turning areas, see Technical study Loading 1.
7.10 Pressure tanks in ISO frames can also be used as process storage tanks, and can be stacked or placed on stillage legs. If placed on a slave trailer, 6 m units can be manoeuvred right into the building and unloaded directly into the process.

Cleaning
7.11 Many tankers, especially those carrying food, require cleaning after discharge. Road tankers can be cleaned in the same bay through discharge connection points. Internal bays should have a high level of extraction to allow for gas escape. Explosive and flammable products should be handled externally where possible. Tanks with opening top hatches, eg milk tankers, are cleaned through pipes manually directed from the tank top catwalk and the fluid discharged through the take-away piping. Steam cleaning is used for some glutinous products. Toxic or flammable liquids must not reach open water; contact the petroleum officer and the Factory Inspec-

10

11a

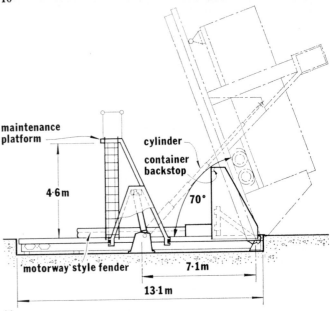
11b

10 *Fuel tank unloading at terminal.*
11a *Dimensions of tipping table.*
11b *ISO container tipped by special skeletal trailer.*

TABLE I Method of discharge of bulk materials

Material	Type of vehicle	discharge method	conveyed by
Powders	tipping tank (see **12**)	through funnel	pneumatic pipe system
	horizontal tanker (see **13**)	through tank base	pneumatic or vacuum pipe system
Granular materials	tipping tank (see **12**)	pit in loading bay floor	screw or belt conveyors
Industrial sands and quarry products	bottom dump hopper truck	pit in loading bay floor	depends on material
Liquids	tanker (see **14, 15**)	side or end valves (light specific gravity liquids have grouped valves)	gravity or pumped system
Heavy liquids (acids or caustic soda)	tanker (see **14, 15**)	single rear discharge	gravity or pumped system
Bulk solids	standard ISO container with disposable liner, on truck body	on skeletal tipper, **11a** or whole vehicle is placed on tipping table, **11b.**	pneumatic or vacuum pipe system or screw or belt conveyor

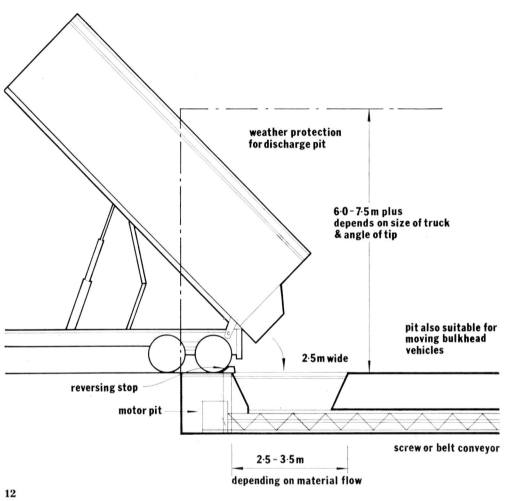

12 *Discharge pit for tippers and for tipping ISO containers. Plastic curtains help to protect pit from driving rain.*
13 *Side view of unloading area for bottom discharge tankers (eg powder and granule tankers). Some products dump straight through a grating, others (eg carbon black) need a flexible pipe connection.*

weather protection for discharge pit

6·0 - 7·5 m plus depends on size of truck & angle of tip

pit also suitable for moving bulkhead vehicles

2·5 m wide

reversing stop

motor pit

screw or belt conveyor

2·5 - 3·5 m depending on material flow

12

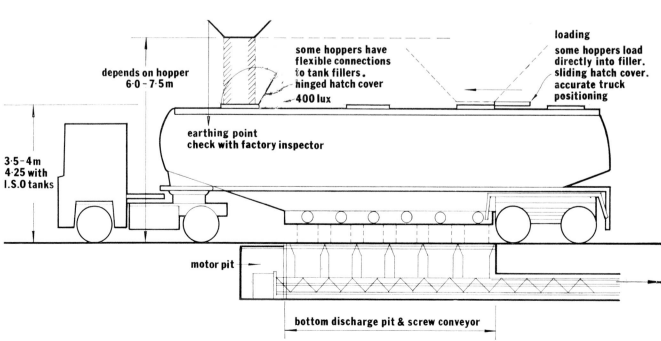

depends on hopper 6·0 - 7·5 m

some hoppers have flexible connections to tank fillers. hinged hatch cover 400 lux

loading
some hoppers load directly into filler. sliding hatch cover. accurate truck positioning

earthing point check with factory inspector

3·5 - 4 m 4·25 with I.S.O tanks

motor pit

bottom discharge pit & screw conveyor

13

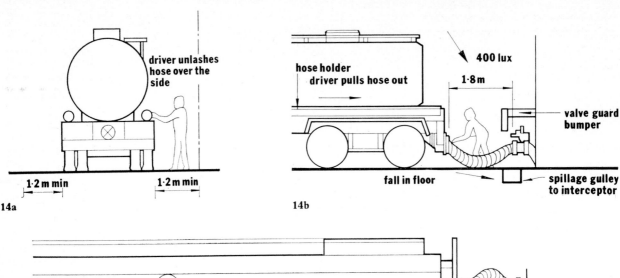

driver unlashes hose over the side

1·2 m min   1·2 m min

14a

hose holder driver pulls hose out

400 lux

1·8 m

valve guard bumper

fall in floor   **spillage gulley to interceptor**

14b

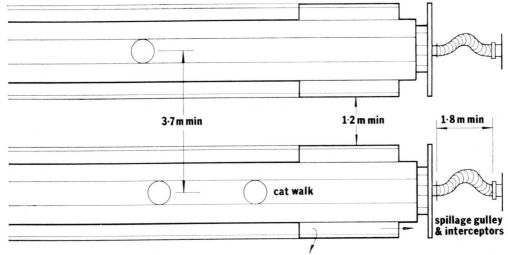

3·7 m min   1·2 m min   1·8 m min

cat walk

spillage gulley & interceptors

14c

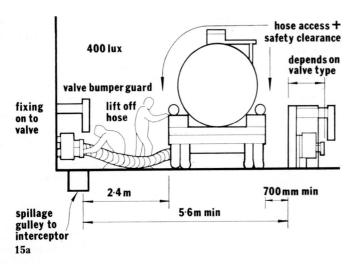

hose access + safety clearance

400 lux

depends on valve type

valve bumper guard

fixing on to valve

lift off hose

2·4 m

700 mm min

5·6 m min

spillage gulley to interceptor

15a

14a *Rear view;* **b** *side view;*
c *plan of unloading area for
rear-valve discharge
tankers. Also suitable for
non-tipping powder tankers.*
15a *Rear view;* **b** *plan of
unloading area for side valve
discharge tankers, eg
petroleum. Interceptors run
to central point for gulley
collection by special service
vehicle.*

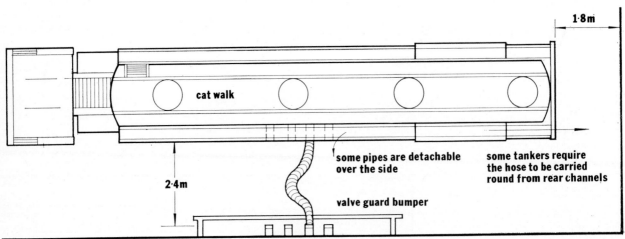

1·8 m

cat walk

2·4 m

some pipes are detachable over the side

some tankers require the hose to be carried round from rear channels

valve guard bumper

**spillage gulley under valves
floor falls to gulley from truck valve point**

15b

torate. Clearance should be allowed for personnel movement on tank catwalks, and for opening hatches. If ISO containers with liners are used, a skip position should be planned for the disposal of the liners.

8 Characteristics of goods

Bulk solids

8.01 Bulk solids have some of the properties of solids, such as elasticity and plastic deformation, but they also resemble liquids in that they can change shape with movement. The most important differences are:

1 Static pressures in a liquid are independent of direction, whereas in a solid they vary with direction. A solid can transmit shear stress under static conditions a liquid cannot. A solid forms a pile when static, whereas a liquid assumes a level surface.

2 When consolidated, many solids retain their shape and possess cohesive strength, retaining a stable arch structure; liquids cannot do this.

In bulk form, non-stick but hard packed or fibrous materials of small particle size tend to break into deeply cracked sections which move in relation to one another. These materials can form an arch or bridge, impeding flow at entry or dispensing points. In certain coarse granule materials, or those which have high mass adhesion, layered movement can occur.

Further information can be obtained from the Powder Advisary Centre.

Bulk liquids

8.02 The characteristics of bulk liquids vary also. Some acids have great mass and flow slowly, while petroleum spirit flows fast and easily. Materials like raw molasses and tar need heating during flow, bulk liquid gases require refrigeration during pumping and storage.

Materials characteristics must be accurately specified in the brief, including factors such as abrasiveness for powders and corrosive characteristics for liquids (see Information sheet Bulk storage 4).

Arch-forming materials

8.03 Typical arch forming materials are:

Chalk, clay, gypsum, coal powder, powdered milk, pyrites, cocoa powder, potato flour, starch, plastics powders, kaolin, bentonite, short fibre asbestos, stone flour and pressed oats.

These materials can be difficult to discharge from silos or transport containers, even with aeration assistance. Their flow characteristics are thought to be greatly improved by the introduction of sound modulated air.

Free-flowing materials

8.04 Free flowing materials include:

Flour, sugar, plastics granules, fertiliser pellets, and cement. These materials have few movement problems.

8.05 Sound modulated air influences slug forming materials, ie those with particles exceeding 5 mm, woodchips, fibrous materials with fibre lengths of more than 3 mm, and damp, heavy materials with excessive mass adhesion like wet sand and certain ore concentrates.

8.06 Many powdered products are explosive when combined with air and detonated with a static electrical charge. Great care has to be taken in designing areas for their transfer and storage.

Sacks

8.07 Sacks should be assembled on pallets without creating voids; this is usually a pin wheel pattern or a row formation with five or six sacks. Pallets or skidboards are often shrink-wrapped for stability and moisture protection, or sacks are banded to the pallet. Sacks shrink-wrapped in heavy gauge sheet, can be lifted from above with vacuum handling equip-

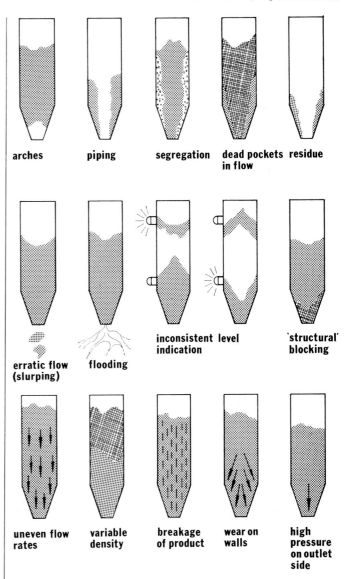

16 *Ways in which hoppers can operate inefficiently if not designed specifically for the characteristics of the solid material stored.*

ment. Jute sacks have a high coefficient of friction and stack well; this produces friction during handling however. Crimping improves the grip between paper sacks. Plastic sacks are inherently slippery, but special printing inks improve adhesion.

8.08 Drums distort if mishandled, and dents in drums can hinder movement throughout the storage system.

9 Sorting

9.01 Bulk solids and liquids are usually transported direct from the loading bay to the hopper or tank. Intermediate bulk containers might need sorting into those going directly to the process buffer stock and those stacked for bulk storage.

The number of intermediate bulk containers arriving at one time should not require buffer space for more than four containers unless in-store travel distances are long. If large numbers of bulk containers are anticipated, full scale bulk handling should be re-examined, as, although hoppers and pipework are costly, their maintenance costs are low compared with mobile and ancillary plant required to tip and handle intermediate bulk containers,

9.02 Pallet loads of sacks and drums can be treated as conventional unit loads as in Technical study Mechanised storage 1, para 9. If sacks are of one product, for block storage, the pallets can be carried direct from the vehicle to the stack. However, if there is a variety of products to move at different user speeds, sorting into racking zones would be required; buffer space should then be provided.

10 Volume calculations

10.01 These should be part of the brief, and of the user specification. They are integral with the production process planned by the user. In bulk storage, volume and flow calculations are largely out of the building designer's hands, but in order that a co-ordinated design can be possible the calculations should be complete at the time of briefing.

11 Turnover calculations

11.01 These are included in volume calculations above.

12 Variety and flow

12.01 These are included in volume calculations above.

13 Type of storage

13.01 Bulk solids are mostly stored in hoppers—a generic term which includes silos and bulk bins. Material is blown, sucked or conveyed into the top of the hopper, and then flows through it by gravity to be discharged as required at the base. The basic theory of flow characteristics should be understood by designers, as it affects the size and shape of the hopper. Poor hopper performance is caused by too large or too small discharge orifices, too tall or too narrow containing walls, and poor design by too steep or shallow walls of the discharge cone. Simulation models are available for testing various materials' flow characteristics in different sizes of hopper.
Material flowing through a hopper is subject to two sets of forces:
1 Compressive force from the mass of material coming into the system.
2 Compressive force exerted on the solid material by the hopper walls.

Mass and core flow
13.02 There are two commonly found flow patterns in hoppers, mass flow and core flow. In mass flow, all the solid material moves from the entry point to discharge together. Mass flow hoppers can be much taller than core flow units.

Friction can cause the material nearest the wall surface to be contaminated by the wall lining. No piping or high pressure build-ups occur. Mass flow hoppers will empty completely so utilising their full capacity, and allowing reliable level control.

Core flow
13.03 Core flow is more complex. Only the central core of material moves, and stationary material builds up next to the container walls. Flow will not necessarily recommence when an obstruction has been removed. Capacity is reduced and control is not so accurate as in mass flow units. Core flow can be converted to mass flow by the addition of a suitable discharge cone. Even in well-designed hoppers flow may not start due to high compacting stresses at the base of the hopper.

Aids to flow
13.04 Flow can be improved by mechanical vibratory impulses on the discharge cone, pulsating discharge panels, mechanical arch breakers or sonic devices. The geometry of the discharge point must be correct for the material. Flow can be hampered by factors outside the hopper itself.
13.05 Sound waves improve the flow of troublesome materials. Sonic activators with air diffusion can shift some materials especially sluggish ones such as short fibre asbestos. For glutinous materials, airbags are inserted in the cone of the hopper, and rapidly inflated and deflated, forcing the sticking material down into the funnel.
13.06 Bulk liquid tanks have simpler flow characteristics, but some liquids have to be heated or cooled to flow easily.

Bulk solids storage
13.07 Some bulk solids, eg lime and sulphur, are stockpiled in heaps in special buildings. The material is conveyed by belt or auger over the storage area, is distributed evenly by a moving distributor head, and is dug out by reclamation conveyors.

Sack storage
13.08 Palletised sacks can be block stacked, but this is usually limited by instability to two to three pallets high. Pallet converters can be used up to five high. Drive-in racking is suitable for sacks requiring high selectivity.
13.09 For small varieties and large quantities, block stacked unpalletised sacks make the greatest use of available volume. Some very large stores work effectively in this manner in Europe. Sacks can be stored at rates of 2000 per hour with only one operator in a remote cabin controlling the automatic loader, fed by continuous loading conveyors. Very high stacks are possible, but this depends on the skill of the personnel and the characteristics of the bagged product.

first in, last out, segregates, ratholes, flushes

first in, first out, de-aerates, remixes, feeds uniformly at at constant density

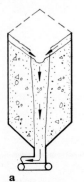
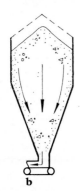
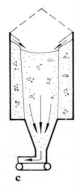

a   b   c

17a *Core flow,* **b** *mass flow*
c *expanded flow (a combination of* **a** *and* **b***, used for certain materials).*

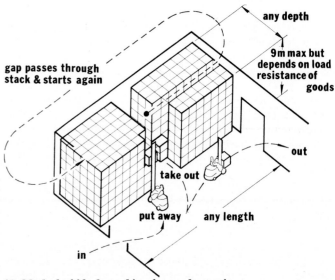

any depth

9m max but depends on load resistance of goods

gap passes through stack & starts again

out

take out

put away   **any length**

in

18 *Method of block stacking for stock rotation.*

13.10 Drums can be stored on pallets, or block stacked by a forklift truck with a special attachment **18**. Drums for paints ingredients need turning to stop the heavier material settling into a solid lump at the base. They are often placed in flow racking and picked on a first-in, first-out principle, the drums rolling down by gravity. Drum silos have been built in Europe, in which groups of drums are elevated up a tower and flow down as drums are removed below.

13.11 Intermediate bulk containers are normally stacked two high when full. Typical capacities depending on density are 1400-2880 litres each.

14 Stock control

14.01 This does not apply to bulk goods.

15 Stock withdrawal

15.01 The basic question facing designers of bulk solids systems is: should the material be *piped* or *conveyed* from the storage medium to the point of use or dispatch?

15.02 Bulk materials are handled by a batch system or continuous system. In the batch system, a fixed quantity of material is blown intermittently from one container into another, or into a flow system. Conveying is either in dilute phase, where discrete particles of the material flow in an air carrier, or dense or pulse phase where the material moves in slugs. The system operates either under positive pressure, when the solids are blown through the pipe, or by vacuum, where the material is sucked. Positive pressure is used where material is conveyed from a single intake point to a number of discharge outlets. A vacuum system is usually employed for a multiple feed to a single discharge point.

Air handling

15.03 The air handling plant is either a fan, multistage turbo blower, scavenger blower or exhauster, reciprocating vacuum pump, or hydraulic steam ejector. The introduction of the solid into the airstream from the hopper should cause as little pressure loss as possible. A rotary valve is often used for this purpose, or else the solid is fluidised in the container before blowing the solid/air mass through the pipe.

Pneumatic handling

15.04 Factors affecting design of pneumatic handling systems are the required solids/air ratio, air velocity, and pressure losses. Variations in pipe diameter, bends, diverters, valves and filtration units all contribute to overall pressure losses. A pneumatic conveyor system should be designed in the context of the total system. Testing programmes are available from the Warren Spring Laboratory, and Loughborough, Bradford and Birmingham Universities.

15.05 Pneumatic conveying has high power and running costs, but low maintenance. At the discharge end of the system, there must be a satisfactory method of separation of the solid from the air carrier. If very fine particles are involved, dust can produce an explosion risk.

Pulse phase conveying

15.06 The Warren Spring Laboratory has developed a new system, pulse phase conveying, which is now being commercially developed, **19**. Bulk solids are in effect chopped into lengths by air pressure, which flow easily through pipelines under low pneumatic pressure. This was designed particularly for adhesive-type materials which are slow and expensive to convey. It could be useful for conveying explosive material, as the slugs could be propelled by an inert gas. Carbon black is also suited to this method.

Hygroscopic materials like ammonium chloride require dried air for transport. This is not expensive with pulse phase conveying, as air quantities are small. Compressed air, in the form of

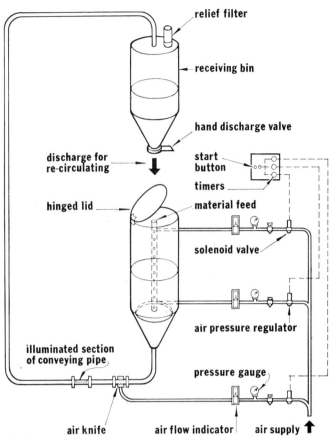

19 *Main features of a typical pulse conveying circuit.*

an air knife, cuts material in blocks and propels it forward.

15.07 For companies doubtful about equipping with pneumatic bulk systems who have kept to augers, belts and intermediate bulk containers with forklift trucks, pulse phase conveying offers a simple system and reduced maintenance at a cost lower than scaling down a larger system. The main problem is power consumption, which can be five times more for long runs.

15.08 Belts and augurs are still specified for some products, although they are space consuming and are comparatively slow. Belts are suited to some particularly glutinous materials that are expensive to handle pneumatically, and grains are efficiently transported by augurs.

In-process weighing

15.09 Both pneumatic and belt conveyors can be equipped with in-travel weighing devices. Load cells are now protected against damp, condensation and dust. Some can measure changes in the permeability of materials. Stock control of bulk solid materials is based on the precise weighing of material in mixing centres at dispatch points and in storage hoppers. Many modern manufacturing processes are designed round an automated weighing system integrated with the materials handling method.

15.10 Weighing installations can be linked to the central data processing computer, becoming an integrated part of the materials flow. In batching installations, a high weighing accuracy does not necessarily mean that materials are accurately dispensed. Variations in the closing time of valves limits the accuracy of dispensed weights to approximately 1 part in 200 or worse. High precision weighing allows the possibility of metering small portions of the same material for packaging in individual sachets; this is useful when only small quantities of material are required in a process, where further bulk handling would be uneconomic.

16 Order picking

16.01 This does not apply to bulk goods.

17 Picking area

17.01 This does not apply to bulk goods.

18 Load build-up

Dispatch sorting

18.01 True bulk materials are delivered directly from the hopper to the loading bay. However, many products stored in bulk are distributed into sacks or drums for further distribution to the consumer.

18.02 *Automatic sacking machines* incorporate in-process weighing and sack manufacture. They are fed from overhead hoppers or, if powders, by pressure pipe to the filling head. Plastic sacks and plastic liners are made from tubular film, which is cut, heat-sealed at the base, filled and heat-sealed at the head in one operation. A manually operated machine works at 120 sacks per hour where an automatic machine can fill 600 or more in the same period.

18.03 *Gravity packers* are designed for granular materials. Material flows from an overhead hopper without any power assistance. The sack is mounted on a weighing head that automatically shuts off the flow at the correct point. 120 sacks per hour are possible per head.

18.04 *Belt packers* are for free flowing materials. Material is propelled between a curved belt and a grooved centrifugal wheel. This is run continuously, and is fed from an high speed automatic weighing hopper. With multiple spout action, filling can be achieved at more than 1 tonne per minute.

18.05 *Screw packers* are designed for meals and fine powders. The screw propels material into the filling spout. For glutinous or sticky materials, an agitator can be fitted over the screw; 8-12 tonnes per hour are normal for single screw machines.

18.06 *Impeller packers* are for ground rock products. The material flows by gravity from overhead hoppers into an impeller rotor, which puts the product into the sack. Full automation cuts the flow by pneumatically pinching the flexible feed tube, controlled by an in-process weighing head. Multi-tube machines can fill at over a tonne a minute, single spout units at 12 tonnes per hour.

18.07 *Pneumatic packers* are fast, dustless in operation, and used mostly with powders. Pneumatic fillers have tended to replace other types. Sacks are supported on a weigh beam, or an inflow load cell is used. High filling speeds are possible.

18.08 After filling, most machines employ continuous heat sealers. A typical method is to squeeze the top of the sack between two steel bands, which pass a heat source, so welding the sack's top; operational speed is approximately 10 m/minute. Faster sealing speeds are possible with multiple jets of heated air and pressure rollers. Other forms used with paper sacks are continuous plastics banders and, for jute and paper, multi-head in-path sewing machines, where speeds of up to 20 m per minute are possible.

18.09 *Feeders* The four basic types of feeder for solids are narrow bore rotary valves, aeration feeders, flat belt feeders, and vibratory feeders.

18.10 Drum filling machines operate in a similar manner to bottle filler lines, but on a larger scale. Empty drums are increasingly stored in silos to save floor space.

18.11 Filled sacks and drums may require placing on pallets prior to dispatch. Sacks are conveyed on belt conveyors, diverted by curving plates or powered belt diverters. Belts normally handle up to 1200 sacks per hour, and can be integrated with elevator/lowerator sections. Conventional palletisers are used for stacking sacks on pallets. Many palletised loads are now shrink-wrapped for ease of handling and external storage. Drums are carried on chain conveyors or slat units to accumulation conveyors for bulk loading, or the drums go through an adapted palletiser. Square section plastic containers make better surface use of pallets.

19 Order and document check

19.01 See Technical study Mechanised storage 1, para 19.

20 Loading and dispatch

20.01 For palletised, sacked goods see Technical study Mechanised storage, para 20. Drums can be assembled on accumulation conveyors, and loaded direct into containers or on to flat vehicles. Alternatively the drums can be block stacked and called forward as required.

20.02 The dispatch of bulk tankered products is similar to unloading. Liquids are pumped, granular products are usually loaded from an overhead hopper by gravity. Powders tend to be pumped under pressure. With standard ISO containers, a plastic liner is suspended from the container walls and a timber restraining end panel fixed, leaving a tubular connection to a blower unit. This is then connected to a hopper, the blower forcing the material into the container, inflating the plastic liner as it goes, **20**.

20.03 All bulk loading can be automatically metered. Materials like acids are carefully pumped and the accuracy of the valve mechanism ensures that there is little spillage. Contact the petroleum officer and Factory Inspectorate.

Bulk solids tankers require weighing before they leave the site. Weighbridge technology has improved with the introduction of load cells and digital read-out facilities. Mechanical systems can transfer the weighing figures direct into a data processing machine and issue the driver with a weighing ticket or a punched card. A mini-computer can be added to integrate the system and to replace the gateman, providing automatic control of the barrier, driver identification, and 'memorising' the tare weight of incoming trucks. Electronic weighing lessens the chance of large-scale fraud. With mechanical systems, the dials on the weigh head have to be very large for accurate reading whereas digital displays are accurate and easy to read, and digital readers are less sensitive to disturbance

20 *ISO container with plastic liner being filled.*

Technical study
Bulk storage 2

Building function

22 Structure

Hopper structures

22.01 Hopper structures must withstand maximum wall pressures, eg pressure from erratic core flow discharge. Any internal wall irregularities, including material joints, seams, and protrusions such as bolts and rivets, reduce performance. To reduce irregularity and reduce frictional properties internal faces of hoppers can be coated. The lining must not generate an electrostatic charge causing fire or explosion.

22.02 Welded hoppers and tanks are specialist structures, calculated for the pressures and stress patterns formed by the product being stored. Tanks can be built of steel, aluminium, cast iron (still effective) or reinforced concrete. Choice depends on hopper size and internal liner. Plastic (filament-wound glassfibre) tanks and bins are used for road and rail transport.

22.03 Hoppers may have to be separate from main building structure owing to the risk of explosion, **1**. Check that the bearing strength of the soil is suitable for large hoppers, whose weight tends to be concentrated on a small area. For positioning of hoppers and pressure tanks for gases, liquid fuels and acids in relation to other buildings, consult the Factory Inspectorate.

Structures for heaped bulk materials

22.04 Heaped bulk materials require special building structures which carry the rehandling machinery. These buildings, usually of steel or concrete, follow the contour of the heaped product. They are often designed within the service offered by the equipment manufacturer, **2ab**.

22.05 For bulk sacked goods, the structure is designed to carry the sack handling plant and to support the cladding.

Silos

22.06 Le Corbusier was very impressed by the great grain silos in Canada when he wrote *Towards a new architecture* in

1 *Plastic hopper, separate from the main building.*

1

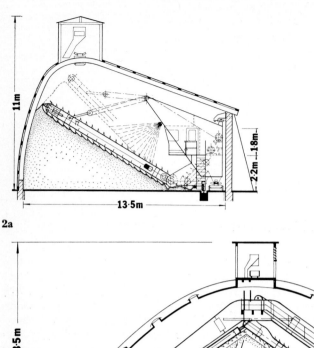

2a

2a, b *Structures for heaped bulk materials. In* **a** *the hopper is loaded from the angled chute above, which moves down the shed. This machine removes from one side only, drawing the material towards the take-away conveyor;* **b** *uses the same principle, but is for larger quantities of material loaded to form a heap. Material is reclaimed from both sides.*

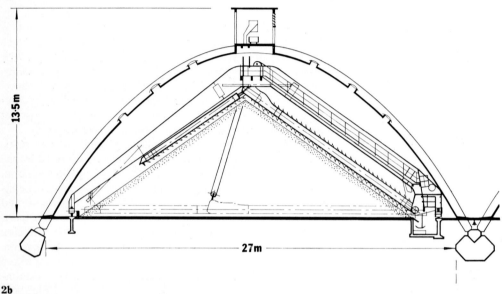

2b

1923. Reinforced concrete is still widely used for silos and proprietary systems offer steel and precast concrete. There is wide choice of height, width and capacity to suit the characteristics of the material to be stored, **3**.

23 Floors

23.01 Floor finishes in bulk handling areas must suit the material, as spillage is inevitable. Some products are highly corrosive to concrete (some lubricants can eat through a 600 mm thick reinforced concrete slab). Specialist flooring contractors offer advice on floors for difficult materials.

23.02 Some industries still recommend quarry tiles as they are resistant to acids and are quickly replaced if cracked. But a tile finish is only as good as its joints and has a greater chance of failure compared with a jointless floor finish. At one installation handling vegetable fats, the fat ran down a cracked joint, was drawn by capillary action some distance under the tile surface and percolated through a concrete slab a long way from the point of failure.

Jointless floors

23.03 Jointless floor finishes consist of a mixture of gap-graded aggregate, bonded with cement and polymer. They are waterproof, oil resistant and can withstand abrasion and the heavy wheel loadings of road tankers. If wheeled tanker

trucks are to be used, plan for wheel loadings of 5 to 6 tonnes. If rail wagons are to be brought into the building, consult British Rail about track foundation details. Jointless finishes can be integrated with sunken railway tracks, as they will not crack and spall against the track members. For very heavy duty areas, where impacts of drums, intermediate bulk containers and the corner castings of ISO tank containers can be expected, use high strength jointless floors, eg Rescon, a trowel-on surface of polyester resin and treated aggregates which can accept high impact loadings, deform and regain its surface without cracking.

23.04 Most jointless finishes are trowelled manually. Power floating is not acceptable, as all the fines are brought to the surface leaving a large dry aggregate base layer causing instability of the floor. Intense acids require an epoxy-based finish. This is strong and resistant to most chemicals but not to impact damage. Several epoxy finishes are self-levelling. Epoxy and polymer based finishes can be filled with non-slip material and can be lapped up wall surfaces to prevent damage from splashback. They are also ideal for tanker cleaning bays.

24 Building services

24.01 In bulk handling, building services must be integrated with special services. Loading areas should have high light levels, 400 lux minimum, as should valve and shut-off positions. Pipelines and valves should not cause reflected glare.

24.02 In tanker loading areas, where liquid tanks are vented as the material is pumped in, the most effective method of extraction is to leave as much of the loading bay open to the air as possible. With toxic and flammable materials dangerous gases can be given off. Most acid gases are heavier than air, sinking to the floor surface. No air inlet or building entry should be within 15 m of the area at risk (consult the Factory Inspectorate). Very toxic gases have to be collected and disposed of separately. In handling powder and granular materials, special in-process dust-extraction machinery reduces the risk of explosion and contamination of machinery and other products, **4**. Sacking areas require dust extraction and filtration. Little dust escapes into the atmosphere when loading powder tankers under pressure.

24.03 Acids and caustic products require large quantities of water to dilute and wash away any that has been spilled accidentally. Drainage should not contaminate surrounding ground or waterways.

24.04 Tanker washing bays require cold water supplies. Water heating is usually supplied with the machinery. A light level of 400 lux is suggested.

24.05 Valves are available with built-in heater elements for external winter conditions. Loading zones with buried wire heaters prevent snow and ice build-up, which is undesirable with tankers carrying dangerous loads.

24.06 Batch weighing and loading control cabins should be sealed and air-filtered in dusty or toxic conditions. Packaged air-conditioners could be used. Electronic hardware requires special filters in dusty conditions.

25 Special services

25.01 Systems for handling both solids and liquids involve quantities of pipework, valves, pumps, mixing chambers etc. The amount of piping and expansion potential of the process within the building affects initial structural design, choice of machine clearances, duct zones and depth of roof construction. Pneumatic piping can be gathered into high density zones, but this might conflict with the requirement for maintenance access.

25.02 Some powders and granular materials need controlled hopper environments, depending on size of hopper and climate of the area. Specialist advice is required.

26 Building fabric

26.01 Owing to the explosion risk in bulk powder installations, light blow-away cladding should be used. Hoppers normally have blow-off panels in their roofs. Cladding is often fixed with shear bolts to release pressure. Ideally bulk-loading bays should be, like storage tanks and hoppers, out of the main building. Translucent, corrugated sheet provides good weather protection and is easy to replace. There are regulations for spark prevention and guarding the building fabric in danger areas (consult the Factory Inspectorate).

27 Fire control

Explosion control

27.01 Few powders, if correctly handled, offer a risk of frequent explosions but, given air and an electrostatic charge, explosion is always possible. Big hopper surface areas and pneumatic conveying can generate electrostatic charges. Flour is particularly difficult to handle. Previously, conveyors were expected to explode and were fitted with blow-off panels, **5**. Today, sophisticated sensors can detect and contain explosive conditions in 10 microseconds. All sensor points must be accessible for maintenance. Conveyor systems and hoppers should be segregated, and long runs split into compartments to prevent

3

4

5

3 Cereal silo, with pneumatic elevator in foreground.
4 Dust extraction plant filters air which is displaced from the silo (below) as it is fed by the distributor (left).
5 Explosion relief doors on hoppers.

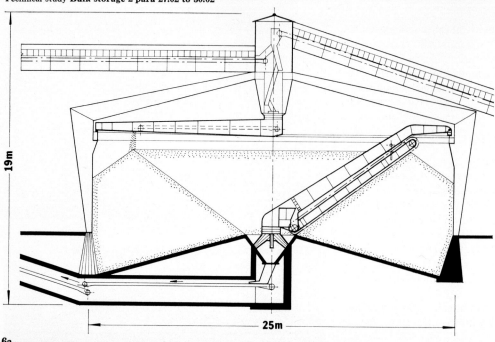

6a *Section through circular site containing central rotating conveyor, which stacks with a circular motion. Capacity is limited to 10 000 m³. Stacking and reclaiming must be alternated.*
b *Open-sided bulk bins fed by overhead gantry.*

6a

6b

flash fires. Explosive materials should not be placed near heat or electrical sources. Hoppers in internal positions should be protected by fire walls from hot processes.

27.02 Dust supression equipment prevents very small particle dust from escaping through rotary valves and filters. Thin layers of fine dust can be activated by electrostatic charges into surface flash fires[1].

27.03 Vehicle loading bays should have earthing points to disperse static charges built up by the flow of granular material.

27.04 Sprinkling can often do more harm than good in a bulk storage area. Consult the Building Research Establishment about the extinguishing method best suited to the material. For petroleum and flammable products stored and used in any process, consult the Factory Inspectorate. Petroleum or flammable materials stored for subsequent sale come under the Explosives Act, so consult the petroleum officer.

27.05 Special handling equipment, such as conveyors with air motors and pneumatic control, is used in spark-proof zones. Care has to be taken when routing piping and cables through these zones.

28 Security

28.01 Intruders must not gain access to premises where dangerous products are handled. Sophisticated electronic security systems are used in driver-operated petrol terminals: they have card readers and automatic gate control. A high level of lighting and a perimeter fence with an outward sloping top section also improves security.

28.02 The surrounding area must be secure from explosion or contamination by liquids and gases. Loading bays for flammable products and toxic chemicals come under the regulations for hazardous materials, and doorways to main building should be not less than 15 m away. Gulleys should be trapped and spillage collected in containers for disposal.

29 External works

29.01 Ranked filling positions for tankers should be well lit and clearly marked and have personnel walkways. External areas for intermediate bulk containers and drums should be drained so that water cannot collect round the container base and cause corrosion. Parking space should be provided for idle tankers. For railway points radii and permissible gradients, consult British Rail.

30 Structure-based plant

30.01 Belt conveyors are used for granular materials and sacks. Care must be taken in routing conveyors near process piping, as covers can blow off and damage services. Other types of structure-based plant are augers which convey material by helical screw, reclamation digger loaders which stock-pile material, and sack stacking and reclamation machines.

30.02 Stock pile reclamation diggers are endless belts or bucket chains, mounted on a mobile base, **6a**. They either attack the stock pile from the end (slewing in both directions to make an efficient cutting pattern) or scrape from the sides with single- and double-sided scrapers which straddle the stock pile to reduce the level evenly. Material is taken away on fixed conveyors. Stock pile buildings are charged by a gantry-slung sliding distributor, **2**, or grab, **6b**, fed by a fixed belt. The charger moves up and down the stock pile, spreading the material evenly. This heavy machinery must be integrated with the structure.

30.03 Intermediate bulk containers require tipping tables, **7a**, or mobile stands for bottom discharge over the process, **7b**. Some systems using intermediate bulk containers need overhead carriers.

31 Mobile plant

31.01 Forklift trucks handle intermediate bulk containers. Mobile plant which stores and handles bulk materials includes mobile conveyors and tractor shovels. Shovel attachments can be used with forklift trucks but cannot be compared in performance with tractor shovels. Mobile drum lifter-tippers are employed for repacking drums or feeding process machinery.

31.02 Mobile sweepers are very useful in bulk stores; they can be electric, or diesel or lpg powered. Diesel is not suitable for internal use, and no internal combustion powered types can be used if there is any risk of explosion. Sweepers can be equipped with solvent tanks and scrubber/scarifier brushes to wash away and collect liquids spilt in loading bays, **8**. This reduces the need for special trapped gulleys and collection tanks. Mechanical sweepers can discharge their load direct into sealed waste skips.

32 Integration of building and plant

32.01 Pipelines, hoppers and other bulk handling plant should be integrated with the building at the design stage. The old navy yard principle—of the first installer being lucky and the last having to thread pipes round all the other valves and joints—can still be seen in some installations. It results in high maintenance costs and increased down time. Pipe runs should not conflict with mobile plant routes or conveyor lines. If there is any risk of explosions, the routing of power cables and hot services should be planned out of the zone.

33 Maintenance

33.01 Maintenance access to all pipe bends and valves, pumps, cyclones and filters should be provided. Powders are not only explosive but also abrasive. Valves and pipe linings need replacement, and areas that have been injected with emergency heat suppressant require cleaning and recommissioning. Conveyors and augers require maintenance of motors and idlers. Chain hoist rails should be fitted over pipe runs or access provided for mobile lifting tackle to be conveniently positioned on the floor. Hydraulic platforms—popular for general purpose maintenance—can be mounted on compact electric vehicles. If pipe runs are at high level, there should be catwalk access to the valves and meters. Although most bulk handling equipment tends to be dismantled and repaired off the premises by outside contractors, first-aid repair facilities should be provided. This welding and cutting gear should be in a fire-proof compartment away from any bulk storage hoppers or equipment. The maintenance area should have access for heavy vehicles, and a 2-tonne overhead chain hoist for unloading valves and pipe sections is useful.

34 Management

34.01 The management of the design, construction and commissioning of bulk installations requires careful organisation. Possible conflicts in installation order and procedure between the various specialists involved—eg bulk transport pipes conflicting with cabling, pipe runs baulked by processing plant substructures—should be identified at the planning stage.

7a

7b

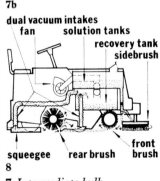

8

7 *Intermediate bulk containers* **a** *on tipping table,* **b** *placed by forklift on stand for bottom discharge into process.*
8 *Sweepers can collect spilt liquids in loading bays.*

34.02 The commissioning of bulk systems often takes time, in achieving the correct hopper discharge rates and pipeline flow speeds. It is at the commissioning stage that explosions occur. In installations carrying corrosive liquids a catch tray should be hung under each valve until it is certain that there is no leakage. The Factory Inspector should be kept informed right through construction and commissioning.

35 Personnel accommodation

35.01 Most bulk storage installations are run by a very small number of control and supervisory personnel. The main labour force comprises loading-bay and maintenance staff. Bulk loading bays are often operated solely by the tanker's driver. Personnel should be kept out of bulk storage and process areas as much as possible.

Office accommodation
35.02 Bulk storage offices are often related to the weighing and transport interface areas. Offices are also required for maintenance personnel. Personnel areas should be dust free and protected from explosion hazards. If office accommodation is positioned near loading bays handling toxic products, make sure that the construction forms an efficient seal against discharges of toxic gas.

36 Amenity

36.01 Drivers require toilet and rest facilities out of the loading-bay zone, and adjacent to a parking area for idle vehicles or those waiting for loading-bay allocation. Some amenity accommodation is necessary for maintenance staff and the few control and supervisory personnel. Some installations have very comfortable control rooms with adjacent rest and washing facilities, all fully air-conditioned. The electronics equipment usually requires air-conditioning; it can produce sufficient heat to necessitate cooling of the control rooms.

37 Security and safety

37.01 Bulk storage and handling zones can be hazardous to operatives. Conveyor belts, crushers, cyclones and blowers should be guarded and fitted with safety cut-off stops. Catwalks should be well lit and clearly marked. Means of escape should be fitted with emergency lighting and be brightly painted for immediate identification in dusty conditions. A first-aid room should be provided, equipped to handle broken limbs, burns and blast shock cases. This room should be air-conditioned if there is any risk of the atmosphere becoming dusty or of escapes of toxic gas in emergency conditions. Ambulance access should be separate from the loading bay, as fires and explosions can occur there.

38 Circulation

38.01 Circulation of materials is an inherent part of the bulk handling system. Truck circulation has been discussed in paras 7 and 20. Car parking should be provided for visiting maintenance staff, and truck access to the maintenance area. Circulation routes for personnel should be clearly marked and guarded from accidentally spilt material. The fire officer should be informed of internal circulation routes for Fire Service use. Cut-out panels in the cladding are useful for firemen's access and to relieve internal pressure: they should be clearly marked. Access for fire engines should take account of the fact that fires in bulk installations often occur at high level, so that water jet and snorkel clearances should be considered.

39 Additional data

Research organisations offering testing facilities for bulk handling problems
Warren Spring Laboratory. Extensive facilities are available for bulk storage, pumping, blending, mixing and weighing. Various test programmes can be requested for hopper characteristics. Work is performed on a contract basis.

British Hydromechanics Research Association. Based at Cranfield Institute of Technology. Assistance in the design and the testing of fluid mechanics, hydraulics and pneumatic systems. Design of large-scale pipe lines for coal, cement, sand, etc. Testing facilities are available for pneumatic conveying.

Particle Technology Group at the Chemical Engineering Department, Loughborough University of Technology. Researches into fundamental properties of pastes, powders, suspensions and all particulate material. Four main research areas are particle characterisation, particle to particle interaction, particle-fluid systems, particle production. Contract work for industry is taken on.

Powder Advisory Centre. This is the clearing house for data for the powder and granular materials handling industry. This organisation has an extensive library, and can suggest consultants for specialist areas. No research or testing is performed.

Industrial Research Laboratories, Public Works Department, Birmingham Corporation, offers contract services for investigating handling systems for cement, aggregates, etc. Materials classification is offered, with density tests, shear tests, etc.

Powder Technology Unit, Bradford University. Academic research into powder technology. Some research and testing of hopper sizes and shapes performed, and powder testing and classification.

Welwyn Hall Research Association. Primarily a design consultancy organisation for bulk storage and handling problems. Contract services are offered as an independent research function. Particular experience in building and construction fields.

British Steel Corporation Corporate Laboratories. Research and testing for raw materials; hoppers and conveyors for bulk ores. Some contract work taken on.

National Coal Board Laboratories. Classification of hopper design and bulk handling research. Some contract services are available at Cheltenham.

Reference
1 DEPARTMENT OF EMPLOYMENT Health and Safety at Work 22 Dust explosions in factories. HMSO, 1960.

9 *External bulk grain tanks.*

10 *Bulk beer tanks.*

11 *Bulk storage hoppers in a brewery.*

12 *Bulk tipper bay: unloading to screw conveyor below.*

13 *Conveyors distributing maize to silos. The material has been raised to the top of the silo by bucket elevator, and will be carried along the* *main conveyor for distribution into the top of each silo. Note the additional space needed above silos in buildings.*

14 *Bulk bags are increasingly popular for handling and storing granular materials. This bag is being emptied into a hopper: note how it is* *carried by a forklift and discharges from the base. Capacity is one ton and bags can be stacked.*

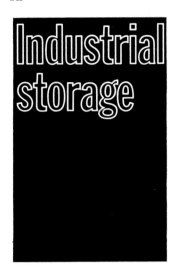

Information sheet Bulk storage 1

Mobile bulk handling plant

This sheet gives dimensions of typical tractor shovels and dumpers.

1 Use

1.01 *Loader shovels* can handle very high throughputs continuously. Small shovels are used in constricted production areas and for cleaning bulk barges and sea-going vessels. Table I gives data on large and small loaders for providing turning space and for suspended floors suitable for laden wheel loadings.

1.02 *Dumpers* range from strengthened commercial chassis to purpose-built machines capable of carrying 100 tonnes at a time. They are used in cement works, crushing and processing plants for quarry products, and ore-processing installations where the material is stockpiled in bulk and rehandled with loading shovels.

1.03 *Forklift trucks* with bucket attachments can move material from stockpiles into hoppers feeding process machinery, and clear spills of granular material. Although versatile, they are no substitute for loader shovels.

Table I Sizes, weights and capacities of mobile bulk handling plant

Type	Capacity kg	Total length m	Weight unladen kg	Max lift m	Max height m	Cab height m	Turning circle radius m
Loader shovel	1 000	3·9	4 040	2·3	3·6	1·9	2·8
	2 500	6·4	8 660	3·52	4·66	3·10	5·09
Dumper	15 400	5·8	24 385	na	5·8 (tipped)	2·9	15·25
	25 000	7·5	39 626	na	7·8 (tipped)	3·2	22·83
Forklift with bucket	2 260	3·1	5 095	varies	4·4	3·3	3·55

Information Sheet Bulk storage 2

Conveyors for bulk materials

This sheet gives information on belt conveyors, spiral conveyors, feeders and other types.

1 Belt Conveyors

1.01 Belt conveyors for bulk materials differ from other conveyors (see Information sheet Mechanised storage 9) as they have a troughed profile to contain granular material, **1**. Side rollers usually have 20-degree angles, although supports allow up to 60-degree angles at the edge of the trough to contain fluffy or light material. Belts of cotton or canvas construction are limited to angles of 30 degrees as the carcase is not flexible enough to trough at steeper angles without damage. Synthetic fibre carcass belts can trough at angles of up to 60 degrees, and can carry a bigger load. Some materials can be carried up inclines with steeper angles, as the greater trough confines the load.
1.02 Most bulk handling conveyors run on closely spaced angled idler rollers, **2**. A wire rope system for supporting and driving long runs is used, which maintains sufficient tension for the fast transport of materials such as ores, but reduces the number of idler brackets.
1.03 The length of trough conveyors is limitless. Slight curves are possible, but transfer to a second belt is normal for direction changes.
Allow 300 to 500 mm over belt width for overall width of conveyor.

Belt surface materials
1.04 Some surfaces are designed for abrasive materials, others for corrosives. Ribbed belts can convey certain materials up inclines. Belt manufacturers will supply information needed to determine suitable flow rates and maximum inclines for the product. Most troughed belts are electrically powered, using a three-phase supply.
Some conveyors for external use and heavy duty work are powered by hydraulic motors.

1.05 Some typical belting materials are listed below:
Polyester with polyurethane coating For foodstuffs, grains, powders. Smooth surface, 1 mm thickness, weight $1 \cdot 2$ k/m². Resistant to humidity, dirt, putrefaction, all solids, oils, fats, and most chemicals and solvents. Not resistant to alkalis and acids.
Polyester with elastomer coating 2 mm thick. For foods, pharmaceuticals, salts, grains, fats. Anti-static and resistant to dirt, wet, dryness, putrefaction, all solids, fats, petrol, most chemicals. Not resistant to more than 10 per cent concentration of caustic soda, 20 per cent of hydrochloric acid, 50 per cent of sulphuric acid. The same surface can be moulded into a heavy grip finish for clinker, scrap iron, glass, bricks etc.
Nylon 1 mm thick. For fast speeds of abrasive goods, broken glass, powders, gravel, clays, stone chips, fertiliser etc. Resistant to humidity and dryness, all solids, fats and most chemicals and solvents. Not resistant to 5 per cent of acetic acid, phenol-derived products and mineral acids.
Nylon with profiled elastomer coating 3 mm thick, weight $3 \cdot 3$ k/m². Specially made for troughed belts and inclines. Suitable for grains, powders, rock products. Anti-static and resistant to dirt, humidity, dryness, putrefaction, all solids, oils, fats, petrol and most chemicals and solvents. Not resistant to acids, alkalis and phenol-based products. The surface is slightly rough for inclines.

2 Vibration or oscillating conveyors

2.01 Vibration conveyors/feed hoppers with abrasive or sharp materials. Material is vibrated up inclines, requiring no belts or moving parts other than the vibration machinery. Power requirements are lower than for belt conveyors, but capacities are also lower, averaging up to 50 tonnes per hour

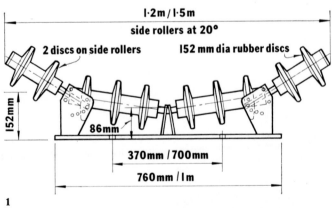

1 *Troughed belt conveyors, supported by idler rollers at each side.*

2 *Typical dimensions of rollers with discs, for belt conveyors.*

for each unit. For in-plant operation, vibration conveyors are more compact than belt units, but may still constrict services and plant movement. Various tray profiles, sizes and duties are available to suit the particular product. For elevating bulk material in confined spaces, spiral vibration conveyors are efficient. These units are particularly suited for processing in transit eg, drying, cooling or moistening. They do not transmit vibration to the floor or structure.

3 Steel plate apron feeders

3.01 Feeders handle bulk materials in large lumps, such as quarry products. They are shallow hoppers, with heavy duty plate conveyor bases, fed by tractor shovel or troughed belt. Feeder widths range from 452 mm to 3047 mm. Power units are electric, fed from three-phase supply. Heavy duty versions feed household refuse and scrap metal.

4 Screw conveyors and elevators

4.01 These handle powdered and granular materials, **4**. Helix diameters range from 160 to 400 mm, but smaller and larger sizes are available. Capacity depends on the type of helix, its revolving speed, and the cross-sectional character of the material (free-flowing materials will fill 45 per cent of a helical section, abrasive products will fill only 15 per cent). A typical 305 mm helix with normal material turning at 80 rpm has a capacity of 30 m^3/h. The pitch of the helix usually equals the diameter. Materials suitable for screw conveying are given in Information sheet Bulk storage 4.
4.02 Capacity of spiral conveyors decreases rapidly as the angle of inclination increases. A closer pitch and a tubular casing should be used for an angle over 20 degrees. A vertical helix should be rotated at a much faster speed than horizontal travel, to give the particles centrifugal force. As friction is produced by the screw action, screw conveyors are unsuitable for fast conveying of abrasive materials.
Screw types
4.02 *Close bladed screws* are the most common. The pitch is equal to the outside diameter, **4a**.
Short pitched screw is recommended for inclines of more than 20 degrees, **4b**.
Screw with notched blades has mixing action for fine granular or flaky materials, **4c**.
Ribbon screw is formed from a flat bar and attached to the axle by radial arms. It is suitable for sticky material that would adhere to a normal screw, **4d**.
Ribbon screw with paddles set at intervals on the shaft give resistance to forward movement; this stirs the material as it is transported, **4e**.
Troughs The most usual form is a U-trough or flared trough. Cover plates fit flanges in the trough tops, **4f**.
4.03 As screw conveyors operate slowly, geared motors are used; they can be electric, hydraulic, or pneumatic for flame-proof areas. Allow 100 mm width over screw diameter for overall width. Screw conveyors can be top or base mounted. Suspension of 3000 mm standard lengths at 1000 mm centres is usual.

5 Other bulk conveyors

5.01 *Drag link conveyors* handle powder or granular materials in depths greater than the chain itself. Skeletal chains and push plates force the material along the casing.
5.02 *Scraper conveyors* scrape the material along a trough. They are simple in operation, and are used for materials such as animal feed stuffs, wood chippings, and in heavy duty form for minerals in lumps; such as bulk ores.
5.03 *Cased bucket conveyors* have either centrifugal or positive discharge (tipping), **5**. Rows of buckets are mounted

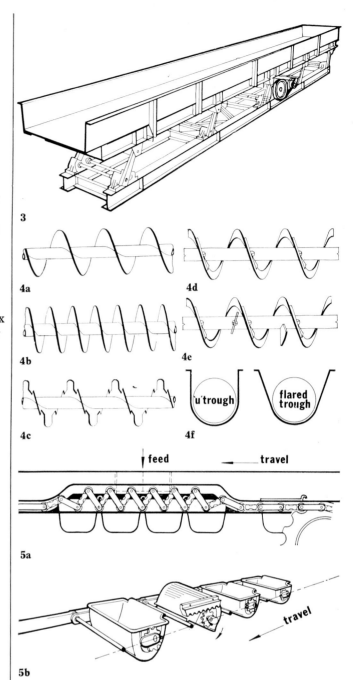

3

4a   4d

4b   4e

4c   4f

u'trough   flared trough

feed   travel

5a

travel

5b

3 *Vibration conveyor,*
1·3 m wide.
4 *Screw types.*
a *close bladed screw.*
b *short pitched screw.*
c *close bladed screw with notched blades.*

d *ribbon screw.*
e *ribbon screw with paddles*
f *troughs.*
5 *Bucket conveyors* **a** *at feed-in position,* **b** *at tipping position.*

on guide chains, and rise vertically or travel horizontally. The self-levelling action of the buckets enables the conveyor to move in complex patterns, incorporating vertical or steeply sloping sections, without spilling. They have been used effectively between bulk hopper truck unloading pits and storage hoppers, and from hoppers to the process. Being flexible they can be routed efficiently. Widths available are 304 mm to 914 mm buckets, but other sizes have been specified. Shaped buckets allow tight horizontal bends as well as vertical direction changes. Typical capacities are 10·8 m^3/h at 18 m/min. Buckets are never filled more than 80 per cent. Allow 280 mm over bucket width for casing, 356 mm over the flanges. The conveyor depth for fitting into vertical duct should be 1100 mm over the casing, 1220 mm over flanges.

Information sheet Bulk storage 3

Bag loading equipment

This sheet gives dimensions of machines for loading bags and sacks. Three basic types of machine are illustrated; for end-loading trucks and containers, for sideloading trucks, and for loading railway wagons through side doors.

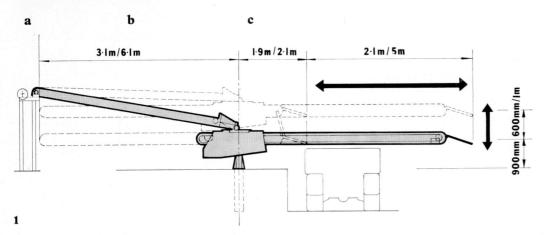

a   b   c

3·1m/6·1m   1·9m/2·1m   2·1m/5m

900mm   600mm/1m

1

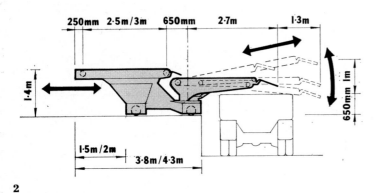

250mm   2·5m/3m   650mm   2·7m   1·3m

1·4m

650mm   1m

1·5m/2m

3·8m/4·3m

2

1 *Truck end or side loaded:*
a *is fixed and has intermediate feed belt,* **b**;
c *elevates, and is telescopic.*
2 *Side loader for trucks. The whole unit advances across the lorry.*
3 *Truck is tail loaded by suspended, swivel mounted, adjustable height conveyor.*

14m/20m

17m/23m

650mm   11m/17m   3·4m   5·5m/6·5m

700mm

5m/6m   2·5m/3·1m

3

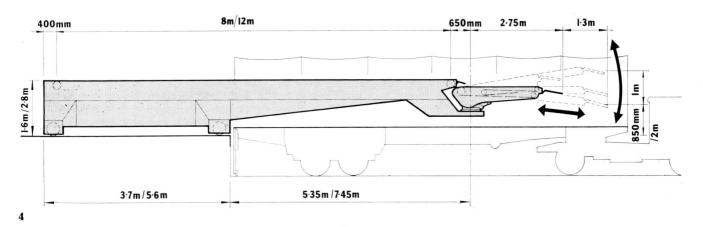

4

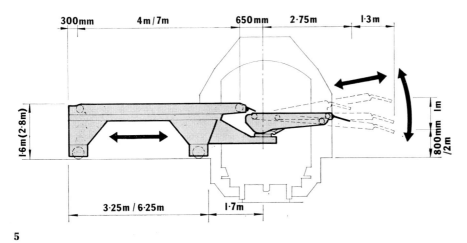

5

4 *Truck is tail loaded by telescopic belt conveyor at dock level.*
5 *Railway wagon is side loaded by swivel-mounted telescopic belt conveyors.*
6a, b *Railway wagon is side loaded by swivel-mounted telescopic belt, capable of lateral movement on rails. Sacks are ploughed from a continuous belt at 90° to the loading conveyor.*

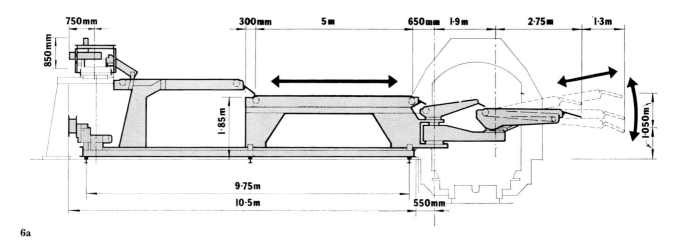

6a

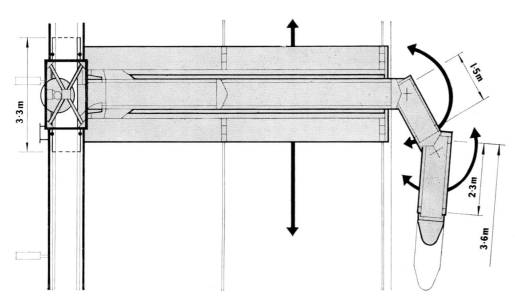

6b

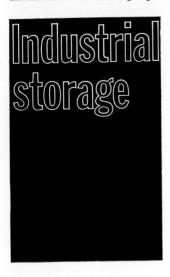

Industrial storage

Information sheet Bulk storage 4

Intermediate bulk containers

This sheet describes types and dimensions of intermediate bulk containers.

1 Size

1.01 General purpose and special products containers are available. Base sizes are usually of standard pallet dimensions (see information sheet Mechanised storage 2 table I). Heights vary according to capacity of bin, and density or specific gravity of the solid or liquid. Sizes and general properties are shown in table I.

2 Types

2.01 *Collapsible containers* are used where storage space is limited and return transport is expensive. Aluminium collapsible containers for liquids can be fitted with disposable liners.

2.02 *Disposable containers* can be pallet mounted or fitted with slings (suitable for one trip only).

2.03 *Metal containers* are of welded construction. Mild steel units are subject to corrosion. Aluminium is widely used because of its high strength/tare ratio, but must not be used for acids, alkalis or caustic materials, **1**.

2.04 *Plastic containers* are more resistant to corrosive materials and to impact damage by forklift trucks. Polypropylene is lighter than high or low density polythenes and is resistant to more chemicals. Polypropylene containers are fabricated, other plastics tend to be moulded.

3 Equipment

3.01 *Vibrator frames* can increase the flow rate of material being discharged from containers, or vibration motors can be clamped to the bin itself.

3.02 *Automated discharge and handling systems,* eg overhead conveyors and automatic tipper/weighers, are used in production buildings where containers feed directly into the process.

1 *Intermediate bulk containers for non-toxic materials.*

Table I Properties of typical intermediate bulk containers

Product	Construction	Capacity m³	Dimensions $\frac{L}{H} \times$ W, mm	Method of discharge	Notes
Powders and granules	Aluminium alloy or steel with steel base frame	1·41 to 3·38	1219 × 1066 1651 to 3353	Base sleeve	Stackable
	Corrugated fibreboard	1·41 to 1·69	1066 diam 1905 to 2235	Slide-in base	Disposable Pallet mounted
	Pvc coated nylon Neoprene coated nylon or polyester	Up to 1·98	1168 diam 1320 to 1981	Slide-in base or sleeve	Collapses to 203 to 330 mm Tubular top frame Stack when full
Free-flowing powders and grain	Reinforced proofed paper	0·99	1066 × 762 1219	Slide or slitting base	Disposable Hoods for exterior use
Cohesive powders	Glass fibre	1·66	1219 × 1118 2032	Fluidising chamber in base	In steel frame Stacks
Slow-flowing materials	Stainless steel	1·36	1219 × 1219 1168	Special base discharge Low angle cone	
Powders and liquids	Low density polythene Moulded	1·98 to 2·54	1168 × 1168 2235 to 2819	Base sleeve or valve	60° cone angle Steel frame
	High density spiral bound polythene or polypropylene	1·41	1219 diam 1219 high	Valve base or slide	Steel frame
Liquids; paints/inks etc	Glass fibre	1·13 1137 litres	1143 × 1143 1575	Sump in base Base valve	Steel frame
	Polyester fabric or Neoprene sandwich	Up to 1·98	1219 × 1219	Base valve	Collapsible Frame gives stability when full

Information sheet Bulk storage 5

Mass densities

Key: Type of material
Abrasiveness
A non-abrasive
B mildly abrasive
C very abrasive
Flowability
1 very free flowing. Angle of repose up to 30 degrees
2 free flowing. Angle of repose 30 to 45 degrees
3 sluggish. Angle of repose 45 degrees plus
Size
4 100 mesh and under
5 fine; 3 mm and under
6 granular; 12 mm and under
7 lumpy; lumps over 12 mm
8 irregular; fibrous, stringy etc
Other characteristics
D degradable or friable
E contains explosive dust
F fluidises, aerates
L very light and fluffy
M matted—resistant to rehandling
P packs under pressure
R mildly corrosive
V very corrosive
Example: material that is non-abrasive, sluggish and contains lumps over 12 mm is coded A37; if it is mildly corrosive as well the code is A37R

Key: Conveyors and elevators
Ch Chain elevator up to 76 m/min
B Belt elevator or conveyor faster than 76 m/min
(Both types have centrifugal discharge)
Pd Positive discharge. Slower speeds for fragile/sluggish materials
Co Continuous overlapping elevator/conveyor
S Screw conveyor/elevator; screws designed for the material handled

This sheet lists mass densities of bulk goods and suggests suitable conveyors to handle them. Many of these materials can also be conveyed pneumatically.

Table I Mass densities and classifications of commodities
Conveyors suitable for handling them

Material	Mass densities kg/m³	Type of material	Suitable conveyor
A			
Alum—lumpy	800–960	A27	Ch
—pulverised	720–800	A25	Ch
Alumina	960	C25	Pd, Co, S
Aluminium—chips	112–240	A38M	Co
—hydrate	290	A26	S
—oxide	1070–1920	B14F	B Co
Ammonium chloride (crystalline)	830	A25	S
Animal feed pellets	480–560	A25D	Pd Co
Asbestos—grit	960	C25	Co
—shred	320–400	B37LP	S
Ashes, coal, dry 75 mm	560–640	B37	Ch S
Asphalt crushed, 12 mm	720	A26	S
B			
Bagasse	112–160	A38FLM	S
Bakelite, fine	480–640	A34	S
Baking powder	660	A24	Pd Co S
Barley	610	A15E	B S
Ballast—dry	1527–1727	B36	B
—wet	1727–1926	B36	B
Bauxite, crushed 75 mm	1200–1360	C27	Ch Co S
Beans, caster, whole	580	A16	Ch Co S
Bentonite 100 mesh	800–960	B24F	Ch Pd S
Bicarbonate of soda	660	A24	S
Bonechar 3 mm	435–640	B25	S
Bonemeal	880–960	B25	Ch S
Borax, powdered	850	A25	Ch Pd S
Boracic acid, fine	880	A25	S
Bran	250–320	A25	Ch Pd S
Brewers grains—(dry)	400–480	A36	Ch S
—(wet)	880–960	A36R	Ch S
C			
Calcium carbide	1120–1280	B27	S
Cast iron—borings	2080–3200	B36	Co
—chips	2080–3200	B36	S
Cattle nuts	610–640	A27D	Pd Co
Cement—Portland	1040–1360	B24F	Ch Co S
—clinker	1200–1280	C27	Pd Co
—kiln, dust	560–640	C14	Ch Co
Chalk—crushed	1360–1440	B37P	Ch Co
—lumps	1360–1440	B37P	S
Charcoal—whole	285–400	B37D	Pd Co S
—pellets	400	B37D	Pd Co
Cinders, coal	640	B37D	Co
Clay, dry (ground)	1015	A24P	B S
wet	1760–1909	B37P	Ch B
Clay and gravel	1593	B38	Ch B
Coal—anthracite	960	B26R	S
—slack	640–770	A36R	Ch Co S
Cocoa—ground	480–560	A34P	Pd Co
—beans	560–640	B26D	Ch Co
Coffee—green beans	500	A26D	Ch Co S
—ground	400	A25	S
Coke—loose	370–500	C37DM	B Co
—petrol, calcined	540–720	C28M	B Co
—breeze 6 mm	400–560	C36	B Pd S
Concrete—cinder	1760	B36P	B S
—dry mix	1246	B36P	B S
—gravel agg	2423	B36P	B S
—limestone agg	2391	B36P	B S
—sandstone agg	2325	B36P	B S
—stone agg	2492	B36P	B S
—wet mix	2394	B36R	B S
Copra—cake, lumpy	400–480	A27	S
—cake, ground	640–720	A25	S
Cork—fine, ground	192–240	A35FL	S
—granulated	192–240	A36	S
Corn—seed	720	A16DE	S
—grits	640–720	A25	S
—Indian	720–770	A16	Ch B
—meal	640	A25	Ch B Pd S
Cottonseed—whole	480–560	A36	Ch
—hulls	192	A35L	Co
—meal	560–640	A25	Ch Pd
Cullet	1280–1600	C27	Ch B Co
Crushed stone	1600	C27	Ch B

Material	Mass densities kg/m³	Type of material	Suitable conveyor
D, E			
Dolomite, crushed	1440–1600	B27	Co
Earth, damp, loose	1246	B37P	Ch B
Earth and gravel—wet	1926	B37	B
—dry	1593	B25	B
Ebonite, crushed 12 mm	1010–1120	A26	S
Epsom salts	640–800	A25	S
F			
Feldspar—ground 3 mm	1040–1200	B25	Ch Co S
—powdered 100 mesh	1200	B34	Pd Co
Ferrous sulphate	800–1200	B26	S
Fertiliser	960	B35V	Pd Co
Fish—meal	560–640	A35	S
—scrap	640–800	A38	S
Flaxseed—whole	720	A15E	B
—meal	400	A25	Ch S
Flour, wheat	560–640	A34	B Pd
Fluorspar	1310	B36	S Ch Co
G			
Gelatine, granulated	640	B25	S
Glass, batch	1440–1600	C27	Ch B Co
Glue—ground 3 mm	640	B25	S
—pearl	640	A16	S
Grains, distillery, spent dry	480	A28L	Ch Co S
Granite—broken	1520–1600	C27	B Co
—chips	2656	C25	B Co
—tarred	1992	C36	B
Grass seed	160–192	A25EL	Co S
Graphite—flake	640	A26	S
—flour	450	A14F	S
Gravel—screened	1440–1600	B27	Ch B Co
—dry	1678–1909	B27	Ch B Co
—wet	2000	B26	Ch B
—and sand, wet	1909	B37	Ch B
Gypsum—calcined 12 mm	850–960	B26	Ch Pd Co S
—raw 25 mm	1440–1600	B27	Ch Pd Co S
Garbage, 75 per cent water content	755	B38R	Ch B
H to L			
Hemp seed	495	A25	Co
Hops, spent—dry	560	A38	Ch S
—wet	800–880	A38R	Ch S
Ice—block	900	A17D	Co
—crushed	560–720	A17	Pd Co S
Lead ore	1700	B37	Co
Lignite, air-dried	720–880	A27	Ch Co
Lime—ground 3 mm	960	A35P	Co S
—hydrated 3 mm	640	A25FP	Pd Co S
—hydrated pulverised	510–640	A24FP	S
—pebble	850–900	A37	Ch Co S
—over 13 mm	850	A37	Ch Co
Limestone—agricultural 3 mm	1090	B25	Ch Pd Co S
—crushed	1360–1440	B27	Ch Co
—rock	4536	B37	B Ch
M			
Magnesium chloride	560	A36	S
Malt—dry, ground 3 mm	350	A25EL	Ch Pd S
—dry, whole	435–480	A26E	Ch S
—wet/green	960–1040	A36	Ch
—meal	580–640	A26	Ch Pd S
Manganese—ore	2000–2240	*	Pd Co
—sulphate	1120	C26	S
Marble, crushed 13 mm	1440–1520	C72	C
Mica—ground	210–240	B25	S
—pulverised	210–240	B25F	S
—flakes	270–350	B15FL	S
Milk—malted	480–560	A34P	S
—dried	570	A35	B Pd
—whole, powdered	320	A35P	S

Material	Mass densities kg/m³	Type of material	Suitable conveyor
Mortar	1370–1900	C36	B Pd
Muriate of potash	1230	C25	S
Mustard seed	720	A15E	Ch S
Mud—wet	1727	B25	B Ch S
—dry	1444	B25	B
O to R			
Oats—whole	415	A16E	B Pd S
—rolled	305	A26EL	Ch Pd S
Oat-meal	620	A25	Pd
Oxalic acid crystals	960	A35	S
Peas, dried	720–800	A16D	Co
Peanuts—in shells	240–320	A27D	S
—shelled	560–720	A26D	Co S
Phosphate—rock	1200–1360	B27	Ch Co
—sand	1440–1600	C25	B Co S
Potash	720	B34F	Pd
Potassium nitrate	1220	B16R	S
Refuse, dry	399	B38	B Ch
Rice—polished	720–770	A15	S
—rough	580	A25E	S
—grits	670–720	A25	S
Rye	700	A15	B
S			
Salt—dry, fine	1120–1280	B25R	Ch B Co
—coarse	720–800	B26R	
Salt cake—dry	1360	B27	
—pulverised	1040–1360	B25	
Saltpetre	1280	A25E	S
Sand bank—dry	1440–1760	C25	B S
—wet	1760–2080	C35	B
Sand—dry, silica	1440–1600	C15	B S
—foundry	1440	C35/C27	B
Sawdust—dry	128–205	A35	Pd
—damp	320	A35	Ch
Shale—crushed	1478	B26	S B
—solid	2757	C26	B Ch
Silica	2169	C15	S
Shingle	1280–1360	B27	Ch
Slag—granulated	960–1040	C26	S
—bank	1113	C27	B Ch S
—machine	1527	C26	B
—sand	880	B25	S
—screenings	1593	C26	B S
—shale	2590	C27	B
Slate—ground 3 mm	1310	B25	S
—crushed 12 mm	1280–1440	B26	S
—dust	1600	B25	B Pd
Soap—flakes	80–240	A250	Pd
—powder	640	A25	B Pd
Soda ash—light	320–560	B24L	Pd S
—heavy	880–1040	B25	Ch Pd S
Sodium nitrate	1150	*	Ch
Sugar beet pulp—dry	190–240	*	Pd
—wet	400–720	*	S
Sugar—raw	880–1040	A35	Ch B
—refined	800	A35	Ch B Pd
—granulated	800–880	B25D	S
Steel chips, crushed	1600–2400	C37	S
Sulphur, lumpy	1280–1360	A27	Ch Pd
Superphosphates	960–1040	A25R	Pd
T			
Talc	800–960	B24F	Ch Pd
Talcum powder	640–960	B24F	S
V, W			
Vermiculite, expanded	255	B36L	S
Wheat—whole	720–770	A16E	B S
—cracked	640–720	A25E	Ch B S
—germ	450	A25	S
Wood chips	190–320	A37	B Pd

Key: Classification of materials
Abrasiveness
A non-abrasive
B mildly abrasive
C very abrasive
Flowability
1 very free flowing. Angle of repose up to 30 degrees
2 free flowing. Angle of repose 30 to 45 degrees
3 sluggish. Angle of repose 45 degrees plus
Size
4 100 mesh and under
5 fine; 3 mm and under
6 granular; 12 mm and under
7 lumpy; lumps over 12 mm
8 irregular; fibrous, stringy etc
Other characteristics
D degradable or friable
E contains explosive dust
F fluidises, aerates
L very light and fluffy
M matted—resistant to rehandling
P packs under pressure
R mildly corrosive
V very corrosive
Example: material that is non-abrasive, sluggish and contains lumps over 12 mm is
coded A37; if it is mildly corrosive as well the code is A37R

Key: Conveyors and elevators
Ch Chain elevator up to 76 m/min
B Belt elevator or conveyor faster than 76 m/min
(Both types have centrifugal discharge).
Pd Positive discharge. Slower speeds for fragile/sluggish materials
Co Continuous overlapping elevator/conveyor
S Screw conveyor/elevator; screws designed for the material handled

Technical study Cold storage 1

Storage process

Cold stores are a specialised building type, and integration between building designer and refrigeration engineer is essential, from the earliest stage. This section gives architects sufficient information to understand the principles involved in cold store design.

Introduction

1.01 Refrigeration slows down the deterioration of perishable products by microbal, chemical and enzymic means, though if putrefaction has already set in, it will not prevent contamination of other products.

Types of cold store

1.02 There are two main types of cold store:
Public cold stores. These are contract facilities, and cater for a wide range of products, and for seasonal demands, eg frozen vegetables. Public cold stores tend to be multi-cellular to segregate products, and to lease areas economically.
Specialist stores, eg distribution centres for ice cream, or reception centres for imported meat products.
Specialist single product cold stores are usually near ports, as until the '50s most refrigerated goods were imported meat and dairy produce.
1.03 The present trend is for both public and special cold stores to increase in size. Ten years ago capacities of 1500 tonnes were normal. Common sizes now range from 3000 to 10 000 tonnes and, in the US some very large cold stores are of over 10 000 tonnes capacity.
1.04 Specialist equipment manufacturers of freezing plant also supply insulation tailored to the environmental requirements of the cell. Some manufacturers offer a packaged deal including the building frame and floor construction.

User specification

1.05 Many distribution warehouses for retail food include refrigerated sections for meat, cheese and frozen foods. Architects will frequently be involved in the design of these, and of cold stores incorporated into food processing factories.
1.06 If extensive cold storage is part of a conventional warehouse, it should be established what proportion of the building it is to be, whether it will be a general purpose zone for seasonal trade, and what will be the development potential of frozen goods as opposed to dry goods. These factors affect the initial form of the building.
1.07 The user specification for a cold store must consider the trading potential of the product, which can be more varied than with conventional goods. Very seasonal trade may demand a change from storing a *low* variety of products requiring similar temperatures to a *wide* variety requiring different temperatures and subject to cross contamination. Some public cold stores have high peaks during the vegetable harvest season, and further peaks for pre-Christmas poultry. If meats are involved, check whether the brief requires frozen meat to be slowly defrosted under closely controlled conditions (ie moving through rooms of different temperatures) thus reducing the area available for general cold storage. Check whether it is necessary to construct cold rooms to cater for a wide range of temperatures, demanded by seasonal space requirements (adaptability in cold stores is very costly).

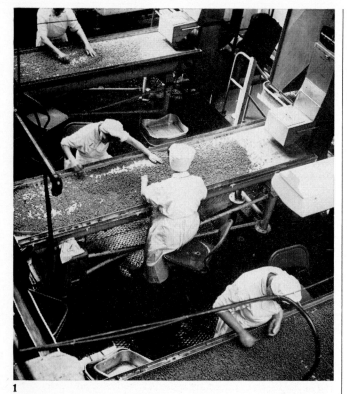

1

2

3

4

1.08 The user specification for a cold store is not a performance specification for the cold rooms, but a detailed operational one for each zone. Through-put and movement of products is more important than in other storage types, as this increases the chance of product damage, and cold loss through doors can increase the required capacity of refrigeration equipment.
1.09 A cold store is often used for activities other than purely storage. Typical uses are:
Cutting up meat carcases into portions for supermarket sale. This involves shrink-wrapping and packaging. Meat processing takes place in a specialist store, is labour-intensive and space consuming.
Packaging frozen vegetables. During the eight to 10 weeks of the vegetable harvest, the product is frozen in bulk as quickly as possible to preserve the quality, **1**. These vegetables require packaging into saleable weights as they are withdrawn from stock, which involves wrapping, packaging and palletising and is not personnel intensive.
Cutting cheese from bulk blocks into saleable portions. Cutting, weighing, wrapping and label printing are all mechanised.
1.10 Any areas for activities peripheral to storage should be specified from the outset, as they are subject to public health regulations for food processing, and can require special floor surfaces and environmental control equipment. This also affects the choice of the number of cold chambers and their distribution in relation to processing and loading.

2 Source of goods

2.01 Frozen goods arrive:
From all over the world, requiring continued temperature controlled storage after transport, and thawing facilities.
From local sources, requiring freezing facilities, or from a cold store acting as a distribution warehouse for seasonal products.

3 Form of transport

ISO containers

3.01 Refrigerated ISO containers known as 'reefers' consist of two types: those fitted with integral cooling equipment, and those equipped with connection plugs for a central source, **2**. Most reefer containers are of the second type and are plugged into a cold air source on the dock at the port of entry, or are fitted with a clip-on individual cooler, operated by a donkey engine or from gas bottles.
3.02 Warehouses expecting large numbers of reefer containers where unloading may be delayed require a portable cooling centre, **3**. A typical centre can handle 22 containers along a central spine which folds into three units of ISO container size when out of use. ISO containers are efficient temporary stores, and in seasonal peak conditions it might be more economic to provide parking and portable cooling for containers than to build extra cold rooms that might be only partially filled for most of the year.
3.03 Once ISO containers are removed from their skeletal semi-trailers or rail wagons, heavy and expensive handling equipment is required. The economic balance rests with the type of trade involved and the development potential.

Refrigerated trailers

3.04 For trade over short sea routes, or national transport, refrigerated trailers are popular. They are similar to reefers, but most have autonomous cooling equipment, either gas or donkey-engine powered, **4**.

1 Frozen vegetable processing.
2 Reefer container which must be connected to cooling *source (ie non-autonomous).*
3 Portable cooler centre.
4 Refrigerated trailer with cooler on front.

Fume build-up

3.05 Where trucks wait for long periods cooler motors may build up fumes and contaminate products. Long, articulated vehicles cause less fumes as the cooler motor is usually outside canopy coverage anyway. Medium-sized inter-town vans and delivery vehicle bays cause more fume build-up.

3.06 Rather than extract fumes at canopy level, some companies run coolers off vehicle batteries during unloading or plug the vehicle into an electrical point at each dock position. In some vehicles the cooler is run entirely off batteries, recharged by the vehicle's motor, and banks of plug positions are provided in the parking area for when trucks are pre-loaded at night, **5**. If leads are fixed to the vehicle there is less damage if the driver forgets to unplug before moving, but these can easily be stolen. Fixed leads are safer and should be on spring-mounted drums to cater for variations on plug-in position. External plug points are equipped with heaters and strong spring-mounted cover plates to prevent icing. Gas connection points have also been used, the vehicle's insulation maintaining the temperature throughout the journey. Gas points and their storage tanks require clearance with the Factory Inspectorate. All plug positions should be clearly marked, fitted with guard rails and well lit.

Rail wagons

3.07 Rail wagons are inherently side loading. The STEF refrigerated fruit trucks from Europe have been a common sight on British railways for some time. Both refrigerated and insulated trucks are used depending on the product. (See Information sheet Loading 6.)

Air handling

3.08 A refrigerated air service has already started for special foods, flowers and temperature controlled pharmaceuticals, **6**. The air cargo industry has been slow to expand generally, but door-to-door containerised air cargo services will be a reality soon. Bellyhold containers are carried on conventional road vehicles, fitted with roller floors.

4 Control of transport

4.01 As much refrigerated produce is imported, Customs facilities may be required. Large public cold stores carry their own Customs clearance, and international traffic must be segregated from traffic that requires no clearance.

4.02 The measures taken to provide efficient traffic control depend on the type of store. As some include packaging or processing operations, vehicles other than refrigerated delivery trucks may use the site. For example for vegetable freezing, vehicles arrive direct from the fields and tip into a pre-freeze hopper, **7**. This should not interfere with the normal vehicle flow. Routes should be clearly marked, and, if it is possible, a separate entry provided for farm vehicles. Road vehicle peaks may coincide with local crop peaks (and a similar situation could occur as at groupage depots, where small vehicles constrict the movement of larger ones) bringing the flow to a standstill.

Loading bays

4.03 Dual-purpose loading bays (ie one bay handling both incoming and dispatch goods), **8**, may be necessary if economies allow only one door per cold chamber. Refrigerated vehicles seldom collect the same product from a contract store as it has delivered, so cross bay circulation for loading

5a *A well-planned parking/plug-in area.*
5b *A row of double lead drum units, showing weather protection and drainage channels. The wide concrete*

apron with deep kerbs around the plugs prevents reversing damage.
6 *Refrigerated air containers.*
7 *Farm vehicles at freezing centre.*

5a

5b

6

7

8 *Dual purpose loading dock*
in a cold store.

goods for dispatch is often necessary. Some operators remove unloaded vehicles back to the accumulation area until a bay near the cold room for the dispatched goods becomes free. This not only reduces on-dock ice build-up but allows time for refrigerated vehicles to be decontaminated (eg venting gas after carrying apples).

4.04 Cold stores serving supermarket chains have the problem of mixing small delivery vehicles with the trunk trucks. The operator may only use medium-sized trucks, but the supplier is likely to use the largest size possible. Many retail organisations receive fruit, meat and dairy produce direct from the Continent so European-sized trucks must be planned for (see Technical study Loading 1).

4.05 In mixed cold and dry goods stores large and small vehicles can be segregated. Maximum size vehicles deliver to the cold store section and the goods are dispatched in conventional delivery trucks in insulated roll pallets, or loaded into refrigerated delivery vehicles that are moved to a parking zone equipped with plug points. These should be segregated from parking zones for conventional trucks by road marking, eg use of the blue international refrigeration sign.

4.06 If rail wagons are mixed with road transport, their times should not coincide as shunting can block a roadway for some time. Contact the client and British Rail concerning shunting tractors.

5 Receipt of goods

Rail wagons
5.01 The platform height for rail vehicles can be critical. With too high a platform certain insulated wagon doors will not be able to open. The height of the base of the doors of European rail wagons is 1·12 m (1·4 m in USA). This dimension is affected by ground conditions, eg banked track (see Information sheet Loading 6).

Road vehicles
5.02 Some reefer containers and refrigerated vans can side and end load. Some cold store operators prefer to handle goods at ground level, using side doors, as the heights of refrigerated vehicle floors differ considerably and hand-unloaded carcases can be dealt with by conveyor. But as cold store floors being insulated are likely to be above ground level, and as nearly all frozen produce is becoming palletised, end loading by forklift trucks should be planned for. Floor levels of insulated containers and vans are up to 100 mm higher than non-insulated and the ceiling 100 mm lower, so forklifts have 200 mm less clearance to work.

6 Form of goods
6.01 *Meat.* Reefer containers from 'deepsea' routes are loaded to maximum volume, carcase on carcase, and require hand

unloading. Some meat products, eg frozen offal, are in blocks on pallets or in bins sized to insulated container dimensions. Where volume is less important than quality and the meat is chilled rather than frozen, the carcases are hung from rails mounted in the top of the van. A variation, popular in general purpose warehousing, is for carcases to be hung from pallet converters, allowing forklift handling and five-high stacking, **9**.
Fruit is normally boxed and palletised. Bulk raw fruit for jam making, etc can be handled in intermediate bulk containers and bulk bins.
Fats are prepacked and palletised.
Poultry tends to be packed in cardboard outers for storage on pallets.
Vegetables are mostly prepacked and stored on pallets. Bulk vegetables are stored in bins or in special pallet converters with plastic liners.
Fish products are prepacked and stored on pallets.
Pharmaceuticals are packed on to pallets; some more delicate products like serums are packed into special expanded polystyrene canisters and shrink wrapped on to pallets.

7 Unloading
7.01 Refrigerated goods should be exposed to the normal atmosphere for the shortest time possible. Unloading procedure follows that of palletised goods, with forklift trucks shuttling in and out of vans.
7.02 Dock equipment may collect rime, which is water vapour in the atmosphere flash frozen when the cold metal surface comes out of the cold room or van. This can build up to

9a

9a *Meat in reefer container.*   **9b** *Carcases on pallet*
converter.

dangerous deposits of ice on the dock surface, and is augmented by ice from the forklift tyres, collected in the cold rooms, and from van floors. To lessen this risk, warm air curtains used on the dockside of the cold room doors will keep the cold air in (though some still escapes at the base). Some operators combine the curtain with scraper pads on the warm side to remove as much moisture from the tyres as possible. Heated dock surfaces and leveller plates have also been successfully used.

7.03 Due to the arrangement of cold room entrances and because products are segregated by temperature and not frequency of movement, the loading dock is liable to act as a cross route. If inevitable, the cross route should be planned with space for two forklift trucks to pass without encroaching on the manoeuvring space of unloading machines. In high use cold stores modified sweepers can scarify the ice away but in the long term under floor heating is more economic.

8 Characteristics of goods

8.01 Meat carcases are awkward to handle, being a difficult shape and slippery when frozen. Pallet converters with meat hooks are an attempt to gain full volume. Packaging for deep frozen products requires special consideration. Unpacked frozen goods should never be stored for reasons of contamination, dust and dehydration. Most goods are placed in a polythene inner lining to avoid air pockets which cause freeze burns.

9 Sorting

9.01 Refrigerated goods should not be left waiting for sorting as they can deteriorate quickly. The forklift should shuttle direct from the truck to the cold room allocated. If sorting into store sections is required for withdrawal speed as well as temperature, buffer space is required. It should be at low temperature, to act as a lobby to the various temperature zones.

Precooling and freezing tunnels

9.02 Some products, eg vegetables, are frozen prior to storage. Many refrigerated warehouses have tunnels for freezing goods in batches **10**. The temperature is lowered quickly by high air velocity to $-30°C$ or $-40°C$. Freezing tunnel efficiency is improved when the goods have been pre-cooled to $0°C$ in a pre-cooling chamber. Pre-cooled products are also of a better quality on arrival in the freezing tunnel, but the process is only economical if the products ripen or deteriorate rapidly, eg soft fruit and pears (apples need not be pre-cooled). Pre-cooling is achieved by high air velocity with controlled humidity (to avoid evaporation), or sprayed ice water or vacuum cooling. Pre-cooling allows the air in the freezing tunnel to be circulated with a uniform temperature, and is most important in a warehouse processing a variety of products to be packed in different sized cartons.

9.03 The freezing tunnel usually uses overhead rails for carcases and boxed goods are placed on pallets. Air circulation is either transverse, with several fans blowing perpendicularly to the main axis or longitudinally with one or two fans discharging parallel to the axis of the tunnel. Most fans are reversible, or are placed at either end to improve the homogeneity of the temperature. Freezing chambers of small dimensions are quicker to load and unload and air distribution with even temperatures is easier to achieve. The optimum capacity will be a compromise between the construction cost and the required throughput.

Freezing methods

9.04 These are as varied as the products themselves. The cold air stream is the most common method and is suitable for

10 *Freezing tunnel for frozen vegetables.*

freezing every type of product, loose or packed. Belt or slat conveyors are used to take the products through the tunnel. Some materials are frozen through direct contact with a horizontal or vertical metal plate or by immersion or spraying with a fluid. Liquefied gases such as nitrogen are also used.

Location in store

9.05 Freezing tunnels are situated in a block of cells close to the refrigeration plant. Air locks link the chambers. If the cold store is part of a slaughterhouse the pre-cooling chambers should be near the slaughtering process to reduce handling. Freezing tunnels often link production plant and cold store. The handling system should integrate the speed of production with packaging and grouping for transport through the freezing tunnel.

Weighing

9.06 Whether coming from the freeze tunnel or out of a container cold store operators like to weigh goods before they are stored in the cold chambers. The weighing machine should not constrict the flow of handling plant. In one installation the weighing machine had been placed so that the forklift had to stop at 90° to the direction of travel across the main route, causing hold-ups. In-process weighing can be used at the end of the freeze tunnel, with roller conveyors equipped with sensor heads electronically recording the weight of each pallet it passes.

10 Volume calculations

10.01 Volume calculations will determine the number and size of the cold rooms. Larger, colder cells allow for greater flexibility. A large range of different products does not necessarily imply an equal number of cold rooms although this is efficient and less subject to cross contamination. As refrigerated warehouses cost approximately four times that of conventional warehouses, the volume must be planned accurately for the trade anticipated. Having determined the principal types of goods to be stored and if they require segregated chambers, examine what quantities of each are likely to be stored, their lead times and what daily requirements are likely to be met at different times of the year. Seasonal and daily peaks should be considered. If a freezing tunnel is involved, daily throughputs and allocation to particular cold rooms should be calculated.

11 Turnover calculations

11.01 Turnover calculation is similar to that described in Technical study Mechanical storage 1, para 11, except that with fixed walls the cold rooms can be considered as separate warehouses within a larger one. As a rough estimate, frozen

11 *Special carcase pallets, stacked three high in a cold store. Carcases can be packed* *more compactly when flat than when hung.*

foods can be calculated as 300 kg/m³ and controlled storage above freezing for products like bananas, 160 kg/m³. In the past densities of 30 per cent were thought adequate with small rooms for special products but this low efficiency is too costly today. A small number of large rooms is preferable.

11.02 Controlled meat thawing requires carcases to move through chambers of rising temperature, spending several days in each. If the refrigeration plant is zoned for various temperatures, carcase thawing can add to the load.

11.03 The production or consumption throughput of frozen products can be seasonal. Vegetables have a steady consumption but input peaks, whereas a product such as ice cream has the opposite flow. Some products are withdrawn for repackaging and take up more space when replaced.

12 Variety and flow

12.01 The withdrawal characteristics of various sizes of packaged frozen goods differ. They are segregated by temperature, the need to avoid contamination, and (within the cold room) by the speed each product is consumed. The products themselves have different speeds of flow according to season, package size and planned factors such as special offers.

13 Type of Storage

13.01 Most products are block-stacked on pallets with pallet converters, adding stability to crushable loads, **11**. These are stored up to 5 high and often 7 to 8 units deep, with gaps left for stock access and rotation. Drive-in racking has been used for refrigerated storage and live racking is effective for fast moving products of similar temperature, where there is little risk of cross contamination.

13.02 The floor should be marked out with pallet positions to avoid contact between walls and packages. Some operators specify a wide gangway right round the room for handling and air circulation.

13.03 Cold chambers should not be placed on both sides of a central corridor. Its walls and services may suffer from condensation and frosting, unless it is air conditioned.

13.04 The pallet stacking method should allow cold air to circulate and goods to be accessible for quick stock checks. The relative amounts of carbon dioxide and oxygen affects storage life, especially with fruit. Chilled products can be spoiled by too dry air or too low temperatures.

13.05 If access is more important to the operator than filling to maximum volume, racking would be used, and the storage process would then be as for Technical study Mechanised storage 1, para 13.

13.06 Automated storage is also used for cold stores. A 12 000 pallet capacity high bay cold store is at present under construc-

tion in Milan for an ice cream company. Mechanical equipment has been well proved in low temperatures. Electronic equipment should be kept clear of the cold environment, or else trace heated.

13.07 Turret trucks have started to be used in several cold stores, **12**. Narrow aisles and high racks reduce volume wastage. Floors must be scarified intermittently to prevent ice build-up.

14 Stock control

14.01 In cold stores this is similar to that for conventional mechanised or automated dry goods stores. Refrigerated stock requires rotation depending on the product's characteristics and the depth of freeze. Planned stock rotation is necessary for all foods, and this is a further argument against deep block stacking, where an operator might overlook the cumbersome shuffling operation it requires.

14.02 Stock control can be complicated by additional repackaging of products such as vegetables. These tend to be withdrawn steadily, tipped out of bulk bins, packed into consumer packs, palletised, and replaced in the cold room. Block-stacked bulk materials and drive-in racks of palletised loads of cartons, can give a high use of volume. The stock rotation of packaged goods and stock withdrawal is made much easier.

14.03 Stock control of refrigerated goods is less of a problem than with dry goods; the packaging has been designed for long periods of storage in cold conditions (see also para 11.02).

15 Stock withdrawal

15.01 The pattern of stock withdrawal depends on the type of order picking, and the organisation of the block stacks. But in cold rooms, different products share the same temperature conditions, and the required air circulation space round stacks

12 *Turret truck used in cold store.*

conflicts with the requirement to maximise volume, often resulting in small aisle widths and shuffling to reach pallets at the rear of a stack. In public cold stores receiving frozen goods from outside manufacturers, some goods are not at the low temperature required on arrival, and cannot be placed next to frozen products for fear of contamination and heat damage. Such suspect incoming goods are block stacked near the cooling plant, and moved into the main stack when freezing has been completed, dispatch and stock being withdrawn from the face away from the incoming goods.

15.02 A simulation of the operation of the cold rooms at design stage, with single product stacks and multiple stacks, would show how much space is lost through leaving air space and circulation area round the combinations of block stacks. Check with the client that the size and shape of the cold rooms will be suitable for future storage patterns, eg different products with the same temperature but requiring segregation.

16 Order picking

16.01 Stock is usually removed from block stacks into racking for order picking. Some users prefer it to be in a special chamber, to reduce heat gain in the main store from frequent opening of the doors.

16.02 In cold stores serving supermarket chains, refrigerated goods must be picked into insulated roll pallets suitable for the delivery transport. The order picking of refrigerated stock is similar to that for dry goods, ie the lower two layers of racking are used for hand picking, and the upper levels for replenishment stock (see Technical study Mechanised storage 1, para 16). Live racking is useful for cartoned goods, combining the storage and picking function. Frozen food manufacturers pack the goods in carton sizes to suit the average shop freezer, and which hold convenient numbers of packets for ordering purposes.

16.03 Carcases that have thawed are picked from hanging hooks either on to hooks on pallet converters, or are carried direct to the vehicle. Carcase handling is diminishing in favour of in-store processing into portion-sized packs. These are placed in cartons and are palletised and picked in the conventional manner.

16.04 Public cold stores and single product stores usually involve full pallet picking. The pallet loads are split into local orders at distribution centres nearer the markets.

17 Picking area

17.01 Safety requirements for personnel in cold stores are discussed in Technical study Cold storage 2 para 37.

18 Load build up

18.01 Insulated roll pallets are handled as normal units and assembled either as part of a dry goods load, or grouped for transport in an insulated vehicle, **13**. Where cold space is precious, vehicle loads are not pre-assembled. Public cold stores shuffle goods to make the stock accessible, and then load directly into the refrigerated truck. The product should be exposed to the untreated atmosphere for the minimum possible time. Many delivery trucks are only insulated, and rely on the goods to withstand the journey time without deterioration. Most refrigerated goods are weighed before dispatch. The weighing machine need not constrict the flow of handling plant. One frozen food producer weighs forklift and load together, on a weighbridge positioned on the main route, rather than having to lower the pallet on to a weighing table each time. The economic requirement for a single door to each cold room congests weighing and cross circulation in peak periods. Generous space provision in this zone is essential to ensure continuous operation in the cross flow conditions dictated by the cold room design.

13 *Incoming empty insulated roll pallets being pushed out of the vehicle to the left. Full dispatch units waiting for loading on the right. Channels are clearly marked,* *and loading bay door is insulated. Incoming units may constrict dispatch units in peak conditions in dual purpose docks.*

19 Order and document check

19.01 In cold stores, this check occurs at the same time as stock withdrawal and loading.

20 Loading and dispatch

20.01 Vehicles running in and out of cold rooms cause ice build-up on the dock and in the cold rooms. Scraper mats squeeze moisture from forklifts tyres and a dock shelter makes the waiting truck an homogeneous part of the cold store atmosphere. Pneumatic seals are also used to prevent ice build-up.

20.02 Icing will still occur as the truck pulls away from the dock, before the door built into the dock shelter has had time to seal the zone. The combination of a dock shelter with a pneumatic seal, a powerful cooler, heated dock surface, and scraper mats would be costly compared to the cost of heating door equipment and intermittent scouring.

20.03 Another method of avoiding ice build-up is to isolate cold room lift trucks, and deliver pallets to the loading bay by conveyor. The conveyor opening need only be one pallet high, plus clearance, and can be fitted with fast pneumatic sliding doors, activated by a sensor on the conveyor. The stuffer forklifts, also isolated, work in a normal atmosphere. Operators using this method claim that the icing problem hardly exists, and that short loading cycle eliminates product deterioration, as long as the van's refrigeration plant is kept operating.

14

14 *Building a cold store: foam glass insulation blocks are being installed.*
15 *Reach truck being used in a cold store for bacon. Standard machines can be used after modifications to the electrical and hydraulic systems.*

15

Technical study Cold storage 2

Building function

Technical study Cold storage 1 dealt with the storage process (paras 1 to 21). This second study (paras 22 to 38) deals with the design of the building.

22 Structure

22.01 Before 1960, most cold stores were multi-storey, because the cube shape has a low surface-to-volume ratio and is thus most economical to refrigerate. This meant highly loaded floors, heavy structures and costly foundations. Now most cold stores are single-storey, **1**, and the trend is towards higher rooms and lower temperatures. The present emphasis is on efficiency of insulation, which can be 15 per cent of the cost of the building.

Concrete frame construction
22.02 Concrete structures can be in situ or precast, and concrete panels or cast walls provide a continuous surface for insulation. There are special problems with cold bridges through concrete structures, outside the scope of this section.

Steel frame construction
22.03 In Europe the steel structure is usually external and insulated cladding forms a sealed box with little risk of heat bridges. The alternative, and now more common method, is to use an internal structure with insulation placed round vertical and horizontal members, the cladding and insulation attached to a sub-frame, and flexible membranes forming corner seals to allow for movement. Some cold stores are constructed with a double frame, the outer forming the main structure, and the inner being buried inside the insulation to support it.

1 *Large single-storey cold store being built.*

Foundations

22.04 Foundations should be designed by specialist structural engineers. They must have continuous insulation to stop cold bridges freezing the ground round the bases and causing frost heave that can displace footings and endanger the whole structure. One monolithic structure heaved sufficiently to dome both floor and rc roof slab.

22.05 Soil profiles and grain size distribution curves should be obtained from bore holes. The susceptibility of soils to frost heave depends on the uniformity of grain sizes, eg sand strata of 10 per cent granular material smaller than 0·02 mm are susceptible. Frost heave also requires water. In one US cold store, grain size and a high water table combined with a cold bridge to freeze the ground to nearly 3 m below foundation base.

23 Floor

23.01 Cold store floors must keep the cold in, to stop soil freezing (causing frost heave). Insulation and sometimes subfloor heating are required, and joints to columns and wall cladding require continuity of insulation. For rooms at 0°C and above (eg for fruit) the wall insulation is carried down to below ground level and a layer of subsoil forms a heat barrier, equivalent (it is claimed) to a layer of insulation.

23.02 To prevent frost heave on very low temperature buildings, either construct a basement, or heat under the slab. If the land is difficult to drain, the basement would be more attractive and should be force-ventilated.

Underfloor heating

23.03 There are several underfloor heating methods: heater mats can be used, or air passed through hollow core tiles, or a heated glycol solution pumped through polythene pipes in the sub-slab beneath the insulation. Typical construction of a solid floor is as **2**:

sub-slab plus heating method

vapour barrier

floor insulation (thickness depends on the material and the internal temperature range)

top slab with a granolithic working surface which should continue at the sides to form a curb, to prevent ice forming between wall insulant and slab. Most operators require permanent thermocouples fixed at various points throughout the building to check subsoil temperature.

Floor finish

23.04 The floor surface should be carefully selected as repairs in a cold store are very expensive. It should be able to withstand scarifying machines and product spills, eg fruit juices and fats. Granolithic screed is acceptable for general purposes, but is not suitable for cold processing zones such as cheese cutting rooms and meat preparation areas. Jointless surfaces suitable for fatty and corrosive applications must still be efficient at low temperatures (some plastic-based products become brittle). Granolithic screeds should have non-slip finishes.

23.05 Damaged floors can be made accessible for repair without defrosting the whole cold room by placing a plastic 'igloo' over the damaged area.

24 Building services

24.01 Air in cold rooms can be contaminated by the products stored inside. Atmospheric segregation can be achieved by drawing external air in over a cooler coil, which reduces the chance of odour inter-communication between cold rooms but does not guarantee fully filtered air. A central system is advantageous in that air can be put into the room at the same temperature and humidity at which it was expelled and at the

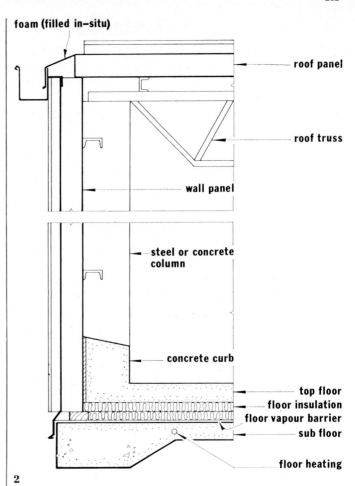

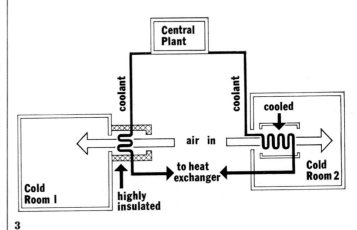

2 *Section through typical cold store.*

3 *Diagram of refrigeration system.*

same time cleaned and disinfected. The air distribution system must minimise condensation and frosting.

Lighting

24.02 Lighting is important for handling and to ensure absolute cleanliness. An overall level of 200 lux is suggested with 400 lux in processing zones. The efficiency of fluorescent tubes falls off rapidly at tube wall temperatures below 40°C. Special tubes are available, one with a double plastic sleeve for insulation. All corners of the cold store must be lit as this is where debris accumulates. Cold room door zones should also be well lit, but without glare as clear vision is essential.

24.03 Building services such as water pipes to amenity areas and electrical services should all be well insulated and detailed to avoid 'cold bridging'. Services should never be run under cold room floors.

4a

4b

5

4a *Plastic faced plywood cladding spalled off by ice build-up. Ice accumulation can be seen on the output face.*
4b *Output side of cooler bank is badly positioned, near a corner and frequently*

opening door. Ice is spread into the corner by the fans, and down to cover electric trunking.
5 *Typical reciprocating compressor room in large cold store.*

25 Special services

25.01 In cold store design, the special service of refrigeration must be considered together with the building fabric, para 26.

26 Building fabric

Refrigeration systems
26.01 The most common system used is a central plant which supplies liquid coolant to individual cooler batteries, **3,** either mounted in the cold rooms at ceiling level or immediately next to the cold room, discharging through a grille, false ceiling or duct. As in a domestic refrigerator, air is drawn over coils by fans, and the heat that has been extracted from the atmosphere is circulated back to a heat exchanger. If cooler units are mounted in the store room at ceiling level, frost deposits tend to build up on the output side of the fans, drop off the ceiling cladding onto floor or products, and cause the cladding surface to spall away. Cooler units outside the room require a fully insulated plant space.
26.02 In large single-product warehouses, ducted cold air is supplied by one central conditioner, but in multi-product stores, several conditioners must be used to avoid cross contamination.
26.03 Five air changes per hour are usual, less if ozone can be used as a purifier. Ozone is unsuitable for dairy products; activated carbon should be used, but this is unsuitable for

fruit smells as it does not act with ethylene. Air ducts can absorb smells and transfer them to other zones.

Types of refrigeration plant
26.04 *Direct expansion cooling,* produced by evaporation of the refrigerant, is used for cooling tunnels and freezing chambers. Fast temperature reduction is possible, but refrigeration ceases when the compressors stop.
26.05 *Secondary liquid cooling* cools antifreeze liquid down to the operating temperature, and then distributes it to cooler batteries (as in **3**). This is initially more expensive than direct expansion, requiring evaporators and circulation pumps, but allows reserves to accumulate, and is advantageous for multi-purpose warehouses.
26.06 Direct expansion cooling requires reciprocating **5** or turbo-compressors. The former are very noisy (more than 92 dBA has been recorded) and their rooms should be sound suppressed. The use of one compressor per cold chamber is not common, even though it simplifies pipe work. Cold

rooms are usually grouped together by function allowing plant to be positioned centrally to cater for various temperatures and for flexibility. Three different cooling circuits of 0°C, −10°C to −25°C, and −25°C and below, run to each chamber. Their compressors should be similar to simplify maintenance. Very low temperatures result in a rise in compression ratio, requiring multi-stage compressors with inter-stage cooling for the refrigerant.

Condensers

26.07 Condensers are used to dissipate heat. Open circuit condensers use large quantities of fresh water, or sea water if available, as a medium. Fresh water should not exceed 25°C and sea water 18°C. Closed circuit coolers use cooling towers or atmospheric or evaporative condensers. The latter need treatment to prevent calcium scaling. As condenser efficiency depends on the cleanliness of the water side of the exchanger surface, access for cleaning and precautions against algal growth are advised. Condenser fans are noisy and may cause annoyance if sited near housing.

26.08 If brine is used as the cooling medium, valves and pipes must be corrosion resistant. Alternative cooling solutions are calcium chloride, ethyl alcohol, and ethylene-glycol.

Relative humidity

26.09 Relative humidity influences the weight loss of the product during refrigeration and must be controlled to prevent organic growth. Low relative humidity levels can shrivel fruit and cause cold burns. The level can be controlled by varying air flow speed, and (more costly but effective) by combined heating and cooling. Grid type in-chamber coolers cool by natural convection, so that relative humidity remains high. This type of equipment is difficult to defrost.

26.10 Refrigeration designers must include heat gain figures for product and packaging, including pallet, handling equipment, lighting, cooler fan motors, door openings, personnel, defrosting equipment and, if applicable, sorting and re-packaging machinery.

Insulation

26.11 Insulation is an integral part of the cold store fabric. BS CP 406:1952 (Mechanical Refrigeration, HMSO £2) states that insulation thickness should be equivalent to 25 mm of good quality cork for each temperature difference between the inside and the outside of 5·6°C.

26.12 Insulation materials are available in soft board or block form. Some are specially developed for cold stores, and are, of their nature, impermeable (though their joints are not).

Vapour barriers

26.13 Continuous vapour barriers are essential. Failure in walls can cause the insulant to deteriorate and frost to damage fabric and structure; failure in foundations will cause frost heave. An impervious material must be placed on the warm side of the insulant, or the cavity between the insulant and cladding must be vented with dry air with a dew point lower than that of the lowest temperature to be encountered in the building.

26.14 Both insulant and vapour barrier must withstand expansion and contraction without fracture. One contractor foams wall, ceiling, and floor joints in-situ to achieve continuity. If the insulation is in board form, all joints should be well lapped. Corner seals liable to differential movement should be of flexible membrane material.

26.15 The choice of insulant depends on the type of goods stored, and temperature ranges. It should be odourless, anti-rot, have a low linear shrinkage and be vermin resistant. For fire precautions see para 27.

26.16 Rigid foamed glass blocks, protected by lightweight metal cladding combine insulation and the main wall structure.

6 *Detail of cold store facade showing pipe penetration and gutter fixing.*

A typical installation used two layers of 120 mm thick blocks step-jointed to the roof and sealed with a mastic.

26.17 Many aluminium and steel sheet insulating systems incorporate subframing and internal and external cladding. Internal walls are usually left unpainted, as some enamel and aluminium paints can retain water. Cladding sheets are often slightly corrugated to take up thermal movement and lessen insolation. Bonded sandwich panels are rigid, and need little wind bracing. One system joins panels externally by pressing the sheeting with a closure tool, and internally with a vinyl batten, and then integrates joints with in-situ foamed polyurethane, forming a vapour resistant seal.

26.18 In-situ or precast concrete cladding systems whose joints are sealed by grouting are also available.

Drainage

26.19 Rainwater guttering and down pipes should be fixed to the exterior of cold stores, or be well isolated from low temperatures, **6**.

Doors

26.20 Doors to cold rooms should be considered as part both of the insulation and the building fabric, and should have the same thickness of insulation. Surface warmers round the frames combat ice jamming but require drains beneath, **7a**.

26.21 Doors are nowadays electrically or pneumatically powered, activated by pull switches and press pads. These should be easily reached by forklift drivers and pedestrians and should be timed to stay open long enough to allow a loaded truck to pass, with a safety margin, **7b**. Other activation devices include radio control and photo-electric cells. Some operators prefer one set of doors per chamber to reduce heat gain and floor icing. Airlocks, curtains and impact-opening rubber doors can reduce air intrusion but no perfect solution has been found. Warm air will tend to flow in at the top of open doors where cold air seeps out at the bottom, and ice will form on the first cold surface that it strikes. A curtain of hot air blown on the warm side will prevent cold air leaving, but moisture can still collect under doors and cause snow build-up.

27 Fire control

27.01 Conventional water charged sprinkler systems cannot be used. Dry riser systems with fast pressurisation are possible, but with a localised fire the system may become icebound before the fire is controlled. Gas extinguishing systems are available. Contact the insurance company before deciding on any extinguishing method and finalising the refrigeration plant.

Fire control in high bay cold stores
27.02 Multi-injection gas systems and liquid extinguishing systems using a strong anti-freeze solution are possible. Fires can start at very low temperature and immediate sensing, which must not be affected by ice build-up, is essential. (See Technical study: Automated storage 2 para 27.)

Choice of insulant in fire control
27.03 Insurance companies are not convinced by claims that expanded plastic foams are as retardant as materials like fibreglass. Some foams smoulder and give off smoke and noxious fumes which damage concrete structures. They prefer 'traditional' construction (cavity brickwork with foam filler or reinforced concrete) to panel systems.
27.04 Cold stores cannot be vented like conventional warehouses. In one recent case, single access doors to a cold chamber were shut to limit the air supply in an attempt to contain the fire, effectively barring entry to the fire brigade.
27.05 Cold store fires are often started by malfunctioning door heaters, whose wiring should be treated with extra care where it runs through insulation.

Fire control in cold store plant rooms
27.06 The insurance company should be consulted before the refrigerant is finally chosen. A 50 per cent coolant alcohol-water solution is flammable and in a secondary liquid refrigerant system thousands of gallons of it will be circulating through the building. Gas and alcohol tanks should be positioned outside the plant area, and as far from the storage zone as possible.
27.07 Contact the local fire officer at an early stage as the regulations vary between areas. In the Inner London zone, the brigade does not differentiate between cold stores and normal warehouses. If the area is over 23 230 m² Section 20 of the London Building Act 1939 applies.
27.08 Ammonia charged systems may explode if a burst or large leak occurs, and should have special emergency ventilation.

28 Security

28.01 Alarm systems must be provided for operatives shut in freezing tunnels and cold chambers. Alarms should be audible next to the chamber and shown on the control room display. Specify a door system that can be manually operated in case of emergency.
28.02 Ice build-up on floors can cause forklift and pallet trucks to skid, damaging racking and doors. Ice drops from ceiling cooler units builds up round door zones, and forms from moisture brought in on the handling plant. It is aggravated in public cold stores by 'frozen' goods arriving at higher temperatures than that of the cold chamber. Ice on floors can be scarified off from time to time. Whatever measures are taken to avoid ice dropping from coolers and building up behind doors, some is inevitable at low temperatures.

7a

7b

7a Ice has built up round door runner and guide wheel of cold store door. Guard rail and post are well used, as both are badly scuffed.

7b Double sliding cold store doors (closed) showing pneumatic door gear, heavy duty guard rail and set back pull control, activated from a forklift seat.

28.03 For security from theft (see Technical study: Mechanised storage 2, para 28). If drugs and pharmaceuticals are involved, alarm and detection systems are available. (See AJ Handbook of Building Services, sec 13.) If delivery vehicles are parked overnight, bright light is a deterrent against wholesale theft. If the vehicles are attached to plug points, an alarm system can show the position of the intruder on a schematic plan in the control room. Many cold stores operate a night shift, and the security problem is then mostly internal.

29 External works

29.01 Stacking of ISO containers is described in Technical study: External storage 1. Plug-in points for vehicle and container cooling should be guarded and clearly marked. **8ab**. If vehicles are parked back to back, to use grouped plugs, a walkway should give access to plug positions. Lighting blocked by closely parked vans should be at low level plug positions (or incorporated with guard bollards).
29.02 Some public cold store operators provide a wash-down bay to decontaminate refrigerated trucks. Flexible hose lines to reach van corners are necessary. Movable steps allow cleaners to reach trailer floors; a movable gantry gives easy access to autonomous refrigeration units; a platform 2·9 m high has proved effective. The area should be well drained and lit (spotlights ensure cleanliness). The hot water from the heat exchanger can be used in washdown areas.

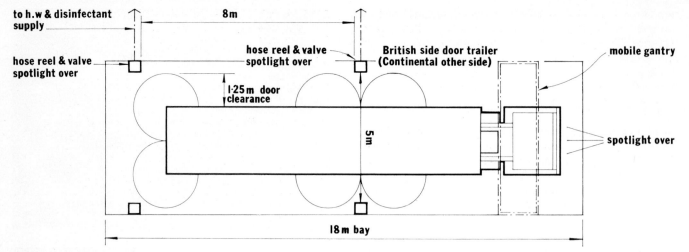

to h.w & disinfectant supply

hose reel & valve spotlight over

hose reel & valve spotlight over

1·25 m door clearance

British side door trailer (Continental other side)

mobile gantry

spotlight over

8m

5m

18m bay

8a *Plan,* **b** *section of refrigerated trailer in container decontamination bay.*

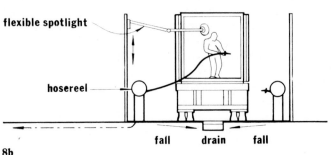

8b

flexible spotlight

hosereel

fall   drain   fall

30 Structure-based plant

30.01 Roller, belt and slat conveyors are used in freezing tunnels and re-packaging areas. Roller conveyors should be galvanised as icing can cause rusting and deterioration. For pallet loads, roller or slat conveyors are used. Packeted goods, though usually moved on belts, may be moved by air conveyors, combining cooling with lift and forward motion. The conveyor surface, often specially developed for cold stores, depends on the product handled, eg steel band and vibration conveyors are used in freezing and repacking areas. Vegetable rehandling is shown in **10**. Account for the heat given off by this plant when calculating cooling capacity.

30.02 Overhead and continuous conveyors are not recommended in cold rooms because of bulk, except for goods moved at regular intervals along the same route. Overhead conveyors are mainly used in single purpose stores. As long as the rail is gap-free, frosting can lower its surface friction.

30.03 Fire regulations often require conveyor lines passing through cold store walls to have fire stop doors with fusible link controls. These may ice and insurers might ask for low output surface heaters. Conveyor fixing to the structure must not form heat bridges.

31 Mobile handling plant

31.01 Handling plant used to suffer from metal fracture at very low temperatures, but has now been improved by use of sealed hydraulic systems, special hoses and wiring for cold store use. Turret trucks **11** and narrow aisle reach trucks, allow higher racking and therefore higher store capacity. Lift trucks moving in and out of cold chambers may ice through moisture collection.

31.02 Battery charging maintenance areas should be well away from any foodstuffs. Gases given off during battery charging, if sucked into a cold chamber, can cause contamination.

32 Integration of building and plant

32.01 Wiring has caused trouble in the past, usually because its insulation was unsuited to the very low temperatures. In automated stores control signals can be affected by icing. Some cabling has fluids in the sheathing to prevent brittle fracture.

33 Maintenance

33.01 Maintenance checks are essential, especially for foods,

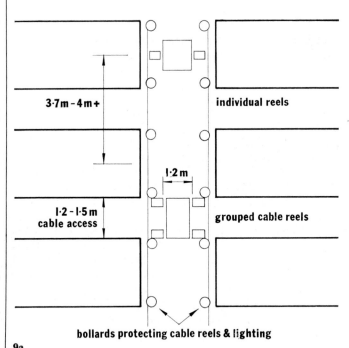

3·7m – 4m+

individual reels

1·2m

1·2 – 1·5 m cable access

grouped cable reels

bollards protecting cable reels & lighting

9a

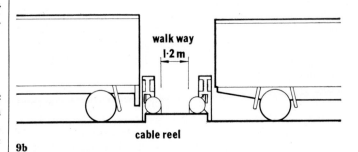

walk way

1·2 m

cable reel

9b

9a *Plan,* **b** *section through refrigerated vehicle park, showing electric plug positions and walkway.*

where contamination is very easy. In temperatures below 0°C heat exchanger coils become blocked with ice, reducing efficiency. Frost does not affect heat transfer unless air flow is blocked. Smaller cooling coils need more frequent defrosting. Primary refrigeration is defrosted by hot gas, secondary circulation systems by hot brine. Conditioner units have manual or automatic defrosting. Wet-type coolers are not defrosted but brine deposits must be cleared with ethyleneglycol solution.

33.02 Floor cleaning avoids dirt build-up in corners. Industrial sweepers for cold stores are convertible into ice scarifiers. Forklift trucks can have sweeper attachments, useful as the lift allows cleaning of upstands and curbs, **12**.

33.03 Planned maintenance should be programmed from the outset. Refrigeration plant is now tending to be maintained on contract by specialist engineers. All structural joints should be examined at frequent intervals for moisture penetration, and metal surfaces should be galvanised or sheathed in plastic. Plant rooms should have vehicle access. Compressors are heavy and a chain hoist or space for a mobile hoist would be useful. Overhead hoists are often not practical as there is so much overhead pipework.

34 Management

34.01 The supply and fixing of insulation and refrigeration plant is usually by a nominated sub-contractor who is a manufacturer of plant and material. Tenders should be obtained from an insulation and refrigeration plant contractor nominated before the main building contract goes to tender, to ensure co-ordination of all building requirements by the general contractor.

34.02 The nominated refrigeration sub-contractor is one of the building team's most important members, with a specialised knowledge of refrigeration problems and particular knowledge of his own plant and insulation materials. There must be the closest working conditions throughout between the general contractor and the refrigeration sub-contractor, because both have an important joint responsibility for the good working of plant and building.

35 Personnel accommodation

35.01 Cold store work needs heavy protective clothing (see **11**). Changing rooms should have large locker accommodation for padded clothing, and drying cabinets are needed.

35.02 Hot showers are advantageous as heavy clothing leads to perspiration and hot water is warming after a shift at very low temperatures.

Office accommodation

35.03 Office areas will vary with the type of cold store and the duty it is performing. Administration personnel and any expansion must be listed in the Brief. Administration often requires a building separate from the cold store—perhaps attached to a processing area. For offices for store management and operatives see Technical study: Mechanised storage, para 35.

36 Amenity

36.01 Men working in low temperatures require 10-15 minutes rest per hour or 30 minutes every two hours, and a maximum of a six hour shift has been suggested. Rest rooms should be warm, away from the cooled zone, and provide hot drinks. Working in very cold chambers is tiring and comfortable seating helps relaxation. Most accidents happen through carelessness due to fatigue. Rest and toilet accommodation should also be provided for truck drivers. If refrigerated trucks are expected from Europe there should be a

10 *For vegetable rehandling, bin tippers empty the bulk bins into an intermediate hopper which distributes vegetables to a vibrating conveyor for sorting foreign bodies, and then to a packaging machine.*

11 *Turret truck and forklift; note protective clothing in cold store.*

separate parking area where drivers can sleep in their cabs and cook.

37 Security and safety

37.01 Cold chambers should have emergency alarms and also intercoms in freezing tunnels to ensure that operatives are not forgotten (see **8b**). Some operators place an axe in every cold chamber in case a power failure jams the door gear.

37.02 Some refrigerated products (eg apples) give off noxious gases requiring face masks and oxygen packs. The refrigerant medium itself can leak dangerous gas accumulations. Plant rooms should be fitted with powerful extraction equipment, as gases from coolants like ammonia can quickly overcome operatives.

37.03 A first aid room, outside the refrigerated zone, should be kept warm and equipped to handle cold burns, broken limbs, crushing and asphyxiation. Access for ambulances with a quick route to the first aid room should be planned. The loading bay is not suitable for emergency access in cold stores unless it is open to normal atmosphere.

37.04 Oxygen equipment and face masks should be stored where in emergencies operatives can reach them quickly from most parts of the store—adjacent to the loading bay and cold chamber doors if possible. Similar equipment should be positioned in plant rooms.

38 Circulation and parking

38.01 Parking should be provided for store operatives, office staff and visiting maintenance personnel. Trucks must be able to drive into the plant area to unload heavy equipment close to the installation position. Access should be considered for the fire service, and the fire officer should be contacted. As access to cold chambers is limited, firemen might have to cut their way in from an outside wall. Parking for container handling equipment should be provided if it is used.

12 *Useful sweeper attachment to a forklift truck.*

13 *Cold storage palletising area for bacon products. Note cooling coils below ceiling.*

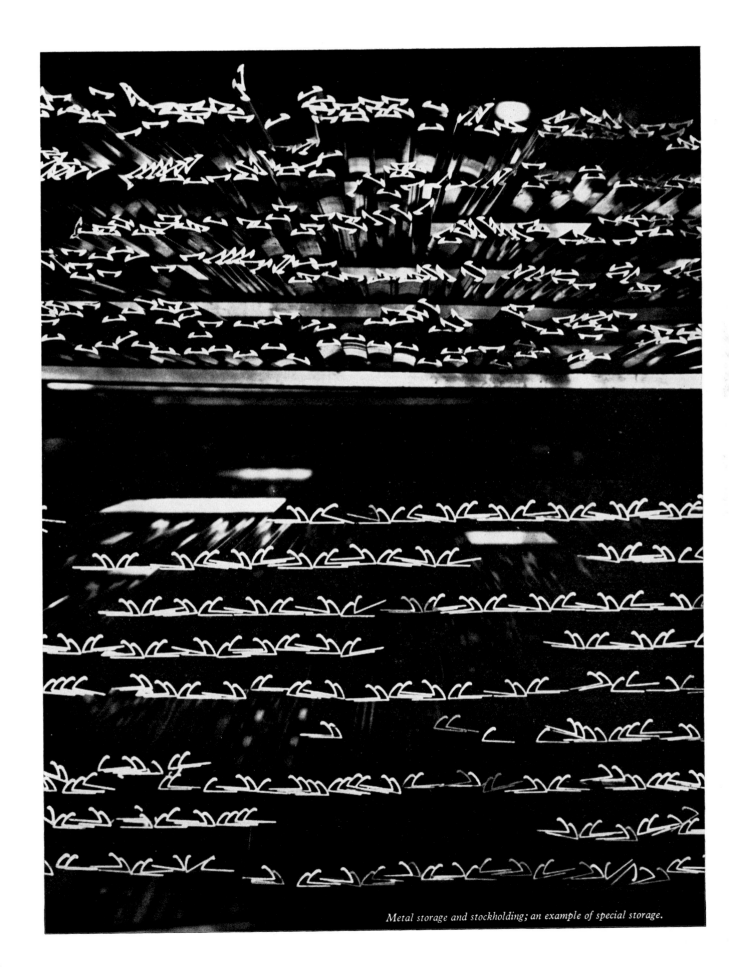

Metal storage and stockholding; an example of special storage.

Technical study Special storage 1

Storage process

Previous sections examined the most commonly required storage types. But there are others which deal with a product requiring special storage conditions.

Most of these would fall into the following categories.

1 Sheet materials (metal, glass, asbestos, plastic).
2 Tubular materials (metals, glass, asbestos, plastic).
3 Non-standard unit loads, eg air cargo.
4 Easily damaged material.
5 High security material.
6 Potentially dangerous material, eg radioactives, explosives.
7 Combination of difficult shapes, large heavy units and fast turnover, eg vehicle spares.
8 Material requiring specific method of handling, eg cable, wire.
9 Combinations of large difficult shapes, low throughput and high selectivity, eg furniture storage.
10 Inter-process storage in production buildings, ie varied throughout, outsize loads, small parts, or special environments.

These categories of storage are 'special' in that the ways and means of storing the product differ, but the basic principles (outlined in previous sections) remain the same. As an example of how these principles are applied in a specialist situation, this section studies in detail steel stockholding (paras 1-38), storage which is special because it has extra heavy loads, and very high throughput. Apart from these factors, which inevitably affect building structure and dimensions, a steel stockholding warehouse is designed on the same principles as a mechanised storage warehouse. Furniture storage is also briefly described in para 1 as an example of large non-standard unit loads, with high volume and selectivity but low turnover.

1 Introduction

Furniture Storage

1.01 Furniture storage is inherently space consuming. Previously it was manhandled and stored in old buildings on the ground to a level as high as a man could lift. Since access gangways had to be left, the resulting volume efficiency was very low.

1.02 In the last two years furniture storage has become containerised. Containers are fast and easy to handle, make greater use of volume, and protect from dust, vermin and moth. But most existing furniture storage buildings and vehicles particularly are unsuitable for container use.

1.03 Warehouses for containerised furniture can be treated in the same way as those for block stacked goods using forklift trucks. One company uses $2 \cdot 4$ m $\times$ $2 \cdot 4$ m $\times$ $2 \cdot 7$ m containers, stacking two high. Containers are block-stacked, or disposed either side of an aisle, depending on speed of stock movement. From past records and experience, removers can predict high user stock. They still must cater for the unplanned withdrawal of one particular piece of furniture from a large consignment.

1.04 Where furniture lots are too small for containers to be used economically, mobile racking is effective, **1**. Cantilever racking with adjustable bearers, wide shelves and mobile bases can store furniture to great heights and densities. Some companies use standard pallets, and store furniture like normal packaged goods (in pallet racking). This is more realistic with new furniture, which is taken apart and packed into cartons.

Removers do not like breaking down used furniture since they use the odd space for packing small objects, and so achieve compact loads in the containers.

1.05 Furniture depositories do not need temperature or humidity control, except to ensure that the stock is kept above freezing point. Heating creates breeding conditions for moth and vermin.

1.06 Fire is a major problem to depository operators. Storage in containers will reduce the risk from inside, but once a fire starts will hardly contain it. Most furniture containers are of timber and board construction. Sprinklers would be required in a new installation. Contact the user's insurers.

1.07 New furniture is usually dismantled and placed in cartons on pallets. If bulky, eg armchairs and settees, it is often shrink-wrapped. Demountable body systems are now widely used in the furniture manufacturing industry, allowing preloading and fast vehicle turn-round.

1.08 Works of art and carpets require special temperature and humidity controlled storage conditions. Such a store should be treated as a sealed unit, eg as a cold store, to ensure freedom from vermin and high security. The design requirements are likely to come from the operator's insurers.

1.09 Design of a furniture depository requires care, and can affect the whole removal system, including the type of vehicle used, and the number of staff employed.

Metal stockholding

1.10 Metal stockholding is a supply service which, by virtue of its dealing with a basic commodity, is a highly competitive business. Success in this field depends on the ability to cope with orders, from a few kilogrammes to many tonnes, in a wide variety of materials at very short notice. The cost effectiveness of plant and buildings is therefore critical.

1.11 The principle of stockholding as a buffer between the primary raw material producer and smaller consumers has been operative since the early days of manufacturing industry. This was essentially a basic wholesaling operation with simple block storage in low cost buildings. However, realisation by the producer mills of rolling programme economics within the last 20 years has tended to direct distribution of smaller orders to the stockholders. The effect has been, notably in steel, for the larger stockholders to become production orientated and take over some of the final mill processes and services. This trend, starting in the USA, was closely followed by the UK, and must be ultimately accepted throughout Europe and the other major industrial nations. In the US and UK some 40 per cent of steel strip mill output passes through the service centres, as the stockholding operations have become, and of this nearly 75 per cent is processed in one form or another.

1.12 The basic stockholder buying-in material in finished form still remains, alongside the service centre, notably in non-ferrous metals. Such an operation normally requires only a simple racking or block stacking system. However, when processing is required, whether for flattening and cutting strip or sawing bars and profiles, more sophisticated handling systems are generally necessary: the more progressive companies demand plans for increasing automation and computer controls.

1.13 The facilities required by a company must be tailored to its closely defined market objectives, and experience has shown that it can be dangerous to generalise too much on the plant requirements of ostensibly competing organisations.

2 Source of goods

2.01 The bulk of steel and aluminium supplies still come from within the UK. However, developments in the continental European industry are already bringing about growth in imported material in addition to that regularly purchased from the Far East to mitigate against adverse UK production patterns. Space should be allowed for the removal of ocean packing.

3 Form of transport

3.01 Coils, **2**, are carried on special well-bodied articulated vehicles, one or two at a time. Tube and bars arrive in bundles on flat vehicles. Imported sheet and other forms of metal arrive in ISO containers, or in articulated trailers from Europe (from the US, in containers or as break-bulk cargo). Special half-height containers are now used for handling metals, with tilt tops and detachable sides for easy unloading, **3**. Standard ISO containers and box trailers have caused problems on arrival at stockholders, as they are not designed to be handled from the top or side, and without a dock, end unloading of metals is difficult and requires manual assistance. TIR-type 'tilt' trailers are time-consuming to unsheet, and block circulation within the store, vehicles usually being driven into the building for full weather protection. Ideally, a buffer space for unroping or unsheeting operations should be provided within the building, clear of circulation routes.

4 Control of transport

4.01 Vehicle peaks are common, and check that the planned delivery pattern does not generate a loading peak when vehicles are likely to arrive from mills. Some truck parking should be provided, both for empty delivery vehicles and for

1

2

3

1 *Mobile furniture racking with hand-crank travel system.*
2 *Special semi-trailer for*
carrying metal coils.
3 *Open, half height container used for carrying steel.*

large mill trucks that can arrive at periods when it is inconvenient to unload them immediately. The number of loading doors should be kept to a minimum and unloading should be at ground level within the building. Each door reduces storage space and is an additional security hazard.

5 Receipt of goods

5.01 Receipt of goods is as described in Technical study Mechanised storage 1, para 5.

6 Form of goods

6.01 Steel can arrive from mills in unit loads of up to 15 tonnes in the case of coil and up to 20 m long in the case of heavy sections. Use of coils weighing 25 tonnes will be a requirement of some of the larger companies, and encouragement by mills for acceptance of 35 tonne coils has been predicted, although such is unlikely to be profitable for all but a very few in the foreseeable future. Bars and tubes are usually bound into one or two tonne lots. Aluminium for sheet can arrive in coil form, but as yet is more often delivered from the mill in half and one tonne stacks of sheets packed in polythene-lined crates.

7 Unloading

7.01 For weather protection, trucks are driven right into the warehouse. Coils must be offloaded by overhead cranage, fitted with special grabs, C-hooks, or slings, in view of the variation in the axial position of coils to be found on the incoming vehicles. Large profiles may be handled by sideloader, while much bar and tube material may also be handled by normal forklifts, **4abc**. Overhead cranes can only operate efficiently on one section of track at a time, which limits unloading speed for multiple units, but does not affect the handling of heavy coils, as there are only one or two per vehicle. Heavy duty sideloaders and forklift trucks require large manoeuvring areas. (See Information sheet External storage 2, as machines are adapted from container carrying units). Where forklifts and sideloaders are to unload over the sides of trucks, a straight-through covered loading area at the perimeter of the building allows normal handling operations to continue undisturbed, and several vehicles can be handled at once **5**. A buffer stacking area is required, accessible to the unloading equipment and storage plant. The size and throughput of the installation will decide whether an island or peripheral straight-through loading area is the most suitable. Consider future extension possibilities and the chance of increasing throughput.

8 Characteristics of goods

8.01 Coils arrive from mills firmly bound. Tube and bar stock tends to 'whip' even when bound in bundles. Fork heads for handling bars are available. Special long pallets help bulk handling and order picking.

9 Sorting

9.01 Buffer space at input allows stacker crane schedules to be flexible. Coils are block stacked on frames on the floor, fitted with adjustable coil stops. The turnover and cranage requirements for supplying process machinery will determine whether separate handling plant is needed for unloading and the initial sorting function.

9.02 Buffer space should also be provided for bars, tubes, and sheet bundles and pallets. This could include full pallets awaiting storage and empty pallets awaiting transfer of goods from the delivery truck. These pallets can be 6 m or more long. Unpacked sheet crates require disposal or storage for collection. A skip positioned in this area can collect polythene liners, broken crates, and general refuse. It should be sited where it will not obstruct handling plant, but can be easily collected by its carrier.

10 Volume calculations

10.01 See para 11, Turnover calculations.

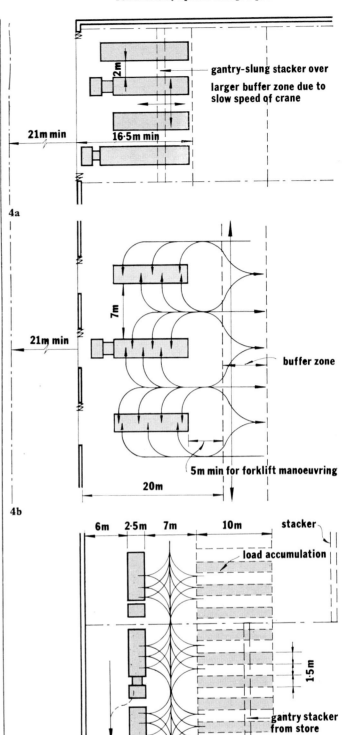

4c

4a *Loading bay using gantry crane is slower than* **b** *but uses less area.*
4b *Loading bay using forklift trucks (load preassembly necessary).*
4c *High throughput straight through loading bay using*

forklifts. Load preassembly necessary. Load accumulation depends on size of load and number of trucks. Fork lift trucks need to pass between parked vehicles to unload both stacks.

11 Turnover calculations

11.01 Assuming that rapid handling systems in large-scale stockholding incorporating a processing line are used, the range of order lines to be produced and the replenishment

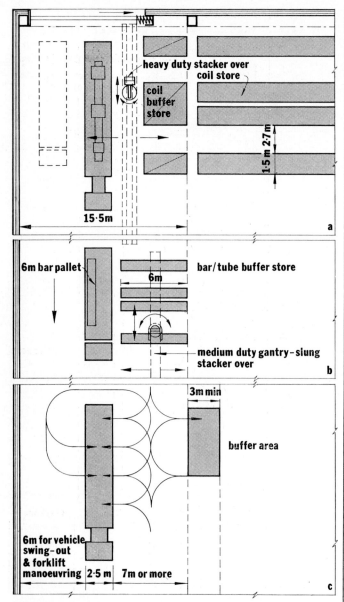

5 *High throughput straight through loading bay showing alternative methods of loading* **a** *heavy coils by stacker crane,* **b** *bar and tube by stacker crane* **c** *sheet and bar by forklift. An island loading bay is similar to* **5**

but has storage on both sides. Island bays tend to constrict plant movement. Where there is a single door trucks reverse into the unloading bay. Unsheeting position should be nearest the door.

period restrict the rate of stock turnover. Once the output/ order mix has been defined, their relationship, plus a comparison of the cost of storage against bulk order discounts will define optimum and maximum coil sizes. The number of coils to be stored can then be calculated. The following should be quantified from the outset:
1 the required throughput for the product range;
2 the gross return on capital expected as a result of trading.
The former will generate the basic specification for the processing plant, while the two factors combined will define the annual stock turnover to be achieved. The processing plant requires buffer storage zones between activities. The flow of material through the plant should be able to maintain a rate commensurate with the fastest conditions on the processing line.

11.02 The general metal stockholder must keep a very wide range of sheet and bar sizes both in steel and non-ferrous metals, which move at various speeds. Aluminium alone has 32 basic 'super standard' sizes, on which there are many variations. Turnover is also likely to expand as producers continue to rationalise output. A typical installation in the

London area dealing in both ferrous and non-ferrous metals handles over 550 orders a day, turning over more than £25 000 worth of material.

12 Variety and flow

12.01 Efficiency of the processing plant in a large-scale stockholding warehouse depends on:
1 the operational efficiency of the bulk coil store;
2 the ratio of running-time to down-time of the processing line.
These are inter-related, and the overall performance laid down for the plant creates a design requirement for the bulk coil store. Even though volume efficiency is lowered as a result, every coil should be directly accessible. The loss of volume efficiency can be minimised by random coil storage.
12.02 *Primary processing:* ie conversion of wide strip coil into flat sheet or narrow strip, variously coated or formed. These can be continually processed. Primary is often automatic. A computer controlling stock movement can also programme processing machinery, and plan the storage of finished goods and dispatch pattern. *Secondary and tertiary processing*, eg, special finishes, grading, blanking, profiling, may also be assisted by a computer, but tend to be more labour intensive.
12.03 General purpose metal stockholders are faced with an ever increasing variety of stock. Some can be very fast moving, but accurate predictions are not easy, even for expert consultants; this is one of the reasons why some operators overstock.

13 Type of storage

13.01 Typical systems in operation with varying degrees of success are:
1 block stacking with overhead cranes (mostly for coils);
2 medium height storage using overhead cranes, sideloaders, forklift trucks or four-way travel reach trucks, for coil, bar and tube stock;
3 mobile racking for sheet, bar and tube (up to 160 tonnes per rack);
4 high bay storage, with stacker cranes or special high lift sideloaders for bar and tube;
5 specialised systems with varying degrees of automatic operation. Many custom built systems incorporate one or more of the former handling methods.
6 'A' frame racks for plates.
7 Floor racks for large profiles.
Choice of hardware depends on space and labour saving needs in relation to the range and turnover of stock held, and a consequent balance between storage density and speed of access to stock.
13.02 Block stacking with overhead cranes is the traditional method for handling coils. With such, random access is not possible and coil damage is increased by additional handling. Furthermore the system must be carefully designed to prevent coils slipping or springing out of position.
13.03 Medium height storage (up to 6m) is a common solution, and is as high as coils can go economically. If stock control, order planning and process machinery control is computer based, the coil storage area should be planned for eventual on-line control of the handling plant (depending on throughput and expenditure). Automation of a coil store requires careful design of the racking and plant so that it can be adapted with as little machine redundancy as possible. One such store (designed for later automation) using a manually controlled gantry-slung stacker crane to handle 15 tonne coils has an interesting rack construction. Special fir-tree racking is designed with staggered peg positions. Coils slot into the spaces left by the units above and below. The pegs of the racking to support the coils are of double bar construction, to allow the crane's peg to enter between them, and accurately

position the coil. A closed circuit television camera is mounted at the end of the stacker's carrier peg to help location. This rack design is the most efficient for combining volume efficiency, individual coil selection, and accurate handling.

13.04 The most commonly found form of coil rack is a 'pallet type', with the coils supported on cradles mounted in a rectangular frame. On considerations of volumetric efficiency this suffers from the 'round peg in square hole' concept and would be inefficient in a fully automated concept. Such racking can be supplied with adjustable cradle heights; a typical rack is 2·4 m deep and 5·5 m high, with a capacity of a 10 tonne coil on the top level, 2 × 15 tonne coils on the 2nd and 1st levels, and a further coil resting on the floor.

13.05 Overhead, suspended stacker cranes are efficient for use in coil stores; a 2·7 m wide aisle can be used with 1·5 m wide coils, allowing full mobility. Sideloaders are also used, but are not so flexible, even with four-wheel steering, since they require substantial turning space.

13.06 *Bar and tube stock* is stored in special pallets. Fir tree racking with parallel pins is used, and both overhead stackers and sideloaders, **7**, are employed. Areas for bar and tube storage require more space at the ends of aisles for manoeuvring. With an underslung stacker, the turning area can be taken as the radius of the load from the centre of the mast. With a sideloader, **8**, swing-out with long bars can be considerable, and the curve complicated. Plant manufacturers supply turning diagrams.

13.07 Mobile racking has been used successfully for bar and tube stocks. Heavy duty cantilever racking is mounted on motorised bases, and operates as conventional mobile rack-

8

9

6

7

6 Coil racking using overhead suspended stacker crane.
7 Narrow aisle sideloader picking from fir-tree racking.
8 Heavy sideloader picking from fir-tree racking.
9 Semi-automatic stacker crane for picking metal sheet. The work cycle is programmed into the control panel (centre) from a position at the end of the aisle.

ing, only one aisle at a time being open. This increases the volume efficiency without reducing access (important for bar stocks, as they generate very low spacial efficiency solutions). Sideloaders or an overslung stacker crane would be used with mobile racking.

13.08 *Cut sheet for individual sheet picking* is stored in timber crates on shallow racking, or in special sheet pallets, thus achieving quite high densities. Bulk sheet tends to be block stacked in crates (a one-tonne 2·4 m × 1·2 m lot of aluminium sheet is approximately 304 mm high in its crate). Clearance should be allowed in the racking for forklift manoeuvring of the sheet crates, and for order pickers to reach in to lift out sheets without fouling the racking structure. Aluminium extrusions can be stacked on end to save space, but in this situation mechanical handling is difficult. Aircraft industry approved stock is segregated from normal metal stock.

13.09 Partially or fully automated high bay storage of sheet and bar is now widespread in the USA, but as yet relatively uncommon in Europe. One steelworks store in Germany employs a high bay semiautomated configuration with the potential of full automation. Cantilever racking 18·6 m high supports special pallets carrying bar stock up to 6 m long. Stacker cranes are adapted to handle the extra-long pallets. There is considerable potential for high bay storage for tube and bar stock, as this is inherently space-consuming.

13.10 Profiles over 6 m in length or large cross-section are normally floor-stacked by overhead crane fitted with a spreader bar from which slings, clamps, or magnets are attached.

13.11 Plates can be stored in 'A' frame racks with overhead cranes fitted with clamps. Thicker material tends to be floor-stacked and handled with overhead cranes fitted with clamps, magnets, or vacuum lifters.

14 Stock control

14.01 Stockholding was previously considered to be keeping as much metal as possible to offset unpredictable deliveries from the mills. This is a costly gamble. By the careful monitoring of the market, and by realistically restricting the product range, a balance can be achieved between stored material and output.

14.02 There are two levels of stock control.

1 The main coil store, supplying steel to processing lines, must operate smoothly; and

2 Further control is required between primary and secondary processing, as well as between final processing, packaging and loading delivery vehicles.

14.03 Manual stock control methods are still used successfully and should be employed unless staff are fully familiar with the disciplines of a computer. If such is the case, then computer stock control systems will offer considerable advantages to the larger companies.

15 Stock withdrawal

15.01 Heavy gantry-slung stacker cranes retrieving 15 tonne coils tend to 'crab' when loaded eccentrically. The drive and control method best suited to the application should be considered when the store is being planned.

16 Order picking

16.01 Special sideloaders with elevating picking-platforms can be used, as can fixed path stacker cranes. Bar and tube stock is either bound into packs or stored loose in pallets for order picking. Orders tend to accumulate on the picking unit before being dropped at the load build-up position. Often in the smaller installations, the order picking machinery loads vehicles direct.

17 Picking area

17.01 Bars and tube are available in such a great variety of sizes and grades that their order picking areas tend to waste space, as easy access to the stock and clearance between racks are required. Mobile racks for bars and tubes provide a solution to this problem, and a high bay system has considerable potential.

18 Load build-up

18.01 Load build-up depends on delivery cycles and type of vehicles in service. Trucks must be kept moving for as much of the time as possible. Large orders of bulk stock can be loaded direct from the storage position and placed on the truck bed by overhead crane or sideloader. Small orders collected for an area delivery round can cause delay. Some operators load goods direct onto articulated trailers which are parked in strategic positions in the store. The tractor returns the empty trailer and immediately leaves with the full one. Demountable bodies are also used in this way. Other operators prefer to separate loading from general in-store handling, and allocate an area for load assembly. This can be space consuming, as (unlike packaged goods and roll pallets) metal must be spread out on the floor to prevent snagging, and to build up a delivery pattern. A forklift truck or sideloader then loads the vehicles as quickly as possible. The accumulation area required will depend on the number of orders built up at a time and the size of the vehicles used.

19 Order and document check

19.01 This is similar to the process described in Technical Study Mechanised Storage 1, para 19.

20 Loading and dispatch

20.01 Vehicles are usually fitted with special bodies for carrying metal products. Trucks are driven into the warehouse. If trailers or swop bodies are preloaded, parallel parking is used. Space can be saved by loading with an overhead crane, although this is slower than using forklifts. If loads are accumulated prior to a vehicle's arrival, a straight-through loading bay is efficient, with trucks loaded over the side by forklifts. If a weighing machine is required at the loading area (to check picked stock), it should be accessible to loading bay plant without blocking circulation routes.

10 *Block stacked coils in store.*

Technical study Special storage 2

Building function

Technical study Special storage 1 dealt with the storage process (paras 1 to 21). This second study (paras 22 to 38) deals with the design of the building.

22 Structure

22.01 To carry gantry cranes handling 15 tonne coils, the structure must be substantial. Some operators sacrifice efficiency and the possibility of automation by using side-loaders which allow a lighter structure.

23 Floor

23.01 Floors in metal stockholding warehouses need to be very strong. Double sided cantilever racking for coils can carry up to 90 tonnes per vertical bay, with an additional 30 tonnes resting on the floor. Block stacked coils also impose heavy weights, but with different distribution, **1**. Mobile racking has special problems; one installation that recently upgraded its storage capacity by placing cantilever racking on mobile bases increased the floor loading per bay from 300 to 640 tonnes. This was achieved by using very wide spreader plates for the rail support.

1 *Distribution of loads for foundations and floor in coil stores.*

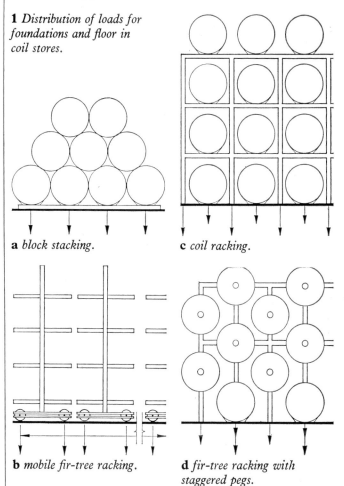

a *block stacking.*

c *coil racking.*

b *mobile fir-tree racking.*

d *fir-tree racking with staggered pegs.*

23.02 Foundations for metal stockholding must be designed by specialist engineers to take impacts from the heaviest coils, which can fall from machinery and 'pop' out of block stacks. Design for 5-6 tonne wheel loadings where trucks run into the store for loading. If heavy duty side loaders or forklift trucks are used for coil handling, plan all plant circulation areas to their wheel loading, up to 15 tonnes, but check with plant manufacturer. The floor must be suitable for slitting and processing machinery, which may need special bases and foundations. In some warehouses the floor is divided up into bays of different capacities to save money initially. This also restricts flexibility of store organisation and handling.

24 Building services

24.01 In storing metals, oxidisation by the atmosphere must be prevented. Aluminium stockholders have special requirements for metals used by the aircraft industry, which set standards for environmental control. These range from conventional blown air or radiant panel heating (to keep the temperature above dew point), to full humidity control. The level of control depends on local environmental conditions, and particular care has to be taken in maritime climates. A temperature level of 10-12°C is suggested.

24.02 Consult the operator about temperature and humidity ranges. Air-conditioning in large-scale special-purpose warehouses can save money (eg, car bodies stored between production and final painting can be left as bare metal, unprimed and ungreased, if air-conditioning is used, and greasing and degreasing cut out).

24.03 Suggested artificial lighting levels are 200 lux for general storage zones, and 400 lux or more for in-process and loading zones. Natural lighting can be used as heat and light do not harm stock. If internal combustion handling plant is used, eg heavy duty side loaders, extraction should be installed to prevent fume build-up.

25 Special services

25.01 Three-phase power supplies are required for overhead cranes, and most processing machinery. If slitting lines are used, contact the plant manufacturer for his plant requirements.

26 Building fabric

26.01 Insulated cladding is advisable for metal stockholding. Some operators use the warehouse cladding as advertising, using metal sheet materials with striking external finishes. Waterproofing is very important as metal, especially stacked sheet, deteriorates when wet. Stacked sheets of galvanised steel wet-stain very fast, and the plastic-lined crates for aluminium can contain moisture. For this reason, operators seldom allow rainwater down pipes to run through storage areas, and prefer flank glazing and ventilation to roof lights. If aisles follow the building perimeter, cladding should be protected from impact damage.

27 Fire control

27.01 This is dealt with in Technical study Mechanised storage, para 26.

28 Security

28.01 Internal security, such as theft by warehouse staff, often working with delivery drivers, may be a problem. Gatehouse security checks will prevent this, and also control traffic. However, storage of high value metals, particularly when in the form of small fittings, may require special internal security enclosures. Weighbridges counter-check weighing during loading. A high fence, strong lighting and alarm systems fitted to doors and windows will deter intruders. Vehicles and handling plant parking areas should not adjoin low roofs or windows, as they act as a convenient stepladder. Many stockholding warehouses operate at night, which reduces the external security problem.

29 External works

29.01 Some steel sheet, eg Cor ten weathering steels, can be stored externally. These areas should be drained, and surface water laden with oxidisation products must not come into contact (by flow or splashing) with surfaces where staining would be unacceptable.

30 Structure-based plant

30.01 Heavy duty gantry-slung stacker cranes, **2**, are very sophisticated, and movement controls can now position the crane in the racking very accurately. They can load and retrieve from fir tree racking and block stack coils, place coils onto processing lines, and unload coils from lorries. A gantry-slung stacker crane carrying a 15 tonne coil has considerable momentum, and there have been problems of mast whip and gantry crabbing.

30.02 For tube and bar stock, a conventional gantry crane with a sling attachment is sometimes used, though a 3-5 tonne capacity gantry-slung stacker with extendable fork heads is faster. The latter can also remove piles of sheet from a cutting

2

3

2 Large gantry-slung stacker handling coil.
3 Advanced slitting line in use (coil shown right, with *coil store in background).*

line and transport them to a pre-dispatch buffer store. If stackers are also used for loading lorries, the mast must be telescopic to at least 2·5 m above floor level, to clear the truck bed and load.

30.03 Primary processing lines for steel strip are normally for flattening and cutting to length, or for slitting into narrower coils. In either case, special foundations will be required and space allowed for a floor buffer store of two or three coils prior to the decoiler unit. The finished product is either a stack of flat sheets, palletised or unpalletised, or a batch of narrow coils which may be palletised 'eye horizontal', strapped to skids 'eye vertical', or simply strapped together 'eye vertical'. Stacks of sheet are not normally in units greater than five tonnes, while slit coil from a service centre is normally limited to unit loads of three tonnes maximum.

31 Mobile plant

31.01 Mobile plant includes sideloaders, **4**, normal and heavy duty forklift trucks and special purpose free path order picking machines. Heavy duty plant is diesel powered, so fume extraction equipment must be installed. Low pressure gas power is popular for normal forklifts and sideloaders as fume levels are low.

31.02 Special purpose free path stacker/order pickers allow narrow aisles as in conventional stores. With 5 tonne capacity order pickers, 1·8 m wide aisles between rack arms are possible. The operator's control platform rises with the fork head, and the base runs between guide rails at floor level. Some models have sliding masts, allowing stacking and picking at both sides of the aisle. There is a wide variety of fork heads for special purpose handling. Many of the heavy duty machines for handling steel have little suspension, and solid tyred wheels. This may cause extra vibration and should be accounted for when calculating floor loadings.

32 Integration of building and plant

32.01 For mechanised plant, see Technical study Mechanised storage 2, para 32.

33 Maintenance

33.01 Provision should be made for crane and mobile plant maintenance. If heavy processing machinery is not covered by overhead craneage, then access must be available for mobile craneage. Normal size forklifts are usually taken off site for maintenance, but large coil-carrying equipment is unsuitable for roads, and tends to be maintained on the premises.

33.02 Building maintenance is mostly repairing impact damage, eg a misplaced 15 tonne coil can buckle racking and cradles. Coils, if they get out of control, can smash through external cladding. Breakables, eg electrical controls, should be protected.

34 Management

34.01 If processing is involved, the integration of production and storage consultants is important.

35 Personnel accommodation

35.01 Locker accommodation should be provided for operatives. Working with metals can be dirty and washing and grease removal facilities should be installed.

Office accommodation

35.02 The amount of office accommodation depends on how much administration is handled from site. Several new metal stockholding warehouses have incorporated large offices. Offices for warehouse and process personnel are required on the warehouse floor.

36 Amenity

36.01 This is dealt with in Technical study Mechanised storage, para 36.

37 Security and safety

37.01 Safety is important in a metal stockholding warehouse. Personnel routes should be segregated from heavy plant, eg carrying coils. All processing machinery should be guarded and clearly marked (contact the Factory Inspectorate). A first aid room equipped to handle crushing injuries should be placed out of the storage area, with easy access for ambulances.

4 *Large side loader handling metal sheet.*

5 *Side loader handling coils into racking.*

6

7

6 *A useful machine for constricted premises: the Matbro swing lift reach truck incorporates a side reach mechanism for side loading in narrow aisles, and a rotating mast for conventional forklift use.*
7 *Diesel forklift handling bound bar stock in fir tree racking.*
8 *Dual weighbridge (one incoming, one despatch) with digital read out for rapid throughput. Cycles of one minute per vehicle are possible. Note strategic siting on circulation route.*

8

38 Circulation and parking

38.01 Internal circulation is inherent in the planning of the storage area and the choice of the handling plant. Parking should be provided for operatives and administrative staff, and for empty delivery vehicles.

Appendix 1

Vehicle dimensions and loadings: Australia and USA

Axle and group loads: state by state (Australia)

State	Per tyre	Per axle with 2 tyres	Per axle with 4 tyres	Per 'Tandem' axle group 40in to 8ft	Per 'Spread Tandem' 8 ft to 9 ft	Axle group controls
Queensland	tons cwts. 2 5	tons cwts. 4 10	tons cwts. 8 —	tons cwts. 13 —	tons cwts. 15 —	By distance between extreme axles of group, or between extreme axles of vehicle. 15 tons at 8ft. 27 tons 10 cwts. at 40ft.
New South Wales	— —	4 14	8 6	13 16	15 9	By distance between extreme axles of vehicle, or between internal axles or group of axles. 15 tons 9 cwts. at 8ft (2 axles). 31 tons 7 cwts. at 40ft (5 axles). 29 tons 13 cwts. at 40ft (4 axles).
Victoria	2 5	4 10	8 —	13 —	15 —	By distance between extreme axles of group, between extreme axles of vehicle, or between axle groups. 15 tons at 8ft. 31 tons at 40ft.
Tasmania	2 5	4 10	8 —	13 —	15 —	By distance between extreme axles of group, between extreme axles of vehicle, or between axle groups. 15 tons at 8ft. 27 tons 10 cwts. at 40 ft.
South Australia	— —	6 10	8 —	16 —	16 —	Nil. Maximum tonnage must not exceed 32 tons, excluding front axle.
Western Australia	2 5 (5000) lbs.	4 10 (10 000) lbs.	8 — (18 000) lbs.	13 — (29 000) lbs.	13 7	By distance between extreme axles. 13 tons 7 cwts. at 8ft. 23 tons 4 cwts. at 40ft.

Dimensional limitations (Australia)

Unit	New South Wales	Queensland	South Australia	Tasmania	Victoria	Western Australia
Length-Feet:						
Truck	31	31	66	35	31	31
Truck and semi-trailer	47	47	66	45	47	47
Truck and trailer	50	50	66	50	50	50
Omnibus	33	35	66	35	33	35
Width-feet:						
All vehicles	8	8	8	8	8	8
Omnibuses	8	8·2½	8	8	8·2½	8·2½
Height-feet:						
All vehicles	14	14	14	12½	13	14
Omnibuses	14½	14½	14	12½	12½	14

State size and weight laws, USA current status (as of 15th December, 1973)

Bold figures after entries refer to footnotes on pp. 283-4.

State	Maximum gross weight practicable (pounds)	Axle loads in thousands of pounds) Single	Tandem	Width (inches)	Height (feet)	Rigid truck	Semi-trailer S.T.	Tractor and semi-trailer T.S.T.	Twin trailer Combination
Alabama	73 280	18·0 2	36·0 3	96 4	13½	40	NR	55	NP
Alaska	100 000	20·0	34·0	96 4	13½	40	45	65	70
Arizona	76 800	18·0	32·0	96	13½	40	NR	65	65
Arkansas	73 280 1	18·0	32·0	96	13½	40	NR	55	65
California	76 800	18·0	32·0	96 4	14	40	NR 7	60	65
Colorado	85 000 1	18·0	36·0	96	13 5	35	NR	65	65
Connecticut	73 000 1	22·4 2	36·0 3	102	13½	50	NR	55	NP
Delaware	73 280	20·0	36·0	96	13½	40	NR	55	65
Dist. of Columbia	70 000	22·0	38·0	96	12½	40	NR	55	NP
Florida	66 610 1	20·0 2	40·0 3	96	13½	40 6	NR	55	NP
Georgia	73 280	20·3 2	40·7 3	96	13½ 5	55	55	55	55
Hawaii	73 280	24·0	32·0	108	13½	40	NR	55	65
Idaho	105 500 1	20·0 2	34·0 3	96	14	35 6	NR	60	98 9
Illinois	73 280	18·0	32·0	96	13½	42	45	55	65 9
Indiana	73 280	18·0 2	32·0 3	96	13½	36	NR	55	65
Iowa	72 634 1	18·0 2	32·0 3	96	13½	35	NR	55	60
Kansas	85 500 1	20·0 2	34·0 3	96 4	13½	42½	NR	60	65
Kentucky	73 280 1	18·0 2	32·0 3	96	13½	35 6	NR	55 8	65 9
Louisiana	73 280 1	18·0 2	32·0 3	96	13½	35	NR	60	65 9
Maine	73 280 1	22·0	32·0 3	102 4	13½ 5	55	45	56½	NP
Maryland	73 280 1	22·4	40·0 3	96 4	13½	40	45	55	65 9
Massachusetts	73 000	22·4	36·0	96 4	13½	35	NR	55	NP
Michigan	sub. to axle 1	18·0	26·0 3	96 4	13½	40	NR	55*	65 9
Minnesota	73 280	18·0	32·0	96	13½	40	NR	55	65 9
Mississippi	73 280 1	18·0	32·0 3	96	13½	35	NR	55	55
Missouri	73 280 1	18·0 2	32·0	96 4	13½ 5	40	NR	55	65 9
Montana	105 500 1	20·0 2	34·0 3	96	13½	35	NR	60	65 9
Nebraska	95 000 1	20·0 2	34·0 3	96	13½	40	NR	60	65
Nevada	128 000 1	18·0	32·0	96	NR	40	NR	70	105 9
New Hampshire	73 280	22·4	36·0 3	96	13½	35	NR	55	NP
New Jersey	73 280	22·4 2	32·0 2	96	13½	35	NR	55	55
New Mexico	86 400 1	21·6 2	34·3 3	96	13½	40	NR	65	65
New York	71 000	22·4	36·0	96	13½	35	NR	55	55 9
North Carolina	70 000 1	18·0 2	36·0 3	96	13½	40 6	NR	55	NP
North Dakota	82 000 1	20·0 2	34·0 3	102 4	13½ 5	40 6	NR	65 8	65 9
Ohio	78 000 1	19·0	32·0	96	13½	40	NR	55	65
Oklahoma	90 000 1	20·0 2	34·0 3	102 4	13½	40	NR	65	65
Oregon	76 000	20·0 2	34·0 3	96	13½ 5	35	35 7	50 8	105 9
Pennsylvania	71 145 1	22·4 2	36·0 3	96	13½	35	NR	55	NP
Rhode Island	73 280	22·4	36·0 3	102	13½	40	NR	55	NP
South Carolina	73 280	20·0	36·0 3	96	13½	40 6	NR	55	NP
South Dakota	95 000 1	20·0 2	34·0 3	96	13½	35	NR	60 8	65
Tennessee	73 280	18·0 2	32·0	96	13½	40	NR	55	NP
Texas	72 000 1	18·0 2	32·0 3	96	13½	45	NR 7	55	65
Utah	130 000 1	20·0 2	34·0 3	96	14	45	45	60	105 9
Vermont	73 280	22·4 2	36·0 3	102 4	13½	55	NR	55	NP
Virginia	70 000	18·0	32·0	96	13½	35	NR	55	NP
Washington	105 500 1	20·0 2	34·0 3	96	13½ 5	35	45	65 8	65
West Virginia	73 280 1	18·0 2	32·0 3	96	13½ 5	40 6	NR	50 8	NP
Wisconsin	69 350 1	18·0 2	32·0	96 4	13½	35	35 7	55	NP
Wyoming	101 000 1	20·0 2	36·0	102 4	14	50 6	NR	75	75

Footnotes to 1973 tables

* A number of states also provide for added length or 'overhang' for carriers of specific commodities (eg, automobiles, boats, pipes, poles).
NP Not permitted
NR No restriction (or not stated)

1 Gross weight
Arkansas On designated highways. 64 000 lb on other highways.
Colorado Except 75 200lb on Interstate system.
Connecticut 2 per cent tolerance allowed, but maximum is 73 280lb including tolerance.
Florida 10 per cent tolerance allowed.
Idaho Except 76 800lb on interstate system.
Iowa 8 per cent tolerance allowed, but maximum is 73 280lb including tolerance.
Kansas Except 73 280lb on interstate system.
Kentucky On Class AAA roads. AA roads = 62 000lb, A roads = 44 000lb, and B roads = 30 000lb.
Louisiana Based on 9000lb steering axle.
Maine 5 per cent tolerance allowed, but maximum is 73 280lb including tolerance, 10 per cent tolerance on farm products, building and construction materials, and refrigerated products. Also 15 per cent tolerance for forest products in December, January and February except on interstate system.
Maryland On 5-axles. 4-axle limit = 65 000lb (except bulk milk haulers who receive 5 per cent tolerance to maximum of 68 250lb). 3-axle limit = 55 000lb. 1000lb overall maximum tolerance.
Michigan Limited to 11 axles. 73 280lb for 5-axle combinations.
Mississippi On designated highways. Other designated limits are 55 980lb and 57 650lb.
Missouri On interstate system, major state roads and parts of state supplementary system which contain no bridges.
Montana By regular permit, except 76 800lb practical limit on interstate system.
Nebraska Except 71 146lb plus 3 per cent tolerance on interstate system.
Nevada Except 76 800lb on interstate system.
New Mexico Plus 20 per cent tolerance when hauling certain products.
North Carolina 5 per cent tolerance allowed, but maximum is 73 280lb including tolerance.
North Dakota Except 73 280lb on interstate system.
Ohio Plus 3 per cent tolerance.
Oklahoma Except 73 280lb on interstate system.
Pennsylvania 3 per cent tolerance allowed.
South Dakota Except 73 280lb on interstate system.
Texas 5 per cent tolerance allowed.
Utah Except 79 900lb on interstate system.
Washington Except 72 000lb (and by permit 76 000lb) on interstate system.
West Virginia Including tolerance on designated roads. Otherwise 60 800lb.
Wisconsin 73 000lb including tolerance.
Wyoming Based on 7 axles and 70ft spacing. Except 73 950lb on interstate system.

2 Single axle weights
Alabama 10 per cent tolerance allowed.
Connecticut 2 per cent tolerance allowed.
Florida 10 per cent tolerance on scale weight allowed.
Georgia 18 000lb plus 13 per cent tolerance.
Idaho Except 18 000lb on interstate system.
Indiana 22 400lb on roads designated by Highway Commission.
Iowa 3 per cent tolerance allowed.
Kansas Except 18 000lb on interstate system.
Kentucky On A, AA and AAA roads. Also 5 per cent tolerance allowed.
Louisiana Tolerance, if unintentional: vehicles transporting natural resources—10 per cent; all other vehicles—5 per cent.
Missouri 22 400lb allowed vehicles operating exclusively in or within two miles of corporate limits of cities of 75 000 or more inhabitants.
Montana Except 18 000lb on interstate system.
Nebraska Except 18 000lb on interstate system. Also 5 per cent tolerance allowed.
New Jersey 5 per cent tolerance allowed.
New Mexico 20 per cent tolerance allowed when hauling certain products.
North Carolina 1000lb tolerance allowed on any one axle.
North Dakota Except 18 000lb on interstate system.
Oklahoma Except 18 000lb on interstate system.
Oregon Except 18 000lb on interstate system.
Pennsylvania 3 per cent tolerance allowed.
South Dakota Except 18 000lb on interstate system.
Tennessee Front axle limited to 12 000lb.
Texas 5 per cent tolerance allowed.
Utah Except 18 000lb on interstate system.
Vermont Not applicable to interstate system which is limited only by gross weight. Also 5 per cent tolerance except on interstate system.
Washington Except 18 000lb on interstate system.
West Virginia 5 per cent tolerance allowed.
Wisconsin 1500lb tolerance allowed.
Wyoming Where overall wheelbase exceeds 50ft; except 18 000lb on interstate system.

3 Tandem axle weights
Alabama 10 per cent tolerance allowed.
Connecticut 2 per cent tolerance allowed.
Florida 10 per cent tolerance allowed on scale weight.
Georgia 36 000lb plus 13 per cent tolerance.
Idaho Except 32 000lb on interstate system.
Indiana 36 000lb allowed on routes designated by Highway Commission.
Iowa 3 per cent tolerance allowed. 18 000lb limit if less than 40 inches apart.
Kansas Except 32 000lb on interstate system.
Kentucky On A, AA and AAA roads. Also 5 per cent tolerance.
Louisiana Tolerance, if unintentional: Vehicles transporting natural resources—10 per cent; other vehicles—5 per cent.
Maine 36 000lb on other than interstate system.
Maryland Either axle of tandem allowed 22 400lb.
Michigan 32 000lb on two tandems when gross does not exceed 73 280lb. 32 000lb on one tandem for other vehicles on designated roads (June to February).

3 Tandem axle weights—*continued*

Mississippi On designated roads. 28 700lb on other roads.
Montana Except 32 000lb on interstate system.
Nebraska Except 32 000lb on interstate system. Also 5 per cent tolerance allowed.
New Hampshire Gross of 3-axle straight trucks limited: 40 000lb with one powered axle, and 47 500lb when both tandem axles are powered.
New Jersey 5 per cent tolerance allowed.
New Mexico 20 per cent tolerance allowed when hauling certain products.
North Carolina 1000lb tolerance on each axle.
North Dakota Except 32 000lb on interstate system.
Oklahoma Except 32 000lb on interstate system.
Oregon Except 32 000lb on interstate system.
Pennsylvania 3 per cent tolerance allowed.
Rhode Island By ruling.
South Carolina Except 32 000lb on interstate system. Also 10 per cent tolerance allowed.
South Dakota Except 32 000lb on interstate system.
Texas 5 per cent tolerance allowed.
Utah Except 32 000lb on interstate system.
Vermont Except interstate system which is limited only by gross weight.
Washington Except 32 000lb on interstate system.
West Virginia 5 per cent tolerance allowed.

4 Width

Alabama 102in for loads of pine or cedar logs except on interstate system.
Alaska Plus 6in for safety devices and load binders.
California 100in for loads of plywood, except on interstate system.
Kansas Additional 6in allowed for wheels and tyres.
Maine Except 96in on interstate system.
Maryland 102in for tobacco hogsheads.
Massachusetts Up to 10in additional for mirrors on vehicles over 10 000lb gross.
Michigan 104in for forest products and concrete pipe.
Missouri 108in allowed in, or within two miles of, corporate limits of cities of 75 000 or more inhabitants.
North Dakota On designated highways.
Oklahoma Except 96in on interstate system.
Vermont Except 96in on interstate system.
Wisconsin 102in for pulpwood logs.
Wyoming Except 96in on interstate system, paved roads less than 20ft wide, and on unpaved roads.

5 Height

Colorado 13½ft allowed on designated highways.
Georgia Annual overheight permits available.
Maine Plus 6in load extension above maximum structural height of vehicles.
Missouri 15ft allowed in, or within two miles of, corporate limits of cities of 75 000 or more inhabitants.
North Dakota 15½ft by special permit.
Oregon 14ft for auto transporters by permit or resolution.
Washington 14ft for auto transporters.
West Virginia On designated roads, and for auto transporters. Otherwise 12½ft.

6 Truck length (see also * general note)

Florida 2-axles = 35ft; 3-axles = 40ft.
Idaho 40ft on designated highways.
Kentucky On designated highways. Otherwise 26½ft.
North Carolina For 3-axle trucks. 2-axle trucks = 35ft.
North Dakota 2-axles = 35ft; 3-axles = 40ft.
South Carolina 2-axles = 35ft; 3-axles = 40ft.
West Virginia 35ft for 2-axle trucks. Also 10 per cent tolerance.
Wyoming 65ft by permit.

7 Semitrailer length (see also * general note)

California Unless distance from kingpin to rear axle exceeds 38ft.
Oregon 40ft allowed by permit.
Texas If total combination length does not exceed 55ft.
Wisconsin Measured from extreme rear of tractor chassis to rear of semitrailer.

8 Tractor semitrailer length (see also * general note).

Kentucky Class AA and AAA Highways. Otherwise 30ft.
North Dakota On designated roads.
Oregon 60ft allowed by permit.
South Dakota 65ft allowed on designated roads.
Washington 70ft for stinger-steered units.
West Virginia 55ft on designated roads.

8 Twin trailer combination length (see also * general note)

Idaho On designated highways for combinations of three or more units. Otherwise 73ft.
Illinois On all 4-lane plus designated 2-lane highways.
Kentucky On 4-lane highways plus designated radii operations on 2-lane roads. By annual permit.
Louisiana On 4-lane highways plus a 10 mile radius.
Maryland On 4-lane highways plus 2-lane highways to most direct point of origin or destination.
Michigan On designated highways.
Minnesota On 4-lane plus other designated highways by annual permit.
Missouri On designated highways.
Montana By annual permit.
Nevada By regular permit.
New York Except in New York City, and in Suffolk and Nassau counties.
North Dakota On designated highways.
Oregon Under permit or resolution for combinations of four units. Otherwise 65 to 75ft.
Utah By annual permit. Otherwise 60 to 65ft.

* Michigan: Allows 60ft auto transporters on any highway plus 3ft front and 4ft rear overhang. 65ft truck-semitrailer auto transporters on designated routes plus 3ft front and 4ft rear overhang.

Industrial storage

Appendix 2

Interprocess storage in small factories

1.01 There are basic laws for materials distribution that are especially important in planning production buildings with small floor areas, and using essentially manual handling: this applies as much to conversion work as in new building.
1 Keep goods off the floor: ie plan to prevent clutter.
2 Only allow goods to stand in properly planned stores or buffer zones.
3 Handling areas are for materials movement.
In small premises, especially if adapting existing installations, space is often at a premium; a major failing is lack of sufficient provision for sorting after unloading into planned sections of the storage accommodation. Sorting numbers of small loads in loading areas quickly generates heaps, constricts vehicle handling and leads to pilferage.
1.02 Sorting: Components and materials in small plants can arrive both by bulk loads, usually stacked on pallets or in post pallets, or as unit loads in light vans. In the former case, a simple mechanical lifting device can be used for unloading and handling (see Information Sheet 3 p.100) but more often, the material is off-loaded manually. The goods have to be checked off, and then stored prior to use: an area must be provided close to the loading bay and the storage area for this purpose, and should not be combined with material awaiting dispatch. There are two ways in which components are handled for storage prior to distribution to the production zone:
a Bulk material is stored on pallets in racking: the whole pallet is then picked and the material repacked into tote boxes or on to shelves when stock in the production supply store becomes low. Material can either be packed into loads for supplying one manufacturing operation with several machines (ie making a large batch) or picked into individual operator's supplies.
b The material can be sorted directly into tote bins or on to shelves for distribution straight to the shop floor. In this case, re-ordering procedure has to be efficient: order picking is a more complicated function than in the former case, as all material is in effect back-up stock, and orders of small numbers of discrete items have to be picked from bulk stock. This can lead to poor use of the volume, but reduces in store handling. The choice of either method depends on the production characteristics, throughput and size of installation (see also Mechanised Storage, Information Sheet 8).
1.03 Turnover: Some components are used more frequently than others: for example for a popular product in a range or where the produce requires more than one of the components. These 'fast mover' items should be positioned in the store at the output end: this can be in the form of a whole aisle if there are a high number of popular items, or the end pallet or bin

positions at the output end of the aisles for quicker selection (T.S. Manual Storage 1, 13 a, b). The latter form of storage is often used where production can change frequently, and there develops a hierarchy of turnover speeds even within the 'high user' section.
1.04 Variety and flow: Planned materials flow is vital in manufacturing, even in factories small enough for manual handling. Unless flows are carefully calculated and a rigorous stock control method instigated, production can be hindered. One of the most common faults found in small factories are heaps of half-finished parts and raw components waiting to be processed. This constricts materials handling and impinges on the work station. Some manufacturing and assembly operations are quicker than others, demanding buffer holding areas. In batch production, often with a wide variety of small batches, the flows and buffer storage requirements can differ greatly as separate elements of production machinery accept different emphases. The designer must therefore plan a flexible materials supply and handling system, even for small scale plants. The stores of small manufacturers often need to keep a wide variety of stocks, though in comparatively small quantities. These components or materials can vary in size and weight from printed circuits to steel bar stock, and production patterns can demand rapid changes to the stocking arrangement. The interprocess handling method and storage areas should also be adaptable to changing manufacturing conditions: many small manufacturers survive on their production flexibility.

Interprocess stores
1.05 In a manufacturing process, interprocess handling can be considered as a form of dynamic storage. Ideally, the time the component is stored between processes is only the time it takes to move between them: however, machine tools work at varying speeds depending on what and how much has to be done to the workpiece. Work study sets out to ensure that production machinery is kept working at maximum capacity. For instance, a fast primary process through one machine might feed a slower secondary operation; or a number of machines might be used, requiring a buffer store to keep the secondary process supplied. There is a tendency to make a separate buffer close to each production machine, often placing bins or plattens of material on the floor where there is space. This can quickly constrict the manufacturing area: although theoretically demanding more handling, a planned buffer store supplying a number of production machines should be provided. Material is then only withdrawn as required by each operator. In practice, it is notable that this philosophy promotes less

handling, as material randomly accumulating near work stations leads to constant shuffling.

Interprocess materials handling and storage can be a unit load concept. Depending on the type and characteristics of the material being processed, the load can be built up of a number of smaller units, tote bins for example, or the unit could be a post pallet, bin, or stillage. In the former case, small parts would be placed in tote bins at each machine and the bins stacked on a pallet or hung on a louvre panel trolley. This is a typical condition in the electronics industry. In the latter case, the bin or stillage can be placed in a collection zone common to a number of work places as is more usual at individual stations. It is important that handling space is planned into production machine layouts: this is often overlooked especially in small factories.

Mechanical handling for interprocess storage.

1.06 Pallet trucks, manually controlled lift trucks and stillage trucks are used to transport material to the buffer position. Turning dimensions, equipment types and pallet dimensions can be found in Information Sheet Manual Storage 3, Information Sheet Mechanised Storage 2, Pallets, Information Sheet Manual Storage 1, Tote boxes. For small components in tote bins, louvre panels on trolley bases are effective; wheeled bins are also popular. The choice of a wheeled bin or a palletised method depends on whether the buffer space available necessitates stacking the units, and on the weight of the components. 25 kg should be the design limit for manual lifting.

An effective and flexible manual handling and storage system involves tracking bolted to the floor. In effect, plattens have been fitted with castors, which run in the tracks: the castors are designed to turn through 90° by the operative depressing a foot pedal at track junctions, allowing right angle direction changes. Buffer storage areas can be built up by forming a matrix of track where required. The track can be quickly bolted to concrete floors and is of sufficiently low profile not to hinder personnel or mechanised plant movement, although it needs to be bridged for pallet trucks.

In that they provide first-in, first-out throughput, roller conveyors are also effective buffer stores. **1** shows how a conveyor and a tracking system can be combined to provide supply, transport and interprocess delays, each chosen for performance and for characteristics commensurate with the particular manufacturing process; **2** shows tracking providing a materials buffer; **3** shows how tracking can be fitted with carriages equipped with roller beds, feeding another form of buffer, roll through conveyor track. For a small variety and a high throughput, live storage provides a very effective and flexible buffer; cambered roller conveyor sections can be quickly bolted to the floor and tracking rearranged to them with little disruption. Rearrangements can be achieved over a weekend with this type of equipment.

In larger scale manufacturing overhead conveyors are used for both transport and as buffer storage. There are two types: overhead conveyors running in a continuous loop, acting as a dynamic store, material being removed manually as required; and 'power and free' conveyors which also run on a loop, but which can accumulate into storage lanes. This type of conveyor has been developed up to have full on-line control for supplying production machinery automatically.

Buffer storage provided by overhead conveyors places considerable loads on the structure, which change dependent on the stock level and the throughput of the process. Overhead conveyors can also conflict with services and route for mobile plant. (See Information Sheet Mechanised Storage 10, para 6). Another development in automated interprocess handling is the transporting of small metal and plastics components between work stations by pneumatic tubes, storage being provided by hoppers at positions.

Stock control: For production processes, this is a work study function and is outside the scope of this handbook.

1

2

3

Industrial storage   Design guide

(Readers outside the UK should refer to locally equivalent statutory bodies, legislation and building codes.)

Inception and primary brief

This stage (A and B of the RIBA 'Plan of work') is to establish enough information about the client's overall requirements to assess feasibility of the project and set the broad framework within which architect and consultants work.

Nature of the problem

See Ts Intro 1.
See Ts Intro 2.
Unit load handling,
Hulett, Gower Press.

Types of client organisation

The essential difference between clients is the origin and destination of goods stored. These facts decide methods of operation and, therefore the design of the storage building. Establish knowledge of client's administrative organisation.

Manufacturer
operating store — Holds raw materials or brought in parts or assemblies necessary for any stage of the manufacturing process.

ancillary store — Holds commodities essential to factory, but which do not go directly to a manufacturing process.

auxiliary store — Temporary store required for, say, seasonal demand variations.

despatch store or finished goods warehouse — Holds items awaiting despatch. Often a storage function must be accommodated in a production building.

Stockholder — Receives raw materials and stores them in bulk prior to sale for further processing.

Builder's or other trade merchant — Receives bulk goods from home and overseas and distributes without further processing (other than breaking bulk) to members of a trade or trades.

Wholesaler — Receives finished bulk goods from manufacturers and distributes them in smaller, probably mixed, quantities to retailers. Client may operate a customer collect service, delivery service and/or 'cash and carry' warehouse. The storage building may be a main, central warehouse or a local distribution depot served by a parent warehouse.

Mail order warehouse — Similar to wholesaler, but central depot receives goods, which are then sent out by mail.

Distribution centre for multiple retail organisation — An organisation with several retail outlets carrying out its own wholesaling.

Bottler or canner — Receives the product in bulk and fills, stores and distributes.

Public storage, goods forwarding and/or contract packing — Handles a wide range of goods without owning them at any stage. Only group which earns money from storage.

groupage depot — Centre for collecting export goods into economic loads and 'breaking bulk' of import loads. Often includes Customs and Excise facilities. Some demand for storage.

repository — Building for any long term storage, eg furniture.

Local authority — May need a new market for wholesalers. Similar problems of handling distribution but little storage.

Site selection

Sizes and shape — Must meet design requirements. Does site allow expansion?

Convenient for transport

Available within planning and cost — Is there government or local control on location of industry? Is Industrial Development Certificate required?

Establish details of site — Consult client re cost.

AJ Guide to site investigation [(A35)] Ts Intro 2, 5.01. Consult LA.

See AJ Guide, Site investigation.

Administration

Architect's appointment	Establish extent of service to be provided and basis for fees.	
Appointment of design team		See Ts Intro 1, para 2.01 to 2.07.
Liaison procedures	Establish who will be in charge of overall liaison between client bodies and architect, and degree of responsibility.	See Ts Intro 1, para 2.06.
Form of client's agreement	Establish the form the client's agreement to architect's and consultants' decisions should take.	
Client's advisers	Determine function and responsibilities and whether direct approach by the architect is permissible.	
Fees	The architect must inform the client about fees for services of specialist members of the design team and obtain his agreement.	
Contracts	Establish method of selecting general contractor and principal subcontractors: selective tendering, negotiated, or preliminary tenders for subsequent negotiation. Discuss appropriate terms of contract: firm price, fluctuation.	
Preliminary programme	Establish any unavoidable requirements affecting feasibility etc.	
completion dates	Any firm dates by which the building must be occupied.	
programme for next stages	Confirm immediate future programme and dates for joint meetings for submission of design/cost assessments for approval, submissions for statutory and building regulation consents.	

Legislation

	Study current legislation and effect on siting, design and construction.	The Building Regulations 1972, the Building (1st amendment) Regulations 1973 and the Building (2nd amendment) Regulations 1974. The Building Standards (Scotland) (Consolidation) Regulations 1971 and the Building Standards (Scotland) Amendment Regulations 1973.
	Is Industrial Development Certificate or Office Development Permit required?	Check with LA and DOE.

Future developments

Consider possible future developments, ie
- increase in quantity or rate of demand;
- anticipated expansion or retraction of storage area;
- change of use; development or change in item stored;
- change of size of item stored;
- developments in transportation or handling methods;
- change in required environment.

Some will affect proposed height, which may allow expansion without increasing area.

Economic factors

Establish cost limitations If the client imposes cost limits, ensure that in doing so he has taken into account the benefits to be gained in time, labour, space, operating and maintenance costs, as well as in customer goodwill, through modernisation of storage facilities and procedures.

2 Feasibility

Quality of building

Quality depends on planned life span. Will building be added to or altered (and is building adaptable to changes)? Is building speculative? Will facade act as advertisement?

Classify materials for handling and storage

Does project justify use of materials handling consultant? If so call in now.

Type of material

solids

—bulk

—unit load

See Is Bulk 5 for properties, mass densities and handling. See table IV, Is Mech 1 for type of unit load related to handling storage.

liquids

—bulk

—unit load

See Is Bulk 5 for properties mass densities and handling. See table III, IV, Is Mech 1 for type of unit load.

plate materials

See table III, IV Is Mech 1 for type of unit load.

Size, shape, weight

Analyse unit load in relation to packaging, transport required and environment (eg temperature, vibration). Are units suitable for palletisation?

See Is Mech 2.

Weight per item

—load per m^2 at base

—side pressure (if loose)

—pressure per m^2 (liquids and gases)

—density

Condition

—fragile

—perishable

—explosive

—flammable

—corrosive

Substance

—hard or soft

See Is Bulk 5 for properties, Is Mech 1 for unit loads.

—rigid, plastic or elastic

Special characteristics

—biological properties

—chemical composition

—coefficient of expansion

—specific heat

—viscosity

—normal freezing point

—thermal conductivity

—surface emissivity

—emission of radiation

—electronic or electrolytic conductivity

—odorous quality

—absorptive quality

—inherent strength

—angle of repose

Information from client or client's supplier.

Source of goods

Where received from

(eg from local, UK or international sources from another factory, or same factory). This will influence form of transport and goods

How received

eg finished, semi-finished or unfinished, packed or unpacked.

See para 2 'Source of goods' of appropriate warehouse section, eg Ts manual 1, 2.01

Form of transport

Does project justify use of transport consultant. If so call in now.

Road vehicles

Some operators insist on their own transport fleet for prestige purpose even where contract hired vehicles are more economical.

See para 3 of appropriate section for discussion.

—company owned collection and/or delivery vehicles

—contract hire vehicles

—suppliers' vehicles

—customers' collection vans

—post office vehicles

How many and what capacity, size and weight?

See Is Loading 1.

Rail	Is rail transport physically or economically essential? Determine length of loading platform from number of wagons expected each day, availability of shunts from nearest railhead.	See Is Loading 6. Contact British Rail divisional superintendent.
Waterway	Barge service: type of barge, eg Lash, Seabea.	
Air	Air container or igloo.	
Pipeline	Special vehicles and dock floors. Special packaging.	
—for bulk transport	Pipeline or belt conveyor.	
Effects of possible changes in transport charges and fuel costs	These will influence: ● site requirements ● loading and unloading facilities ● queuing space ● layout of storage building.	
Relative volumes of different goods or raw materials		
Size of individual consignments		

Dock design

For unit loads by road and rail	How are goods off- and on-loaded/checked?	See para 7 Unloading, eg Ts Man 1, 7.01 ff, Ts Mech 1, 7.01 ff. For rail only see Is Load 6.
	Consider dock equipment.	See Is Load 5.
For bulk goods	How are goods off- and on-loaded/checked?	See Ts Bulk 1, para 7.01 ff.
	Consider dock equipment.	See Is Bulk 3.

Volume, turnover and stock control

		See paras 10, 11 and 12, 14 under appropriate warehouse Ts eg for manual store. Ts Man 1, para 10.01, 11.01, 12.01 ff etc.
Supply and demand —average rate —normal and peak periods —seasonal variations	Stock turnover for each item stored decides storage layout.	
Rate of deterioration **Variety of items**	Note need for selective withdrawal.	
Volume of items	Varied or seasonal. Identify peak demands, seasonal goods changes.	
—time factor	Rate of turnover of goods or materials.	
—frequency factor	For movement, ie continuous or intermittent.	
—quantity factor		
—economic storage period	Relate economic period and quantity to be stored to: ● supply and demand rate ● rate of deterioration ● cost of environmental control ● accidental interruption of supply	
—cost per unit	Relate cost per unit stored, or cost per unit of storage space to: ● value when supplied ● cost of storage ● value at demand.	
Daily pattern	Will depend on transport arrangements.	See Ts Man 1 para 7 'Unloading'.
Weekly pattern	Eg heavy weekend buying of foodstuff.	
Seasonal pattern	Establish seasonal patterns, eg stocking up by the wine and spirit trade to meet a seasonal peak.	

Type of storage

	Determine nature and details of storage components.	See para 13 'Type of storage' in appropriate warehouse Ts, eg Ts Mech 1 para 13.01 ff.

Pallets		See Is Mech 2 Pallets.
Fixed storage components		See Is Man 1 Tote boxes.
		See Is Man 2 Shelving.
		See Is Mech 1 Racking.
Mobile storage components		See Is Mech 1 Racking.

Material handling sequence within storage area

Outline ideas only, to decide schedule of accommodation.

See paras 14, 15 and 16 in appropriate sections.

Movement of materials and goods

How will materials and goods be conveyed:
● at floor level (eg by fork truck, trolley);
● overhead (eg crane monorail, conveyors)?

Ts Mech 1 para 16 'Order pickings'.

—circulation patterns

For personnel see *AJ Handbook: Building services: Section 8: Circulation* [(5-)].

Mechanical handling

This has a greater impact on design and construction than any other single aspect.

Design principles
—equipment
—movement
—time
—handling
—accessibility
—production work flow

Choose the right handling equipment for the job.
Movement should take place in the shortest possible distance and time.
Consider time element in every operation.
Avoid handling wherever possible.
Design for accessibility of all items when required.
Design handling operations during any production process to facilitate the flow of materials in a logical order.

Handling equipment

From analysis of items, type of storage and work process, determine the most suitable handling equipment for each stage of the process.

—cranes

See Is Mech 8, Is Auto 1.
See Is Man 3, Is Mech 3, Is Mech 6.

—industrial trucks

See Is Man 3, Is Mech 3, Is Mech 6.

—forklift trucks
—conveyors and elevators

See Is Mech 7, Is Mech 9, Is Mech 10.

Effect of equipment on design and other elements

● structure (will it take cranes and conveyors, vibration?)
● building height, working height
● natural light interference
● services and connections
● noise
● safety

—trucks

For trucks check also:
● floor loading and finishes
● doorways: height, width, construction, operation
● damage to building fabric.

—conveyors

For conveyors check also:
● openings in walls and floors; fire proofing, fire divisions
● work flow
● physical obstruction to other circulation routes.

Accommodation for handling equipment

Determine accommodation requirements for mobile equipment.
NB is battery charging area required?

See Is Mech 5.

Environmental requirements of items stored

Client's views should be sought on the optimum environment for storage of his type of goods. Manufacturers may have clearer ideas than those engaged solely in storage.

See para 24 of appropriate warehouse type, eg Ts Mech 2 para 24.01 ff.

Thermal requirements

May often be critical but what is acceptable to workpeople may often satisfy storage requirements. It may waste money to heat whole building when workers are only occupying order picking area. Should order picking then be in separate zone?

—design criteria	Optimum levels of temperature, relative humidity, air movement and so on, may be different in different parts of the storage space. Note special requirements for cold storage.	
—zone control	Do any areas require precise control of thermal environment?	
—temperature control	Establish permissible range.	
—humidity control	With hygroscopic products (eg paper) can be as critical as temperature. Establish permissible range	
—ventilation control	Need may be influenced by density of storage. In a hot summer, mechanical ventilation may be the minimum practicable means of achieving adequate thermal conditions for goods in which temperature is critical.	
—refrigerated (cold store) areas	Ascertain needs.	See Ts Cold 2, para 24.
—air-conditioning	Need for precise control of thermal environment may indicate requirement for air-conditioning.	

Other requirements

—need for control of daylight	Where light would cause colour fading of goods or packaging.	
—need for very high standard of cleanliness including freedom from dust		
—need for very high standard of hygiene.	eg foods, repackaging (cheese).	
—need for absolute freedom from damp	eg electronics and electrical equipment.	
—tainting of stock	Certain goods (eg tobacco) become tainted as a result of odours, fumes. Check on mixture of goods in cold stores.	See Ts Cold 1.
—explosion hazard	eg powders during bulk handling.	See Ts Bulk 1, paras 1.02, 27.01.
—high fire risk	Compartmentation for fire and smoke.	See para 27 of appropriate Ts
—pest infestation problem	Especially in food industries.	
—corrosive atmosphere	Consider effect on structure and finishes type.	
Storage requiring especially resistant finishes	Resistant to water, grease, acid, sugar, abrasion etc, liquids and vapour. Define areas where special finishes are required.	

Users of the building

Establish numbers, sex and status of all likely users of the building

Staff
—store operatives and general warehouse and order picking staff;
—office staff;
—executive staff;
—checking and packaging staff;
—lorry drivers (including company and visiting drivers);
—salesmen (including company and visiting salesmen);
—gatemen;
—security staff (and their dogs);
—casual/seasonal labour (extra wc or canteen facilities may be required).

Executives of supplier companies

Customers
May be hundreds if warehouse is wholesale centre. Note:
● security and control
● car parking
● wc accommodation.

Interested individuals or groups
eg members of a trade, sightseers (found particularly in food and drink warehouses).

Environmental requirements of users

Environmental requirements of people working in the warehouse space, as well as overriding requirements of the items stored.

See para 24 of appropriate warehouse type, eg Ts Mech 2, para 24.01 ff. section 3, and Offices, See Factories Act 1961, Shops and Railway Premises Act 1963, chap. 41. See *AJ Handbook: Building environment* [(E6)]: Design guide, Lighting, Sound.

—visual environment
—thermal environment

—acoustic environment

Outline schedule of accommodation

This will be determined largely by the information already obtained on items to be stored, turnover, transport arrangements, pattern of activity and users of the building. A schedule should now be made using the check list below.

Warehouse:
Bulk storage area
Order picking area

Number of orders is related to variety of goods and quantity of items picked.
Sales volume of each type of goods stored.
Number of days supply of each to be kept in stock area.

Goods pre-assembly area Where loads are assembled in the correct 'drop off' sequence of loading into the vehicle (not unit loads).

See para 18, Load build-up of Ts Mech 1.

—method of storage Open (flat) pallets
Post pallets
Intermediate bulk containers
Containers.

See Ts Load 1, 5.06, and Is Mech.
See Is Bulk 4.
See Is Ext 1.
See Ts Load para 5.06.

—time allowance for completion or orders How many hours ahead of dispatch can orders be completed (affects volume)?

—danger of theft What precautions are to be taken?

Pre-load accumulation area For roll pallets and pallets.

Packing materials store

—type, material and size of packing Cardboard or plastic packing stores flat.

—method of handling Usually by fork truck.

—disposal of waste To be compressed and sent back to paper and cardboard manufacturers.

See Is Load 3.

Loading and unloading area transfer method from pre-assembly areas to delivery vehicle
daily and weekly pattern and peaks

See Ts Load 1
See para 20 and para 7 of appropriate Ts.

inspection area Usually combined with unpacking area. May need:
● weighing facilities
● storage for damaged goods, space for repacking cases damaged in transit
● space for repair of cases (where returnable packages are used) and repair pallets.

See Ts Load 1, para 5.16.

check-off area If required. Often combined with inspection area.

Empties store

—returnable containers Must be stored and returned to the factory of origin for repair, cleaning and repacking. Storage can sometimes constitute a sizable problem. Space for repair.

—non-returnable containers Disposed of by the retailer or other person responsible for 'breaking bulk'.

Bonded accommodation For goods on which duty is payable; concerns wines, spirits, tobacco, and goods grouped for forwarding by trailer or container.

Discuss proposals with HM Customs and Excise (local office address from Kings Beam House, 39/40 Mark Lane, London EC3).

Security rooms A separate lock-up store for more expensive goods.

—security cages and roll pallets Security cages containing loads are locked on the warehouse side before doors at opposite ends are opened for loading.

Contact police.

—returned goods Must be kept separate.

—hazardous goods Separate or underground storage areas for materials, eg fireworks or matches which constitute an extreme fire risk.

Contact Factory Inspectorate.

Trade counter

—security

—communications Contact appropriate office for credit and stock control, on line facilities print out etc.

—staffing Counter staff may have other jobs elsewhere in the store warehouse.
Picking lists.

Administration

—general office For minimum a depot manager and one or two clerks (order-taking and invoicing).

For detailed briefing see *AJ Handbook: Office building* [32]: Design guide.

—executive offices For local directors or other managerial staff.

—supervisor's office The warehouse supervisor and assistants must supervise the flow of goods into and out of the warehouse.

—transport office Transport officer's duties include:
● general maintenance of all trucks.
● route planning. This is vital in distribution depot, as vehicle route determines way in which it is loaded.
Print-out facilities sometimes required.

See para 4 'Control of transport' of appropriate warehouse type, eg Ts Mech 1, para 4.0 ff.
See also Ts Load 1, para 2.02

—customs office	Needed only in bonded warehouses.	
—salesmen's office	Room where salesmen can work (eg writing up orders) outside working hours.	
—interview rooms	For visiting salesmen.	
—showroom	Either linked to reception or, usefully, within trade counter area.	
—reception area	With cloakrooms and wcs for visitors. Size and finish depends on client.	
—gatehouse	Very important, especially in automated stores. Agree with client that the gatehouse for security reasons should be the only entrance to the site. Security checkout.	See Ts Load 1, para 2.0, Is Load 2, para 2.0.
—weighbridge	Discuss weighbridge with client. Usually placed near main entrance, often constricts flow.	See Ts Load 1, para 5.16.

Welfare

—washrooms, wcs and locker rooms	Client to decide on separate wcs for different staff. Warehouse staff also need lockers for protective clothing.	See Factories Act 1961. See para 37 of appropriate warehouse Ts, eg Ts Mech 2 para 37.01 ff.
—rest room with locker space, wcs (lorry drivers)	Separate room for drivers, to do paper work and prevent them from entering warehouse. Also special rest room for continental drivers (groupage depots).	See *AJ Handbook: Services and circulation* [(5-)]: Section 2, Sanitary appliances.
—rest room for female staff	Especially for order-picking staff.	
—special dressing rooms	To allow complete change of clothing for certain industries.	
—'dry' and 'wet' wcs	For certain industries.	
—search rooms	Where this form of security and control is required.	
—provision for tea breaks	Area separate from store.	See Factories Act 1961.
—smoking	Ascertain policy: time, place.	
—vending machines		
—canteen	If provided is usually shared by warehouse and office staff, but generally not used by drivers because of their irregular hours of work.	See *Restaurant planning and design* [512]: Fred Lawson. The Architectural Press, 1973.
—first aid room	Ascertain scope of facilities to be provided. Position ambulance bay where access is unrestricted.	
—clocking in area		

Transport

—maintenance garage	Does company operate its own fleet? Enable day to day maintenance to be carried out by the drivers (eg pit or ramp, and a store for spare parts and tyres). Vans are usually washed at night on the premises, so time is saved by washing machine.	See *AJ Metric handbook*, Chapter 14: Garages and service stations', p82, The Architectural Press, 1973. See Ts Cold 2, **8**, **9**.
—petrol pumps	Establish requirements. Large establishments have both petrol and/or diesel oil pumps, lubricating oil and water. Facilities for pumping up tyres must also be available. Plug points to refrigerated trucks.	Contact fire officer, petroleum officer.
—car parking and cycle storage	For parking of staff, customers' and visitors' cars, and delivery vehicles. Establish client's needs and check local planning requirements. Often critical in site purchase as car parking will restrict heavy vehicle areas when demanded at late stage.	
—pallet and fork truck maintenance		See Is Mech **5**.

Site layout

| **General site layout** | Place boiler house, transformer, offices and transport premises on site perimeter. Note yards are more useful than roads. Main door entrances, works offices and laboratories on permanent walls, leaving removable walls at side and rear free for expansion. Visitors and cars should be kept clear of the loading/unloading area. Light vans should be segregated from heavy trucks. | See Ts Load 1, para 1.01 ff. |

Delivery and dispatch
by road

	Adequate space for vehicles to stand under cover.	
—bay widths and depths	For side or end loading (within store).	See Is Load 2, para 1.01 ff.
—road and accumulation area layout		
—parking area required	For trucks; handling equipment; staff and visitors' transport. Agree standards with local planning authority.	See Ts Load, para 2.01 ff.

—traffic movement	Check space required for traffic flow to avoid congestion.	See Ts Load 1, para 2.01 ff.
by rail	Length of unloading area may stretch building. Consider gradients and transition curves from main line to siding.	See Is Load 6.
—height of platform	Heights of wagons vary. Note spring deflection.	
—unloading within building	Can rail siding run into the building? Use of railway locomotives and wagons in factory premises.	Railway regulations 1906 no 679.

Planning relationships

Loading and unloading	Can assembly and loading be combined in one bay to minimise movement? This simplifies access layout and is useful for returned empties, which can be unloaded as full containers are being loaded enabling fast turn-round times. May cause constricting cross-circulation.	Ts Load 1. See Ts Load 1.
Storage areas	Consider speed of turnover and ease of handling fast-moving or awkward items, should be close to loading point.	See paras 34, 35 of appropriate Ts, eg Ts Mech 2, para 34.
Offices	The traffic office should adjoin loading bay.	
Trade counters	Placing trade counter beside representative stock area avoids duplication of stock and makes for ease of operation.	
Showroom and reception	Should be close to the general offices and well removed from the loading bay.	
Computer rooms	Computer control of stock is important in processing orders, labelling, invoicing, stock and credit control, traffic touring.	
Circulation	● Keep movement to minimum. ● Allow access to all stock at all times. Positioning the loading area in one corner produces similarly equal accessibility to all parts. The building can subsequently be extended if necessary, without altering the position of the core or the system of circulation. Prepare a basic flow design.	

Plan area and height of warehouse

	Determine plan area of warehouse according to volume of goods stored, and height of stacks.	
Annotating storage items	Determine comprehensive method of annotating all storage. This will be governed by: ● position and method of supervision ● method of controlling inventories ● location of items ● systematised storage or filing systems, eg letters, symbols.	
Layout of storage	Determine layout of storage components and hence basic cube requirements.	
—number of items in one unit load	Depending on: ● accessibility required ● safety ● packaging and type of container ● work process (possibly).	
—capacity for stacking	Depending on: ● inherent strength of item, container or enclosure ● permissible load on basic support or ground.	
—depth of stack	Depending on: ● accessibility ● method of handling ● work process (possibly).	
—height of stack	Depending on handling device, floor loading, and factors above. Minimum headroom 7·3 m for future use. Buildings using modern methods of racking may go up to 10 m. In fully automatic warehouses using stacker cranes up to 30 m can be required. (On very large projects with a high floor to wall ratio a building with 9 m height may cost initially only about 5 per cent more than one of 4·5 m height.)	
Height of building	Storage buildings should be single-storeyed for flexibility of layout, heavy-duty floors at minimum cost, economics in handling equipment and plant layout. Add clearances for structure and services to obtain overall building height.	
Space between storage components	Decide between more space required for forklift trucks and less space and high racks with narrow aisle trucks. Determine clearances between storage components and gangway width. This will depend on: ● size of storage component ● space required for movement of handling equipment ● space required for turning, loading, unloading	See Ts Mech 3. See Ts Mech 3.

● space required for other traffic.
Alternative schemes are then compared on the basis of:
● total cube of space needed to house each
● manpower requirements
● type of building required
● cost of building on m² basis and of site, viewed together.
● cost of storage and handling equipment.
● operational costs.

3 Outline proposals

Before this stage, return to 'Feasibility' and go through in more detail, inserting flow figures, sizes, clearances, and deciding on one storage system out of several possibilities.

Structure

Establish any special requirement of the client or of the goods stored.

See para 22, 'Structure', appropriate warehouse.
See *AJ Handbook: Building structure* [(2-)].

Structural framework
—support for equipment loads (including floor loading)

Especially handling equipment.
Determine design load/m² and if required throughout.
(NB Turret trucks wheel loads).

—support for services

Determine design load/m² and if required throughout.

—choice of structural material

Steelwork is most favoured choice for single-storey structures, except in special conditions (eg high fire risk, corrosive atmosphere).

See Ts Mech 1, 22.01 for discussion.

—fire protection

May influence choice of structural material and form.
Also explosion in bulk stores.

See para 27 'Fire Protection'.
Consult insurance company, district surveyor, fire officer.

—impact damage potential

May influence choice of structural material or need local protection.

—maintenance

Any specially corrosive atmospheres, especially in cold or bulk stores.
May influence choice of structural material and/or form.
Consult factory inspectorate.

Loadbearing elements

Must span storage space and support cladding.

Select basic structure

Use column-free floor space (or place stanchions to suit storage plan).

See para 22, 'Structure', of appropriate Ts.

—solid loadbearing wall

Only for small stores with no chance of expansion and with fire and/or theft hazards.

—steel frame

Allows big uninterrupted spans in two directions; rapid erection and flexibility. Overcome rusting by galvanising or anti-rust finishes.
Many members may make maintenance difficult.

—concrete frame

Fire protection and low maintenance but little flexibility and may have close grid of stanchions.

—combined concrete roof and support members

Good fireproofing but inflexible. Difficult to put holes through roof, and support heavier loads.

—composite roof or steel and concrete

Can span over 60 m but needs heavy foundations and close stanchion grid.

—low cost portal framed structures

Cheap solution for block stacking where insulation is not required.
Steel or concrete. Reduced headroom at gutters and close spacing of stanchions in one direction constricts racking.

See Ts Mech 1, para 22.

Decide floor construction
—floor loading

Design for future heavier weights.

See para 23, 'Floor', of appropriate Ts, eg Ts Mech 2, para 23.01 ff.
For types of floor see Ts Mech 2, para 23.04.
For forklift weights see Is Mech 3.

—suspended floors

Three times greater than in uniformly loaded floor.
Floor slabs and beams need to be specially designed.

Storage component
Materials

Consider in detail any special characteristics necessary in selection of materials for storage components.

As listed in feasibility study.

Selection or design of storage component
—manufactured components
—specially designed components

Consider:
● cost;
● construction and finishes;
● serviceability;

● availability of component or basic materials;
● whether flexible, demountable, interchangeable;
● appearance.

Enclosing elements and finishes

Establish special requirements or preferences.

See *AJ Design guide: Industrial production— Buildings* [27], para 33.

External walls

Distinguish between:
● non-extendable perimeter walls (near site boundaries)
● walls of substantial construction for fire protection
● removable walls for extension
● security.

Internal walls

Distinguish between fire walls, space divisions, security boundaries, screening for offices.
Non-loadbearing partitions should be removable.
Dry construction avoids dust problems.

Roof
—sheeted construction

Assess use of pitch against running costs and handling plant conditions.

—continuous membrane

Flat roof, wide spans. Leakage may be catastrophic.

See Ts Mech 2, **1ab**

Finishes
to floors, walls, ceilings, also to structural framework:
—high humidities or wetting

In washing plant or bottling line.

—chemical attack

In chemical stores.

—abrasion by heavy equipment
—impact or wheeled traffic

eg steel post pallets. Avoid use of steel-wheeled trucks.

—high standards of cleanliness (eg freedom from dust)
—high standards of hygiene

eg food, cheese-cutting.

—anti-static, non-conductive (eg freedom from sparks)

eg automated stores.

—effect on general level of noise

Especially towcarts.

—appearance

Floor finishes

Floors must be precisely level if mobile racking or high stacking in narrow aisles is used.

Windows

Danger of glare, especially for turret truck drivers, and package fade.

Doors

Judge economic balance between wide doors (convenient but heat loss) and narrow doors (damage by vehicles).

See Is Load 4, Doors.

House style

Any special demands of house style, materials, colours, livery?

Colour

Use to aid lighting, for colour coding of racking and tote bins and safes.

BS4880; BS2929; BS1710.

Environment
Thermal environment

See para 24 of appropriate Ts, eg Ts Mech 2, 24.01.
See *AJ Handbook: Building environment* [(E6)].

—ventilation

Consider ventilation with heating costs.
Low labour density requires few air changes per day.

—loading area

A loading area in the building should be screened off from storage or work areas by a 3 m (min) door to ensure that diesel or petrol fumes do not enter the store.

—air blowers

Hot air should not blow over goods at close range.

—hygroscopic products

eg paper—relative humidity is more critical than temperature. Meet requirements by partitioning but keep general temperature within comfort range.

—dust

Often main environmental hazard. Choose suitable floor finishes and sweep regularly.

Heating

Compromise between human comfort (for moving workers requiring 15°C temperature approximately) and ideal storage conditions (may be different). Where low value goods are

stored, heating may be a serious on-cost. For goods
bulk-stored for long periods which are little worked, omit
heating altogether. Areas of high human activity, eg order
make-up areas and checking, heat up to 15°C. Van manual
loading is best done within the building in a semi-heated
area, behind closed doors. Where the doors are frequently
opened, use radiant heat.

—low pressure hot water
Operated by solid fuel, oil or gas. For large storage buildings
requiring accurate temperature control and where a plenum
system is used. Fresh air during summer gives good cool
working conditions.

—hot air heaters
Operated by gas or oil. Cheapest in first cost, and with
ducting can operate satisfactory in quite large store buildings.
Cool air can be introduced during the summer through
the unit.

—hot air heaters
(steam-operated)
Provided by solid fuel, oil or gas boiler. Effective if process
steam is required for other purposes (eg bottle washing).

—radiant sources
From low pressure water, steam, hot air or electricity.
Effective in loading areas and for raising local temperature
for operatives where normal temperature is below 12·8°C.
But provide separate ventilation systems in summer.

summer cooling
In large storage buildings temperature can be kept under
15°C by blowing cool night air (from 9 m above ground level)
through the store.

effect of ceiling height
In very large storage buildings, ceiling height has little
effect on heating costs as the number of air changes can be
reduced as volume increases. The main heat loss is through
the roof, which is the same regardless of building height.

Lighting
See Ts Mech 2, paras 24.03
to 24.15.

Noise
Concentrations of road vehicles and handling of bottles
particularly; mobile handling equipment will be the main
source of noise.
Site loading bay and access roads to cope with materials flow,
and in relationship to external environment.

Services
Design of services
  —supply services
  —disposal services
  —environmental services
  —mechanical services
  —special services

See paras 24, 'Building
services' and 25,
'Special services' of
appropriate Ts.
See *AJ Handbook:
Building services* [(5-)].

Routeing of services
Space frame or lattice truss construction allows services to be
carried in roof space. Where bulky piped and cable services
must be run below floor level, eg cold stores, a service tunnel
may be required (minimum 1·8 × 2·4 m) with access at
either end and the necessary fire escapes.
The floor itself should be left clear of services.
Design drainage system so that it will keep itself clear.
Any manhole, gulley or duct cover is vulnerable to the
heavy weights of fork lift trucks. Vertical pipes should be
protected. Consider walkway in roof trusses for access to
services.
Liquid and trade effluents (as found in bottling stores) may
be pumped up into the roof space, to run through drains
which can be serviced or altered in course without having
to dig up the floor.

Waste disposal
A common problem is the disposal of outer packaging
materials. Compactors can solve this.

Unpacking near unloading area can prevent waste spreading
into the storage area.

See Ts Load 3, 'Waste
handling equipment',
para 1.01 ff.

Communications

Establish overall requirements for following systems.

—telephones	GPO and/or private internal systems.
—signals	Bells, buzzers, lights.
—personal call system	Loop.
—broadcast relay systems	For 'music while you work', personal calls.
—impulse timing systems	Clocks.
—closed circuit tv	For inspection and control.
—monitoring	Special equipment, for the environment in critical areas, may be automated, to run continuously without supervision. Such equipment may be monitored back to a central control panel.
—on/off line computer links	Print-out. Stock picking lists—Real time plant control.

Security and protection

Consider requirements and effects on design or protection system:

See *AJ Handbook: Services and circulation* [(5-)]: Section 13, Security and fire.

Fire protection:

—subdivision of storage area

—means of escape

Compromise between needs of fire protection.

See para 37, 'Fire control' of appropriate Ts. Discuss requirements with local fire authority and factory inspectorate.

—fire alarm

—fire fighting equipment

Whether to be linked to fire station.

There are special requirements for equipment in certain cases.

Check with factory inspectorate. (See Ministry of Labour Booklet 16 and Building Regulations).

Burglary

Problems are greatest where small, high-value articles are handled, where customers are not closely controlled; where a storage building is on the outskirts of an industrial estate, rather than on a well-lit main road.
Answers are:
● to have only one entrance to, and exit from, the entire site;
● to split up lorry drivers and trade customers with pick-up vehicles after they enter the gate;
● to keep the site and exterior walls well lit at night;
● to pay particular attention to goods after made up into orders for dispatch, when most theft occurs;
● store goods at a high level, out of normal reach;
● use locking cages for high-value goods;
● institute random searching of staff;
● install an adequate burglar alarm system.

Prevention of accidents:
—legislation

Design to prevent order picking staff from exposure to machinery except where necessary.

Factories Act 1961 has general requirements that workplaces must be kept safe.

Defence

Protection of classified material.

Requirements of insurance companies

These will sometimes be more stringent than either the functional or statutory requirements.

Special hazards

Including those to personnel and neighbouring industrial plants or residential areas.

Cleaning and maintenance

Consider maintenance and cleaning—internal and external—in relation to capital cost (normally higher initial capital cost reduces maintenance, lower initial capital cost increases maintenance costs) and fiscal factors.

See para 33, 'Maintenance', of appropriate Ts.

Cost studies

This design guide is not continued beyond the 'Outline proposals' stage, as by then all major factors in the project will have been considered. 'Scheme design' and 'Detail design' are described in stages D and E of the RIBA 'Plan of work' (*RIBA Handbook* part 3.220) and are common to all projects.

For procedure see *AJ Guide to cost planning and cost control* [(A4)].

Index

This book consists of nine sections, design guide, appendixes and index. Each section contains technical studies usually followed by information sheets. The design guide is not referred to in the index. The document referred to in each of the following entries is identified in the following manner: page number/type of document/reference keyword/number of document. For example: 225 Ts Bulk 1 2.01 = page 225, Technical study Bulk storage 1, paragraph 2.01.